Praise for *Crisis Economics*
by Nouriel Roubini and Stephen Mihm

"A succinct, lucid, and compelling account of the causes and consequences of the great meltdown of 2008. . . . Essential reading for anyone interested in getting a crisp, if opinionated, overview of how the global financial system seized up in the fall of 2008 and what may happen in the months and years to come if serious reforms and new regulations are not embraced."

—Michiko Kakutani, *The New York Times*

"A very good primer on how finance gone bad can wreck an otherwise healthy economy."

—Paul Krugman and Robin Wells, *The New York Review of Books*

"Readers hungry for more of the professor's grim analysis will appreciate [Roubini's] erudition. Even people who aren't finance buffs ought to read and heed his words." —*The New York Times Book Review*

"This book is a tightly argued, convincing assault on the free-market ideology that allowed the finance sector to hijack the global economy. . . . This is a wake-up call." —*The Guardian*

"*Crisis Economics* explains succinctly how the global financial system went into a downward spiral in the fall of 2008 as a consequence of government mistakes over an extended time." —*Sarasota Herald Tribune*

"[*Crisis Economics* is] a sober and sensible analysis of what has gone so badly wrong in finance in the past few years, coupled with a list of proposals about what could now be done to fix these woes. . . . One of the most readable and sensible accounts to date of the financial disaster." —FT.com

"An impressive, timely argument on behalf of transparency and stability for a financial system conspicuously lacking both." —*Kirkus Reviews*

"It is no surprise that Roubini's contribution should be so broad, well-argued, and easy-to-digest a précis of how we got to this point." —*The Independent*

ABOUT THE AUTHORS

Nouriel Roubini is professor of economics at New York University's Stern School of Business. He served in the White House and the United States Treasury department from 1998 through 2000. He is the founder and chairman of Roubini Global Economics (www.roubini.com), an economic and financial consulting firm, and regularly attends and presents his views at the World Economic Forum at Davos. He appears frequently on Bloomberg, CNBC, CNN, and NPR. *Foreign Policy* magazine named him one of the "Top 100 Public Intellectuals" in the world in 2008, *Forbes* magazine named him one of the top 10 academic gurus whose views and ideas should be known by any business executive, and *Prospect* magazine named him the second most important public intellectual in the world.

Stephen Mihm writes on economic and historical topics for *The New York Times Magazine*, *The Boston Globe*, and other publications. He was the Newcomen Postdoctoral Fellow in business history at Harvard Business School from 2003 to 2004. He is currently an associate professor of history at the University of Georgia, where he teaches courses on American political, cultural, and economic history.

Crisis Economics

A CRASH COURSE IN THE FUTURE OF FINANCE

Nouriel Roubini

and

Stephen Mihm

PENGUIN BOOKS

PENGUIN BOOKS
Published by the Penguin Group
Penguin Group (USA) Inc., 375 Hudson Street, New York, New York 10014, U.S.A. • Penguin Group (Canada), 90 Eglinton Avenue East, Suite 700, Toronto, Ontario, Canada M4P 2Y3 (a division of Pearson Penguin Canada Inc.) • Penguin Books Ltd, 80 Strand, London WC2R 0RL, England • Penguin Ireland, 25 St. Stephen's Green, Dublin 2, Ireland (a division of Penguin Books Ltd) • Penguin Books Australia Ltd, 250 Camberwell Road, Camberwell, Victoria 3124, Australia (a division of Pearson Australia Group Pty Ltd) • Penguin Books India Pvt Ltd, 11 Community Centre, Panchsheel Park, New Delhi–110 017, India • Penguin Group (NZ), 67 Apollo Drive, Rosedale, North Shore 0632, New Zealand (a division of Pearson New Zealand Ltd) • Penguin Books (South Africa) (Pty) Ltd, 24 Sturdee Avenue, Rosebank, Johannesburg 2196, South Africa

Penguin Books Ltd, Registered Offices:
80 Strand, London WC2R 0RL, England

First published in 2010 by The Penguin Press,
a member of Penguin Group (USA) Inc.
This edition with a new afterword published in Penguin Books 2011

1 3 5 7 9 10 8 6 4 2

THE LIBRARY OF CONGRESS HAS CATALOGED THE HARDCOVER EDITION AS FOLLOWS:
Roubini, Nouriel.
Crisis economics : a crash course in the future of finance / Nouriel Roubini and Stephen Mihm.
p. cm.
Includes bibliographical references and index.
ISBN 978-1-59420-250-6 (hc.)
ISBN 978-0-14-311963-0 (pbk.)
1. Financial crises. 2. Business cycles. 3. Economics. I. Mihm, Stephen, 1968– II. Title.
HB3722.R68 2010
338.5'42—dc22
2009053925
Printed in the United States of America
DESIGNED BY AMANDA DEWEY

Nouriel Roubini: To H.H., K.S., L.S., M.M., and M.W.

Stephen Mihm: To my family

Contents

Introduction

In January 2009, in the final days of the Bush administration, Vice President Dick Cheney sat down for an interview with the Associated Press. He was asked why the administration had failed to foresee the biggest financial crisis since the Great Depression. Cheney's response was revealing. "Nobody anywhere was smart enough to figure [it] out," he declared. "I don't think anybody saw it coming."

Cheney was hardly alone in his assessment. Look back at the statements that the wise men of the financial community and the political establishment made in the wake of the crisis. Invariably, they offered some version of the same rhetorical question: Who could have known? The financial crisis was, as Cheney suggested in this same interview, akin to the attacks of September 11: catastrophic, but next to impossible to foresee.

That is not true. To take but the most famous prediction made in advance of this crisis, one of the authors of the book—Nouriel Roubini—issued a very clear warning at a mainstream venue in the halcyon days of 2006. On September 7, Roubini, a professor of economics at New York University, addressed a skeptical audience at the International Monetary Fund in

Washington, D.C. He forcefully sounded a warning that struck many in the audience as absurd. The nation's economy, he predicted, would soon suffer a once-in-a-lifetime housing bust, a brutal oil shock, sharply declining consumer confidence, and inevitably a deep recession.

Those disasters were bad enough, but Roubini offered up an even more terrifying scenario. As homeowners defaulted on their mortgages, the entire global financial system would shudder to a halt as trillions of dollars' worth of mortgage-backed securities started to unravel. This yet-to-materialize housing bust, he concluded, could "lead . . . to a systemic problem for the financial system," triggering a crisis that could cripple or even take down hedge funds and investment banks, as well as government-sponsored financial behemoths like Fannie Mae and Freddie Mac. His concerns were greeted with serious skepticism by the audience.

Over the next year and a half, as Roubini's predictions started coming true, he elaborated on his pessimistic vision. In early 2008 most economists maintained that the United States was merely suffering from a liquidity crunch, but Roubini forecast that a much more severe credit crisis would hit households, corporations, and most dramatically, financial firms. In fact, well before the collapse of Bear Stearns, Roubini predicted that two major broker dealers (that is, investment banks) would go bust and that the other major firms would cease to be independent entities. Wall Street as we know it, he warned, would soon vanish, triggering upheaval on a scale not seen since the 1930s. Within months Bear was a distant memory and Lehman Brothers had collapsed. Bank of America absorbed Merrill Lynch, and Morgan Stanley and Goldman Sachs were eventually forced to submit to greater regulatory oversight, becoming bank holding companies.

Roubini was also far ahead of the curve in spotting the global dimensions of the disaster. As market watchers stated confidently that the rest of the world would escape the crisis in the United States, he correctly warned that the disease would soon spread overseas, turning a national economic illness into a global financial pandemic. He also predicted that this hypothetical systemic crisis would spark the worst global recession in decades, hammering the economies of China, India, and other nations thought to be impervious to troubles in the United States. And while other economists were focused on the danger of inflation, Roubini accurately predicted early on that the entire global economy would teeter on the edge of a potentially crippling deflationary spiral, of a sort not seen since the Great Depression.

Roubini's prescience was as singular as it was remarkable: no other economist in the world foresaw the recent crisis with nearly the same level of clarity and specificity. That said, he was not alone in sounding the alarm; a host of other well-placed observers predicted various elements of the financial crisis, and their insights helped Roubini connect the dots and lay out a vision that incorporated their prescient insights. Roubini's former colleague at Yale University, Robert Shiller, was far ahead of almost everyone in warning of the dangers of a stock market bubble in advance of the tech bust; more recently, he was one of the first economists to sound the alarm about the housing bubble.

Shiller was but one of the economists and market watchers whose views influenced Roubini. In 2005 University of Chicago finance professor Raghuram Rajan told a crowd of high-profile economists and policy makers in Jackson Hole, Wyoming, that the ways bankers and traders were being compensated would encourage them to take on too much risk and leverage, making the global financial system vulnerable to a severe crisis. Other well-respected figures raised a similar warning: Wall Street legend James Grant warned in 2005 that the Federal Reserve had helped create one of "the greatest of all credit bubbles" in the history of finance; William White, chief economist at the Bank for International Settlements, warned about the systemic risks of asset and credit bubbles; financial analyst Nassim Nicholas Taleb cautioned that financial markets were woefully unprepared to handle "fat tail" events that fell outside the usual distribution of risk; economists Maurice Obstfeld and Kenneth Rogoff warned about the unsustainability of current account deficits in the United States; and Stephen Roach of Morgan Stanley and David Rosenberg of Merrill Lynch long ago raised concerns about consumers in the United States living far beyond their means.

The list goes on. But for all their respectability, these and other economists and commentators were ignored, a fact that speaks volumes about the state of economics and finance over recent decades. Most people who inhabited those worlds ignored those warnings because they clung to a simple, quaint belief: that markets are self-regulating entities that are stable, solid, and dependable. By this reasoning, the entire edifice of twenty-first-century capitalism—aided, of course, by newfangled financial innovation—would regulate itself, keeping close to a steady, self-adjusting state of equilibrium.

It all seems naïve in retrospect, but for decades it was the conventional wisdom, the basis of momentous policy decisions and the rationale for grand-scale investment strategies. In this paradigm, not surprisingly, economic crises had little or no significant place. Indeed, if crises appeared at all, they were freak events: highly improbable, extremely unusual, largely unpredictable, and fleeting in their consequences. To the extent that crises became the object of serious academic study, they were generally considered to afflict less developed, "troubled" countries, not economic powerhouses like the United States.

This book returns crises to the front and center of economic inquiry: it is, in short, about crisis economics. It shows that far from being the exception, crises are the norm, not only in emerging but in advanced industrial economies. Crises—unsustainable booms followed by calamitous busts—have always been with us, and with us they will always remain. Though they arguably predate the rise of capitalism, they have a particular relationship to it. Indeed, in many important ways, crises are hardwired into the capitalist genome. The very things that give capitalism its vitality—its powers of innovation and its tolerance for risk—can also set the stage for asset and credit bubbles and eventually catastrophic meltdowns whose ill effects reverberate long afterward.

Though crises are commonplace, they are also creatures of habit. They're a bit like hurricanes: they operate in a relatively predictable fashion but can change directions, subside, and even spring back to life with little warning. This book sets out the principles by which these economic storms can be tracked and monitored and, within reason, forecast and even avoided. Using the recent crisis as an object lesson, it shows how it's possible to foresee such events and, no less important, prevent them, weather them, and clean up after them. Finally, this book seeks to show how we can rebuild our financial levees so as to blunt the effects of future storms. For what we just lived through is a taste of what is to come. Crises will figure in our future.

To understand why, we will tackle a host of unresolved, lingering questions about the recent disaster, beginning with the most obvious: Why did the bubble behind the worst financial meltdown in decades first form?

Was it a function of excessive risk taking by financial institutions, made possible by lax regulation and supervision? Or was it the inevitable consequence of excessive government interference in financial markets? These questions cut to the core of very different, even antagonistic ways of understanding financial crises. They also point toward radically different remedies.

This book also examines why the recent crisis hit when it did. Was it merely a collapse of confidence, a withering of what John Maynard Keynes called the "animal spirits" of capitalism? Or was it the inevitable consequence of the fact that some portions of the economy were (and arguably remain) excessively leveraged and effectively bankrupt? Put differently, did the crisis result from a mere lack of liquidity or from a more profound lack of solvency? If the latter, what does that portend for the future?

From there the questions multiply. In the midst of the crisis, central bankers around the world became "lenders of last resort" for vast swaths of the financial system. Did their actions prevent something worse from happening? Or will they only encourage excessive risk taking in the future, setting us up for bigger and more destructive bubbles and busts? Likewise, what will be the result of the rush to reregulate? Will it produce a more robust and resilient financial system and more stable growth, or will its effects be merely cosmetic, incapable of preventing more virulent bubbles and crises in the future?

None of these questions are hypothetical. John Maynard Keynes, a giant in twentieth-century economics, once rightly observed that "the ideas of economists and political philosophers, both when they are right and when they are wrong, are more powerful than is commonly understood. Indeed, the world is ruled by little else. . . . Madmen in authority, who hear voices in the air, are distilling their frenzy from some academic scribbler of a few years back." Keynes wrote those oft-quoted words more than seventy years ago, but they are equally pertinent today. Much of our framing and understanding of the worst financial crisis in generations derives from a set of assumptions that, while not always wrong, have nonetheless prevented a full understanding of its origins and consequences.

We want to make it clear at the outset that we are not devotees of any particular economist's thought; almost every school of economics has something relevant to say about the recent crisis, and our analysis relies on a range of thinkers. Keynes has his say, but so do other voices. In fact, we believe that understanding and managing crises requires a more holistic and eclectic approach than is perhaps customary. It's necessary to check ideology at the door and look at matters more dispassionately. Crises come in many colors, and what works in one situation may not work in another.

That same pragmatism pervades this book's assessment of the financial system's future. Going forward, it asks, should we worry more about inflation or deflation? What will be the long-term consequences of policy measures like the stimulus packages implemented by many countries, never mind the emergency measures undertaken by the Federal Reserve and other central banks? And what is the future of the Anglo-Saxon model of unfettered laissez-faire capitalism? What is the future of the dollar? Does the recent crisis mark the beginning of the end of the American empire, and the rise of China and other emerging economies? Finally, how can we reform global economic governance in order to mitigate the damage from future crises?

The modest ambition of this book is to answer these questions by placing the recent crisis in the context of others that have occurred over the ages and across the world. After all, the past few years conform to a familiar, centuries-old pattern. Crises follow consistent trajectories and yield predictable results. They are far more common and comprehensible than conventional wisdom would lead you to believe. In the pages that follow, we'll move between past and present, revealing how the foregoing questions were asked and answered in the wake of previous crises.

Along the way we'll explain several intimidating and often misunderstood concepts in economics: *moral hazard, leverage, bank run, regulatory arbitrage, current account deficit, securitization, deflation, credit derivative, credit crunch,* and *liquidity trap,* to name a few. We hope our explanations will prove useful not only to financial professionals on Wall Street and Main Street but also to corporate executives at home and abroad; to undergraduate and graduate students in business, economics, and finance; to policy makers and policy wonks in many countries; and most numerous of all, to ordinary investors around the world who now know that they ignore the intricacies of the international financial order at their peril.

This book follows a straightforward arc, starting with a history of older crises and the economists who analyzed them. It then addresses the very deep roots of the most recent crisis, as well as the ways this catastrophe unfolded in a very predictable pattern, conforming to time-honored precedents. Finally, the book looks to the future, laying out much-needed reforms of the financial system and addressing the likelihood of other crises in the coming years. Chapter 1 takes the reader on a tour of the past, surveying the many booms, bubbles, and busts that have swept the economic landscape. We focus in particular on the relationship between capitalism and crisis, beginning with the speculative bubble in tulips in 1630s Holland, then ranging forward to the South Sea Bubble of 1720; the first global financial crisis in 1825; the panic of 1907; the Great Depression of the 1930s; and the many crises that plagued emerging markets and advanced economies from the 1980s onward. Crises, we argue, are neither the freak events that modern economics has made them seem nor the rare "black swans" that other commentators have made them out to be. Rather, they are commonplace and relatively easy to foresee and to comprehend. Call them white swans.

In most advanced economies, the second half of the twentieth century was a period of relative, if uncharacteristic, calm, culminating in a halcyon period of low inflation and high growth that economists dubbed the "Great Moderation." As a result, mainstream economics has either ignored crises or seen them as symptoms of troubles in less developed economies. To gain a more expansive way of viewing and understanding crises of the past, present, and future, one must go back to an earlier generation of economists. Chapter 2 introduces economic thinkers who can help us do just that. Some, like John Maynard Keynes, are reasonably well known; others, like Hyman Minsky, are not.

Chapter 3 explains the deep structural origins of the recent crisis. From the beginning, it has been fashionable to blame it on recently issued subprime mortgages that somehow infected an otherwise healthy global financial system. This chapter challenges that absurd perspective, showing how decades-old trends and policies created a global financial system that was subprime from top to bottom. Beyond the creation of ever more esoteric and opaque financial instruments, these long-standing trends included the rise of the "shadow banking system," a sprawling collection of nonbank mortgage lenders, hedge funds, broker dealers, money market funds, and other institutions that looked like banks, acted like banks, borrowed and lent like banks, and otherwise became banks—but were never regulated like banks.

This same chapter introduces the problem of moral hazard, in which market participants take undue risks on the assumption that they will be bailed out, indemnified, and otherwise spared the consequences of their reckless behavior. It also addresses long-standing failures of corporate governance, as well as the role of government itself, though we do not subscribe to the usual contradictory explanations that the crisis was caused by too much government or too little. The reality, we argue, is much more complicated and counterintuitive: government did play a role, as did its absence, but not necessarily in the way that either conservatives or liberals would have you believe.

Several subsequent chapters focus on the crisis itself. Numerous accounts already exist, but almost all have painted it as a singular, unprecedented event particular to twenty-first-century finance. Chapter 4 dispels this naïve and simplistic view by comparing it to previous crises. We argue that the events of 2008 would have been familiar to financial observers one hundred or even two hundred years ago, not only in how they unfolded but in how the world's central banks attempted to defuse them by serving as lenders of last resort. The particulars of the crisis differed from those of its predecessors, but in many ways it stuck to a familiar script, amply illustrating the old adage that while history rarely repeats itself, it often rhymes.

History confirms that crises are much like pandemics: they begin with the outbreak of a disease that then spreads, radiating outward. This crisis was no different, though its origin in the world's financial centers rather than in emerging markets on the periphery made it particularly virulent. Chapter 5 tracks how and why the crisis went global, hammering economies as different as Iceland, Dubai, Japan, Latvia, Ireland, Germany, China, and Singapore. We break with the conventional wisdom that the rest of the world merely caught a disease that originated in the United States. Far from it: the vulnerabilities that plagued the U.S. financial system were widespread—and in some cases, worse—elsewhere in the world. The pandemic, then, was not indiscriminate in its effects; only countries whose financial systems suffered from similar frailties fell victim to it.

While other books on the financial crisis focus heavily or exclusively on the United States, this one frames it as a broad crisis in twenty-first-century global capitalism. By tracing its sometimes surprising international dimensions, chapter 5 uncovers truths about global finance, international macroeconomics, and the cross-border implications of national monetary and fiscal policy. The crisis can tell us a great deal about the workings of the global economy in both normal times and not-so-normal times.

All crises end, and this one was no exception. Unfortunately, the aftershocks will linger on for years if not decades. Chapter 6 shows why they do, and why deflation and depression loom large in the wake of any crisis. In the past, central bankers used monetary policy to counter crises, and now they've revived some of these approaches. At the same time, many financial crises force central bankers to innovate on the fly, and the recent crisis was no exception. Unfortunately, while these emergency measures may work, they can, like any untested remedy, end up poisoning the patient.

That's the case with fiscal policies as well. In chapter 7 we examine how policy makers used the government's power to tax and spend in order to arrest the spread of the crisis. Some of these tactics were first articulated by Keynes; many more represented a massive, unprecedented intervention in the economy. This chapter assesses the future implications of the most radical measures, particularly the risks they may create down the line.

The level of intervention necessary to stabilize the system challenges the sustainability of traditional laissez-faire capitalism itself; governments may end up playing a much larger direct and indirect role in the postcrisis global economy, via increased regulation and supervision. Chapters 8 and 9 lay out a blueprint for a new financial architecture, one that will bring new transparency and stability to financial institutions. Long-term reforms necessary for stabilizing the international financial system include greater coordination among central banks; binding regulation and supervision of not just commercial banks but also investment banks, insurance companies, and hedge funds; policies to control the risky behavior of "too big to fail" financial firms;

the need for more capital and liquidity among financial institutions; and policies to reduce the problem of moral hazard and the fiscal costs of bailing out financial firms. These chapters also grapple with the vexing question of what future role central banks should play to control and pop asset bubbles.

Chapter 10 tackles the serious imbalances in the global economy and the more radical reforms of the international monetary and financial order that may be necessary to prevent future crises. Why have so many emerging-market economies suffered financial crises in the last twenty years? Why has the United States run massive deficits, while Germany, Japan, China, and a host of emerging-market economies have run surpluses? Will these current account imbalances—which were one of the causes of the financial crisis—be resolved in an orderly or a disorderly way? Could the U.S. dollar crash, and if so, what would replace it as a global reserve currency? What role can a reformed IMF play in reducing global monetary distortions and financial crises? And should the IMF become a true international lender of last resort?

This part of the book recognizes an inescapable truth: the ability of the United States, much less the G-7, to dictate the terms of these reforms is limited. These changes in global economic governance will play out under the watchful eye of a much more extensive group of stakeholders: Brazil, India, China, Russia, and the other countries that make up the ascendant G-20. These increasingly powerful nations will profoundly shape the handling of future crises; so will a host of new players and institutions in the global financial system, like sovereign wealth funds, offshore financial centers, and international monetary unions.

The final "Outlook" section surveys the road ahead, taking a hard look at the many dangers that await the world economy. The crisis that gave us the Great Recession may be over for now, but potential pitfalls and risks loom large. What issues will determine the future volatility of the world economy and its financial system? Will the global economy return to high growth, or will it experience a long period of subpar and anemic growth? Has the loose monetary policy adopted in the wake of the crisis created a risk of new asset bubbles that will go bust? How will the U.S. government and other governments deal with the massive amounts of debt assumed on account of the crisis? Will the government resort to high inflation to wipe out the real value of public and private debts, or will deflation pose the bigger danger? What is the future of globalization and of market economies? Will the pendulum swing toward greater government intervention in economic and financial affairs, and what will be the consequences of such a shift? While many commentators have assumed that the future belongs to China and that the United States is destined for a long decline, this look to the future sets out various scenarios in which both existing and emerging economies might survive and thrive—or struggle and collapse.

More generally, the final chapters of the book wrestle with several open questions: How will globalization affect the probability of future crises? How will we resolve the global imbalances that helped create the recent crisis? How, in other words, will we reform global capitalism? Here too the lessons of the past may have some bearing. After all, we've been down this road before, many times. In 1933 John Maynard Keynes declared, "The decadent international but individualistic capitalism, in the hands of which we found ourselves after the [First World] war, is not a success. It is not intelligent, it is not beautiful, it is not just, it is not virtuous—and it doesn't deliver the goods. In short we dislike it, and we are beginning to despise it. But when we wonder what to put in its place, we are extremely perplexed."

That perplexity was eventually resolved, and it will be once again. This book contributes to that resolution, giving some sense of how to reform a capitalism that has delivered serial crises instead of delivering the goods on a consistent and stable basis. Indeed, while market-oriented reforms have taken many emerging market economies out of endemic poverty and underdevelopment, the frequency and virulence of economic and financial crises have increased in both emerging markets and industrial economies. To that end, we offer a road map, not merely of how we got into this mess, but how we can get out—and stay out.

Chapter 1

The White Swan

When did the boom begin? Perhaps it began with the sudden mania for flipping real estate, when first-time speculators bought and sold subdivision lots like shares of stock, doubling and tripling their profits in weeks if not days. Or possibly things got out of balance when the allure of a new economy founded on new technology and new industries drew ordinary people to wager their life savings on Wall Street.

Politicians and policy makers, far from standing in the way of these get-rich-quick schemes, encouraged them. No less an authority than the president of the United States proclaimed that government should not bother business, while the Federal Reserve did little to stem the speculative tide. Financial innovation and experimentation were hailed for their tremendous contributions to economic growth, and new kinds of financial firms emerged to market little-understood securities to inexperienced investors and to make extensive lines of credit available to millions of borrowers.

At some point the boom became a bubble. Everyone from high-flying banks to ordinary consumers leveraged themselves to the hilt, betting on the dubious yet curiously compelling belief that prices could only go up. Most economists blessed this state of affairs, counseling that the market was always right; it was best not to interfere. The handful of dissidents who warned of a coming crash found themselves mocked if not ignored.

Then came the crash, and as it echoed up and down in the canyons of Wall Street, venerable institutions tottered, besieged by fearful creditors. During lulls in the storm, some declared that the worst had passed, but then conditions worsened. Financial firms slid toward the abyss, and though a few investment banks—most notably Goldman Sachs—managed to escape the conflagration, other storied firms collapsed overnight. Lines of credit evaporated, and the financial system's elaborate machinery of borrowing and lending seized up, leaving otherwise creditworthy companies scrambling to refinance their debts.

As the stock market crashed, foreclosures mounted, firms failed, and consumers stopped spending. Vast Ponzi schemes came to light, as did evidence of widespread fraud and collusion throughout the financial industry. By then the sickness in the United States had spread to the rest of the world, and foreign stock markets, banks, and investment firms came crashing down to earth. Unemployment soared, industrial production plummeted, and falling prices raised the specter of deflation. It was the end of an era.

What we're describing didn't happen a couple of years ago; it happened more than eighty years ago, on the eve of the Great Depression. Then as now, speculative bubbles in real estate and stocks, minimal financial regulation, and a flurry of financial innovation conspired to create a bubble that, when it burst, set the stage for the near collapse of the financial system on Wall Street, a brutal economic downturn on Main Street, and a worldwide bust. That the recent crisis bears so many eerie similarities to a catastrophe that unfolded decades ago is not a coincidence: the same forces that gave rise to the Great Depression were at work in the years leading up to our very own Great Recession.

Even more striking, the irrational euphoria, the pyramids of leverage, the financial innovations, the asset price bubbles, the panics, and the runs on banks and other financial institutions shared by these two episodes are common to many other financial disasters as well. Change a few particulars of the foregoing narrative, and you could be reading about the infamous South Sea Bubble of 1720, the global financial crisis of 1825, the boom and bust that foreshadowed Japan's Lost Decade (1991–2000), the American savings and loan crisis, or the dozens of crises that hammered emerging markets in the 1980s and 1990s.

In the history of modern capitalism, crises are the norm, not the exception. That's not to say that all crises are the same. Far from it: the particulars can change from disaster to disaster, and crises can trace their origins to different problems in different sectors of the economy. Sometimes a crisis originates in the excesses of overleveraged households; at other times financial firms or corporations or even governments are to blame. Moreover, the collateral damage that crises cause varies greatly; much depends on the scale and appropriateness of government intervention. When crises assume global dimensions, as the worst ones so often do, much hangs on whether cooperation or conflict characterizes the international response.

The stakes could not be higher. When handled carelessly, crises inflict staggering losses, wiping out entire industries, destroying wealth, causing massive job losses, and burdening governments with enormous fiscal costs. Even worse, crises have toppled governments and bankrupted nations; they have driven countries to wage retaliatory trade battles. Crises have even paved the way for wars, much as the Great Depression helped set the stage for World War II. Ignoring them is not an option.

Creatures of Habit

Early in 2007, when signs of a looming housing and subprime mortgage crisis in the United States appeared on the horizon, the initial reaction was disbelief and denial. In March, Federal Reserve chairman Ben Bernanke confidently told Congress, "At this juncture, however, the impact on the broader economy and financial markets of the problems in the subprime market seems likely to be contained." That summer Treasury Secretary Henry Paulson dismissed the threat of the subprime mortgage meltdown: "I don't think it poses any threat to the overall economy."

Even after the crisis exploded, this refusal to face facts persisted. In May 2008, after the collapse of Bear Stearns, Paulson offered a characteristically upbeat assessment. "Looking forward," he said, "I expect that financial markets will be driven less by the recent turmoil and more by broader economic conditions and, specifically, by the recovery of the housing sector." That summer saw the collapse of mortgage giants Fannie Mae and Freddie Mac, yet even then many remained optimistic.

Perhaps the most infamous bit of cheerleading came from stock market guru and financial commentator Donald Luskin, who on September 14, 2008, penned an op-ed in *The Washington Post* laying out the case for a quick recovery. "Sure," he conceded, "there are trouble spots in the economy, as the government takeover of mortgage giants Fannie Mae and Freddie Mac, and jitters about Wall Street firm Lehman Brothers, amply demonstrate. And unemployment figures are up a bit too." But "none of this," he forcefully argued, "is cause for depression—or exaggerated Depression comparisons. . . . Anyone who says we're in a recession, or heading into one—especially the worst one since the Great Depression—is making up his own private definition of 'recession.'" The next day Lehman Brothers collapsed, the panic assumed global proportions, the world's financial system went into a cardiac arrest, and for two quarters the global economy experienced a free fall comparable to that of the Great Depression.

As it became apparent that the crisis was real, many commentators tried to make sense of the disaster. Plenty of people invoked Nassim Nicholas Taleb's concept of the "black swan" to explain it. Taleb, whose book of that title came out on the eve of the crisis, defined a "black swan event" as a game-changing occurrence that is both extraordinarily rare and well-nigh impossible to predict. By that definition, the financial crisis was a freak event, albeit an incredibly important and transformational one. No one could possibly have seen it coming.

In a perverse way, that idea is comforting. If financial crises are black swans, comparable to plane crashes—horrific but highly improbable and impossible to predict—there's no point in worrying about them. But the recent disaster was no freak event. It was probable. It was even predictable, because financial crises generally follow the same script over and over again. Familiar economic and financial vulnerabilities build up and eventually reach a tipping point. For all the chaos they create, crises are creatures of habit.

Most crises begin with a bubble, in which the price of a particular asset rises far above its underlying fundamental value. This kind of bubble often goes hand in hand with an excessive accumulation of debt, as investors borrow money to buy into the boom. Not coincidentally, asset bubbles are often associated with an excessive growth in the supply of credit. This could be a consequence of lax supervision and regulation of the financial system or even the loose monetary policies of a central bank.

At other times asset bubbles develop even before the credit supply booms, because expectations of future price increases are sufficient to foster a self-fulfilling rise in the asset's price. A major technological innovation—the invention of railroads, for example, or the creation of the Internet—may lead to expectations of a brave new world of high growth, triggering a bubble. No such new technology prompted the current housing-driven crisis, although the complex securities manufactured in Wall Street's financial laboratories may qualify, even if they did little to create real economic value.

But that would not be new either. Many bubbles, while fueled by concrete technological improvements, gain force from changes in the structure of finance. In the last few hundred years, many of the most destructive booms-turned-bust have gone hand in hand with financial innovation, the creation of newfangled instruments and institutions for investing in whatever is the focus of a speculative fever. They could be new forms of credit or debt, or even new kinds of banks, affording investors novel opportunities for participating in a speculative bubble.

Regardless of how the boom begins, or the channels by which investors join it, some asset becomes the focus of intense speculative interest. The coveted asset could be anything, but equities, housing, and real estate are the most common. As its price shoots skyward, optimists feverishly attempt to justify this overvaluation. When confronted with the evidence of previous busts, they claim, "This time is different." Wise men and women assert—and believe—that the economy has entered a phase where the rules of the past no longer apply. The recent housing bubble in the United States followed this script with remarkable fidelity: real estate was said to be a "safe investment" that "never lost value" because "home prices never fall." The same was said of the complex securities built out of thousands of mortgages.

From such beginnings, financial disasters proceed along a predictable path. As credit becomes increasingly cheap and abundant, the coveted asset becomes easier to buy. Demand rises and outstrips supply; prices consequently rise. But that's just the beginning. Because the assets at the heart of the bubble can typically serve as collateral, and because the value of the collateral is rising, a speculator can borrow even more with each passing day. In a word, borrowers can become leveraged.

Again, this pattern played out from 2000 in the United States: as home values rose markedly and wages stagnated, households used their homes as collateral in order to borrow more, most often in the form of a home equity withdrawal or home equity loans; people effectively used their homes as ATM machines. As housing prices climbed, borrowers could borrow even more, using what they'd purchased—home improvements, even second homes—as additional collateral. By the fourth quarter of 2005, home equity withdrawals peaked at an annualized rate of a trillion dollars, enabling millions of households to live well beyond their means. At the same time, the household savings rate plunged to zero, then went into negative territory for the first time since the Great Depression. However unsustainable, this debt-financed consumption had real economic effects: households and firms purchasing goods and services fueled economic growth.

Such a dynamic creates a vicious cycle. As the economy grows, incomes rise and firms register higher profits. Worries about risk drop to record lows, the cost of borrowing falls, and households and firms borrow and spend more with ever greater ease. At this point, the bubble is not just a state of mind but a force for economic change, driving growth and underwriting new and increasingly risky business ventures, like housing subdivisions in the desert.

In the typical boom-and-bust cycle, people are still saying, "This time is different," and claiming that the boom will never end, even though all the elements of a speculative mania—"irrational exuberance" and growing evidence of reckless, even fraudulent, behavior—are in place. American homeowners, for example, enthusiastically embraced the fiction that home prices could increase 20 percent every year forever, and on the basis of that belief they borrowed more and more. The same euphoria held sway in the shadow banking system of hedge funds, investment banks, insurers, money market funds, and other firms that held assets that appreciated as housing prices boomed.

At some point, the bubble stops growing, typically when the supply for the bubbly asset exceeds the demand. Confidence that prices will keep rising vanishes, and borrowing becomes harder. Just as a fire needs oxygen, a bubble needs leverage and easy money, and when those dry up, prices begin to fall and "deleveraging" begins. That process began in the United States when the supply of new homes outstripped demand. The excessive number of homes built during the boom collided with diminished demand, as excessively high prices and rising mortgage rates deterred buyers from wading any further into the market.

When the boom becomes a bust, the results are also predictable. The falling value of the asset at the root of the bubble eventually triggers panicked "margin calls," requests that borrowers put up more cash or collateral to compensate for falling prices. This, in turn, may force borrowers to sell off some of their assets at fire-sale prices. Supplies of the asset soon far outstrip demand, prices fall further, and the value of the remaining collateral plunges, prompting further margin calls and still more attempts to reduce exposure. In a rush for the exits, everyone moves into safer and more liquid assets and avoids the asset at the focus of the bubble. Panic ensues, and just as prices exceeded their fundamental value during the bubble, prices fall well below their fundamental values during the bust.

That's what happened over the course of 2007 and 2008. As homeowners defaulted on their mortgages, the value of the securities derived from those loans collapsed, and the bust began. Eventually the losses suffered by highly leveraged financial institutions forced them to hunker down and limit their exposure to risk. As happens in every bust, the banks overcompensated: they trimmed their sails, curtailed lending, and thereby triggered an economy-wide liquidity and credit crunch. Individuals and firms could no longer "roll over," or refinance, their existing debt, much less spend money on goods and services, and the economy began to contract. What started as a financial crisis spilled over into the real economy, causing plenty of collateral damage.

That's the recent crisis in a nutshell, but it could be the story of almost any financial crisis. Contrary to conventional wisdom, crises are not black swans but white swans: the elements of boom and bust are remarkably predictable. Look into the recent past, and you can find dozens of financial crises. Further back in time, before the Great Depression, many more lurk in the historical record. Some of them hit single nations; others reverberated across countries and continents, wreaking havoc on a global scale. Yet most are forgotten today, dismissed as relics of a less enlightened era.

The Dark Ages

Financial crises come in many shapes and guises. Before the rise of capitalism, they tended to be a result of government malfeasance. From the twelfth century onward, governments of countries and kingdoms as diverse as Spain and England debased their currencies, cutting the gold or silver content of coins while maintaining the fiction that the new coins were worth as much as the old. These naked attempts to discharge debts in depreciated currency became even easier with the advent of paper money. Governments could literally print their way out of debt. The Chinese pioneered this practice as early as 1072; European nations adopted it much later, beginning in the eighteenth century.

A government that owed money to foreign creditors could take a more honest route and simply default, much as Edward III did in the mid-fourteenth century. Having borrowed money from Florentine bankers, he refused to pay it back, sowing chaos in Italy's commercial centers. It was a harbinger of things to come; plenty of other sovereigns took this route, with predictable consequences for their creditors. Austria, France, Prussia, Portugal, and Spain all defaulted on their debts at various times from the fourteenth century onward.

While important and destabilizing, these episodes were crises of confidence in overindebted governments, not of capitalism. But with the emergence of the Netherlands as the world's first capitalist dynamo in the sixteenth and seventeenth centuries, a new kind of crisis made its appearance: the asset bubble. In the 1630s "tulip mania" gripped the country, as speculators bid up the prices of rare tulip bulbs to stratospheric levels. While historians continue to debate the consequences of this bit of speculative fever (and some economists even deny it was a bubble, arguing that all bubbles are driven by fundamentals), it set the stage for larger bubbles whose destructive effects are not in doubt. Most infamous was John Law's Mississippi Company, a sprawling speculative venture that dominated the French economy in the late 1710s. At its peak in 1719, Law's company controlled several other trading companies, the national mint, the national bank, the entire French national debt, and for good measure much of the land that would become the United States.

Not to be outdone, the British caught the bubble bug around the same time. At the center was a corporation known as the South Sea Company, which at its height effectively controlled much of the British national debt. Speculation in its shares gave rise to a mania for stocks of all kinds, including many fraudulent corporations. After the company's stock price increased by 1,000 percent, the day of reckoning came: the stock market crashed, leaving the economy in shambles and a generation of British investors wary of financial markets. An even more devastating crisis hit France at the same time, as Law's schemes unraveled spectacularly, stunting the development of financial institutions for decades.

These crises figure significantly in any standard history of speculative manias, panics, and crashes, but they did not trigger global financial crises. By contrast, the panic of 1825 reverberated around the world. It began in Britain and had all the hallmarks of a classic crisis: easy money (courtesy of the Bank of England), an asset bubble (stocks and bonds linked to investments in the emerging market of newly independent Peru), and even widespread fraud (feverish selling of the bonds of a fictitious nation called the Republic of Poyais to credulous investors).

When the bubble burst, numerous banks and nonfinancial firms in Britain failed. It was, the English economist Walter Bagehot recalled, "a period of frantic and almost inconceivable violence; scarcely anyone knew whom to trust; credit was almost suspended; [and] the country was . . . within twenty-four hours of [entering] a state of barter." Bagehot, one of the first writers to argue that a central bank should act as a lender of last resort when a panic and bank run occurs, lamented that "applications for assistance were made to the Government, but . . . the Government refused to act." The financial crisis quickly spread to the rest of Europe, and panicked investors pulled money out of Latin America. By 1828 every country on the continent except Brazil had defaulted on its public debt. It took three decades for the flow of capital to the region to return to earlier levels.

No less global in scope was the panic of 1857. The boom began in the

United States, with speculation in slaves, railroads, financial instruments, and land. The bubble burst, and banks in New York City panicked, curtailing credit and trying to shore up their positions, but to no avail: holders of the banks' obligations presented them for redemption, draining the banks of gold and silver reserves, a classic case of a bank run. A little over a month later, panic hit London, and the Bank of England's reserves were drawn down with similar speed. The panic spread to the rest of Europe and from there to India, China, the Caribbean, South Africa, and Latin America. Countries around the world saw their economies suffer, and the crisis put an end to one of the longest economic expansions in modern times.

The most dramatic nineteenth-century global meltdown may have been the crisis of 1873. Once again, investors in Britain and continental Europe made enormous speculative investments in railroads in the United States and Latin America, as well as other projects. Worse, reparations paid by France to Germany in the wake of the Franco-Prussian War sparked a speculative boom in German and Austrian real estate. When this boom collapsed, the stock markets in Vienna, Amsterdam, and Zurich imploded, prompting European investors to liquidate overseas investments. This put strain on the United States, which itself was in the grip of a speculative boom in railroad securities. When the investment banker Jay Cooke failed to find buyers for securities issued to underwrite construction of the new Northern Pacific Railroad, both his bank and the railroad collapsed, triggering a massive panic on Wall Street. This calamity sparked further secondary panics in Europe, and much of the world plunged into a brutal economic depression and a deflationary spiral. In the United States a quarter of the nation's railroads went under, while soaring unemployment and wage cuts led to bloody riots and strikes. The collapse in the global economy had particularly pernicious effects outside the United States and Europe, hitting the Ottoman Empire, Greece, Tunisia, Honduras, and Paraguay.

This account is but a sampling of the crises that plagued the nineteenth century; there were many, many more: the panics of 1819, 1837, 1866, and 1893, to name a few. All had their unique qualities, but many shared a common set of features. Typically they began in more developed economies after excessive speculative lending and investments went bust, triggering a banking crisis. As the global economy sputtered and slowed, countries on the periphery that depended on exporting commodities saw their economies wither. Government revenue collapsed, leading some countries to default on their domestic debt, if not loans from overseas. In some cases, these defaults spurred additional meltdowns at the economic core, as investors in these emerging markets lost their shirts.

The early twentieth century saw its shares of panics too. The crisis of 1907 began in the United States after a speculative boom in stocks and real estate collapsed. So-called trust companies—lightly regulated commercial banks bound together by complicated chains of ownership—suffered runs on their reserves, and panic spread throughout the country. The stock market crashed, and as the crisis spiraled out of control, the nation's most powerful banker, J. P. Morgan, convened a series of emergency meetings with New York City's banking establishment to stop the bank run. On the first weekend of November, Morgan, in a famous act of brinksmanship, invited the bankers to his private library. When they failed to agree to come to one another's aid, he locked them in a room and pocketed the key. The bankers eventually agreed, and the crisis came to an end shortly thereafter. While Morgan received credit for averting a catastrophe, the events of 1907 persuaded many of the need for a central bank to provide lender-of-last-resort support in future crises, and six years later the Federal Reserve was born.

In theory, a central bank like the Federal Reserve can serve as a bulwark against financial crises, providing lender-of-last-resort support in the event of a bank run. But during the catastrophic crash of 1929, as the crisis spun out of control, the Fed stood idly by. Rather than pursuing an expansionary monetary policy, it tightened the reins, making a bad situation even worse. As a consequence, the money supply sharply contracted between 1929 and 1933, leading to a severe liquidity and credit crunch that turned a stock market bust into a banking crisis and eventually into a severe economic depression.

The reaction of the rest of the federal government wasn't much better. Andrew Mellon, Herbert Hoover's Treasury secretary, believed a purge was necessary. Hoover described Mellon as a "leave-it-alone liquidationist" who had no pity for those caught in the crisis. "Liquidate labor, liquidate stocks, liquidate the farmers, liquidate real estate," Mellon was said to have counseled. Mellon believed that financial panic would "purge the rottenness out of the system. High costs of living and high living will come down. People will work harder, live a more moral life."

Perhaps, but from 1929 to 1933 the United States plunged into the worst depression in its history. Unemployment rates shot from 3.2 percent to 24.9 percent; upwards of nine thousand banks suspended operations or closed, and by the time Franklin Delano Roosevelt took office, a good part of the nation's financial system had effectively collapsed, much as it had in other countries around the world. Many of those other countries experienced comparable rates of unemployment and economic decline. Currency wars led to trade wars. In the United States the infamous Smoot-Hawley Tariff triggered retaliatory tariffs across the world and contributed to a breakdown of world trade. Many nations in Europe eventually depreciated their currencies, debased their debts via inflation, and even formally defaulted on debts, including Germany, where the crisis paved the way for Hitler's rise to power and the worst war in human history.

For all its horrific consequences, World War II made possible a wholesale transformation of the world's financial system. In 1944, as the end of the war drew near, economists and policy makers from the Allied nations met in Bretton Woods, New Hampshire, to hammer out a new world economic order. Their deliberations gave rise to the International Monetary Fund, as well as the forerunner of the World Bank, and a new system of currency exchange rates known as the Bretton Woods system or dollar exchange standard. In this system, every nation's currency would be exchanged into dollars at a fixed rate. Foreign countries that held dollars then had the option of redeeming them for U.S. gold at the price of thirty-five dollars an ounce. In effect, the dollar became the world's reserve currency, while the United States alone remained on a gold standard in its dealings with other countries. Thus began a remarkable—and extraordinarily anomalous, given the previous centuries' crises—era of financial stability, a *pax moneta* that depended on the dollar and on the military and economic power of the newly ascendant United States. That stability rested as well on the widespread provision of deposit insurance to stop bank runs; strict regulation of the financial system, including the separation of American commercial banking from investment banking; and extensive capital controls that reduced currency volatility.

All these domestic and international restrictions kept financial excesses and bubbles under control for over a quarter of a century.

All good things come to an end, and the postwar era was no exception: the Bretton Woods system fell apart in 1971, when the United States finally went off the last vestiges of the gold standard. The reason? The twin U.S. fiscal and current account deficits (which we will discuss in chapter 10) triggered by the Vietnam War caused an accumulation of dollar reserves by the creditors of the United States—primarily Western Europe and Japan—that became unsustainable. In effect, the creditors of the United States realized that there wasn't enough gold to back up the dollars in circulation. When that happened, Bretton Woods collapsed, the dollar depreciated, and the world moved to a system of flexible exchange rates.

This move unshackled monetary authorities that, freed of the constraints of a fixed-rate regime, could now print as much money as they wanted. The result was a rise in inflation and commodity prices, even before the 1973 Yom Kippur War led to an oil embargo and a quadrupling of oil prices. Stagflation, a deadly combination of high inflation and recession, followed the two oil shocks of 1973 and 1979 (the latter triggered by the Iranian Revolution) as well as the botched monetary policy response to these shocks. It took a new Federal Reserve chairman, Paul Volcker, to set things right. He sharply raised interest rates to stratospheric levels, triggering a severe double-dip recession in the early 1980s. While brutal, this shock treatment worked, breaking the back of inflation and ushering in a decade of growth.

Every silver lining has its cloud: Volcker's policies also helped trigger the Latin American debt crisis of the 1980s. In the 1970s many Latin American governments embarked on massive economic development projects financed with foreign capital. The resulting fiscal and current account deficits were financed with loans brokered by banks in the United States and Europe. The interest rates on these foreign currency loans were linked to a benchmark short-term interest rate known as the London Interbank Offered Rate (LIBOR). When Volcker hiked interest rates, the LIBOR rate rose sharply as well, making it impossible for Latin American countries to service their debts. Even worse, the real value of these debts rose as these countries' currencies depreciated.

As a consequence, multiple governments defaulted on their debt. In Mexico in 1982, the default ushered in an economic collapse that led to the nationalization of Mexico's private banking system and then a devastating recession; Brazil, Argentina, and other countries in Latin America soon followed suit. In many ways, these defaults replayed earlier crises, as events in the world's leading economies reverberated in less developed countries.

The Latin American debt crisis had profound consequences: lost growth, political instability, and social unrest throughout the region. Only in the late 1980s, when the loans were reduced in face value and converted into bonds (the "Brady bonds"), did the region start to recover. Many banks in the United States and Europe struggled to recuperate as well. It took an enormous amount of regulatory forbearance and international crisis management, led by the United States and the IMF, to stop the banks from going under.

The Not-So-Great Moderation

By the mid-1980s Volcker had defeated inflation, and central bankers around the world reaffirmed their commitment to low inflation. At the same time, the ordinary business cycle of the advanced industrial nations became markedly less volatile: recessions came and went with fewer ill effects, and expansions lasted longer. In the United States, flirtations with disaster and financial crisis, like the stock market crash of 1987, did not metastasize into anything more destructive: the 1987 crash did not cause a recession, and the 1990–91 recession was relatively short and shallow, lasting only eight months. And so the Great Moderation was born: an era of low inflation, high growth, and mild recessions.

What accounted for the Great Moderation was anyone's guess. Some economists argued that the climate of business and financial deregulation and technological innovation had created a more flexible and adaptable economic system, one that could more readily handle the ups and downs of the business cycle. Others suggested that growing globalization and free trade—and the rise of China and other emerging economies capable of producing ever-cheaper goods—would keep global inflation at bay even as global growth accelerated. Still others stressed that the decline of organized labor helped keep wage growth in line with productivity.

Some ascribed the Great Moderation to monetary policy. Ben Bernanke, in a speech delivered in 2004, made a forceful argument along these lines. Bernanke declared himself "optimistic for the future" and noted that only one advanced industrial nation didn't display the much-celebrated combination of financial stability and short, shallow recessions: Japan, which he observed suffered from a "distinctive set of economic problems."

That was an understatement. Japan in the 1980s fell into the grip of an unprecedented speculative mania rooted in stocks and real estate. The bubble originated with the usual suspects. Easy money, courtesy of the Bank of Japan, kept rates low; the bank raised them only at the very end of the boom. There was financial innovation and deregulation, as banks moved aggressively into real estate lending, an area outside their traditional expertise. And there was the usual irrational euphoria, the belief that prices could only go higher. The domestic stock market index, the Nikkei, went from roughly 10,000 to nearly 40,000, and real estate prices displayed a similar trajectory: residential real estate prices nearly doubled in the late 1980s, and commercial real estate tripled. At the peak of the boom, the land beneath and surrounding Tokyo's Imperial Palace—several hundred acres in total—had by some estimates market value equivalent to all the real estate in California.

The market leveled off in late 1989, and when the Bank of Japan began raising rates in order to end speculation, the bubble burst. After an early crash in the stock market, the economy collapsed in slow motion: stock prices continued to drift downward, as did land values. The 1990s in Japan have a name—*ushinawareta junen*—the Lost Decade. For over ten years the Japanese economy lurched in and out of recessions, never again growing at its earlier breakneck pace of 4 percent; annual growth averaged only 1 percent. Though many corporations and banks were effectively insolvent, regulators looked the other way as firms and banks engaged in creative or fraudulent accounting devices to hide the extent of their losses. Failure to undertake aggressive corporate and bank restructuring kept zombie banks and firms alive for too long. The eventual closure of banks, and the waves of consolidation in the banking sector and recapitalization of financial institutions in the late 1990s, finally helped resolve some of these issues, but prices of land and equities never recovered.

Bernanke had argued in his 2004 speech that Japan was the exception, not the norm. But was it? In fact, a financial crisis engulfed Norway in the late 1980s and persisted into the early 1990s, when much of the banking system in both Finland and Sweden collapsed, a casualty of the collapse in Russian demand for Scandinavian goods after the fall of the Berlin Wall. In the United States in the late 1980s and early 1990s, savings and loan associations saw their loans go bad as the real estate bubble popped. Upwards of 1,600 banks eventually went under, and although this banking crisis was not as severe as the recent global financial meltdown, it nonetheless led to a credit crunch, a painful recession in 1990–91, and significant fiscal costs of nearly $200 billion (in 2009 dollars).

While the United States did see volatility subside in the 1990s, countries in Latin America and Asia endured a number of crippling crises that centered on speculative booms and excessive debt in different sectors of the economy. After the resolution of the Latin American debt crisis of the 1980s, investors returned to the region, only to be burned again. Capital inflows resumed, but the same problems resurfaced. In 1994 Mexico edged toward crisis, thanks to unsustainable deficits and an overvalued currency. The peso plunged in value after doubts spread about the health of the nation's banking system and the government proved unable to roll over its large stock of short-term foreign-currency-denominated debt, the *tesobonos*. Only when the United States and the IMF intervened with a large bailout package did Mexico stabilize. But the damage was significant: after the government bailed out the nation's banks, taxpayers footed the bill, which totaled some $50 billion.

This was the first of a number of "capital account crises" in emerging-market economies. All had one thing in common: unsustainable current account deficits that were financed in risky ways. By relying so heavily on short-term debt—and on debt denominated in foreign currencies—these countries set themselves up for a catastrophic fall. When foreign investors panicked and refused to roll over short-term debts, overvalued local currencies collapsed. Worse, as the relative value of local currencies declined, the real value of debts denominated in dollars and other foreign currencies soared, making default all the more likely.

In 1997 and 1998 emerging economies throughout the world fell prey to this kind of crisis. Investors from more developed nations plowed money into Thailand, Indonesia, South Korea, and Malaysia, sparking speculative booms in each. Equities markets became overvalued; real estate bubbles formed; banks made increasingly risky loans; current account deficits ballooned as excessive and low-return private investment outstripped national savings. Worries about the ability of the Thai government to prop up its currency (the baht) made the country ripe for a panic. When foreign investors pulled their money out of Thailand and the country consequently ran out of the foreign currency reserves necessary to maintain the value of the baht, banks, stock markets, and real estate prices all collapsed. The panic spread to Indonesia, Korea, and Malaysia. Like Thailand, each of these countries saw its currency depreciate and its debt explode. The costs of bailing out the economy ended up on the backs of taxpayers; millions of those same taxpayers plunged into poverty in the ensuing contraction.

Russia's turn came in 1998. Buffeted by the Asian financial crisis and the declining price of oil, Russia's economy entered a tailspin. Doubts grew about its ability to maintain the value of the ruble and its commitment to honor its debts. In the summer of 1998 investors fled the country, and the value of the ruble collapsed. The Russian government defaulted on debt owed to its citizens and stopped payments on most of the debt owed to foreign creditors.

The effects of these actions reverberated around the world. Long-Term Capital Management (LTCM), a hedge fund based in the United States, had placed extremely complicated bets on the prices of other countries' government bonds that failed to factor in the possibility of a financial crisis. As panic over Russia's default spread, the usual relationships among different kinds of bond prices went haywire, and LTCM was forced to liquidate its assets in order to survive. Fears that such fire sales might force down the value of other financial firms' assets led the Federal Reserve to orchestrate a private bailout of LTCM, which stopped the spreading panic.

Crises continued to materialize in emerging markets, though none of them threatened the global financial system. In 1999 Ecuador and Pakistan suffered sovereign debt crises, while Brazil experienced a currency crisis. Other financial crises soon followed: Ukraine (2000), Turkey and

Argentina (2001), and Uruguay and Brazil again (2002). Like earlier emerging-market crises, these disasters came in many different guises. In Argentina, for example, the crisis crippled every sector of the economy. Households could no longer service their personal debts, particularly mortgages and consumer credit, which were often denominated in foreign currency; corporations had similar problems with commercial debt. Angry depositors besieged the nation's banks, desperately trying to withdraw their life savings, while the government defaulted on its debt and saw the value of its currency collapse.

As is so often the case, a speculative boom and an excessive acccumulation of debt stood at the center of many of these crises. Governments, corporations, individual households, or some combination thereof borrowed too much money, much of it denominated in foreign currencies. At the same time, banks and other financial institutions lent too much against collateral of shaky value. This situation was unsustainable, and eventually doubts about the viability of all those loans triggered a panic. The resulting crisis necessarily hit both excessively indebted borrowers and excessively leveraged lenders.

In the end, the costs of the emerging-market crises were staggering. Currencies were devalued, governments fell, and millions of people sank into poverty. Many countries experienced political turmoil. The Russian crisis marked the beginning of the end for Boris Yeltsin's presidency and the return of an authoritarian state under Vladimir Putin. In Indonesia the events of 1998 put an end to thirty years of rule by Suharto. And in Argentina, bank runs and street riots in 2001 ultimately toppled the presidency of Fernando de la Rúa, ushering in a period of political and economic chaos.

These events do not seem to have registered in any significant or sustained fashion on the consciousness of most investors and policy makers in the United States. The Great Moderation was alive and well. Some skeptics reasonably wondered whether the calm that reigned in most of the advanced industrial nations was an illusion: after all, the mania for Internet stocks and high-tech companies that dominated the American economy in the late 1990s looked like a consummate bubble, with a financial crisis waiting in the wings. But when the bubble burst and the stock markets collapsed, the effect was relatively mild: a limited recession and a sluggish recovery. While thousands of dot-coms went bust, no banking crisis materialized, because most of the funding had come from shares sold to domestic and foreign investors in capital markets, rather than from bank loans.

But trouble was brewing beneath the surface. The symptoms of crisis that had been glimpsed in the 1990s emerging-market meltdowns started to materialize in the United States. Worse, with interest rates at historic lows after the Fed aggressively countered the fallout of the tech bust, a housing bubble began to inflate, first in the United States and then in many other countries. Indeed, the same problems of easy money, easy credit, and lax supervision and regulation first witnessed in the United States surfaced in many economies: the United Kingdom, Ireland, Spain, Iceland, Estonia, Latvia, Dubai, Australia, New Zealand, and even China and Singapore.

By 2006, credit had become so readily available in the United States that the spread between the yield on high-risk junk bonds and low-risk Treasury bonds shrank to historic lows of less than 2.5 percent. A handful of economists raised the alarm, but few listened. As with every other bubble, plenty of boosters stepped forward to claim that the fundamentals justified soaring prices. David A. Lereah, chief economist for the National Association of Realtors, was arguably the most visible. "There is no national housing bubble," Lereah told *The Washington Post* in 2005. "Any talk about the housing market crashing is ludicrous."

Crisis Redux

Aldous Huxley once observed that "the charm of history and its enigmatic lesson consist in the fact that, from age to age, nothing changes and yet everything is completely different." While the recent crisis shared much in common with past crises, many of its causes were unique, or at the very least, they played a bigger role in the twenty-first-century global financial system than they did in the past.

Take the most obvious, tired explanation of the crisis: greed. When the financial levees first broke, countless commentators claimed that Wall Street's unbridled lust for money had wrecked the financial system. That implausibly assumed that the financiers of 2007 were greedier than the Gordon Gekkos of a generation ago. In fact, what made a difference was not the magnitude of greed but new structures of incentives and compensation that channeled greed in new and dangerous directions. Over the previous two decades, bankers and traders had increasingly been rewarded with bonuses tied to short-term profits, giving them an incentive to take excessive risks, leverage up their investments, and bet the entire bank on astonishingly reckless investment strategies.

That's precisely what happened in the recent crisis: financial wizards set up "insurance" in the form of credit default swaps (see chapter 8). These swaps yielded staggering profits and bonuses in good times but set firms like AIG up for catastrophic collapse when the sailing got rough. Yes, traders were greedy—and arrogant and foolish too—but that alone would not have triggered the financial equivalent of a nuclear meltdown had the bonus system not become the dominant kind of compensation in the financial sector.

In theory, the firms' shareholders should have put an end to these practices. In reality, corporate governance failed long before the entire financial system did: conflicts of interest were rife among the boards of directors charged with minding the store. This was nothing new, but the financial system that emerged in the late twentieth century was particularly opaque and impenetrable. In the process, the interest of shareholders and the interests of the bankers, traders, and managers who were the agents of those shareholders diverged.

Regulators could have stepped into the breach. But like so many eras of booms gone bust, the late twentieth century was an era of free-market fundamentalism. Regulators and supervisors in the United States—not only the Federal Reserve but dozens of other federal and state authorities—were asleep at the wheel, unaware or willfully ignorant of how financial institutions were circumventing everything from capital adequacy requirements to accounting regulations. In fact, many of these regulators actively encouraged the financial innovations that would become the catalysts for the crisis: interest-only mortgages, negative amortization loans, teaser rates, and option adjustable-rate mortgages, along with the increasingly esoteric securities that derived their value from these toxic assets. Many of the same conditions prevailed in the United Kingdom.

Markets know best and never fail: this was the conventional wisdom in Washington, London, and elsewhere in the English-speaking world. Alan Greenspan, perhaps the most visible advocate of letting the financial system regulate itself, claimed that markets would sort things out, warning in 1997 that when it came to financial innovation, "we should be quite cautious in enacting legislation or creating regulations that unnecessarily fetter market development." Greenspan even defended the rise of subprime lending, claiming in 2005 that "lenders are now able to quite efficiently judge the risk posed by individual applicants and to price that risk appropriately."

In retrospect, these remarks seem laughable. In fact, financial innovations rendered irrelevant the question of whether lenders bothered to assess risk: rather than make loans and hold them on their books, banks and other financial institutions made loans regardless of the applicants' creditworthiness, then proceeded to funnel the loans—mortgages, auto loans, student loans, and even credit card debt—to Wall Street, where they were turned into increasingly complex and esoteric securities and sold around the world to credulous investors incapable of assessing the risk inherent in the original loans. Securitization was the name of the game, and banks and other Wall Street firms made hefty fees while passing along the risk to unwitting investors.

The various ratings agencies—Fitch, Moody's, Standard & Poor's—could have and should have prevented this from happening. But they too made hefty fees from securitization and were more than happy to help turn toxic loans into gold-plated securities that generated risk-free returns. Far from criticizing this cozy relationship, Greenspan and other cheerleaders of financial innovation blessed it.

Greenspan also performed a key action in adopting easy-money policies, slashing the rate at which the Federal Reserve lent money to the larger financial system. From early 2001 through the middle of 2003, Greenspan cut the Fed funds rate by some 5.5 percent (or in banking parlance, by 550 basis points). He then kept rates low for too long a time, an easy-money policy that would help foster the unsustainable credit and housing boom. But the story is even more complicated. After all, the Fed raised rates in 2004–6, yet long-term interest rates and fixed mortgage rates barely moved; monetary tightening had no traction. As it turned out, there were plenty of sources of easy money overseas. Over the course of the past decade, China, Japan, and Germany had accumulated massive stockpiles of savings that were lent back to the United States, financing budget deficits and excessive borrowing by everyone from households to corporations. In effect, China lent Americans the rope they used to hang themselves. Again, nothing changes, and yet everything is different.

The onset of the crisis was likewise a mixture of old and new. Housing prices eventually leveled off, and in late 2006 and early 2007 the first nonbank mortgage lenders specializing in subprime loans failed after growing defaults among borrowers. Then in June 2007 two highly leveraged hedge funds managed by Bear Stearns, which had invested in securities backed by subprime mortgages, collapsed, triggering a flight from all securities associated with the subprime market. As awareness mounted that exposure to subprime mortgages was ubiquitous throughout the global financial system, panic spread.

As with so many panics, uncertainty drove decisions. Thanks to securitization, credit risk was transferred from banks to investment banks and then to other financial institutions and investors around the world. But by the time the crisis hit, this process was incomplete: banks kept some of the toxic assets on their own balance sheets or else stowed them in "structured investment vehicles" and "conduits" that did not show up on official balance sheets until the crisis forced banks to acknowledge their losses.

News that venerable banks had transferred only part of the risk to outside investors—holding the rest on their own balance sheets—sowed more panic. The dawning realization that every major and minor player throughout the global financial system had some exposure to toxic assets sparked a full-blown crisis. No one knew who was holding toxic assets or how much. A financial system that thrived on opacity and complexity began to unravel.

It had the makings of a classic panic, complete with bank runs, except that the "banks" this time weren't only commercial banks like the ones besieged during the Great Depression. These "banks" were also nonbank mortgage lenders, conduits, structured investment vehicles, monoline insurers, money market funds, hedge funds, investment banks, and other entities. These institutions, which belonged to the new shadow banking system (discussed in greater detail in chapter 3), had one thing in common: they borrowed from the "depositors" (for example, purchasers of commercial paper) who lent these entities money on a short-term basis. The shadow banks then sank this money into illiquid, risky, long-term securities: mortgage-backed securities, CDOs, and other assets with mysterious acronyms. When panic struck this system, the "depositors" who had made the short-term loans demanded their money back or refused to renew loans, forcing the shadow banking system to liquidate these complex, difficult-to-value securities at fire-sale prices.

That process gathered speed in 2008. After more than three hundred nonbank mortgage lenders collapsed, shadow banking beasts born of regulatory evasion—structured investment vehicles, conduits, and other off-balance-sheet entities, which were also holding highly toxic mortgage-backed securities and other, even more esoteric forms of structured finance—began to collapse as well. The next step was the swift demise of Wall Street's major investment banks, which perished as their lifeblood—very short-term loans known as "overnight repo financing"—dried up. Bear Stearns was first, followed later that year by Lehman Brothers. Merrill Lynch would have collapsed too, had it not been sold to Bank of America. Goldman Sachs and Morgan Stanley dodged the bullet by turning themselves into bank holding companies, gaining access to lender-of-last-resort support from the Federal Reserve in exchange for submitting to greater regulatory oversight.

The run on the shadow banking system continued with a run on the $4 trillion money-market-fund industry. Thanks to exposure to Lehman Brothers, one of these supposedly safe funds, the Reserve Primary Fund, "broke the buck," meaning that a dollar invested with it was no longer worth a dollar. This was a fateful step: investors panicked and began to stage a run on the trillions of dollars of assets in these funds. To avoid a financial meltdown, the government was forced to provide a blanket guarantee—the equivalent of deposit insurance—to all existing money market funds.

The panic did not end there. The demise of the shadow banking system continued with the collapse of the market for still more exotic instruments (ARSs, TOBs, VRDOs, and a whole alphabet soup's worth of securities) used by state and local governments to finance their spending. These markets disintegrated when the imperiled investment banks pulled the plug on these instruments, sending interest rates for borrowers—even safe state and local governments—through the roof.

Then it was the hedge funds' turn. The financial distress of the primary brokers—who financed hedge funds with overnight funds—and the losses that many of these funds experienced in the market turmoil of 2008 led to the equivalent of a bank run on hedge funds, forcing hundreds to close shop and others to reduce their leverage and their assets, driving prices of a host of exotic assets still lower.

This process reached new and dangerous levels in late summer and fall of 2008, when the entire shadow banking system suffered a massive run on its assets. Lehman Brothers crumpled, AIG teetered on the brink, and the Federal Reserve did what had eventually been done in the Great Depression: it became the lender of last resort and gave deposit insurance to a new generation of banks. Nonetheless, the fallout from Lehman's collapse and the resulting financial meltdown in the fall of 2008 led global credit and money markets to seize up. The humdrum business of global imports and exports threatened to collapse, as companies could no longer secure the financing necessary to move goods from one country to another.

By the end of the year, the crisis had spread far beyond the United States, reverberating from China and Japan to Ireland and Iceland. The reasons went beyond the general collapse of credit; there were underlying troubles in economies around the world. Many of the same problems that bedeviled the United States—a real estate bubble, overleveraged banks, excessive current account deficits, and overvalued currencies—were present throughout the world. In Europe banks had made high-risk loans in Romania, Hungary, Ukraine, and the Baltic states. Indeed, many economies in "emerging Europe," the twenty-plus countries formerly under Soviet control, were very fragile, being heavily dependent on overvalued currencies and high current account deficits for their continued prosperity.

No one was immune to the crisis. As the recession in the United States worsened, China, Japan, and other countries heavily dependent on exporting manufactured goods saw their economies crumble; likewise, commodity exporters in the Middle East and elsewhere saw demand collapse. In time, economies as diverse as Latvia and Dubai fell victim to what was quickly becoming a financial pandemic. As credit dried up in the United States, it evaporated overseas too, and as economies contracted, manufacturing giants like China and commodity exporters like Russia caught the virus.

Toward the end of 2008 the pandemic worsened, and the history of long-forgotten crises became increasingly relevant for explaining what was happening. So too did the writings of economists who had languished in obscurity for many years. John Maynard Keynes came back into vogue, as did Joseph Schumpeter, Hyman Minsky, Irving Fisher, and even Karl Marx. Their sudden reappearance was significant, if portentous: all had made their mark studying how capitalism could collapse in crisis. They may have drawn wildly different conclusions as to why and how, much less what to do about it, but the fact that their names were uttered with a quiet respect was a sign that a sea change was at hand. Economists who had preached the virtues of deregulation, the efficiencies of markets, and the benefits of financial innovation suddenly seemed outdated compared with these more unconventional thinkers. But who were they, and what could they tell us?

Chapter 2

Crisis Economists

Ask economists why booms and busts occur, and you'll get a wide range of responses. Some will tell you that crises are the inevitable consequence of government meddling in markets; others will maintain they occur because government didn't meddle enough. Still others will claim that there is no such thing as a bubble: markets are perfectly efficient, and if housing values double or triple in the space of a few years and then crash back down to earth—well, that's just the market responding to new information.

The same contradictions can emerge if you ask economists what to do once a crisis has hit. Some will maintain that government must intervene, becoming a lender of last resort and providing a massive fiscal stimulus in order to counter the plunge in private demand. Others will dismiss that approach as laughable, arguing that government must never intervene in the machinery of the market. Doing so, they insist, will only prolong the hangover from the crisis and will lead to a dangerous accumulation of public debt. And some economists will claim with a straight face that the very idea of a crisis is illusory, a fiction perpetrated by those who doubt the market's ability to allocate goods and resources with astonishing efficiency.

All of this can seem baffling to noneconomists. After all, economics strives to be a science, complete with equations, laws, mathematical models, and other trappings of objectivity. But behind this facade of a single scientific truth lies a tremendous diversity of conflicting opinions, particularly when it comes to the vexed subject of financial crises. This was true in the nineteenth and twentieth centuries; it remains true today.

While it's tempting to dismiss these differences as nothing more than obscure academic debates, doing so would be a grave mistake. These debates have profoundly shaped our response to the recent crisis, guiding everything from central bank policies to the embrace of stimulus spending. As John Maynard Keynes memorably observed, "Practical men, who believe themselves to be quite exempt from any intellectual influences, are usually the slaves of some defunct economist." Ideas matter, and without an understanding of the economic ideas in play during the recent crisis, it's impossible to understand how we got into this mess and, more important, how we can get out.

This chapter surveys these disparate ways of understanding crises, in an attempt to gather the materials for a unified field theory. It is is an admittedly selective history of economic theory, but its ambition is straightforward: to highlight what's useful. As always, pragmatism informs our choices. Keynes is here, as is his most radical interpreter, Hyman Minsky, but so are economists from other camps: Robert Shiller, one of the most visible proponents of behavioral economics; Joseph Schumpeter, the grand theorist of capitalist "creative destruction"; and economists of a historical bent, from Charles Kindleberger to Carmen Reinhart and Kenneth Rogoff. Their disparate strands of thought inform our idiosyncratic approach to understanding crises.

When Markets Behave Badly

Crisis economics is the study of how and why markets fail. Much of mainstream economics, by contrast, is obsessed with showing how and why markets work—and work well. This preoccupation arguably dates back to the origins of the profession of economics, beginning with the Scottish thinker Adam Smith. In his *Wealth of Nations*, he advanced the now-famous metaphor of the "invisible hand" to capture the seemingly miraculous process by which the selfish and divergent interests of individual economic actors somehow coalesce into a stable, self-regulating economic system. Out of the chaos of innumerable individual choices comes order.

Smith, however, did not acknowledge capitalism's many vulnerabilities. This was understandable: like other early economists, he was interested in explaining how capitalist markets succeed, not why they fail. In the next century, however, many economists refined and reworked Smith's ideas. In fact, if nineteenth-century economics had a consensus, it was the idea that markets are fundamentally self-regulating, always moving toward some magical equilibrium. A host of economists—David Ricardo, Jean-Baptiste Say, Léon Walras, and Alfred Marshall—refined Smith's insights and started to build a mathematical edifice to prove this point.

Faith in the fundamental stability of markets gave rise to an important corollary: if markets are fundamentally self-regulating, and their collective wisdom is always right, then the prices of assets bought and sold in the market are accurate and justified. Early-twentieth-century economists tried to give this theory some mathematical validity. They relied in part on the work of French mathematician Louis Bachelier, whose *Théorie de la spéculation*, completed in 1900, argued that an asset's price accurately reflects all known information about it. There is no such thing, in his view, as an undervalued or overvalued asset; the market is a perfect reflection of the underlying fundamentals. To be sure, asset prices change, often dramatically, but merely as a rational and automatic response to the arrival of new information.

Though they remained somewhat obscure in France, Bachelier's ideas became popular in the United States. On the eve of the crash that inaugurated the Great Depression, Princeton economist Joseph Lawrence confidently declared, "The consensus of judgment of the millions whose valuations function on that admirable market, the Stock Exchange, is that stocks are not at present overvalued." Lawrence evidently believed in the wisdom of crowds, challenging anyone to "veto the judgment of this intelligent multitude."

In theory, the Great Depression should have put an end to this sort of nonsense, but postwar academic departments of economics and finance breathed new life into the old fallacy. Much of the credit—if that's the word—goes to the economics department at the University of Chicago. A professor named Eugene Fama and others sympathetic to laissez-faire economic policies began to construct elaborate mathematical models aimed at proving that markets are utterly rational and efficient.

Again, they believed that the price of any given asset at any time is always completely correct. In other words, an asset cannot be overvalued or undervalued; the current price is the right price, nothing more and nothing less. This theory posited that all public information is immediately and accurately incorporated into the asset's price, and any future price changes must depend on things not yet known. Therefore, predicting where prices will move next is impossible. This insight begat the "random walk" theory: that when it comes to picking stocks, there is no point trying to beat the market. By this logic, it is far better to simply select random stocks and stick with those choices, ignoring the movement.

The scores of economists who embraced this thesis in the postwar years gave it nuance, acknowledging that markets may be more or less efficient depending on certain variables. But its overall thrust—that markets are efficient and incorporate all known information into prices—remained a truism in business schools and economics departments. By the 1970s the Efficient Market Hypothesis had become conventional wisdom, preached from academic pulpits at the University of Chicago and elsewhere.

However, not everyone bought into it. A popular joke among economists neatly captures its logical absurdities. An economist and his friend are walking down the street when they come across a hundred-dollar bill lying on the ground. The friend bends down to pick it up, but the economist stops him, saying, "Don't bother—if it were a real hundred-dollar bill, someone would have already picked it up."

Whoever came up with the joke was on to something: markets look remarkably inefficient; savvy investors manage to pick up plenty of genuine hundred-dollar bills. Many economists, moreover, have poked holes in the Efficient Market Hypothesis, not with anecdotal evidence but with rigorous statistical analysis. The most trenchant critic is Yale economist Robert Shiller. In the early 1980s, Shiller conducted research demonstrating that stock prices exhibit far more volatility than the Efficient Market Hypothesis can possibly explain. By the end of that decade, he and other critics had amassed a remarkable body of evidence showing that asset prices rarely rest in a state of equilibrium but rather fluctuate wildly. On any one day, investors may overreact optimistically about an asset, bidding up its price to new and dizzying heights. The next day they may panic, abandoning the asset at fire-sale prices. These movements are not rational; they are the irrational impulses of the crowd. Or as Shiller observed, "While markets are not totally crazy, they contain quite substantial noise, so substantial that it dominates the movements in the aggregate market."

Questioning the myth of the efficient market was one thing; explaining precisely why markets are inefficient was another. That job fell to the practitioners of a new field, behavioral economics and behavioral finance. Researchers in these fields, Shiller later explained, develop "models of human psychology as it relates to financial markets." In recent years these twin fields have attracted countless economists. Many researchers have conducted real-time experiments to determine how, exactly, participants in the stock market can behave in ways that contribute to disruptions like asset bubbles and financial panics.

Recent research in behavioral finance has indeed revealed several ways that speculative bubbles can inflate, becoming self-sustaining until they eventually burst, raining destruction on the larger economy. Feedback theory, for example, suggests that investors who watch prices go up will jump on the bandwagon, sending prices still higher—which, in turn, only attracts more investors, who inflate the bubble still further. Eventually, the feedback mechanism causes prices to become untethered from any rational basis, spiraling skyward until they can go no higher. Then they crash, creating a "negative bubble," in which prices plummet precipitously. Such declines can be equally irrational, and just as prices can overshoot on the way up, they can drop far below what's justified on the way down.

Behavioral economists have identified a host of factors that aggravate this kind of feedback mechanism—"fundamental parameters of human behavior," as Shiller calls them. One is "biased self-attribution," in which investors in a speculative bubble attribute their growing profits not to the fact that they and thousands of other equally deluded fools are participating in a bubble but to their own perspicacity. A host of biases, distortions, and other irrational inclinations tend to feed speculative bubbles and the curious justifications that inevitably accompany them, most notably the claim that old rules of doing business no longer apply now that the economy has entered a new era.

All this attention to irrational economic behavior has yielded a less flattering portrait of how markets do—or don't—work. The work of Shiller and others suggests that capitalism is not some self-regulating system that hums along with nary a disruption; rather, it is a system prone to "irrational exuberance" and unfounded pessimism. It is, in other words, extraordinarily unstable.

That insight is both new and very old. Long before the behavioral economists punctured the myth of the efficient market, a host of nineteenth-century thinkers observed that, for all its remarkable ability to generate wealth, capitalism was prone to remarkable booms and busts. Though these thinkers are rarely read today, they are important because their ideas highlight the fault lines that still divide our understanding of crises and their consequences.

The Cradle of Crisis Economics

Americans have a reputation for optimism, which may be why they did the most to popularize the Efficient Market Hypothesis. Europeans, by contrast, are often viewed as dour and gloomy, so appropriately some of the first economists to write about crises hailed from Europe.

The political-theorist-turned-economist John Stuart Mill was arguably the first to write about crises in a sustained way. In his widely read *Principles of Political Economy* (1848), Mill tried to generalize about what caused the booms and busts that had become commonplace in his lifetime. The language that Mill used to describe these phenomena anticipated that of contemporary behavioral economists like Shiller. Bubbles, Mill believed, begin when some external shock or "some accident"—a new market, for example—"sets speculation at work." As prices rise, the sight of others growing rich "call[s] forth numerous imitators, and speculation not only goes much beyond what is justified by the original grounds for expecting rise of price, but extends itself to articles in which there never was any such ground: these, however, rise like the rest as soon as speculation sets in." Price gains beget more price gains, and a self-sustaining bubble forms.

The bubble alone does not create a crisis, Mill recognized: credit and debt play an essential role. As the bubble forms, he argued, "a great extension of credit takes place. Not only do all whom the contagion reaches employ their credit much more freely than usual; but they really have more credit, because they seem to be making unusual gains, and because a generally reckless and adventurous feeling prevails, which disposes people to give as well as take credit more largely than at other times, and give it to persons not entitled to it." Invariably, the boom ends when the unexpected failure of a handful of firms causes a "general distrust" in the marketplace, spreading uncertainty and making credit next to impossible to secure, except on onerous terms. Unable to service their debt, firms collapse, and bankruptcies soar. As credit evaporates, prices fall, and panic seizes the market; a "commercial crisis" ensues, as does, in "extreme cases, a panic as unreasoning as the previous over-confidence." Just as the feedback mechanism works to drive prices up, it operates to send prices down. Falling prices invariably overshoot, Mill observed: prices "fall as much below the usual level, as during the previous period of speculation they have risen above it." The crash spills over from the financial sector to the rest of the economy, destroying businesses, driving up unemployment, and contributing to a "condition of more or less impoverishment."

Mill provided a pretty accurate model of a classic boom-and-bust cycle, complete with features that apply to the world we inhabit today as much as they did to Mill's: an external shock or catalyst for a boom; a speculative mania driven by psychology, not by fundamentals; a feedback mechanism that sends prices skyward; easy credit available to almost everyone; and the inevitable crash of the financial system, followed by plenty of collateral damage on the "real economy" of factories and workers. If Mill were alive today, he would immediately recognize the contours of the recent crisis, although many of our more esoteric financial instruments might puzzle him a bit.

Mill was succeeded by several other thinkers who tried to generalize further about what was increasingly called the business cycle. One of the most influential was William Stanley Jevons, whose theory is laughable from a twenty-first-century vantage point but is nonetheless revealing. Like Mill, Jevons believed that some external disruption sets in motion events that culminate in a crisis. Those periodic disruptions, Jevons believed, are caused by . . . sunspots. These solar variations disrupt the planet's weather, which affects agricultural production, which changes eventually knock the economies of advanced nations like Britain out of balance. Voilà! With such disruptions, speculative fever flourishes, paving the way for a crisis.

As preposterous as it now seems, Jevons's underlying thesis—that crises are born of events completely external to and separate from capitalism—had tremendous appeal in the nineteenth century, and it continues to resonate today. The problem, Jevons was saying, originates not within the system but outside it—in his case, from outer space. Sunspots aside, the external cause idea remained highly appealing to members of the classical school of economics, which held that markets are fundamentally self-regulating; they can be disrupted by external events but are fundamentally resilient and could not collapse.

A darker vision was offered by a more controversial thinker. Unlike Mill and Jevons (and most nineteenth-century economists), Karl Marx believed that crisis was part and parcel of capitalism and was a sign of its imminent, inevitable collapse. Indeed, if Adam Smith wrote to praise capitalism, Karl Marx wrote to bury it. History, Marx believed, is defined by a struggle between two antagonistic social groups: a capitalist class, or bourgeoisie, that owns the factories and other "means of production"; and an ever-growing landless proletariat class. Central to Marx's analysis was his argument that the real value of goods depends on the human labor that goes into making them. As capitalists replaced workers with machines in an attempt to cut costs, profits would perversely decline. This decline would spur capitalists to cut costs even more, eventually driving the economy into a crisis born of overproduction and underemployment. At that point a brutal shakeout would trigger waves of bankruptcies and consolidations. Eventually, Marx believed, a final crisis would usher in a revolution of the working class.

In *The Communist Manifesto*, published in 1848 (the same year Mill published his *Principles*), Marx captured this instability in vivid prose. "Modern bourgeois society," he observed, "is like the sorcerer who is no longer able to control the powers of the nether world whom he has called up by his spells." "Commercial crises," he asserted, "by their periodical return put on trial, each time more threateningly, the existence of the entire bourgeois society." The crises would only intensify. "How does the bourgeoisie get over these crises?" he asked. "On the one hand by enforced destruction of a mass of productive forces; on the other, by the conquest of new markets, and by the more thorough exploitation of the old ones." But those solutions would only defer the final day of reckoning by "paving the way for more extensive and more destructive crises, and by diminishing the means whereby crises are prevented."

Marx's ideas, which are far more sophisticated than this précis suggests, remain controversial. But what matters here is that Marx was the first thinker to see capitalism as inherently unstable and prone to crisis. In his estimation, capitalism is chaos incarnate; it will inevitably plunge into the abyss, taking the economy with it. Marx thus stood apart from an earlier generation of political economists who saw capitalism as a system that would reliably govern itself. Capitalism, he warned, is doomed. So far Marx has not been proved right. But his larger point—that crisis is endemic to capitalism—is a hugely important insight: after Marx, economists had to reckon with the possibility that capitalism contains the seeds of its own demise. Crises aren't a function of something as banal as the opening of new markets or shifts in investor psychology, much less sunspots. Capitalism *is* crisis; it introduced a level of instability and uncertainty that had no precedent in human history.

But Marx's vision was not widely shared. Most mainstream economists in the late nineteenth and early twentieth centuries advanced the idea that the economy is a self-regulating, self-correcting entity, one that will, if left to its own devices, generally move toward a state of equilibrium, with stability and full employment as inevitable results. For sure, crises come and go, but they will not stay.

This quaint confidence disappeared in the Great Depression. That event transformed the discipline of economics as well as government policy. For this reason, the Great Depression looms large in the debate over how to handle the recent crisis. What happened some eighty years ago shaped the immediate response to the crisis in 2007 and 2008; it continues to shape economic and financial policies today.

The Long Shadow of John Maynard Keynes

The most important economist to emerge out of the Great Depression—and arguably, the most important in the last century—was John Maynard Keynes. The son of a respected British economist, Keynes was born the year Marx died. He attended Eton and Cambridge, where he swiftly distinguished himself in mathematics and, ultimately, economics. He eventually became a lecturer in economics at Cambridge, where he wrote on everything from monetary policy to the science of probability.

Keynes was no ordinary economist. He collected contemporary art, married a Russian ballerina, and was a key member of the Bloomsbury Group, a coterie of bohemian writers, painters, and intellectuals who made their home in London in the first few decades of the twentieth century. Witty, urbane, and vivacious, he was comfortable beyond the confines of academia and served in the British government on several occasions.

Keynes's most famous work was *The General Theory of Employment, Interest and Money*, published in 1936. As he finished it, he told George Bernard Shaw that "I believe myself to be writing a book on economic theory which will largely revolutionize . . . the way the world thinks about economic problems." His bland choice of title notwithstanding, Keynes delivered on his promise: much of the research agenda of economics in the twentieth century was an explicit or implicit engagement with Keynes's ideas.

The General Theory is an exceedingly complex work and defies easy interpretation. Perhaps the simplest way to understand Keynes is to look at how he parted ways with economists of the classical and neoclassical schools. In the 1930s most of these economists believed that the economy is capable of regulating itself. Moreover, they assumed that full employment is the natural state of things, and that when wages go too high, the economy will necessarily contract. As unemployment rises, wages will start to fall. The conventional wisdom was that as wages fall, entrepreneurs will start to hire again, lured by the prospect of increased profits. The cycle then begins anew.

Keynes approached the problem from an entirely different perspective. What really determines employment levels, he argued, is effective or aggregate demand—the collective demand for goods and services within a particular economy; if wages are cut and workers are fired, people will consume less, and demand will falter. The argument essentially contradicted the era's conventional wisdom. As demand drops, entrepreneurs will become more reluctant to invest, which will lead only to further wage cuts or layoffs. Likewise, ordinary consumers will save more and spend less—laudable goals to be sure, but ones that dampen demand still further, a conundrum that came to be known as the "paradox of thrift." This kind of retrenchment, Keynes theorized, would become a self-fulfilling cycle, as the economy entered into "underemployment equilibrium," a state of suspended animation in which workers remain unemployed and factories shuttered. Then, as demand falls below the aggregate supply of goods, firms would be forced to cut prices to sell the inventory of unsold goods; this price deflation—which was severe in the Great Depression—would lead to a further fall in their profits and cash flows.

The process is driven as much by the heart as by the mind, Keynes realized: in a collapse like the Great Depression, the "animal spirits" of capitalism, the "spontaneous urge to action rather than inaction," would wither away, he thought, even when there were profits to be made. Keynes recognized that economic decision making isn't merely a rational mathematical calculus; it is impulsive and conditioned by events, uncertain and contingent. "If the animal spirits are dimmed and the spontaneous optimism falters," he observed, "leaving us to depend on nothing but a mathematical expectation, enterprise will fade and die." It didn't matter whether the underlying "fundamentals" justified a return to prosperity; absent the return of the "animal spirits," the economy would sink into a permanent state of torpor.

For Keynes, the solution was simple: government would step into the breach and create demand, reversing the downward spiral. This insight became orthodoxy in the postwar years, as governments around the world adopted Keynesian prescriptions in order to keep economic slumps from deepening. The most enthusiastic and optimistic adopters believed they could use Keynes's ideas to maintain something approximating "full employment." An intervention that had originally been proposed as an emergency measure to forestall a full-blown depression became instead a means of keeping a nation's economy on an even keel. In 1965 a *Time* cover story hailed Keynes as a visionary. The title of the story was a quotation—"We Are All Keynesians Now"—that captured the era's mood. In a bit of wicked irony, the person who uttered those words was the conservative economist Milton Friedman.

Friedman later disavowed his comment, and with good reason: he was the father of the monetarist school of economics, which argues that instability within any given economy can be explained by fluctuations in the money supply. Friedman and his coauthor, the economist Anna Jacobson Schwartz, posited a very different interpretation of the Great Depression from Keynes's. According to Friedman and Schwartz, the Great Depression was not caused by a collapse in demand, as Keynes averred, but rather was a direct consequence of a decline in the quantity of bank deposits and bank reserves, which plummeted when frightened depositors withdrew their savings and banks shut down. According to the monetarists, this collapse in the money supply, or what they dubbed the "Great Contraction," caused aggregate demand to collapse, which in turn reduced spending, income, prices, and eventually employment.

Friedman and Schwartz opposed government intervention on principle—especially if it was government spending à la Keynes—but they believed that a drop in the money supply could have been avoided had the Federal Reserve aggressively cut the rates at which banks could borrow from it. More important, the monetarists blamed the Federal Reserve for not acting as a lender of last resort, making lines of credit available to faltering banks and financial institutions. Had the Federal Reserve prevented the waves of bank failures in the early 1930s, they argued, the Great Depression would not have been so great, and the nation would have suffered through an ordinary recession before recovering.

The monetarist interpretation of the Great Depression has some merit: the collapse of the money supply in the 1930s certainly exacerbated the credit crunch, and the Federal Reserve only made matters worse. But other economic historians, most notably Peter Temin, have since argued that the collapse in aggregate demand was the primary catalyst for the disaster. Keynes, they argued, was mostly right: only increased public spending could have sustained aggregate demand, even if a more aggressive monetary policy would have contributed to the eventual recovery.

Nonetheless, it was Friedman, not Keynes, who became increasingly influential in the 1970s and 1980s. One reason was that what little remained of Keynesian economics by this time was a pale imitation of the original. Significant portions of Keynes's writings—not only *The General Theory* but his earlier *A Treatise on Money*—contained plenty of other insights that the postwar generation of economists ignored in their attempt to reconcile Keynes with earlier schools of economic thought, particularly the classical economists. That effort, which came to be known as the neoclassical synthesis, was a mixed bag. (One critic called it "bastard Keynesianism.") The great economist's belief in the power of government to stimulate demand was retained, but almost everything else Keynes wrote was ignored.

Not everyone discounted the other implications of Keynes's work, however. Hyman Minsky, a professor of economics at Washington University in St. Louis, dedicated his life to building a theoretical edifice on the foundation that Keynes had laid. Minsky authored an intellectual biography of Keynes and an elaboration of his own distinct interpretation, pointedly titled *Stabilizing an Unstable Economy*.

In these works, along with numerous articles, Minsky argued that Keynes had been misunderstood. He focused on several neglected chapters of *The General Theory* that dealt with banks, credit, and financial institutions, and he synthesized them with insights from *A Treatise on Money*. Keynes, Minsky argued, had made a powerful argument that capitalism was by its very nature unstable and prone to collapse. "Instability," Minsky wrote, "is an inherent and inescapable flaw of capitalism."

According to Minsky, instability originates in the very financial institutions that make capitalism possible. "Implicit in [Keynes's] analysis," he wrote, "is a view that the capitalist economy is fundamentally flawed. This flaw exists because the financial system necessary for capitalist vitality and vigor—which translates entrepreneurial animal spirits into effective demand for investment—contains the potential for runaway expansion, powered by an investment boom." This runaway expansion, Minsky explained, can readily grind to a halt because "accumulated financial changes render the financial system fragile."

Minsky repeatedly came back to Keynes's observation that financial intermediaries—banks, most obviously—play a critical and growing role in modern economies, binding creditors and debtors in elaborate and complex financial webs. "The interposition of this veil of money," wrote Keynes, ". . . is an especially marked characteristic of the modern world." According to Minsky, Keynes offered a "deep analysis" of how financial forces interact with variables of production and consumption, on the one hand, and output, employment, and prices on the other.

All of this stood in stark contrast to the economics profession in the postwar era: the equations and models deployed by architects of the neoclassical synthesis had little or no place for banks and other financial institutions, despite the fact that their failure could wreak havoc on the larger economy. Minsky set out to change this state of affairs by showing how banks and other financial institutions could, as they became increasingly complex and interdependent, bring the entire system crashing down. The centerpiece of his analysis was debt: how it is accumulated, distributed, and valued. Following Keynes, he saw debt as part of a dynamic system that would necessarily evolve over time. Again, per Keynes, he recognized that this dynamism injected uncertainty into economic calculations. In good times, the promise of continuing growth and profits allayed uncertainty. But in bad times, uncertainty would prompt financial players to curtail lending, reduce risk and exposure, and hoard capital.

In itself, this view was not entirely revolutionary. But Minsky's Financial Instability Hypothesis had another dimension. He categorized the debtors in a given economy into three groups, according to the nature of the financing they used: hedge borrowers, speculative borrowers, and Ponzi borrowers. Hedge borrowers are those who can make payments on both the interest and the principal of their debts from their current cash flow. Speculative borrowers are those whose income will cover interest payments but not the principal; they have to roll over their debts, selling new debt to pay off old. Ponzi borrowers are the most unstable: their income covers neither the principal nor the interest payments. Their only option is to mortgage their future finances by borrowing still further, hoping for a rise in the value of the assests they purchased with borrowed money.

During a speculative boom, Minsky believed, the number of hedge borrowers declines, while the number of speculative and Ponzi borrowers grows. Hedge borrowers, now flush with cash thanks to their conservative investments, begin lending to speculative and Ponzi borrowers. The asset at the center of the boom—real estate, for example—rises in price, prompting all borrowers to take on even more debt. As the amount of unserviceable debt balloons, the system becomes ever more ripe for financial disaster. In Minsky's view, the trigger is almost irrelevant: it could be the failure of a firm (much as the failure of hedge funds and major banks marked the end of the bubble in 2007 and 2008) or the revelation of a staggering fraud (like the Bernard Madoff scheme, exposed in 2008).

When pyramids of debt start to crumble and credit dries up, Minsky realized, otherwise healthy financial institutions, corporations, and consumers may find themselves short of cash, unable to pay their debts without selling off assets at bargain-basement prices. As more and more people rush to sell their assets, the prices of those assets spiral downward, creating a self-perpetuating cycle of fire sales, falling prices, and more fire sales. As the level of aggregate demand falls below the supply of goods, the larger economy suffers from price deflation: with every passing day, each dollar purchases more than it did the day before.

It sounds like a blessing, but for debtors it's a curse. Irving Fisher, a Great Depression economist who coined the term "debt deflation" (see chapter 6) to describe this process, observed that if the price of goods falls faster than debts are reduced, the real value of private debts will rise over time. For example, imagine that someone borrows a million dollars to buy a house with no money down. The house is worth a million dollars; the owner owes a million dollars. Then deflation kicks in, and prices fall across the economy; everything from the price of the house to the salary of the owner declines. Everything costs less, but everyone has less money. Unfortunately, the real size of that mortgage has increased: a million dollars' worth of debt is now a bigger burden than it was previously.

Because deflation increases people's debt burden, it also increases the probability of default and bankruptcy. As defaults and bankruptcies soar, the downward spiral continues, dragging the economy into a depression. Between October 1929 and March 1933, for example, the liquidations of assets reduced the nominal value of private debts by 20 percent. But thanks to deflation, the real burden of those debts increased by a whopping 40 percent.

In order to avoid a repeat of the Great Depression, Fisher (and for that matter, Friedman and Minsky) counseled that a central bank—the Federal Reserve, in the case of the United States—should step in to play the role of lender of last resort, providing the necessary financing for banks and even for corporations and individuals. In extreme cases, Fisher argued that the government should pursue "reflation," reviving the economy by flooding it with easy money.

That's exactly what has been done in our own time. Over the course of 2007 and 2008, as the financial crisis deepened, American policy makers looked to the lessons of the Great Depression and acted accordingly. Rather than let thousands of banks and corporations go under, as Hoover had done in the early 1930s, the Federal Reserve made available unprecedented lines of credit. That enabled investment banks, insurers, hedge funds, money market funds, and others to avoid insolvency and eventually halted the vicious cycle of fire sales, falling prices, and more fire sales. Likewise, major firms like Chrysler and General Motors were given lines of credit to prevent them from falling into Chapter 7 bankruptcy proceedings, where their assets would have been liquidated. Instead, the government steered them into Chapter 11, where they could be reorganized and reborn. It was all a far cry from the "leave-it-alone liquidationists" of the Hoover administration.

The policy response on the fiscal level also starkly contrasts with what happened during the Great Depression. As the early 1930s crisis spiraled out of control, the idea of using government spending to take up the slack in demand was still a glimmer in Keynes's eyes. Instead, governments across the world insisted on balancing the budget, which prompted cuts in government spending and tax hikes, both of which arrived at the worst possible time. But in 2009 the Obama administration passed the biggest stimulus bill in the nation's history, which included plentiful tax breaks. Between monetary policy (the government's various levers of control over the money supply) and fiscal policy (the government's means of taxing and spending), everything that should have been done was done, however imperfectly.

So regardless of their theoretical inclinations, economists of all stripes should be happy with the handling of the recent crisis, right? Wrong. There's another way of looking at financial crises, one that points to an entirely different understanding of the Great Depression of the 1930s, the Japanese near depression and Lost Decade of the 1990s, and the Great Recession of our own time.

To Austria and Back

The Austrian School originated in the late nineteenth and early twentieth centuries with a loosely affiliated group of Austrian economists: Carl Menger, Ludwig von Mises, Eugen von Böhm-Bawerk, and Friedrich Hayek. These economists and their many students, including Joseph Schumpeter, were a fractious bunch and are next to impossible to categorize. The same can be said of those twenty-first-century economists who consider themselves heirs to the Austrians.

Nonetheless, a few generalizations are possible. Being an Austrian economist today is tantamount to holding libertarian economic beliefs. Indeed, a deep skepticism of government intervention in the economy—especially in the monetary system—is a pillar of the Austrian School. For example, most Austrians make a strong distinction between sustainable economic expansion financed by private savings and unstable, ill-fated expansion financed by credit from a central bank. While they would agree with Keynes and Minsky that excessive asset and credit bubbles lead to dangerous crises, they don't blame capitalism for that problem. Instead, they point to government policies, namely easy monetary policy, along with regulations and interventions that allegedly interfere with the workings of the free market.

This skepticism toward government intervention goes hand in hand with another hallmark of the Austrian approach: a focus on individual entrepreneurs as the unit of economic analysis. Though he was hardly a libertarian, Joseph Schumpeter developed a powerful theory of entrepreneurship that is often distilled down to a pair of powerful words: *creative destruction*. In Schumpeter's worldview, capitalism consists of waves of innovation in prosperous times, followed by a brutal winnowing in times of depression. This winnowing is to be neither avoided nor minimized: it is a painful but positive adjustment, whose survivors will create a new economic order.

For those who embrace the Austrian point of view, the Great Depression is an object lesson in the perils not of doing too little in the face of a crisis but of doing too much. According to some Austrian economists, Roosevelt prolonged the Great Depression by intervening in the economy. The Austrians even criticize Herbert Hoover, arguing that by overseeing the Reconstruction Finance Corporation, a government agency that made loans to beleaguered banks and local governments, he too stood in the way of the necessary but painful process of "creative destruction."

This dispute over distant crises may seem academic, but it's not: Austrian School economists make a historical case that the policy response to the recent crisis will eventually give us the worst of all worlds. Instead of letting weak, overleveraged banks, corporations, and even households perish in a burst of creative destruction, thereby allowing the strong to survive and thrive, governments around the world have meddled, creating an economy of the living dead: zombie banks that cling to life with endless lines of credit from central banks; zombie firms like General Motors and Chrysler that depend on government ownership for their continued survival; and zombie households across the United States, kept alive by legislation that keeps creditors at bay and that spares them from losing homes they could not afford in the first place.

In the process, private losses are socialized: they become the burden of society at large and, by implication, of the national government, as budget deficits lead to unsustainable increases in public debt. In time, the assumption of these crushing debts can strain government finances and reduce long-term economic growth. In extreme cases, this kind of burden will lead the government to default on its debt, or alternatively, to start printing money to buy back its debt, a maneuver that can swiftly trigger bouts of dangerously high inflation. In either case, the Austrians argue, the best course of action would have been to let the inevitable liquidations take place as quickly as possible. If Andrew Mellon were alive today, he would find friends in the Austrian camp.

Economists of the Austrian persuasion are also deeply skeptical of the rush to regulate that so often occurs in the wake of a crisis. In their view, too much regulation was the cause of the crisis in the first place, and adding more will only make future crises worse. This seems counterintuitive: how can regulation cause a crisis? The Austrians would respond that innovations like deposit insurance and lender-of-last-resort support, while offering security to anyone with a savings account, have nonetheless increased bankers' appetite for risk. Much as someone who wears a seat belt may be tempted to drive faster, banks assumed greater risks—and the potential for accruing greater profits—secure in the knowledge that if they failed, the federal government would make things right with their depositors.

This same logic extends to any number of other government interventions in the economy. Earlier this decade, Wall Street analysts spoke of the "Greenspan put"—the belief that the Federal Reserve would rescue financial firms with easy money, special lines of credit, and lender-of-last-resort support. (A put is an option that an investor can purchase to hedge against a sharp market downturn.) The Greenspan put is precisely what happened when the crisis hit: the Federal Reserve stepped into the breach, rewarding incompetent risk taking with monetary largesse—or at least, that is how the Austrians would interpret it. In the process, they argue, it only fostered a bigger and more disastrous boom-and-bust cycle down the line.

Austrians argue that many of the common cures for financial disasters are worse than the disease. On the one hand, if governments run fiscal deficits in order to keep the economy afloat, levels of public debt become unsustainable. Eventually, governments are forced to raise interest rates, killing off whatever recovery may be under way. The Austrians are equally critical of the easy solution to this problem: printing money to "monetize" deficits. Doing so, they argue, will invariably lead to inflation and anemic economic growth comparable to the stagflation that crippled the United States in the 1970s. Either way, the Austrians believe, government can only make a bad situation worse and plant the seeds of a bigger bubble down the line, as everyone comes to believe that in the event of a future financial crisis, a bailout will be forthcoming.

Much of the Austrian vision seems extreme, or at the very least heartless. It is the antithesis of Keynesian thinking, much as Joseph Schumpeter was the most significant rival of Keynes when both were alive. If Keynes advanced a vision of capitalism that might occasionally become imbalanced (but could readily be stabilized with government intervention), Schumpeter believed instability to be the necessary consequence of the kind of innovation that made capitalism possible in the first place.

From the Austrian perspective, the fear now is that the United States is heading down the road that Japan paved in the 1990s, when it responded to its own slow-motion financial crisis by propping up zombie banks and corporate firms and by dropping interest rates down to zero, flooding the economy with yet more easy money. The government also ran enormous fiscal deficits to finance the kind of stimulus spending that Keynes prescribed. Instead of allowing "creative destruction," the Japanese built bridges to nowhere that merely put enormous amounts of debt on the shoulders of the national government. The result, the Austrians maintain, was Japan's Lost Decade.

Does the Austrian view have any merit? Economists who swear fealty to Keynes argue that Japan failed to implement the appropriate fiscal stimulus and monetary policy in time. They point out that the government waited two years after the collapse of the bubble to start its stimulus spending. Even worse, the Bank of Japan took eight years to cut interest rates from 8 percent to 0 percent. Then it moved away from this zero-interest-rate policy (better known as ZIRP) too soon. Just as FDR curtailed fiscal and monetary policies in 1937, ushering in a severe recession, Japan triggered a recession that lasted from 1998 to 2000. By the same logic, the United States, should it curtail stimulus spending or tighten the monetary reins while the recovery has barely started, risks repeating this mistake today.

In short, the Austrian approach is misguided when it comes to short-term policies. As Keynes and Minsky recognized, in the absence of government intervention, a crisis caused by financial excesses can become an outright depression, and what begins as a reasonable retreat from risk can turn into a rout. When the "animal spirits" of capitalism vanish, the "creative destruction" hailed by the Austrians can swiftly turn into a self-fulfilling collapse of private aggregate demand. As a consequence, distressed but still-solvent firms, banks, and households can no longer gain access to the credit necessary for their continued survival. It's one thing if truly insolvent banks, firms, and individual households go under; it's another altogether when innocent bystanders to an economic crisis are forced into bankruptcy because credit dries up.

In order to prevent this kind of collateral damage, it makes sense to follow the playbook devised by Keynes in the short term, even when the underlying fundamentals suggest that significant portions of the economy are not only illiquid but insolvent. In the short term, it's best to prevent a disorderly collapse of the entire financial system via monetary easing and the creation of bulwarks: via lender-of-last-resort support, for example, or capital injections into ailing banks. It's also best to prop up aggregate demand through stimulus spending and tax cuts. Doing so will prevent a financial crisis from turning into something comparable to Japan's Lost Decade or, worse, the Great Depression.

But when it comes to the medium term and long term, the Austrians have something to teach us. Even Minsky correctly pointed out that resolving a financial crisis over the medium and long term requires that everyone from households to corporations to banks reduce their level of debt. Putting this off is always a serious mistake. By failing to reduce private leverage, banks, firms, and households drown in debt, unable to lend, spend, consume, or invest. Likewise, socializing these losses—via unending government bailouts—is untenable. So too is the impulse to get rid of these debts by trying to inflate the currency. These actions merely move the problem from one part of the economy to another. In the long term, it is absolutely necessary for insolvent banks, firms, and households to go bankrupt and emerge anew; keeping them alive indefinitely only prolongs the problem.

In general, the followers of Keynes and the followers of Schumpeter don't talk to each other. That's unfortunate, because both thinkers—and the larger schools of economic thinking they represent—have something to say about what should be done. The insights of both schools can be synthesized and brought to bear on the problems we face now; indeed, the successful resolution of the recent crisis depends on a pragmatic approach that takes the best of both camps, recognizing that while stimulus spending, bailouts, lender-of-last-resort support, and monetary policy may help in the short term, a necessary reckoning must take place over the longer term in order to achieve a return to prosperity.

What we counsel is a kind of controlled "creative destruction." Financial crises are a bit like nuclear energy: they are enormously destructive if all the energy is released at once, but much less so if channeled and controlled. The massive interventions by the Federal Reserve and governments around the globe brought the financial crisis under control. But much remains to be done: radioactive assets the world over must be acknowledged, contained, and disposed of. Regulations must be written, and international financial institutions reborn.

How to manage that task is the pressing question of our time. Keynes once observed that "economists set themselves too easy, too useless a task if in tempestuous seasons they can only tell us that when the storm is long past the ocean is flat again." The waters will eventually stop churning, but how long it takes them to subside depends on how economists approach the problem, craft solutions, and make difficult decisions.

In facing these challenges, it's worth adding one more arrow to the quiver of crisis economics. The study of crises cannot be confined to economic theories alone. A final perspective is necessary, one that is not easily distilled to a school of thought, a model, or an equation: the study of the past.

The Uses of History

In June 2009 the legendary economist Paul Samuelson sat down with an interviewer. Samuelson, who remained as productive as ever into his nineties, is widely considered the greatest economist of the last half century. A founder and codifier of the neoclassical school, he oversaw his profession's embrace of esoteric mathematical models as a way of describing timeless economic phenomena. But when the interviewer innocently asked, "What would you say to someone starting graduate study in economics?" Samuelson gave an unexpected answer. "Well," he said, "this is probably a change from what I would have said when I was younger. Have a very healthy respect for the study of economic history, because that's the raw material out of which any of your conjectures or testings will come."

Samuelson is right—economic history is important, far more than theories of efficient markets and rational investors would lead one to believe. That's not because history repeats itself in some simplistic, cyclical way, though parallels between past and present are plentiful. Rather, history is useful precisely because its raw material can inform and inflect economic theories. It injects gritty, real-life detail into elegant mathematical models, like those devised by Samuelson and his peers. That's a good thing: an almost religious faith in models helped create the conditions for the crisis in the first place, blinding traders and market players to the very real risks that had been accumulating for years. History promotes humility, a quality that comes in handy when assessing crises, which so often come on the heels of arrogant proclamations that ordinary economic rules no longer apply.

We are hardly alone in our desire to harness history. As long as there have been crises, there have been attempts to put them in historical context. Amateurs like the Scottish journalist Charles Mackay, whose *Extraordinary Popular Delusions and the Madness of Crowds* was published in 1841, began the effort. Though only partially concerned with economic crises (and chock-full of inaccuracies), Mackay's book may have been the first attempt to draw lessons from the history of economic crises. His main conclusion—that human beings are an irrational lot, prone to fits of economic exuberance and euphoria—anticipated both behavioral economics and the thrust of much historical writing on crises.

Several professional historians and economists followed in Mackay's footsteps, but not until the economist Charles P. Kindleberger wrote *Manias, Panics, and Crashes* in 1978 did someone try to articulate an overarching historical theory of crises. It became a cult classic, and though its conclusions were evidently ignored in the years leading up to the recent disaster, its spirit of inquiry animates much of our thinking. So too does it animate the systematic and rigorous work of Carmen Reinhart and Kenneth Rogoff. In *This Time Is Different: Eight Centuries of Financial Folly* (2009), these two economists assembled a massive collection of historical data on crises, showing that while the details of currency crashes, banking panics, and debt defaults change, the broader trajectory of crises varies little from decade to decade, century to century.

This work, along with the work of numerous other historians and economists of a historical bent, helps us understand the deep origins of crises as well as their lingering aftereffects. Clearly the best way to understand crises is to see them as part of a broader continuum of causes and effects, extending long before and long after the acute phase of the crisis. In this spirit, we turn next to tracking some of those deeper structural forces that over many years set the stage for a crisis.

Chapter 3

Plate Tectonics

A familiar account of the current economic crisis goes something like this: A housing bubble in the United States got out of control sometime around 2005 or 2006. People took out mortgages they couldn't afford and eventually defaulted on them. Having been securitized, however, those mortgages went on to infect and topple the global financial system.

This account blames a few bad apples, subprime borrowers, for the catastrophe. It's reassuring but wrong: while the housing bubble rested in part on subprime mortgages, the problems were more pervasive and widespread. Nor were these problems of recent origin; they were rooted in deep structural changes in the economy that date back many years.

In other words, the securitization of bad loans was but the beginning; long-standing changes in corporate governance and compensation schemes played a role too. Government also shoulders some share of the blame, most obviously the monetary policies pursued by Alan Greenspan. So too do decades of government policies favoring home ownership.

In the end, however, the significance of government intervention was dwarfed by the significance of government inaction. For years federal regulators turned a blind eye to the rise of a new shadow banking system that made the entire financial system dangerously fragile and prone to collapse. These new financial institutions battened on the easy money and easy credit made available not only by the Federal Reserve but by emerging economies like China.

These changes may have been invisible to most market watchers, or at the very least, their importance was not fully recognized. Subprime mortgages were but the most obvious sign of a deep and systemic rot. This fact underscores a cardinal principle of crisis economics: the biggest and most destructive financial disasters are not produced by something so inconsequential as subprime mortgages or a few reckless risk takers. Nor are they merely produced by the euphoria of a speculative bubble.

Rather, much as with earthquakes, the pressures build for many years, and when the shock finally comes, it can be staggering. In 2006–8 it was not simply the subprime securities that collapsed in value; the entire edifice of the world's financial system was shaken. The collapse revealed a frightening if familiar truth: the homes of subprime borrowers were not the only structures standing on the proverbial fault line; countless towers of leverage and debt had been built there too.

Financial Innovation

Many bubbles begin when a burst of innovation or technological progress heralds the dawn of a new economy. In the 1840s Great Britain endured a mania driven by a new technology: the railroad. In 1830 the first commercially successful railroad began carrying passengers between Manchester and Liverpool; thereafter investors bought shares in companies that would build even more profitable lines. During the height of the boom in 1845–46, share prices of railroad stocks soared, and corporations built thousands of miles of track, much of it redundant and unnecessary. While that boom ended with a brutal bust, it was justified in part by fundamentals: a new technology begat new business opportunities. Even though most of the railway companies of the 1840s went bankrupt, they left behind a new transportation infrastructure that was essential to the nation's economic expansion throughout the nineteenth century.

The same argument could be made for the dot-com boom of the 1990s. Though it swiftly became a speculative bubble, it was at least partly justified by a new technology—the Internet—and its many promising applications. When this bubble collapsed, plenty of new companies survived, as did a new communications infrastructure of coaxial cable lines, cell phone towers, and other tangible technological improvements.

The recent crisis, by contrast, has left behind few tangible benefits: abandoned housing subdivisions in Las Vegas are next to useless. Worse, no technological revolution underpinned the housing boom: houses built in 2006 were no different and no more efficient than houses built a decade or two earlier. The most recent boom was that rare creature, a boom without any change in fundamentals. It was a speculative bubble and nothing more.

But if technological innovation wasn't driving the housing boom, what was? In fact, there was plenty of innovation—that's the good news. The bad news is that most of it percolated in one sector of the economy, the financial services industry. In itself, this was not a problem. After all, plenty of financial innovations in centuries past—insurance, for example, and commodity options—have proved their value again and again, enabling market participants to manage and contain risk.

At first that same spirit animated the current crop of financial innovations. Indeed, they were attempts to improve on the older model of making loans. Several decades ago banks that made home loans followed the "originate and hold" model. A prospective homeowner would apply for a mortgage, and the bank would lend the money, then sit back and collect payments on the principal and interest. The bank that originated the mortgage held the mortgage; it was strictly a transaction between the homeowner and the bank.

Financial innovation changed that. In the 1970s the Government National Mortgage Association (better known as Ginnie Mae) put together the first mortgage-backed securities. That is, it pooled mortgages it had originated, then issued bonds on the basis of that pool. Consequently, rather than waiting thirty years to recoup the proceeds from a mortgage, Ginnie Mae could receive a lump sum up front from the purchasers of the bond. In turn, the investors buying these new bonds would receive a certain portion of the revenue stream from the thousands of homeowners paying off their mortgages.

This scheme was revolutionary. Thanks to what was quickly dubbed securitization, illiquid assets like mortgages could now be pooled and transformed into liquid assets that were tradable on the open market. These new instruments had a name: mortgage-backed securities. In time other government agencies like Freddie Mac and Fannie Mae joined the securitization business. So too did investment banks, brokerages, and even home builders, all of whom brought together growing numbers of home mortgages into new and ever more profitable pools. Investors around the world snapped them up. After all, according to conventional wisdom, home prices never went down.

Investment banks typically guided the creation of pools of mortgage-backed securities. Working with whoever had originated the pool of mortgages—a bank, a nonbank lender, or a government-sponsored entity—an investment bank would help set up a "special purpose vehicle" (SPV). The SPV would then issue bonds, or mortgage-backed securities, selling them to investors. In theory, everyone got what he wanted with this system. The homeowner got a loan, and the mortgage broker and the appraiser earned their fees. The mortgage lender made a tidy profit without having to wait thirty years. The investment bank earned a fat fee for its assistance even as it unloaded the risk of the mortgage onto someone else. And last but not least, the investors who purchased the securities looked forward to receiving a steady revenue stream as homeowners paid off their loans.

Though mortgage-backed securities became increasingly popular in the 1980s, it was not until the 1990s that they really took off. In an ironic twist, the savings and loan (S&L) crisis cemented the popularity of securitization. In that debacle more than sixteen hundred thrifts went bust because they'd made a bunch of bad residential and commercial real estate loans that they'd kept on their books (as "originate and hold" transactions). That would not have happened had the loans been securitized—or at least that's the lesson that many bankers drew from the S&Ls' collapse. The new thinking was simple enough: far better to sell off the loans and pocket a tidy profit up front than hold the loans and risk having them go bad later. Distributing the loans to those better able to shoulder the risk—pension funds, insurance companies, and other institutional investors—could lessen the risk of a systemic banking crisis. "Originate and distribute" replaced "originate and hold."

It's a sound principle as long as the buyers of the securities can accurately assess the risk inherent in them. But if you're a bank selling off newly minted mortgages via the securitization pipeline, your primary objective is to unload as many mortgages as quickly as possible. Each sale gives you more money with which to make more loans. Unfortunately, because the bank no longer faces the consequences of making bad loans, it has much less incentive to properly monitor the underlying risk of the mortgages it originates. When originate and hold becomes originate and distribute, a bad mortgage is passed down the line like a hot potato.

As securitization became increasingly commonplace in the 1990s and 2000s, mortgage brokers, mortgage appraisers, ordinary banks, investment banks, and even quasi-public institutions like Fannie Mae and Freddie Mac no longer subjected would-be borrowers to careful scrutiny. So-called liar loans became increasingly common, as borrowers fibbed about their income and failed to provide written confirmation of their salary. Most infamous of all were the "NINJA loans," in which the borrower had No Income, No Job, (and no) Assets.

Securitization did not stop there. Financial firms oversaw the securitization of commercial real estate mortgages along with many kinds of consumer loans: credit card loans, student loans, and auto loans. Corporate loans were securitized as well, such as leveraged loans and industrial and commercial loans. The resulting bonds—asset-backed securities—proved popular, and securitization soon spread elsewhere. As one textbook on risk management concluded in 2001, "Sometimes it seems as though almost anything can be securitized." That was no exaggeration: by the time the crisis hit, securitization had been applied to airplane leases, revenues from forests and mines, delinquent tax liens, radio tower revenues, boat loans, state and local government revenues, and even the royalties of rock bands.

Many of these newfangled products suffered from the same problems and temptations associated with the first generation of mortgage-backed securities: the bank or firm originating the securities had little incentive to conduct the oversight and due diligence necessary to confirm that the underlying loans would be paid off. The investment banks that had midwifed the birth of these pools of securities did not perform this duty either: they intended to sell the bundled loans and thereby move them off their balance sheets.

In theory, the ratings agencies—Moody's, Fitch, Standard & Poor's—should have sounded the alarm. But relying on the ratings agencies was much like relying on the fox to guard the henhouse: they had every possible incentive to give a high rating to the securities under review (see chapter 8). Doing so earned them a nice fee from the very entities they were evaluating and the promise of future business; giving a realistic assessment, by contrast, could mean losing the commission, along with any future commissions. Far better to award a bank the financial equivalent of a *Good Housekeeping* Seal of Approval and hope for the best. On the eve of the crisis, the ratings firms made upwards of half their profits from handing out AAA ratings, many of which were undeserved, to exotic structured finance products.

But there is more to the story than corrupt ratings agencies. In fact, the ratings agencies may have had a genuinely difficult time figuring out the likelihood of defaults on the loans pooled into these securities, as very little historical data about the new subprime mortgages and their default rates were available. This was particularly the case with the new, exotic, and complicated mortgage-backed and asset-backed securities first crafted by investment banks in the 1980s. These securities go by different names and different acronyms: collateralized mortgage obligations (CMOs), collateralized debt obligations (CDOs), and collateralized loan obligations (CLOs).

All of them worked according to the same principle. Anyone holding a plain-vanilla mortgage-backed security necessarily took on a certain amount of risk: the homeowner might default, for example, or simply prepay the loan, thereby depriving the lender of the additional interest payments it would earn if the loan was paid off on schedule. Financial "engineers" on Wall Street came up with an elegant solution: the CDO. The CDO would be divided into slices, or tranches. The simplest CDOs had only three tranches: equity, mezzanine, and senior. The purchasers of an equity tranche got the highest return but took on the greatest risk: if any homeowners in the underlying pool defaulted, the holders of the equity tranche would see losses before anyone else. The mezzanine tranche was less risky, but its purchasers would still suffer losses if a larger percentage of homeowners in the underlying pool defaulted. At the top was the senior tranche. While it paid the lowest rate of return, it was supposed to be risk free or pretty close to it. The holders of the senior tranche got paid first and sustained losses last.

This impressive edifice of structured finance rested on shaky foundations. It depended on a sleight of hand: a bunch of dodgy and risky BBB-rated subprime mortgages would be bundled into a BBB mortgage-backed security and then sliced into tranches in which the senior tranche—approximately 80 percent of the total underlying assets—would be given an AAA rating. The process transformed toxic waste into a gold-plated security, even though the underlying pool of mortgages was just as risky as it was before.

Securitization achieved even more bizarre levels of complexity. It became fashionable, for instance, to combine CDOs with other CDOs, then split them up into tranches. These CDOs of CDOs (sometimes called a CDO^2) paled next to the more baroque products coming out of the labs on Wall Street: CDOs of CDOs of CDOs, better known as CDO^3; and synthetic CDOs, which assembled a bunch of credit default swaps to mimic an underlying CDO. Some of these more esoteric products had far more than three tranches: they might have fifty or even one hundred, each of which represented a certain level of risk tolerance.

In hindsight, the peril of this kind of financial innovation is easy to understand. Slicing and dicing credit risk and transferring it around the world suffused the system with financial instruments that were exotic, complex, and illiquid. These creations became so fiendishly complex and unique that it became difficult to value them by conventional means. Instead of market prices, financial firms resorted to mathematical models to value them. Unfortunately, these models relied on optimistic assumptions that minimized measured risk. The net result was an utterly opaque, impenetrable financial system ripe for a panic.

This state of affairs may seem unique and unprecedented, and it was, but only in the particulars. Lack of transparency, underestimation of risk, and cluelessness about how new financial products might behave when subjected to significant stress are recurrent problems in many crises, past and present.

Moral Hazard

While the financial engineers who gave us monstrosities like the CDO[3] deserve plenty of blame, many other problems were accumulating that went far beyond the obvious flaws in the securitization food chain. The faulty ways in which financial firms governed themselves helped lay the groundwork for the recent crisis as well.

The key to understanding this situation is the concept of "moral hazard." Simply put, moral hazard is someone's willingness to take risks—particularly excessive risks—that he would normally avoid, simply because he knows someone else will shoulder whatever negative consequences follow if not bail out those who took those risks. For example, someone who has auto theft insurance may be more willing to park his car in a place where it might be stolen, or neglect to buy an anti-theft device, than someone who lacks that insurance. The car owner knows that the insurance company will cover the loss; the problem will fall on someone else's shoulders. Likewise, someone who leases an automobile with a service contract is more likely to drive in ways that subject the car to wear and tear than someone without such a contract. Again, the lessee knows any damage will be someone else's problem.

Moral hazard played a significant role in the recent economic crisis. In the securitization food chain, a mortgage broker who knowingly brought a liar loan to a bank got compensated for his efforts but bore no responsibility for what would happen as the mortgage moved down the line. Likewise, the trader who placed enormous bets on a CDO would be rewarded handsomely if he succeeded but was rarely punished if he failed. Even if he was terminated, he would get to keep whatever compensation he'd accrued over the years. The fallout of his decisions became someone else's problem—namely, the company that employed him.

This observation is pretty familiar. Less well known is the fact that moral hazard was especially rife in the financial services industry because of the way these firms provided compensation. Rather than simply paying employees a salary, the traders and bankers who worked at investment banks, hedge funds, and other financial services firms were rewarded for their performance via a system of annual bonuses. While bonuses have long played a role in compensation at these firms, they soared in recent years, and all the major investment banks—Goldman Sachs, Morgan Stanley, Merrill Lynch, Lehman Brothers, and Bear Stearns—paid ever more staggering sums. In 2005 the big five firms paid $25 billion in bonuses; in 2006 they paid $36 billion; and a year later, $38 billion.

More to the point, the ratio of bonuses to base pay skyrocketed. In 2006 the average bonus accounted for 60 percent of total compensation at the five biggest investment banks. In some cases, the figure was much higher: bonuses ten or even twelve times the size of base salaries became commonplace in many firms at the center of the meltdown. Even after these firms ended up on life support, they continued to pay bonuses.

The bonus system, which focused on short-term profits made over the course of a year, encouraged risk taking and excessive leverage on a massive scale. Nowhere was this more evident than at AIG, which specialized in selling insurance on events—the bankruptcy of Lehman Brothers, for example—that were unlikely to materialize in any given year. In the short term, this willingness to wager huge amounts of money insuring against catastrophes yielded large revenues, profits, and bonuses for traders and banks. In the long term, the inevitable happened, and when it did, companies like AIG nearly collapsed. The consequences of these gamblers' decisions ended up being shouldered by someone else—namely, American taxpayers.

In theory, this outbreak of moral hazard should have been prevented, but it was not. Why? The answer lies with what economists call the principal-agent problem. In large-scale capitalist enterprises, the principals (the shareholders and board of directors) must hire other people such as managers (the "agents") to carry out their wishes and mind the store. Unfortunately, the agents invariably know more about what's going on than the principals and can pursue their own self-interest to destructive effect.

Think, for example, of the problem of a store owner who has employees minding the cash registers. This is a very basic example of the principal-agent problem. It's obviously in the interest of the store owner to have employees behave honestly and not line their own pockets. But the store owner is not omniscient; he can't see everything that's going on beneath him. He suffers from what economists call the asymmetric information problem, in which the principal (the store owner) knows less than the agent (the cashier). The store owner needs to make his employees serve his interests, and that's no easy task.

Now imagine this problem multiplied many times, with many layers of employees or agents, all of whom have the ability to pursue their own interests at the expense of the "principals" who oversee them. Moreover, many employees are both principals (responsible for overseeing people below them) and agents (responsible for answering to someone above them). Worse, the problem here is no longer that employees will steal, but that they will use the firm's resources to place outsize, risky bets in order to collect the maximum bonus, even if that means putting the firm in jeopardy.

This, more or less, is the structure of a typical financial firm, and the dangers of this arrangement became increasingly evident over the course of the recent financial crisis. The collapse of AIG may be the most extreme example of the dangers of moral hazard, principal-agent problems, and asymmetric information. There, the actions of a small group of employees based in London brought the entire company to its knees, along with the global financial system.

In theory, shareholders should be able to prevent such disasters: they are the last link in the chain, the ultimate owners of the financial firm. But in fact, shareholders generally don't have much incentive to rein in reckless bankers, traders, and managers. Why? Financial firms rely far more heavily on borrowed money to finance their operations than do ordinary corporations, so when it comes to the firm's day-to-day operations, shareholders don't have much skin in the game. They have little incentive to steer traders away from taking big risks; in fact, they have plenty of incentive to do the opposite. If those risks pay off, shareholders win big. If they don't, shareholders may end up losing their small stake in the company. That's bad news, for sure, but when compared to the potential gains realized by playing with other people's money, it's a risk worth taking. Thus, shareholders with little skin in the game were "gambling for redemption."

In theory, one final firewall exists to keep moral hazard in check: the people who lend money to banks and other financial firms. If any party has a strong incentive to monitor banks, they do. After all, they stand to lose their shirts if the bank does something stupid. Unfortunately, this is another example of the law of unintended consequences. Funds lent to most ordinary banks come in the form of deposits. However, most deposits are subject to deposit insurance. So even if a bank recklessly gambles with depositors' money, the depositors can sleep well at night knowing that deposit insurance will make them whole. That removes any incentive for them to take actions that might punish the bank for its bad decisions.

In principle, unsecured creditors of banks and other financial institutions could impose market discipline; their funds, after all, could be jeopardized if the institutions took too much risk. But in the recent crisis, even these unsecured creditors did not impose market discipline. The reasons were various: the unsecured claims were too small to make a difference; the unsecured creditors were treated mostly like secured creditors (insured depositors) and did not experience losses as they were bailed out; the lender-of-last-resort support of central banks prevented the working of market discipline.

Not all financial institutions are covered by deposit insurance, but if there's one lesson of financial crises that does get remembered by everyone, it's that when the going gets rough, a lender of last resort will appear to save the day. Ever since the Great Depression, central banks have consistently stepped into the breach and acted as the lender of last resort. It happened in the LTCM crisis in 1998, when the New York Fed orchestrated a private bailout, and it happened again in the midst of the recent crisis, when the Federal Reserve made unprecedented levels of liquidity available to institutions like investment banks and others that fell outside the aegis of deposit insurance.

Knowing that a probable lender of last resort existed reduced financial institutions' incentive to hold a large amount of liquid assets as a buffer against a bank run. It also helped remove any remaining incentive that the de facto depositors had to monitor these institutions' performance: should a crisis strike, they knew, central banks around the world could be counted on to save the day. And in this respect, the calculations of all the financial system's players proved remarkably correct: in both the United States and abroad, central banks fell all over themselves to provide lifelines to ailing firms. There was one dramatic attempt to address the problem of moral hazard—by letting Lehman Brothers fail—followed by frantic efforts to bail out huge swaths of the financial system.

If there was ever an argument for tightly regulating banks and other financial firms, this is it. Banks have to be forced to hold enough liquidity, and shareholders must have enough skin in the game and an incentive to monitor the firms they supposedly supervise. And these requirements mean that government must play a major, if controversial, role. Unfortunately, in the years leading up to the crisis, government was nowhere to be found. In fact, government helped foment this crisis, not merely through its absence, but through its not-so-subtle interventions as well.

Government and Its Discontents

The Federal Reserve is arguably the most powerful instrument of government control over the economy. Its power can be used for good or for ill, as the career of Alan Greenspan amply suggests. That Greenspan presided over the Federal Reserve is ironic. After all, as a young man he became smitten with the power of the free market. In the 1950s he even became an acolyte of Ayn Rand, whose hard-core libertarian beliefs he admired. Yet Greenspan's growing conviction that government should stay out of the economy did not prevent him from serving in government when the opportunity arose.

Greenspan's first major appointment came in 1974 as chairman of President Gerald Ford's Council of Economic Advisers. But this service paled in importance compared to his 1987 appointment as chairman of the Federal Reserve. His ambivalence about government's role in regulating the free market was evident from the beginning. Four months after his appointment, the stock market crashed, and Greenspan immediately rode to the rescue. Out the window went any principled opposition to government intervention. As he memorably put it, "In a crisis environment . . . we shouldn't really focus on longer-term policy questions until we get beyond this immediate period of chaos." If Greenspan could acknowledge that the central bank had a role to play in mitigating the effects of a financial crisis, he declined to do anything to prevent such crises from developing. He seems to have had little interest in a long-standing central banking philosophy that these powerful institutions should prevent bubbles from forming in the first place. Nicely summarizing that belief, former Federal Reserve chairman William McChesney Martin,

Jr., once said that the job of the central banker was to "take away the punch bowl just as the party gets going."

Greenspan revealed himself to be unwilling to take it away. In 1996, as the stock market spiraled into a giddy bubble focused on tech and Internet stocks, he warned of "irrational exuberance," then did next to nothing to stop the bubble from inflating, aside from instituting a token increase of 25 basis points in the Federal funds rate. When the dot-com bubble finally popped in 2000, Greenspan poured plenty more alcohol into the proverbial punch bowl. In the wake of the attacks on September 11, he kept cutting the funds rate, even after signs of a recovery started to appear. When he finally resumed raising rates in 2004, he did so in tiny and slow and predictable (a policy of "measured pace" tightening) increments of 25 basis points every six weeks, when the Federal Open Market Committee met. This policy kept rates too low for too long and normalized them too late and too slowly.

The result was the housing and mortgage bubble. By pumping vast quantities of easy money into the economy and keeping it there for too long, Greenspan muted the effects of one bubble's collapse by inflating an entirely new one. This policy was the inevitable consequence of the contradiction at the heart of his approach to central banking: helplessly watching bubbles on the way up, and moving frantically to arrest the downward slide. Unfortunately, it created a Greenspan put. By the end of Greenspan's final term as chairman of the Federal Reserve, the Greenspan put was an article of faith among traders: the markets believed that the Fed would always ride to the rescue of reckless traders ruined after a bubble collapsed. It created moral hazard on a grand scale, and Greenspan deserves blame for it.

Greenspan also deserves blame for refusing to use the power of the Federal Reserve to regulate markets. For example, in 1994 Congress passed the Home Ownership and Equity Protection Act in order to crack down on predatory lending practices. Under its terms, Greenspan could have regulated subprime lending, but he refused to do so. He continued to refuse even after Edward Gramlich, one of the members of the Federal Reserve Board, beseeched him to do so. Greenspan later defended his refusal to monitor subprime lenders: "For us to go in and audit how they act on their mortgage applications would have been a huge effort, and it's not clear to me we would have found anything that would have been worthwhile without undermining the desired availability of subprime credits."

Revealing words, these. Greenspan considered the advent of subprime lending to be entirely a good thing, the inevitable consequence of letting markets run free. Until very recently he continued to praise the role that financial "innovation" played in making credit available to growing numbers of Americans. At one public event in 2005 he hailed the way financial innovation had "led to rapid growth in subprime mortgage lending, . . . fostering constructive innovation that is both responsive to market demand and beneficial to consumers."

In all fairness, Greenspan had plenty of company in the relentless drive toward deregulation. For the previous three decades, freeing financial markets from "onerous" regulations had been an article of faith among conservatives. It also became public policy. From the 1980s onward, tight regulations of the financial system instituted during the Great Depression were phased out or eliminated.

The most notable casualty was the Glass-Steagall Act of 1933. Part of that landmark legislation had created a firewall between commercial banks (which took deposits and made loans) and investment banks (which underwrote, bought, and sold securities). Those provisions suffered death by a thousand cuts. Beginning in the late 1980s, the Federal Reserve Board permitted commercial banks to buy and sell a range of securities. At first commercial banks could derive only 10 percent of their profits from securities operations, but in 1996 the Federal Reserve Board raised that threshold to 25 percent. The following year Bankers Trust became the first commercial bank to purchase a securities firm; other banks soon followed suit.

The catalyst for the final repeal of Glass-Steagall was the proposed merger of Travelers with Citicorp. This combination, which brought commercial banking, insurance underwriting, and securities underwriting under the same roof, forced the issue: the new financial behemoth was illegal under existing laws. Late in 1999, after intense lobbying, Congress repealed the remnants of Glass-Steagall via the Financial Services Modernization Act, paving the way for additional mergers between investment banks, commercial banks, and insurers.

One of the key players in the repeal of Glass-Steagall was Republican economist-turned-senator Phil Gramm. Gramm continued to lead the crusade against financial regulation, most famously in 2000, when he attached the Commodity Futures Modernization Act to a budget bill. This act, which was never debated in the Senate or the House, effectively declared huge swaths of the derivatives market off-limits to regulation. Among the instruments thus removed from regulation were credit default swaps, which permitted a purchaser to buy "insurance" to protect against defaults on bonds both very simple (such as those issued by an automaker) and extremely complex (collateralized debt obligations backed by pools of mortgage-backed securities). Credit default swaps, which mushroomed to reach a notional value of over $60 trillion by 2008, became one of the most important sources of "systemic risk"—perils that threaten the entire financial system. (For more on credit default swaps, see chapter 8.)

The push for deregulation also took place outside Congress. In 2004 the five biggest investment banks lobbied the Securities and Exchange Commission (SEC), hoping to persuade it to loosen rules that restricted the amount of debt their brokerage units could assume. Obtaining an exemption would allow the firms to tap billions of dollars hitherto held in capital reserve should they sustain major losses on their investments. It would allow cuts in the cushion these firms had maintained, even as it magnified their potential for profits. In a unanimous decision, the SEC complied with the banks' request, though not without some recognition that the move might be risky. "We've said these are the big guys," observed one commissioner at the sparsely attended hearing, "but that means if anything goes wrong, it's going to be an awfully big mess." Investment banks reacted to this deregulation by massively increasing their leverage (ratio of assets to capital) to ratios of 20, 25, or even more, well above the ratio of 12.5 imposed on the more regulated commercial banks.

Not everyone thinks that deregulation alone is to blame for the crisis. Some conservative commentators have claimed that it was the product of too much government, not too little. The key claim here is that the Community Reinvestment Act of 1977 helped inflate the bubble. That piece of legislation, which prevented banks from discriminating against low-income neighborhoods when they made loans, made it easier for the poor and minorities to obtain mortgages. In the conservative interpretation, the original and the amended legislation—with the assistance of Fannie Mae and Freddie Mac—helped spur the subprime market and caused the eventual meltdown.

It's an interesting argument but misplaced. The huge growth in the subprime market was primarily underwritten not by Fannie Mae and Freddie Mac but by private mortgage lenders like Countrywide. Moreover, the Community Reinvestment Act long predates the rise of the housing bubble. True, legislation passed in the 1990s compelled Fannie Mae and Freddie Mac to purchase mortgages that effectively included subprime loans. In 1997, for example, some 42 percent of the loans they purchased had to come from borrowers whose income was below the average for their neighborhood. Some of these loans were subprime, though the precise number is not known with certainty. Regardless, overblown claims that Fannie Mae and Freddie Mac single-handedly caused the subprime crisis are just plain wrong.

What is true is that the federal government has long sponsored and subsidized home ownership, making it a far less expensive and burdensome proposition than it would otherwise be. Its subsidies include allowing homeowners to deduct property taxes and mortgage interest payments on their federal income tax returns. Similarly, it does not tax a certain portion of capital gains from the sale of a primary home. Most important of all, several government-sponsored enterprises—not only Fannie Mae, Freddie Mac, and FHA but the Federal Home Loan Banks, among others—support and subsidize the housing and mortgage market. These subsidies may not have caused the housing bubble, but they certainly created conditions that encouraged and sustained its growth.

The Shadow Banks

If government policies helped inflate the bubble, and deregulation helped remove existing constraints on financial firms, the failure of government to keep pace with financial innovation also played a role. This failure goes far beyond merely neglecting to regulate exotic derivatives, or leaving the bonus system favored by the financial services industry untouched. It goes to the heart of the dramatic if unheralded rise, over the past thirty-plus years, of what Pacific Investment Management Company's Paul McCulley dubbed the "shadow banking system."

The shadow banking system consists of financial institutions that look like banks, act like banks, and borrow and lend and invest like banks, but—and here's the important part—are not regulated like banks. Think for a moment about what constitutes a bank. In simplest terms, a bank borrows money on a short-term basis, usually in the form of deposits "lent" to it by depositors. These deposits constitute most of the bank's liabilities: at any moment the depositors can demand their money, and the bank has no choice but to give it back.

But banks don't just sit on deposits; they lend them out in the form of mortgages and other long-term investments, such as a ten-year loan to a corporation. In other words, they borrow the deposits, make loans, and thereby make a profit for themselves via the interest they charge. However, there's a catch: while the bank's liabilities are liquid (they're in the form of deposits), its assets are illiquid (they're tied up in land, new equipment on a factory floor, and other things that can't immediately be turned into cash).

Normally, this disparity isn't a problem; it's highly unlikely that all the depositors will rush to the bank at once, demanding their money back. But occasionally they do precisely that, and the Great Depression is the example of what happens when panicked depositors flood a bank. The perils of this dynamic were beautifully dramatized by Frank Capra's *It's a Wonderful Life*, which profiles the ups and downs in the life of small-town banker George Bailey.

One day, as Bailey is besieged by anxious depositors demanding their money back, he gives an impromptu lesson on banking. "You're thinking of this place all wrong," he tells the depositors, who cling to the idea that their money is simply lying idle in the vaults. "As if I had the money back in a safe," he remonstrates. "The money's not here. Your money's in Joe's house. . . . And in the Kennedy house, and Mrs. Backlin's house, and a hundred others." The liquid deposits, in other words, have been transformed into illiquid investments that are not readily converted back to cash. As Bailey explains to the depositors, "you're lending them the money to build, and then, they're going to pay it back to you as best they can."

Bailey's predicament was typical of banks in the darkest hours of the

Great Depression. He was grappling with the "maturity mismatch" between liabilities that are short-term "demand deposits," and assets held for the long term that can rarely be turned into cash on the spur of the moment. As a consequence, it's next to impossible to use the one to pay off the other without incurring tremendous costs. A bank caught in a run might sell off its assets, such as mortgages and other loans it has made. Unfortunately, if a general panic has seized the banking system, every bank will be trying to do the same thing, and these sales will fetch only a fraction of what they would command in normal times.

So in practice, banks that fall victim to liquidity runs can swiftly go from being illiquid to being insolvent. Sometimes banks deserve that fate, as when their assets are insufficient to accommodate the demands of depositors, regardless of the price at which they are sold. But in plenty of other cases, a bank is solvent but has simply made illiquid investments. As a consequence, its short-term liabilities far outweigh its liquid assets. During the Great Depression, banks failed for both reasons. Some could never have made good on the obligations to their depositors, whether there was a bank panic or not. Others could have made good on their obligations if they'd had help.

That help could have come in two forms: lender-of-last-resort support and deposit insurance. The first was available during the Great Depression, but the Federal Reserve failed to use it effectively; the second came into being when New Deal banking legislation created the Federal Deposit Insurance Corporation (FDIC). These two antidotes to bank runs are slightly different. Lender-of-last-resort support stops a bank run by giving banks ready access to cash so they can pay off their depositors, thus sparing them having to liquidate assets at fire-sale prices. Deposit insurance, by contrast, prevents bank runs from occurring in the first place: it reassures depositors that they will get their money back if the bank becomes illiquid or even insolvent.

In the postwar era, both lender-of-last-resort support and deposit insurance became the norm, not only in the United States but in most capitalist nations. These protections came at a cost for the participating banks: they had to give up some of their autonomy in order to avoid the problem of moral hazard. They thus submitted to regulation and supervision in the form of controls on their liquidity, leverage, and capital, which necessarily limited how much money they could make. As a result, banking became a rather humdrum if dependable business. A running joke had it that banking operated according to the 3-6-3 rule: bankers paid their depositors 3 percent interest, lent it out at 6 percent interest, and lined up to tee off at the golf course by three P.M. A slight exaggeration, perhaps, but the joke had more than a grain of truth.

As if that weren't enough to tame banking, international regulations imposed further restrictions. In 1974 central bank governors from the countries that made up the G-10 established the Basel Committee on Banking Supervision, named after the Swiss city that is home to the Bank for International Settlements, a linchpin of the global financial system. In 1988 the committee introduced a capital adequacy system that laid down methods for determining the relative risks of different kinds of assets held by banks around the world. This system, called the Basel Capital Accord, spelled out in no uncertain terms how much capital banks had to hold, relative to the risk of the assets in their custody. The core of the agreement held that banks had to maintain a minimum capital standard of 8 percent, that is, hold reserves equivalent to or exceeding 8 percent of the total value of their "risk-adjusted assets" (which meant that riskier assets would incur higher capital charges). Though the committee had no legal authority over member nations, its recommendations were adopted in most countries throughout the world.

The committee did not rest on its laurels: in succeeding years it issued additional recommendations. The stakes of those revisions were clear. As one 1997 report of the committee noted, "Weaknesses in the banking system of a country, whether developing or developed, can threaten financial stability both within that country and internationally." That spirit informed a revision to the Basel Capital Accord in 2006, known as Basel II. Unlike the first accord, not all the recommendations of Basel II have been implemented. (For more on the Basel accords, see chapter 8.)

Why? Simply put, not everyone in banking was looking for stability and security. A growing number of people who joined the financial services industry from the 1980s onward realized that they could make plenty of money, so long as they were willing to walk the banking tightrope without a safety net underneath. There were ways to conduct banking free of regulations, but also free of the protections afforded ordinary banks. So began a game of "regulatory arbitrage," the purposeful evasion of regulations in pursuit of higher profits. This quest gave rise to the shadow banks.

The shadow banks didn't have tellers; they didn't stand on street corners in neighborhoods across the country. They had funny acronyms, or what Paul McCulley aptly called a "whole alphabet soup of levered up non-bank investment conduits, vehicles, and structures," many of which lurked off the balance sheets of conventional banks. The shadow banks came in all shapes and sizes: nonbank mortgage lenders; structured investment vehicles (SIVs) and conduits, which financed themselves with complex short-term loans known as asset-backed commercial paper; investment banks and broker dealers, which financed themselves with overnight "repos," or repurchase agreements; money market funds, which relied on short-term funds from investors; hedge funds and private equity funds; and even state- and local-government-sponsored pools of auction-rate securities and tender option bonds, both of which had to be rolled over at a variable rate in weekly auctions. Most of these shadow banks had one thing in common: a profound maturity mismatch. They mostly borrowed in short-term, liquid markets, then invested in long-term, illiquid assets. They looked quite different from Bailey Bros. Building & Loan, but they suffered from the same vulnerability to a bank run.

This would not have been a problem had the shadow banks made the same bargain as regular banks, submitting to increased regulation in exchange for access to lender-of-last-resort support and the equivalent of deposit insurance. But they did not. Even worse, these institutions grew to rival the conventional banking system, lending comparable amounts of money. It's little wonder that the shadow banking system was at the heart of what would become the mother of all bank runs.

A World Awash in Cash

All of these factors—financial innovation, failures of corporate governance, easy monetary policy, failures of government, and the shadow banking system—contributed to the onset of the crisis. In many aspects, the United

States and other countries in the English-speaking world took the lead. But the rest of the world helped set the stage for the crisis, even if it was hardly their intent to do so.

Alan Greenspan was one of the first to recognize the problem. He rightly noted that when he raised the federal funds rate from 1 percent to 5.25 percent between 2004 and 2006, long-term interest rates and fixed-rate mortgage rates barely moved. Greenspan's belated policy of monetary tightening had had no effect. This was not what the textbooks would have predicted. In theory, long-term interest rates and mortgage rates should have crept upward in tune with the rate hikes.

Greenspan called it the "bond market conundrum," but it turned out to have an explanation. In an integrated world economy, the rates at which the United States could borrow money were increasingly determined in global markets. And in global markets there was a surplus of savings from Japan, Germany, China, and a range of emerging economies. All that savings had to be invested somewhere, and in the end, it went into purchasing debt generated by the United States. But the low rates of return on the federal government's short-term and long-term debt understandably caused investors to prefer debt paying a higher rate of return. So they purchased the debt of Fannie Mae and Freddie Mac, along with the mortgage-backed securities guaranteed by those institutions. All were implicitly guaranteed by the U.S. Treasury.

But overseas investors did not stop there. Private creditors of the United States—particularly investors and financial institutions in Europe—became major purchasers of securitized products. Estimates vary, but between 40 and 50 percent of the securities generated by American financial institutions ended up in the portfolios of foreign investors. In other words, the income stream from credit card debt, home equity loans, auto loans, student loans, and mortgages ended up in the portfolios of foreign investors via the process of securitization. By making those purchases, foreign creditors helped finance the borrowing binge that drove the bubble.

Just how much foreign investors underwrote the boom remains an open question. Much rides on the answer: some commentators have used the "global savings glut" hypothesis to blame the crisis on China and the other creditors of the United States. That misplaced analysis wrongly shifts the blame from problems in the United States. But what is indisputable is that this pool of savings in search of investments ended up in the United States. In the process, it inadvertently helped the United States live far beyond its means for far too long. Indeed, had the United States been an emerging economy instead of the world's sole superpower, its creditors would have pulled the plug long ago.

But they didn't. Instead, easy money poured into the United States, and this powerful global trend sustained the boom. Combined with lax monetary policy, reckless financial innovation, the problems of moral hazard and poor corporate governance, and the shadow banking system, easy foreign money helped brew a disaster of epic proportions. Still, none of these developments could alone cause a crisis. An essential, additional factor made a catastrophe all but inevitable: the fact that almost everyone connected to the financial system was increasingly reliant on debt or leverage.

The Lure of Leverage

Let's recall Minsky's taxonomy of borrowers (see chapter 2). The most conservative are the hedge borrowers, whose short-term income flow can cover payments not only of interest but of principal too. More risky are the speculative borrowers, whose income can cover only payments on interest; they must roll over the principal each time it comes due. Most dangerous are the Ponzi borrowers, who can service neither the principal nor the interest and must take on new debt just to stay afloat.

Minsky grasped an essential truth: that an economy would become vulnerable to collapse should its various players resort to debt to finance their activities. He believed that the greater the reliance on debt and leverage, the more fragile the financial system.

Leverage has been on the increase for years. From 1960 to 1974 the leverage ratios of banks in the United States increased by some 50 percent. This process only accelerated from the 1980s onward. Look, for example, at the statistics on debt for households, financial institutions, and the other corporations that constitute the private sector. In 1981 the debt of the

U.S. private sector was equal to 123 percent of the gross domestic product (GDP); by the end of 2008 it had soared to 290 percent.

Debt soared in every part of the private sector. The corporate sector was the most prudent: its total debt increased from 53 percent to 76 percent of GDP. Households showed less restraint. In 1981 household debt in the United States was 48 percent of GDP, but by 2007 it had risen to 100 percent. The household-debt-to-disposable-income ratio went from 65 percent in 1981 to a staggering 135 percent by 2008. Much of this debt came in the form of leverage in the housing sector, as home buyers purchased increasingly expensive homes with less and less of their own equity. Indeed, at the height of the housing boom, homes could be purchased with no money down, thanks to "innovations" like piggyback loans and other contrivances.

But if debt increased among households and corporations during this period, the financial sector came to rely on debt in a big way: between 1981 and 2008 its debt went from 22 percent of GDP to 117 percent, more than a fivefold increase. The use of debt to supplement investment is known as leverage. For example, an investment bank that finances the purchase of $20 million worth of mortgage-backed securities by putting up $1 million of its own capital and borrowing the other $19 million is leveraged at the rate of twenty to one.

Leverage comes in many flavors. Plain-vanilla leverage is the sort just described, but embedded leverage offers the potential for gains (and losses) that are many times the value of the underlying asset. For example, CDOs, as we have seen, come in different tranches, the riskier ones taking the brunt of the losses in the event things go south. That means in practice that for holders of certain slices of the CDO, losses are magnified to astonishing levels; a tiny loss on the underlying portfolio can hit certain investors particularly hard. Much of this kind of leverage is invisible to the market at large; there's no way to measure it, but when it unravels, the consequences can be dramatic.

Then there's systemic or compound leverage, in which one opening bit of leverage becomes the tip of a vast inverted pyramid of debt. Suppose, for example, that a wealthy individual borrows $3 million from a bank, adds $1 million of his own equity, and invests it into a "fund of funds" that invests in other hedge funds. At this point he has leverage of four to one. Then suppose this fund of funds takes that $4 million and borrows another $12 million from another bank, and sinks it into yet another hedge fund. Again, the leverage is still only four to one, but the initial stake of $4 million has grown to $16 million. Now imagine that this hedge fund borrows another $48 million—again, a leverage of four to one—to invest a total of $64 million in some high-risk tranches of a CDO. In an illustration of the power of exponential math, a tiny initial stake of $1 million has become the basis of a $64 million bet.

That's all fine if the value of those securities holds steady or, better yet, increases. But it's altogether different if the value of the assets declines. Consider the simple example of leverage given above, where the investment bank is levered twenty to one. Recall that the investment bank's equity totals a million dollars. But let's say the value of the asset falls from $20 million to $19 million, a drop of 5 percent. Should that happen, the investment bank's equity has been wiped out; the effective return on its investment is a rather unpleasant *negative* 100 percent. The same logic applies no matter what the level of leverage. If the leverage ratio was one hundred to one (a dollar of equity for every ninety-nine dollars of debt) even a minuscule drop of 1 percent in the value of the asset wipes out the underlying equity.

To make matters worse, lenders often expect leverage ratios to remain constant, even when the asset purchased with the loan loses some of its value. Say, for example, that a hedge fund borrows $95 million from an investment bank, kicks in $5 million of its own money, and purchases a CDO worth $100 million. Then the market price of the asset falls to $95 million. The equity has been wiped out. That's not necessarily a problem: the price may rebound to $100 million in due course. But the investment bank may get worried and make a margin call, demanding that the original leverage ratio be restored. That means that the hedge fund must come up with $4.75 million in new equity ($4.75 million is one twentieth of $95 million). If the hedge fund can raise the money, things may work out. If not, the hedge fund has to sell the asset at $95 million and see its equity wiped out.

That alone is hardly a tragedy: margin calls happen, and people (or hedge funds) lose their shirts all the time. The bigger problem is the risk that the hedge fund scrambling to raise equity is not alone. What if many such hedge funds and other financial institutions suddenly have to answer a margin call? It could happen if the asset that everyone is using leverage to obtain is the object of a speculative bubble, and prices have risen to unsustainable levels. In the recent crisis, that asset was real estate, not only land and buildings but the exotic securities that derived their value from timely mortgage payments.

When the value of an asset plateaus, then falls—say, because some subprime loans go sour, and the revenue stream of a CDO slows to a trickle—the effect ramifies throughout the financial system. Suddenly countless investors are seeing their $100 million CDO fall in value to $95 million. Suddenly all of them get margin calls, demanding that they put up more equity. Perhaps some of them can raise it, but many more will be forced to sell their CDO at whatever the market will bear. And if too many of them do this at once, the CDO may no longer fetch $95 million; it may drop to $90 million or $85 million.

When that happens, borrowers must sell off even more of their assets to meet new margin calls. This creates a cascade of fire sales, as too many sellers chase too few buyers. Even worse, lenders nervous about the solvency of borrowers may start requiring an even greater equity margin and lower leverage ratios as a condition of rolling over the debt. This adds fuel to the fire, and selling pressures intensify. Of course, borrowers may sell other assets to make margin calls: Treasury bonds or plain-vanilla equities. Unfortunately, if everyone pursues that strategy at the same time, the same dynamic that played out with CDOs will affect these other assets too: there will be too many sellers and too few buyers, and prices will fall in a range of asset classes.

In this way, what began as a problem in, say, housing, can suddenly spread to other markets. And what began as a subprime problem can suddenly become everyone's problem. Sound familiar?

Chapter 4

Things Fall Apart

Walter Bagehot was a giant in the nineteenth-century British financial world. Aside from editing *The Economist* for many years, he wrote extensively about financial crises, most famously in *Lombard Street*, published in 1873. Writing about the great banks of his day, Bagehot complained that they "are imprudent in so carefully concealing the details of their government, and in secluding those details from the risk of discussion." That veil of secrecy was all well and good in prosperous times, he observed, but in a downturn it could become a terrible liability. Suppose, he wrote, that one of the "greater London joint stock banks failed." The result "would be an instant suspicion of the whole system. One *terra incognita* being seen to be faulty, every other *terra incognita* would be suspected." In short, he concluded, "the ruin of one of these great banks would greatly impair the credit of all."

If Bagehot had been alive in 2007, he would have recognized a familiar but deeply unsettling scene: Citigroup, a financial institution with impeccable credentials but an impenetrable balance sheet, was ailing because of mysterious dealings with shadowy SIVs and conduits and a baffling assortment of structured financial products. A big bank was in trouble, and the extent of its problem was not apparent. Other financial institutions came under suspicion; uncertainty and unease roiled the markets.

What happened next was precisely as Bagehot anticipated. The first failures of 2007 set the stage for a collapse of confidence and an evaporation of trust, not merely in the shadow banks but in conventional banks as well. In no time at all, the ordinary bank-to-bank lending that supports global finance collapsed. The reason was simple: the entire financial system was one great *terra incognita*. As one market economist at the doomed firm Lehman Brothers observed late in the summer of 2007, "We are in a minefield. No one knows where the mines are planted." The result was the paralysis of the entire financial system.

That paralysis was a function of not knowing which banks were merely illiquid and which banks were truly insolvent. To have trouble rolling over some debt because of a seizure in the markets was one thing; to be bankrupt was altogether another. In a panic, it's difficult to tell which is which, and absent any clarification, panic can only grow. When that happens, institutions can swiftly slide from illiquid to insolvent, as asset values drop amid countless fire sales.

The only thing that can reliably arrest the descent into fear and terror is a lender of last resort. Bagehot is generally credited with coming up with the idea. He believed that a bank of banks—something like the Bank of England or the Federal Reserve—must step up to the plate and lend to those caught in the crunch. The holders of what he called the "cash reserve" must "advance it most freely for the liabilities of others. They must lend to merchants, to minor bankers, to 'this man and that man,' whenever the security is good." After all, he observed, "in wild periods of alarm, one failure makes many, and the best way to prevent the derivative failures is to arrest the primary failure which causes them." Yet Bagehot was against indiscriminate bailouts: only solvent institutions should be able to gain access to loans, which would be made at penalty rates so as to discourage all but the most desperate. His philosophy has often been distilled to its essence: "Lend freely at a high rate, on good collateral."

Over the course of 2007–8, Bagehot's perceptive diagnosis, along with a deeply flawed version of his prescription, played out dramatically. Panic struck the markets, uncertainty spread, liquidity evaporated, and central banks around the world threw lifelines to banks large and small and to financial institutions of every stripe. It was a rescue effort on a scale that Bagehot never foresaw. For this crisis, although a textbook case, was bigger, swifter, and more brutal than anything seen before. It was a nineteenth-century panic moving at twenty-first-century speed.

The Minsky Moment

By the spring of 2006, the financial system, with its extraordinary reliance on leverage—and its blind faith that asset prices would only continue to rise—was primed for a breakdown of monumental proportions. Financing increasingly depended on the sort of speculative and Ponzi borrowing that Minsky predicted. Euphoria that began in the housing sector and percolated upward throughout the entire financial system only encouraged further risk taking, and the few skeptics who raised the alarm were not heard. As Minsky himself said of these euphoric moments, "Cassandra-like warnings that nothing basic has changed, that there is a financial breaking point that will lead to a deep depression, are naturally ignored in these circumstances."

And so it was with this boom. Throughout 2006 and into 2007, one of the authors—Nouriel Roubini—warned of the coming collapse, as did a handful of other prescient commentators. In general, their warnings fell on deaf ears, much as Minsky anticipated. Naysayers at the height of a bubble, Minsky observed, "do not have fashionable printouts to prove the validity of their views," and those in the establishment inevitably "ignore arguments drawn from unconventional theory, history, and institutional analysis."

Indeed, by the time a bubble peaks, its participants do more than scorn the skeptics; they proclaim that a new age of prosperity has arrived. The particulars vary from era to era, but the language is the same. On October 15, 1929, the otherwise accomplished economist Irving Fisher announced that having dropped downward from their remarkable highs, "stock prices have reached what looks like a permanently high plateau." Likewise, in December 2005 the somewhat less accomplished (and more subjective) spokesman for the National Association of Realtors, David Lereah, looked at a similar precrash drop and uttered this sage pronouncement: "Home sales are coming down from the mountain peak, but they will level out at a high plateau, a plateau that is higher than previous peaks in the housing cycle."

It seems quaint in retrospect, but what inaugurates a financial crisis is rarely something dramatic or out of the ordinary, merely a leveling off, a movement sideways, and a few unsettling signs. Those arrived in the spring of 2006, as housing starts flattened out, and home prices—which had doubled in real terms over the previous decade—stopped rising. The reason was simple enough: the supply of new homes began to outstrip the demand, and a rise in interest rates made variable-rate mortgages more expensive. Prices leveled off.

At the same time, as in every financial crisis, a "canary in the coal mine" signaled that all was not well: subprime mortgages issued in 2005 and 2006 began to exhibit unusually high rates of delinquent payments. These same mortgages came with features—superlow teaser rates, option ARMs, negative amortization—that depended on refinancing at low rates. But the option of refinancing—particularly for those mortgages that had no down payment and no equity—was available only if home prices kept rising. As a consequence, delinquencies and defaults started to crop up; cracks appeared in the facade.

Still, there was little indication that this was the beginning of a colossal banking crisis. But beginning in late 2006, the shadow banking system became the focus of a slow-motion run that George Bailey himself would have recognized. The hundreds of unregulated nonbank mortgage lenders who had been at the forefront of originating subprime mortgages relied heavily on short-term financing from larger banks. Once subprime mortgages were going into default at accelerating rates, the larger banks refused to renew these lenders' lines of credit. Unable to tap a lender of last resort, the nonbank lenders began to fail, victims of a twenty-first-century bank run.

The first lender to go under was the hilariously misnamed Merit Financial, which had allegedly spent all of fifteen minutes training its loan officers before setting them loose to originate loans with little documention, liar loans, and no-income, no-job NINJA loans. But Merit Financial was not alone. Other nonbank lenders may have kept up professional appearances, but their lending practices were no less suspect. By the end of 2006, ten institutions had gone bust, and the flow of mortgages through the securitization pipeline began to slow. By end of March 2007, the number of nonbank lenders that had collapsed soared to fifty or more. On April 2 the nation's second-largest subprime lender—New Century Financial—went bankrupt after its funding dried up. At the same time, others who had battened on the business of originating mortgages—thousands of small-time mortgage brokers—went out of business.

Most market commentators claimed that the problem was restricted to one small sector of the financial system. This too often happens as financial crises gather steam: the problem is widely seen as "contained"—in this case, to a handful of reckless mortgage lenders and the loans they made. Federal Reserve chairman Ben Bernanke fell into this trap when he appeared before Congress in May 2007. While he conceded that the subprime market had plenty of problems, he portrayed these troubles as an isolated disease outbreak rather than the beginnings of a pandemic.

Then a London-based company called Markit Group introduced something called the ABX Index, which measured stress in the market for subprime securities. It did so by measuring the prices of a basket of credit default swaps, used to transfer the risk of default on securities derived from subprime home loans. The goal, a company spokesman said, was "visibility and transparency." Using the ABX, one could measure the cost of buying insurance—in the form of credit default swaps—against defaults of tranches of mortgage-backed securities and CDOs rated from an abysmal BBB to a supposedly high-grade AAA. Over the course of 2007, the ABX Index went into a free fall, as bottom-of-the-barrel tranches lost upwards of 80 percent of their value. Even the safest AAA tranches lost 10 percent by July 2007.

The fall in the ABX Index revealed that something was going horribly awry. Worse, the ABX figures made all the shadow banks look at their assets and recalculate the value of the securities they held. Collateralized debt obligations that had been worth one hundred cents on the dollar sustained enormous losses, leaving financial institutions with fewer assets relative to their outstanding liabilities. Faced with dwindling reserves, both the traditional and the shadow banks began to hoard cash, refusing to lend on the basis of collateral that looked more dubious by the day.

A sudden aversion to risk, a sudden desire to dismantle the pyramids of leverage on which profits have until so recently depended, is the key turning point in a financial crisis. In earlier times, it was called "discredit" or "revulsion"; more recently it has been called a "Minsky moment." By late spring of 2007, that moment had definitely arrived.

The Unraveling

Hedge funds may not look like banks, but they operate much as banks do, getting short-term investments from individual and institutional investors as well as short-term repurchase agreements, or repos, from investment banks. Like conventional banks, hedge funds invest their short-term borrowings for the long term. For example, two hedge funds run by Bear Stearns sank billions of short-term loans into highly illiquid subprime CDO tranches.

The collapse of those two funds in the summer of 2007 portended the fate not only of hundreds of other hedge funds but of the shadow banking system as a whole. Like many players in this system, these two funds were virtually unregulated but highly leveraged; the riskiest had a debt-to-equity ratio of twenty to one. As the ABX Index revealed the market's growing belief that subprime CDOs might lose much if not most of their value, these two hedge funds started to suffer major losses.

At that point the banks that had lent billions to the two funds made margin calls and threatened to sell the collateral—some AAA CDO tranches—that the two funds had pledged to secure financing. This step was fateful: up until now CDOs and other forms of structured finance had rarely been traded. The ABX Index was merely a proxy for prices, not an actual reflection of the going market price. The hedge fund managers knew that these securities would never fetch their original price; trying to sell them into a panicked market would have revealed that the entire CDO enterprise was, like the fabled emperor, without clothes. Instead, Bear Stearns injected money into the funds. But to no avail: by the summer of 2007, one of the funds had seen 90 percent of the capital put up by the investors of wiped out, while the equity of the more leveraged fund disappeared altogether. Both funds filed for bankruptcy at the end of July. They were not alone: another hedge fund created by UBS perished under similar circumstances.

These early failures showed how hedge funds could fall victim to the equivalent of a bank run on their assets. Institutional creditors could suddenly refuse to roll over the repo loans, leaving them high and dry. Alternatively, those who'd invested equity—wealthy individuals and the like—could demand their money back, just as depositors used to demand money back from old-fashioned banks like Bailey Bros. Building & Loan. Either way, the result was the same: the short-term financing of the hedge funds could readily disappear, forcing them to shut their doors.

The failure of the first three hedge funds conformed to the classic narrative of a financial crisis. Most crises see a few initial high-profile failures, then a period of unsettling uncertainty, as people try to determine whether the troubles that have befallen once-healthy institutions are part of a larger problem. More often than not a larger problem is emerging, and this crisis was no different: in the two years following the failure of the Bear Stearns and UBS funds, some five hundred hedge funds perished, the victims of a slow-motion bank run. The reason was simple: the creditors of the hedge funds couldn't and didn't know how much exposure individual hedge funds had to the toxic assets. Faced with so much uncertainty, they curtailed credit to all of them.

As panic spread in the spring and summer of 2007, the search for toxic assets began apace. Investors desperately tried to figure out who else was exposed to the subprime mess. Suspicion soon fell on the off-balance-sheet vehicles that investment banks and broker dealers had created during the rush to securitization. They came in two varieties: conduits and SIVs. Both had played essential roles in the securitization frenzy: conduits had served as a holding pen at the beginning of the process, and SIVs served as a dumping ground at the end. Together they held upwards of $800 billion in assets.

Here's how they worked. As investment banks assembled mortgages and other assets, they needed a place to park them. Rather than keeping them on their balance sheets—where they would force the banks to maintain higher levels of reserves relative to the value of the assets—the banks parked them in something called a conduit, a kind of shadowy legal entity that had reserve ratios a tenth the size of ordinary banks'. There they would sit until they were turned into mortgage-backed securities, collateralized debt obligations, and other securities. Conduits depended on financing to keep this process humming along, for which they turned to money market funds, pension funds, and corporate treasurers, who gave the conduits short-term loans using asset-backed commercial paper (ABCP).

Crucially, the loans were short-term, but once again the assets—the subprime mortgages and other forms of debt—were illiquid, long-term instruments. The same dynamic was in play at the other end of the securitization assembly line. Once the investment banks had created the securities, they inevitably encountered a bottleneck: they could not possibly shove all the new structured products down the throats of gullible investors right away. Rather than keep the assets on their balance sheets—and incur capital charges—the investment banks came up with the SIV. The purpose of this off-balance-sheet vehicle was to buy up these securities using money siphoned from the ABCP market. This was a bit like an automaker setting up a shell company to buy up unsold vehicles sitting on dealer lots.

Citigroup, which had some seven separate SIVs holding assets of $100 billion, was one of the first to falter. Just as trouble with one hedge fund sparked a panicky scrutiny of all hedge funds, trouble with one SIV sparked a more general rush for the exits by wary investors. It quickly turned into a rout: in the space of four weeks, investors moved $200 billion out of the ACBP market, and the SIVs and conduits alike had to contend with much higher costs for borrowing money from this market. Even worse, some creditors of the SIVs and conduits refused to lend money at any cost, leaving them unable to continue in their current incarnation.

As things spiraled out of control, the banks that had sponsored the SIVs and conduits found themselves in a delicate position. Originally, in order to entice investors, many of them had promised to use the bank's own liquidity in the event of a crisis, and they had even guaranteed the interest rates and value of the instruments. That put the banks on the hook for any losses. After much kicking and screaming, the banks were forced to bring their SIV exposure back onto their balance sheets, sustaining massive losses in the process.

The worst was yet to come. Beginning in August 2007, a much more severe shock—a full-blown liquidity and credit crunch—seized the financial markets, culminating in the collapse of Lehman Brothers and bringing the global financial system to the brink of collapse. During that time the remnants of the shadow banking system collapsed, and even the conventional banking system came under assault. The crisis was just beginning.

Fear of the Unknown

Risk, Uncertainty, and Profit, first published in 1921, contains iconoclastic economist Frank H. Knight's now famous distinction between the concepts of *risk* and *uncertainty*. Risk, he argued, can be priced by financial markets because it depends on known distributions of events to which investors assign probabilities—and price things accordingly. Uncertainty, on the other hand, can't be priced: it relates to events, conditions, and possibilities that can't be predicted, measured, or modeled.

To understand this distinction, imagine two men playing a game of Russian roulette. They take a standard revolver with room for six bullets, put a bullet in the chamber, and spin it. Whoever pulls the trigger first has a one-in-six chance of blowing his brains out. That's risk. While the men playing this game may be suicidal idiots, they know the odds. Now imagine that the two men are handed a mystery gun prepared by someone else. The gun could have one bullet; it could have six; or it could have none. It may not even be a real gun; it could fire blanks instead of bullets. The players don't know. That's uncertainty: they have no idea how to assess the risk. The odds of dying are impossible to quantify.

The distinction between risk and uncertainty helps explain the financial markets from late summer 2007 onward. Until the crisis struck, risk could be reduced to the ratings slapped on various securities: some were riskier than others, and the risk could be quantified—or so it seemed. As the housing market crumbled, however, and uncertainty enveloped these securities, the financial system no longer seemed comprehensible, much less predictable. Bad things had already happened, but they paled next to what might happen next. As one journalist with the *Financial Times* put it that August during a radio interview, "It is not the corpses at the surface that are scary; it is the unknown corpses below the surface that may pop up unexpectedly. Nobody knows where the bodies are buried."

By late summer of 2007, the balance sheets of an extraordinary range of financial institutions showed an unpleasant surprise: a diverse handful of hedge funds, banks, conduits, SIVs, and others had been forced to exhume "bodies" by revealing a bewildering array of toxic assets. Where might others lie? And how many were there? No one could know; uncertainty reigned. Estimated losses on subprime mortgages now ranged from $50 billion to $500 billion and beyond.

This development didn't fit the standard expectations or measurements of risk. When two Goldman Sachs hedge funds lost more than a third of their value late that summer, the firm sought to calm investors by claiming that these losses were "twenty-five standard deviation events." This was statistical shorthand for claiming that what had happened should occur only once in a million years. In actuality, the models used to assess risk were flawed; they used preposterous assumptions—home values could only go up!—and relied on data that went back only a few years.

A deeper appreciation of history might have prepared market watchers for what happened next: uncertainty spread, suspicion grew, and long-time bonds of trust frayed. Bagehot captured this dynamic all the way back in 1873, noting that "every day, as a panic grows, this floating suspicion becomes both more intense and more diffused; it attacks more persons; and attacks them all more virulently than at first." When that happens, the money market—the arena where banks borrow and lend surplus cash—seizes up. In Bagehot's day the epicenter of the global money market was Lombard Street, where the most important banks in England had their headquarters.

In 2007 the seizure occurred in a more amorphous international network of financial institutions—not only in London but in New York, Tokyo, and other financial centers. This was the interbank market, where banks and other financial institutions lend their surplus cash to one another. It all takes place in cyberspace, but in a testament to London's enduring place in financial history, the most important rate at which money is lent is known as the London Interbank Offered Rate (LIBOR).

In normal times, the overnight LIBOR—for loans made for the duration of a day—is only a few basis points above the overnight policy rates set by central banks around the world. The reason for this near convergence is simple: the perceived risk of lending between established banks is only marginally higher than the risk-free lending available from central banks. Similarly, longer-term interbank loans—three-month LIBOR contracts—rarely deviate from rates associated with supersafe investments like three-month Treasury bills.

In August and September 2007 unease was rising. By that time the subprime crisis was in full swing, complete with rising delinquencies and foreclosures. The securitization pipeline clogged as ratings agencies downgraded mortgage lenders and a range of structured products. At the same time, the ABX Index revealed a marked deterioration of confidence in the value of various CDO tranches, while the unraveling of the commercial paper market continued apace. Other ominous portents appeared: stock markets became extraordinarily volatile, and hedge funds that used complicated mathematical strategies to make money off equities suffered enormous losses. Subprime mortgage lenders continued to go under, including giant American Home Mortgage. Credit spreads for corporate firms sharply rose. A run on some money market funds overseen by BNP Paribas only added to the sense that things were going horribly, terribly awry. So did ruptures in the "carry trade," where investors borrowed in low-interest-rate currencies and invested them in high-interest-rate currencies. The crisis was no longer an isolated problem; it was spreading into new and dangerous territory.

As a consequence, the interbank market tightened in August, and the spread between LIBOR and the rates charged by European central banks soared, from 10 basis points to about 70. This was extraordinary, signaling that liquidity in overnight money markets had largely dried up; banks that had previously done business confidently now looked suspiciously at one another's finances, fearful that untold numbers of "bodies" might be lurking on or off the balance sheets. Every bank in Europe and the United States wanted to borrow cash, but no bank would lend it, except at extraordinarily high rates.

Predictably, central banks rode to the rescue—or tried to do so. On August 9 the European Central Bank lent €94.8 billion to some fifty banks; the next day it lent another €61 billion. The Federal Reserve joined the fire brigade as well, lending some $60 billion over the course of two days. Though these infusions helped close the LIBOR spread in the early fall, it widened once more in November and December as bank losses mounted, stock prices plummeted, and panic spread still further. The Federal Reserve cut its rates by 100 basis points that fall, but to no avail. The Fed also made it easier for banks to borrow from its discount window, but there was a stigma associated with doing so. Any bank that needed to go to the Fed for funds might be perceived as weak and on the brink of collapse.

These events followed a familiar pattern. Hard evidence was growing that things were bad and getting worse by the day; it was not a matter of rumor or conjecture. According to the ABX Index, CDO values continued to erode, and even the AAA-rated supersenior tranches were losing value by the day. The ratings agencies, in a rush to compensate for their negligence during the boom years, downgraded the ratings of a range of securities. As for the securitization market, it was effectively frozen. Mortgages and other forms of debt that had served as ingredients in the sausage making of structured finance now accumulated, unused and unwanted.

By the end of 2007, profound uncertainty prevailed. Which banks had bodies buried off their balance sheets? Which hedge funds had placed foolish bets? Who else had invested in subprime CDOs? Unfortunately, it was next to impossible to tell. The financial system was extraordinarily opaque, and much of its activity—credit default swaps, for example—took place outside the purview of regulated exchanges. Increasingly it resembled a vast minefield. A few of the mines had gone off, but most remained buried, waiting for the unsuspecting.

Illiquid and Insolvent

In the late summer of 2007, when the Bank of England first threw a lifeline to British banks, Mervyn King, the governor of that institution, had tough words for insolvent banks begging for a bailout. "We are certainly not going to protect people from unwise lending decisions," he grandly proclaimed.

The subtext was clear: if central banks were going to play their role as lenders of last resort, they would help only the deserving. He was speaking a language that Walter Bagehot would have appreciated. As Bagehot had counseled, "Any aid to a present bad Bank is the surest mode of preventing the establishment of a future good Bank."

Now as then, the difficulty lies in distinguishing between banks that are merely illiquid (the "good" ones) versus those that are insolvent (the "bad" ones). Or to put it another way, the challenge is to figure out which banks have more assets than liabilities, even if these assets can't readily be converted to cash; and which banks have more liabilities than assets, effectively wiping out the banks' capital and thereby driving them into insolvency.

The problem with teasing out this distinction in the midst of a panic is that financial institutions can readily move from one state to another, depending on, say, the changing value of the assets they hold. This question of valuation was particularly complicated in the recent crisis. Take, for example, the CDOs held by banks and other financial institutions. In the early months of the crisis, the ABX Index implied that the value of CDOs was declining. But that was not the actual market value: it was merely a reflection of the cost of insuring against future defaults. Early on, banks reasonably argued that these implied losses were theoretical, not real: the actual default rates on the underlying mortgages had not yet approached the levels implied by the index.

The thinking was that irrational panic was driving the markets. The banks blamed the losses on market psychology alone, be they the declines implied by the ABX Index or even the real declines in the prices of assets such as stocks. Once investors regained their sanity, it was thought, prices would return to their normal levels. The markets would become more liquid, and the threat of insolvency would subside. At least, that was the theory.

This thinking was naïve. The crisis was never merely a function of illiquidity alone; plenty of insolvency was involved as well. That became apparent when the unthinkable happened: rates of delinquency and of defaults on mortgages started to soar, and the cash stream from these assets collapsed. Hypothetical losses on the "safe" supersenior AAA tranches became real losses, and the value of those assets fell. The value of mortgage-backed securities, collateralized loan obligations, corporate bonds, and municipal bonds fell too.

Even the banks' plain-vanilla assets hemorrhaged: that is, ordinary residential mortgages, commercial mortgages, credit card portfolios, auto loans, student loans, and other forms of consumer credit. Banks had also made commercial and industrial loans or helped finance leveraged buyouts of firms. All of these loans deteriorated, especially after the United States entered a recession at the end of 2007.

These developments highlighted that a bank's health is a fleeting, impermanent thing. As long as the prices of underlying assets continued to fall, banks in good standing saw their positions deteriorate, bringing them to the brink of insolvency. Of course, they could also collapse if they suffered a run on their liabilities. The shadow banks were clearly vulnerable on this point, given that they lacked deposit insurance. Conventional banks were not—or so the thinking went.

Nonetheless, once the run on the shadow banking system gathered steam, ordinary banks became targets of bank runs for the first time since the 1930s. One of the first to go was Countrywide Bank, the savings arm of Countrywide Financial, the nation's largest mortgage lender. Founded by Angelo Mozilo, the lender had been at the center of the subprime crisis. As conditions worsened, doubts about the firm rose and eventually spilled over to its banking division. In August 2007 depositors rushed branches of Countrywide Bank, clamoring for their money in a way not seen for decades. One retiree waiting in line outside a branch captured the spirit of the panic when he told a reporter, "I'm at the age where I can't afford to take the risk. I'll gladly put it back as soon as I know the storm is over."

Words like these were uttered during panics in Bagehot's time, but to hear them spoken in the twenty-first century was remarkable. Even more extraordinary, bank runs spread around the world. Northern Rock, a sizable British mortgage lender with a banking arm, suffered Countrywide's fate the following month. Like Countrywide, most of its funding came from sources other than ordinary depositors, but that didn't stop its ordinary depositors from lining up outside its branches in mid-September, under the glaring lights of the global media. The Bank of England intervened, offering emergency lines of liquidity, but still the run did not stop. "I don't think the bank will collapse—but we just don't have the nerves," explained one depositor. "I'm taking the money out to get peace of mind."

As the run continued, fears mounted that other well-regulated banks with deposit insurance might suffer runs as well, then spiral from illiquidity to insolvency. As irrational as these bank runs may have seemed, depositors actually did have reason to worry. Like Countrywide, Northern Rock offered deposit insurance only up to a certain point: $100,000 in the case of Countrywide, and £30,000 in the case of Northern Rock. Plenty of depositors had sums well in excess of these amounts, and should the bank become insolvent—with or without the support of a lender of last resort—they would lose their savings. In fact, in the United States in 2007, some 40 percent of conventional deposits were uninsured. Bank runs, in other words, were rather rational.

The cases of Countrywide and Northern Rock highlighted the difficulties of channeling aid only to "good" banks as opposed to "bad" ones. Banks were well on the road to insolvency, if not there already; by normal standards, they deserved neither lines of liquidity nor additional insurance for depositors. But what sounds good in theory is hard to put into practice during a crisis, when depositors storm banks and the financial system crumbles. The Bank of England's Mervyn King found himself in precisely this awkward position. A month after lecturing the market about letting bad banks fail, he reversed course, promising to insure all of Northern Rock's deposits and offering additional lines of liquidity to the beleaguered bank. That blanket deposit guarantee was soon extended to all banking institutions throughout the United Kingdom. Most other countries eventually followed suit or, at the very least, raised the deposit insurance ceiling.

These interventions were just the beginning, but for a brief period in the winter of 2007 and 2008, some claimed that the crisis was over: the markets seemed to settle down. As any student of crisis economics should have known, this was an illusion. More often than not, crises wane before waxing anew; a period of calm may precede even worse outbreaks of panic and disorder.

The Eye of the Storm

In May 1930 President Herbert Hoover confidently announced that "we have been passing through one of those great economic storms which periodically bring hardship and suffering upon our people. . . . I am convinced we have now passed through the worst—and with continued unity of effort we shall rapidly recover. There has been no significant bank or industrial failure. That danger, too, is safely behind us." Another day in May seventy-eight years later, Treasury Secretary Henry Paulson confidently announced, "The worst is likely to be behind us," adding a week later that "we are closer to the end of the market turmoil than the beginning."

Both Hoover and Paulson were making the classic error of those caught in a financial hurricane, mistaking the eye of the storm for the end of the crisis. They were hardly the only wise men to make such pronouncements in the midst of a meltdown; every crisis has its share of optimists who at some point declare the worst is over. Interestingly, this kind of optimism is usually genuine; it's not an attempt to jawbone markets but generally reflects a real belief that the storm has passed.

Unfortunately, financial crises usually ebb and flow in their severity; they rarely hit once and then subside. They resemble hurricanes in that they gather strength, weaken for a while, and then gain even more destructive power than before. This reflects the fact that the vulnerabilities that build up in advance of a major crisis are pervasive and systemic. They cannot be cured by the collapse or bailout of a single bank, or even the implosion of an entire swath of the financial sector.

Many crises follow this pattern. For example, in Britain the crisis of 1847 erupted in two distinct stages in April and October of that year; the crisis of 1873 was even more complicated, surfacing and subsiding in Vienna in April, reappearing with a vengeance in the United States that September, and then flattening much of Europe in November. The Great Depression was the most complicated of all, with a blowup on Wall Street, multiple bank runs interspersed with periods of relative calm, and different financial centers around the world erupting in panic at different times over the course of three years.

In the winter of 2007–8, surprisingly, a semblance of calm settled over the markets. As the fall turned to winter, write-downs and losses were reducing the capital of financial institutions to new and dangerous lows. Many banks circled their wagons, lending less, increasing their lending standards, and limiting their exposure to risky assets. Nonetheless, the value of assets continued to fall, while liabilities rose. Regulators in both the United States and Europe suggested that banks raise more capital to buttress their balance sheets.

Given that the entire financial system was in the same boat, the banks had few places to turn. Their solution was to go hat in hand to sovereign wealth funds, investment vehicles owned by foreign governments in the Middle East and Asia. The prospect of Saudi Arabian and Chinese investors controlling American and European banks was politically untenable, so the recapitalization of the troubled banks took the form of preferred shares. This meant in practice that sovereign wealth funds received only a minority stake, no board membership, and no voting rights.

Citigroup raised $7.5 billion from a fund in Abu Dhabi; UBS got $11 billion from Singapore's fund and a group of private investors from the Middle East. Singapore's fund sank $5 billion into Merrill Lynch, while China sank another $5 billion into Morgan Stanley. In a smaller-scale effort, American private equity firms pumped $3 billion into Washington Mutual and close to $7 billion into Wachovia.

These infusions helped give the illusion that things might be stabilizing. So did the actions of the Federal Reserve. In December the Fed along with other central banks started to provide long-term loans to banks. The Term Auction Facility (TAF), created in coordination with the European Central Bank and the Bank of England, was designed to unclog the interbank lending market by providing longer-term loans to banks. At the time of its creation, interbank loans lasting one, three, and six months had all but dried up, and the spread between LIBOR rates and central bank rates had risen to unprecedented highs.

At first the TAF was successful in reducing stress in the interbank market. One measure of stress—the LIBOR-OIS spread—fell from 110 basis points to below 50. The measure seemed to give the economy some breathing room, and there was hope that the worst had passed. "I'm optimistic about the economy," said President George W. Bush to the press on January 8, 2008. "I like the fundamentals, they look strong." He acknowledged some clouds on the horizon but remained upbeat: "We'll work through this period of time . . . the entrepreneurial spirit is strong."

In fact, the U.S. economy had formally entered a recession the previous month, and the entire financial edifice was on the verge of crumbling. The crisis was about to enter its most dangerous and dramatic stage. Like Hoover's relief that there had been no "significant" failure in the spring of 1930, Bush's conviction that things had stabilized was extraordinarily complacent. The levees were about to break.

The Reckoning

Like the current crisis, the panic of 1825 was a speculative bubble gone horribly awry. That fall a single bank failure eventually triggered a massive run on all the banks. At first the Bank of England did nothing, refusing to intervene. As the crisis spiraled out of control, pressure built for the government to do something—anything. In December 1825 the Bank of England reversed policy and began lending money in new and unconventional ways. The Bank became the lender of last resort to virtually every participant in the financial system. The results, Bagehot recalled, were dramatic. "After a day or two of this treatment, the entire panic subsided, and the 'City' was quite calm."

This narrative—a central bank compelled to adopt extreme, unprecedented measures to arrest the panic—would play out numerous times in the succeeding decades, and 2008 was no exception. In the recent crisis, however, the Federal Reserve and other central banks could not—and did not—immediately bring the crisis under control. One reason was that central banks were in uncharted territory: the size and scope of the meltdown made many of the usual tools useless. Worse, many of the institutions in the deepest trouble—investment banks and other members of the shadow banking system—lacked ready access to the lifelines that had served central bankers so well in previous crises. The central bankers caught in the midst of the crisis would have to improvise, much as their predecessors had done nearly two centuries ago.

In the spring of 2008 the pressure to do something quickly mounted. By then the securitization pipeline had all but shut down, not only for ordinary mortgages but for credit card loans, auto loans, and other consumer credit products. The securitization of corporate loans and leveraged loans into collateralized loan obligation froze up, a victim of plummeting demand and growing aversion to risk. When the credit markets shut down, banks and investment banks found themselves stuck with the loans, unable to turn them into securities and sell them off. They also found themselves stuck with $300 billion worth of bridge loans that gave temporary financing to private equity funds putting together leveraged buyouts. Banks and broker dealers trying to sell off these loans quickly realized that assets with a par value only a few months earlier were now selling into extremely illiquid markets at a steep discount.

All this was playing out against the backdrop of deterioration in a range of asset classes. The stock market continued to stumble downward, and banks continued to announce write-downs and losses as diverse structured financial products saw their ratings downgraded and their values plummet. Even AAA tranches of CDOs saw their ratings cut, and their prices fell by 10 percent or more. While banks and broker dealers could use accounting tricks to conceal some of the growing losses, structured financial products like CDOs had to be valued at the prevailing market price.

The net result of these declines—in assets both esoteric and conventional—was that banks had to announce write-downs on their asset portfolios. By March 2008 banks around the world announced write-downs of over $260 billion. Citigroup alone took a $40 billion write-down, and other big banks would post comparable figures. Many of those that went public with their losses at this time may not have been insolvent yet, but their days were numbered. Two institutions whose troubles would dominate the headlines in the coming months, AIG and Wachovia, posted write-downs of $30 billion and $47 billion, respectively.

Ordinary commercial banks were suffering, but the investment banks suffered first. Some of them, such as those attached to commercial banks—the units embedded in Citigroup, JPMorgan Chase, and Bank of America—could rely on the support of their parent companies. But the independents—Lehman Brothers, Merrill Lynch, Morgan Stanley, Goldman Sachs, and Bear Stearns—were on their own. Like ordinary banks, they borrowed short and lent long, but they did not have access to a lender of last resort, and their creditors could not rely on deposit insurance if things went awry. Worse, being less regulated, they tended to be much more leveraged. They were also highly dependent on short-term financing in the repo market.

None of the independent broker dealers would remain by the end of the year. The first to go was Bear Stearns in March 2008. Like its counterparts, it had been a big player in running CDO assembly lines, and it had kept plenty of now-toxic securities on its books. Losses mounted in the fall and winter of 2007 as the value of CDOs—particularly AAA tranches—eroded. There was a growing sense of clarity in the market: Bear Stearns was in trouble, and like the depositors who withdrew their money from Countrywide, Northern Rock, and other banks, the hedge funds borrowing from Bear Stearns and other firms lending funds to the ailing investment bank pulled their money. On March 13 the besieged bank reported that 88 percent of its liquid assets were gone, the result of creditors' refusing to roll over short-term financing. Bear Stearns was moribund, and over a frantic weekend the legendary firm was summarily sold off to JPMorgan Chase. The Federal Reserve intervened heavily, facilitating the sale and agreeing to assume most of the future losses tied to the former firm's toxic assets.

The Federal Reserve's move was not a full bailout; Bear Stearns's shareholders were effectively wiped out. But its creditors and counterparties were fully bailed out. Instead, the Fed made a classic central bank move, as if following Bagehot's admonition to rescue the bank whose failure threatents otherwise solvent banks. In Bear Stearns's case, it deemed such intervention necessary: the firm had been a big player in selling credit default swaps against a variety of risky assets held by other banks and investors. Its collapse would have nullified those insurance contracts, potentially triggering "derivative failures" throughout the global financial system.

But the Federal Reserve was not finished intervening. Much as the Bank of England had used swaps in 1825, the Federal Reserve began exchanging liquid, safe short-term Treasury bills for the more illiquid assets that were weighing down the balance sheets of the investment banks. This lending facility (which we will discuss in chapter 6) helped the banks contain the illiquidity trap that the panic created. So did the Federal Reserve's subsequent creation of another lending facility that gave investment banks like Goldman Sachs and Morgan Stanley access to lender-of-last-resort support.

This was a radical break with past precedent: for the first time in decades, the government had opted to provide such support to key members of the shadow banking system.

The creation of the two new lending facilities reduced but did not eliminate the risk that the broker dealers would suffer a run. For starters, the broker dealers did not have access to deposit insurance, arguably the strongest shelter against a bank run. Moreover, their access to the lender-of-last-resort support of the Federal Reserve was conditional and limited. If a broker dealer was truly insolvent, the Federal Reserve would refuse to ride to the rescue. Or so prudent central banking practice would dictate. That almost guaranteed there would be some more high-profile failures.

At the same time, the bailout of Bear Stearns seemed to indicate that the Federal Reserve was unwilling to stand on the sidelines if the failure of a financial institution would sow panic on a global scale. Bear Stearns was but the smallest of the independent broker dealers; surely, the reasoning went, the Federal Reserve would step in to save a bigger victim if doing so would stop the crisis from spreading further. Allowing such a failure would risk a meltdown of the entire global financial system.

Both views had merit. Unfortunately, both turned out to be correct. What happened in the succeeding months sent contradictory messages about whether the Federal Reserve would hold the line on moral hazard.

The Center Cannot Hold

Whenever the narrative of a financial crisis is dominated by a high-profile failure, there's a temptation to see the entire crisis through the prism of that one event, as if all that came before and after can be reduced to a specific inflection point. In the recent crisis, the failure of Lehman Brothers played this role: many market watchers are convinced that it, more than anything else, was responsible for turning the American crisis into a worldwide conflagration.

This interpretation is understandable: reducing a crisis to one spectacular failure simplifies an extraordinarily complex chain of events. Unfortunately, it's misleading. The failure of Lehman Brothers was less a cause of the crisis than a symptom of its severity. After all, by the time Lehman announced it would file for bankruptcy on September 15, 2008, the United States had been in a severe recession for ten months, and other industrial economies were on the verge of entering one. The housing bust was entering its second year, and high oil prices were sending shock waves through the global economy. Some two hundred nonbank mortgage lenders had collapsed, and as securitization ground to a halt, SIVs and conduits had unraveled. Conventional banks were in trouble too: their balance sheets continued to deteriorate in 2008, and new write-downs inevitably followed. After showing some signs of improvement over the winter, interbank lending had seized up yet again in the spring and summer.

The institutions charged with backing up the system—smaller insurers like Ambac and ACA, which specialized in guaranteeing bond payments (also known as monoline insurers), as well as sprawling insurance companies like AIG—were also deep in trouble long before Lehman collapsed. Using credit default swaps, they had insured several trillion dollars' worth of CDO tranches, effectively transferring their own AAA ratings onto a range of structured financial products. As the tide of losses rose, it looked increasingly likely that the insurers would be forced to pay out. Unfortunately, they didn't have the capital, thanks to being wildly overleveraged. The ratings agencies knew this and started to downgrade the monolines in the fall of 2007.

These real and looming downgrades threatened to rob companies like Ambac and AIG of their ability to confer AAA ratings on a range of securities. In the case of the smaller companies like Ambac, that meant not only CDOs but the municipal bonds that had been their original bread and butter. In the spring of 2008 the deepening troubles of the monoline insurers plunged the usually boring (but reassuringly stable) municipal bond markets into turmoil. Many of the investment banks that had previously played a pivotal role in these markets abandoned the field, fearful of potential losses. Auctions of municipal bonds started to fail, and panic spread throughout the market. Much of the more complex short-term financing used by these municipalities—auction-rate securities and tender option bonds—also collapsed. In a matter of months, state and local governments that were otherwise solvent saw the costs of borrowing soar.

This facet of the crisis began as a matter of illiquidity, but here too the specter of insolvency loomed: many municipalities that had profited from rising property values in the good times saw tax revenues fall off a cliff in the face of escalating delinquencies and foreclosures. The growing troubles of California, already evident in the summer of 2008, offered a glimpse of what lay in wait for other states and municipalities. The problem was real; it wasn't merely a matter of investor psychology.

Fannie Mae and Freddie Mac started to falter too. These enterprises, sponsored by the federal government, had leveraged themselves at ratios of forty to one by issuing debt that enjoyed the implicit backing of the U.S. Treasury. They had used part of that supposedly risk-free debt to purchase risky mortgages and asset-backed securities. By 2008 both institutions were sustaining massive losses that rapidly eroded their capital. Those losses came from two sources. For starters, the fee they received for guaranteeing the mortgages that they manufactured into mortgage-backed securities proved insufficient to cover their losses. In the worst housing crisis since the Great Depression, even safe "prime" borrowers started to default, at rates far in excess of what Fannie Mae and Freddie Mac had anticipated. The insurance premiums no longer covered the losses, which now surfaced on the two institutions' balance sheets.

Far more significant was the fact that their investment portfolios were bursting with subprime mortgages and subprime securities. That summer the losses on these investments had become so large—and the two institutions' capital had so dwindled—that investors panicked. Fears grew that the duo might no longer be able to cover the securities they had guaranteed. Even worse, investors who had purchased debt issued by the two giants now openly talked about the possibility of a default. The assumption that the U.S. government stood behind that debt had never been tested.

Here again the question of moral hazard came to the fore. Without a government takeover, the failure of Fannie Mae and Freddie Mac would clearly send financial markets and mortgage markets into a panic of unprecedented proportions, never mind spook the various foreign creditors that had purchased their debt. Here much more was at risk than the market for a bunch of subprime mortgages: the creditworthiness of the United States was at stake. Letting the two institutions fail in the name of sending a message to the markets was not an option.

The result was another government takeover, formalized in September. Its terms protected those who had purchased the debt of Fannie Mae and Freddie Mac, but the common and preferred shareholders alike saw their investments wiped out. Unfortunately, many of the preferred shareholders included scores of regional banks, who overnight saw their "risk-free" investments wiped out. These losses sent further shock waves reverberating through the collapsing financial system.

On the eve of Lehman's failure, much of the damage had already been done. Lehman and the other investment banks, most obviously Merrill Lynch, were floundering, awash in losses due to exposure to a range of toxic assets; their ability to remain liquid, much less solvent, was in serious doubt. All the financial system needed to plunge into a state of utter panic was a little push.

Mere Anarchy Is Loosed upon the World

The panic of 1907 has a special place in the history of financial disasters. More than most, it has a hero, the banker J. P. Morgan, who occupied a singular place in the financial firmament as the biggest and most powerful banker of the day. In fact, in the days before the Federal Reserve, Morgan was the closest thing the United States had to a lender of last resort. The panic had begun in a series of lightly regulated, overleveraged financial institutions that were the forerunners of today's shadow banking system. Like twenty-first-century investment banks, the "investment trusts" of Morgan's day operated with little transparency.

The panic felled some secondary players, then detonated under the mighty Knickerbocker Trust Company. From there it spread swiftly, threatening to consume the other banks and trusts caught in the tangled web that bound together the financial community. Morgan was unable to save the Knickerbocker, but he decided to draw the line at another ailing institution, the Trust Company of America. The crisis seesawed for days and eventually culminated in a private meeting at Morgan's enormous private library, where he gathered together the city's financial movers and shakers on a Saturday.

Morgan asked them to pool their resources and rally behind the Trust Company of America. The bankers initially refused, and deliberations dragged into Saturday night. At some point in the wee hours of the morning, the bankers realized that Morgan had locked them in the library and pocketed the key. He then issued an ultimatum: support the ailing Trust Company, or face the likelihood of complete annihilation in the ensuing panic. As he almost always did, Morgan got his way: the meeting broke up at 4:45 that morning after the bankers signed a mutual aid agreement. The panic was soon over.

On a very similar weekend 101 years later, Treasury Secretary Henry Paulson tried to pull off an equally audacious bit of brinksmanship. As Lehman Brothers and Merrill Lynch slid inexorably toward insolvency, he called the city's financial elite into the office of the Federal Reserve in Lower Manhattan on Saturday, September 13, 2008. Summoning the spirit of Morgan, he told the assembled bankers that the duty of dealing with the panic would rest with all of them. "Everybody is exposed," he reportedly told the assembled bankers, hoping this would prod them to come up with some way of either buying Lehman or organizing its orderly liquidation.

The bankers came back the following morning but left later that day without a deal; Lehman would be allowed to go under. Paulson's attempt to channel J. P. Morgan had failed. By this time Merrill Lynch was rushing into the arms of Bank of America, fearful of sharing Lehman's apparent fate. "We've reestablished moral hazard," claimed one person present at the meetings. "Is that a good thing or a bad thing? We're about to find out."

Much of what happened in the succeeding days and weeks was probably inevitable, even without the dramatic collapse of Lehman. But the speed with which it happened, and the drama that accompanied it, was a function of the shock waves that Lehman's failure sent through the financial markets.

Those shock waves hit AIG first. On September 15, Lehman declared bankruptcy, and all the major ratings agencies downgraded AIG's credit rating. Its losses had been mounting for months, but the downgrade was the coup de grâce: it effectively called into question the guarantees that the insurance giant had bestowed on a half trillion dollars' worth of AAA-rated CDO tranches. The day of the downgrade, the U.S. government threw the firm an $85 billion lifeline; additional funds would flow in the coming months. In exchange, AIG became a ward of the state: most of the firm's common stock now belonged to the government.

It was a bailout not so much of AIG as of all the banks that had purchased insurance from AIG. In the wake of the takeover, the U.S. government went to those banks and bought back the CDO tranches that AIG had insured. It could have demanded that the banks take a "haircut"—a loss—on those tranches as a penalty for their foolishness in trusting AIG to make them whole. But it did not. Instead, the government paid one hundred cents on the dollar—the full value—even though the market value of the tranches had fallen far below that. By this time, any talk of holding the line against moral hazard had gone out the window.

The parts of the financial system that had so far escaped the crisis now descended into the abyss. Money market funds were one of the first to fall. The funds were supposed to operate reliably: they took cash from investors and sank it into safe, liquid short-term securities. Though a handful had stumbled the previous summer, in the wake of Lehman's bankruptcy things went completely awry. One of the most prominent funds, the Reserve Primary Fund, "broke the buck," meaning that a dollar invested with it was no longer worth a dollar. This was almost unprecedented, and it sparked a run on the fund.

Was the run even remotely rational? Yes. It turned out that the Reserve Primary Fund had surreptitiously sunk some of its investors' money into toxic securities such as Lehman's debt. When this fact came out, suspicion fell on the entire $4 trillion money market industry, which became one big *terra incognita*, and the kind of dangerous uncertainty that Frank Knight had first described swept the field. In no time the federal government was forced to provide a blanket guarantee—the equivalent of deposit insurance—to all existing money market funds.

The panic in the money market funds quickly spilled over into other arenas, beginning with the market for commercial paper, the debt that ordinary corporations used as their main source of working capital. Money market funds had been primary purchasers of this kind of debt, and when their fortunes turned, the commercial paper market seized up too. Perfectly solvent corporations found themselves shut out of the market as borrowing rates went through the roof. For a few weeks during this liquidity crisis, corporate borrowing effectively collapsed, and blue-chip firms found themselves short of cash.

Emergency times call for emergency actions. The collapse of the commercial paper market, which handled some $1.2 trillion in loans, posed the risk that otherwise solid corporations would go insolvent because of a run on their short-term liabilities. In order to avoid any further runs, the Federal Reserve opted to extend lender-of-last-resort support to nonfinancial corporations. On October 7 it set up yet another lending facility that made loans to corporations issuing commercial paper, though only firms with an A rating or better could borrow from the Fed. This was a belated gesture at holding the line against moral hazard.

Otherwise the federal government drew no such distinctions. In the wake of the collapse of IndyMac that summer, the threat of further bank runs loomed. Washington Mutual and Wachovia, two of the nation's largest banks, started to bleed deposits. Both were effectively insolvent, yet government officials were eager to prevent their collapse. The Office of Thrift Supervision first took over Washington Mutual before brokering its sale to JPMorgan Chase. Four days after the seizure and sale of Washington Mutual, the FDIC invoked emergency powers to facilitate the sale of Wachovia, initially to Citigroup and ultimately to Wells Fargo.

The two remaining independent investment banks—Goldman Sachs and Morgan Stanley—had opted not to wait for lifelines; both saw their positions erode precipitously in the wake of Lehman's failure, and by the end of September both applied to become bank holding companies. Doing so gave them access to lender-of-last-resort support and, no less important, enabled them to look to more traditional means of underwriting their activities, namely old-fashioned bank deposits. This move came with a steep price tag: much more stringent regulation of their activities. Their conversion marked a pivotal moment in the nation's financial history: in the space of seven months Wall Street had been utterly transformed, with all five independent investment banks destroyed, absorbed, or temporarily muzzled.

Yet the transformation of banking was still not complete. Despite the fact that the Federal Reserve raised the limits on deposit insurance, banks still faced the threat of runs, though from a new quarter. Many banks had other liabilities besides their deposits, most notably the bonds they issued to finance their assets. These bonds came with different maturities and with different levels of seniority. As bank bonds came due in the final months of the financial crisis, banks could not roll over this debt at the same rate. Borrowing money became extraordinarily expensive, and banks faced the prospect of yet another run on their liabilities.

The solution was to have the government guarantee all of the principal and interest on this kind of debt. On October 14 the FDIC announced that it was insuring all new senior debt (the debt that must be repaid ahead of junior "subordinated debt") of regulated financial institutions, including both ordinary banks and bank holding companies. This guarantee was an unprecedented intervention in the banking system. It meant that banks could now issue debt at the sort of low, "no-risk" rates enjoyed by the U.S. Treasury when the government issued debt. Within six months, banks and other financial institutions that qualified managed to roll over a massive $360 billion worth of debt at extremely low rates. Similar guarantees soon fell into place throughout Europe. Early in the fall a number of enormous European banks—Hypo Real Estate, Dexia, Fortis, and Bradford & Bingley—teetered on the brink of collapse. Ireland was the first to guarantee the debt of its banks, followed by the United Kingdom, which announced something called the Credit Guarantee Scheme. In October other European countries along with Canada followed suit, announcing that they too would guarantee the debt of their banks. These blanket guarantees had the desired effect: the risk of a bank run subsided.

By late fall the most dramatic phase of the crisis was subsiding, though all manner of other bailouts and interventions took place; lines of credit were given to everything from car companies like General Motors to finance companies like GE Capital. Most of this was done with little attention paid to whether the recipients were solvent or even worth saving; the only goal was to stop the panic.

This willingness to lend arrested the panic, though the aftershocks would continue for months, if not years. But the uneasy calm came at a great cost. Walter Bagehot and many theorists of central banking had warned against lending indiscriminately in times of panic; lenders should distinguish between the illiquid and the insolvent and lend only at what Bagehot called "penalty" rates. This time around central bankers saved both bank and many nonbank firms, giving access to lines of credit at rates that were far from punitive. Indeed, the mother of all banklike runs had swept nonbank mortgage lenders, SIVs and conduits, hedge funds, interbank markets, broker dealers, money market funds, finance companies, and even traditional banks and nonfinancial corporate firms. Since banks were not lending to each other or to nonbank financial firms or even to nonfinancial corporate firms, central banks were forced to become lenders of first, last, and only resort. The storm engendered little in the way of the "creative destruction" that Joseph Schumpeter would have celebrated. Instead, strong and weak alike remained in a state of suspended animation, awaiting the final reckoning.

Chapter 5

Global Pandemics

An old saying in financial markets has it that "when the United States sneezes, the rest of the world catches a cold." However clichéd, that observation contains plenty of truth: the United States is the biggest, most powerful economy in the world, and when it gets sick, countries that depend on its insatiable demand for everything from raw commodities to finished consumer goods find themselves in trouble too.

This dynamic takes on dangerous potency in times of financial crisis. An outbreak of some financial disease in the world's economic powerhouse can swiftly become a devastating global pandemic. A crash in the stock market, the failure of a big bank, or some other unexpected collapse at the epicenter of global finance can become a countrywide panic and then a worldwide disaster. It's a scenario that has played out many times, whether in Britain in the nineteenth century or in the United States since that time.

Nevertheless, as the United States succumbed to the subprime disease late in 2006 and 2007, conventional wisdom held that the rest of the world would "decouple" from the financially ailing superpower. This idea, first promoted by analysts at Goldman Sachs and then taken up as the consensus, argued that the booming economies of Brazil, Russia, India, and China would rely on domestic demand and get through the crisis unscathed by the subprime meltdown. The world's economic upstarts would escape the curse of history.

So too would Europe, where many people clung to a similar belief. Only the United States, so the thinking went, had practiced *le capitalisme sauvage,* as the French disparaged it, and it alone would suffer the consequences. In September 2008 German finance minister Peer Steinbrück declared, "The financial crisis is above all an American problem," and added, "The other G7 financial ministers in continental Europe share this opinion." But a few days later much of the European banking system effectively collapsed. Germany was forced to bail out banking giant Hypo Real Estate, and Steinbrück conceded that Europe was "staring into the abyss." Bailouts of European megabanks soon followed, and Ireland issued a blanket guarantee for its six biggest lenders. Other nations in Europe followed suit, including Britain, which effectively nationalized much of its banking system. By October 2008 many European countries as well as Canada had gone so far as to guarantee not only the deposits but the debts of the banks as well.

Nor was the crisis confined to Europe and Canada. It hammered countries on every continent, including Brazil, Russia, India, and China. In some cases this shared affliction was a matter of global interdependence: the crisis rippled through various channels, infecting otherwise healthy sectors of other countries' economies. But the contagion metaphor, so frequently invoked, does not fully explain the crisis. It was not simply a matter of a disease spreading from a sick superpower to otherwise healthy countries. Other nations, having long pursued policies that fostered homegrown bubbles, were vulnerable when the crisis struck. Indeed, what initially seemed like a uniquely American ailment was in fact far more widespread than anyone wanted to acknowledge.

All of this caught most commentators by surprise. Having missed the crisis in the United States, many bullish financial pundits clung to the decoupling thesis until it was impossible to defend. By the end of 2008 most of the world's advanced economies had slipped into a recession, and numerous emerging-market economies in Asia, Eastern Europe, and Latin America had succumbed as well. Many of these same economies suffered the stock market meltdowns, banking crises, and other dramatic distresses that had first surfaced in the United States. What began as one country's crisis thus became a global crisis. As usual, this was nothing new or out of the ordinary. The crisis was following a path well worn by centuries of historical precedent. It was, in more ways than one, a blast from the past.

Financing a Pandemic

Crises rarely cripple perfectly healthy economies; usually underlying vulnerabilities and weaknesses set the stage for a collapse. Nonetheless, for economies outside the United States to catch the proverbial cold, some channel had to be in place. The most visible were the institutions that make up the global financial system.

Money markets are one such institution: they're the places where banks and other financial firms borrow and lend money on a short-term basis. These webs of debt and credit have always been fragile in times of panic, spreading problems from one part of the global economy to another. The reason is simple: when one link in the very elaborate chain breaks and defaults on some debt, it can leave creditors dangerously short of funds, unable to guarantee the credit of other firms. In this way, the consequences of one failure can spread throughout the entire money market.

For this reason, troubles in the money market have long been a hallmark of financial crises. In the panic of 1837, the Bank of England refused to roll over loans made to three major British financial firms, whereupon those firms failed. The effect was calamitous: the firms had extended short-term loans to merchants around the world, and their collapse voided tens of millions of pounds' worth of commercial paper. Financiers in Liverpool, Glasgow, New York, New Orleans, Montreal, Hamburg, Antwerp, Paris, Buenos Aires, Mexico City, Calcutta, and elsewhere found themselves short of credit. *The Times* of London lamented, "It must be a very long time, years perhaps, before the entire effect of these failures is known, for they will extend more or less over the whole world."

Those words could well have been uttered in the wake of any of the crises that crippled international money markets in the nineteenth and early twentieth centuries. The worst crises typically followed the unexpected collapse of some venerable firm that occupied a prominent place within the global money market. In the panic of 1873, for example, the failure of Jay Cooke's giant investment house helped trigger a worldwide crisis. In the Great Depression it was the sudden implosion of Austria's biggest bank, Credit-Anstalt. Many of the world's most powerful and important banks had lent money to it, and its failure triggered other bank failures around the globe.

In the intervening decades, financial markets became even more integrated and interdependent. Indeed, in the recent crisis, the complex webs of borrowing and lending that bound together the international financial system were almost impossible to fully understand, much less disentangle. In fact, few people likely understood that stress in the repo or commercial paper market in one country could be quickly transmitted elsewhere. While there had been some crises that crossed national borders, none came close to rivaling the Great Depression; understanding of how the global financial system could—and would—unravel was limited.

That ignorance ended after the collapse of Lehman Brothers on September 15, 2008. When it failed, the hundreds of billions of dollars in short-term debt it had issued—most of it commercial paper and other bond debt—became worthless, triggering panic among the various investors and funds that held it. This panic prompted a run on the money market funds that provided lending to the commercial paper market and sowed further panic throughout the global banking system. Banks that had made short-term loans to foreign banks jacked up their rates by over 400 basis points, an astronomical increase. What overseas investors called the "Lehman Shock" spread fear throughout global money markets, curtailing lending and eventually crippling global trade.

While the failure of Lehman Brothers helped transmit the crisis throughout the world's financial system, it was hardly the only catalyst. A classic mechanism for spreading crises is the otherwise unremarkable fact that investors in multiple countries hold identical assets. In a number of nineteenth-century crises, for example, investors around the world held the same types of railroad securities, a popular international investment. When the bubble behind these securities popped, investors in the United States, Britain, France, and elsewhere simultaneously saw their portfolios go up in smoke. Invariably, they curtailed credit, hoarded cash, and triggered a panic.

The recent crisis was comparable. The subprime meltdown spilled over from the United States to Europe, Australia, and other parts of the world for the simple reason that about half of the securitized sausage made on Wall Street—the collateralized debt obligations and the mortgage-backed securities from which they derived their value—were sold to foreign investors. During the housing boom, foreign banks, pension funds, and a host of other institutions had snapped up these securities. When a subprime borrower in Las Vegas or Cleveland defaulted on his mortgage, it rippled up the securitization food chain, hitting everyone from Norwegian pensioners to investment banks in New Zealand.

Perhaps the largest portion of these securities ended up in the asset portfolios of European banks and their subsidiaries. Some banks had direct exposure to the subprime crisis, holding tranches of CDOs and other instruments as ordinary assets. In other instances, most notably with BNP Paribas and UBS, hedge funds attached to these banks functioned as disease vectors, placing high-risk bets on a range of subprime securities. When those investments soured, the resulting losses ultimately hit the banks' bottom lines.

The losses sustained by these banks caused considerable collateral damage to the corporate sector in Europe. Unlike American firms, which rely more on capital markets for their financing, European firms depend heavily on bank financing. When the subprime crisis started to hammer reputable European banks, they curtailed lending, limiting the corporate sector's ability to produce, hire, and invest. This set the stage for the recession that gripped the region in the final months of the crisis.

The damage did not stop there. Many of these same European banks had subsidiaries in other countries, particularly in emerging Europe—the countries that had been freed of Soviet control after the end of the Cold War. These subsidiaries had pumped significant amounts of credit into Ukraine, Hungary, Latvia, and other countries. Once the parent banks suffered massive losses, they became risk averse and withdrew credit across the board, starving their foreign subsidiaries. The resulting collapse of credit in emerging Europe helped plunge these countries into recession.

In this way, the subprime problem in the United States rippled outward via financial ties. It first affected countries that did plenty of banking business with the United States, then radiated from there to financial institutions in countries on the periphery of the global economy. It was a classic case of contagion, in which the banking system served as the conduit for America's subprime ills.

But banks weren't the only parts of the financial system to sow crisis around the world. Stock markets played an important role as well. At dramatic turning points in the crisis, the American stock market plunged, followed by precipitous drops on exchanges in London, Paris, Frankfurt, Shanghai, and Tokyo, and in smaller financial centers. This spread was partly a function of the remarkable degree of interdependence between international stock markets. In a world in which traders can instantaneously track movements in markets halfway across the globe, investor sentiment can easily spill over from one exchange to another.

Nonetheless, this growing synchronization was not merely a classic case of herd behavior, in which spooked investors in one country's exchange sent investors elsewhere over the cliff. As the portents of disaster accumulated, the stock market became the medium through which investors registered their growing aversion to risk, by dumping equities for less risky assets.

The contagion that raced through the stock markets may have been more pervasive, faster, and more synchronized than in any previous disaster. But it was merely the latest, most sophisticated version of a dynamic that has existed for well over a hundred years. Financial globalization, in other words, is nothing new. In 1875 the banker Baron Karl Mayer von Rothschild, upon observing that global stock markets had plunged in unison, made a simple but timeless observation: "The whole world has become a city."

Integration in Rothschild's day went beyond the stock markets: global trade too was extraordinarily interdependent and sensitive to financial crises. Sadly, little changed in the intervening years. After panic seized the financial system in 2008, international trade helped spread the crisis around the world.

Disease Vectors

In the nineteenth century the British Empire was the reigning economic superpower, and whenever it spiraled into a financial crisis, its trading partners suffered collateral damage, as demand for raw materials and finished goods plummeted. In the twentieth century the United States inherited Britain's mantle, accounting on the eve of the crisis for about a quarter of the world's gross domestic product. Thanks to its $700 billion current account deficit, its real share of the world economy was even bigger. When it slipped into a severe recession, the effects echoed around the world, in countries as various as Mexico, Canada, China, Japan, South Korea, Singapore, Malaysia, Thailand, and the Philippines. China was particularly at risk, as much of its recent growth had depended on exports to the United States. Thousands of Chinese factories shuttered, and employees returned from urban to rural areas, casualties of a collapse half a world away.

The effects of the downturn in China were not limited to trading links. Many Asian countries produced computer chips and exported them to China, where they would be assembled into computers, consumer electronics, and other items, to be shipped to the United States. When the crisis hit the United States, it hit not just China but all the countries that China used in its supply chains. Here decoupling was next to impossible: economies throughout Asia depended heavily on a wide range of direct and indirect trading ties to the United States.

Decoupling was particularly difficult to avoid once Lehman Brothers collapsed; the usually boring world of trade financing was one of the first casualties. Normally banks issue "letters of credit" to guarantee that goods in transit from, say, China to the United States will be paid for when they reach their final destination. Once the credit markets seized up after Lehman's failure, however, banks stopped providing this essential financing. Global trade came close to a standstill; formerly obscure benchmarks like the Baltic Dry Index—a measure of the cost of shipping commodities—plummeted by almost 90 percent. As one expert on global shipping observed shortly after Lehman's collapse, "There's all kinds of stuff stacked up on docks right now that can't be shipped because people can't get letters of credit."

The collapse of global trade that began with the U.S. recession and intensified with the demise of Lehman Brothers was unprecedented: only the Great Depression can compare. At the peak of the crisis in early 2009, exports fell—on a year-over-year basis—by 30 percent in China and Germany, and by 37 or even 45 percent in Singapore and Japan. All these countries save China slipped into a severe recession, and even China saw a dramatic collapse in its annual economic growth from 13 percent to approximately 7 percent, below the threshold of what's considered sustainable in that country.

All this happened with a speed and simultaneity that shocked most market watchers. "The Great Synchronization," as two economists with the Organisation for Economic Co-operation and Development dubbed the international trade collapse, was clearly a function of the global credit crunch, but that alone doesn't explain what happened. As the crisis worsened, despite pledges to the contrary, many nations adopted tariffs, quotas, and other barriers to international trade—legislation forcing government contractors to buy from domestic manufacturers, for example. Such tit-for-tat trade wars had proved inimical to global trade and growth in the depths of the Great Depression, and their recent recurrence, while less pronounced, did not help global trade recover.

Finally, the crisis spread along paths taken not only by goods but by people too. As the United States plunged into recession, migrant workers stopped sending money back to their home countries: Mexico, Nicaragua, Guatemala, Colombia, Pakistan, Egypt, and the Philippines, to name a few. Many of these migrant workers had gained regular work during the housing booms, not only in the United States, but in Spain and Dubai, and when these booms became busts, remittances back home collapsed too. The effect of this drop-off in remittances is hard to overstate. In some Central American countries, more than 10 percent of the national income comes from citizens who work abroad. In this way, the crisis hurt countries that had never participated in reckless financial practices.

While trade and labor ties have often enabled crises to jump national boundaries, commodities and currencies have played an even bigger role. The reason is simple enough: the prices of commodities and currencies are set in world markets. When the price of oil or copper or a dollar rises in one place, it rises everywhere; when it declines, it declines everywhere. For that reason, sudden fluctuations in the prices of commodities and currencies can fuel instability on a global scale.

This level of integration dates back at least two centuries. When the price of cotton in New Orleans rose to bubblelike heights in 1836 and then crashed with the panic of 1837, the pain was felt not only domestically but in cotton-exporting nations around the world. Likewise, when a range of commodity prices fell by as much as 50 percent in the year following the crash of 1929, export-driven economies suffered terribly. As prices fell for everything from coffee to cotton to rubber to silk, the economies of Brazil, Colombia, the Dutch East Indies, Argentina, and Australia were distressed. Even Japan suffered, as a disintegration of demand for raw silk crippled its economy. These countries saw their finances imperiled and their currencies depreciated on account of falling commodities prices.

Commodities prices played a role in the recent crisis too, though in ways that challenge the usual boom-to-bust narrative. Throughout 2007 and 2008 the prices of oil, food, and other commodities rocketed upward. In the summer of 2008 oil prices peaked at around $145 a barrel, up from $80 a year earlier. The increase wasn't remotely justified by economic fundamentals; rather, it was a function of investment or speculation driven by hedge funds, endowment funds, broker dealers, and various commodities funds that had invested some of their portfolios in commodities. While the oil price spike may have benefited the oil exporters, it hit all the oil importers hard: the United States, the Eurozone, Japan, China, India, and others. Several of these countries were already reeling from the effects of the financial crisis; the oil shock probably pushed them into a full-blown recession.

What was true on the way up was true on the way down. Exporters of oil and other commodities who had remained insulated from the financial crisis in 2007–8 struggled when demand from the United States and China collapsed. In the second half of 2008, demand for oil, energy, food, and minerals fell even further, and the effect was comparable to what happened in the Great Depression: commodity exporters in Africa, Asia, and Latin America saw their economies tumble. Oil producers were particularly hard hit: the price of oil fell from its peak to a low of $30 in the first quarter of 2009. But the damage extended to a range of raw materials. In Chile, for example, the collapse of demand for copper hammered that country's export-driven economy, propelling it into a recession. In all of these disruptions, a commodity boom initially helped trigger a global recession among commodity-importing nations; the consequent commodity bust pummeled the exporters.

Fluctuations in currencies displayed a similar dynamic and proved equally disruptive. In 2007, during the opening innings of the crisis, the American economic slowdown and the ensuing reduction in interest rates helped undermine the value of the dollar. This devaluing hit countries that relied on exports to the United States: the United Kingdom, Japan, and many nations in the Eurozone. As their respective currencies strengthened relative to the dollar, the cost of these goods to American consumers rose. This undercut the competitive edge of these countries, setting them up for a recession.

As the crisis worsened, however, the process went abruptly into reverse. The fear and panic that seized the financial markets over the course of 2008 drove international investors to seek safe havens. One of them was, somewhat paradoxically, the dollar. Even though the United States was at the epicenter of the crisis, it seemed a safer bet than any number of emerging economies. As investors piled into dollars, along with the currencies of other developed countries, they simultaneously dumped the stocks and bonds in various emerging markets, further widening the gap between those countries' currencies and the "safer" currencies of the developed nations.

The effects were calamitous. Before the crisis, households and firms in emerging Europe had obtained mortgages and corporate loans from banks in more established countries. They had turned to those banks because the interest rates on euros, Swiss francs, and even Japanese yen were lower than the rates available in their own countries. Firms in Russia, Korea, and Mexico used the same borrowing strategy. But when the crisis hit and investors fled from emerging-market currencies to safe havens like the dollar, the euro, and the yen, the cost of servicing those debts went through the roof, putting enormous strains on the emerging-market economies.

All of this followed a pattern established by crises past. Like the international financial system, and like the global trading links, commodities and currencies served as pathways, enabling one nation's financial crisis to become an economic crisis of global proportions.

That said, there are limits to what the contagion model can explain.

Implicit within it is the idea that a sick country—the United States—gave the rest of the world one hell of a cold. That's a comforting thought, but it's partly wrong. Plenty of other countries hatched their own bubbles independently of the United States and pursued policies no less reckless or foolish. They had little immunity to the subprime sickness because they too had made themselves highly vulnerable to the disease.

Shared Excesses

In 1837 Martin Van Buren, who was just ascending to the U.S. presidency, tried to explain why "two nations"—the United States and Britain—"the most commercial in the world, enjoying but recently the highest degree of apparent prosperity . . . are suddenly . . . plunged into embarrassment and distress." He was referring to the horrific panic of 1837, which was well under way, and while many commentators blamed either the United States or Britain for triggering the disaster, Van Buren recognized that the truth was more complicated. "In both countries," he wrote, "we have witnessed the same redundancy of paper money and other facilities of credit; the same spirit of speculation; the same partial successes; the same difficulties and reverses; and at length nearly the same overwhelming catastrophe."

Van Buren's assessment was not far from the mark. While the United States was arguably the worst offender in its unbridled enthusiasm for high-risk banking and real estate speculation during the 1830s, the British independently engaged in a mania for chartering banks and created a comparable bubble, complete with a "reckless extension of credit and wild speculation" in textiles and railroads. When the American economy started to shake and fall, the British economy did as well. Not only was it inextricably intertwined with the American economy, but it suffered from many of the same vulnerabilities that had accumulated during the boom years. The crisis did not emanate from a sick country to a healthy one; it struck two nations at nearly the same time.

This same pattern can be glimpsed in other crises. When one country's boom goes bust, other countries that have racked up the same kind of excesses tend to collapse as well. In 1720, for example, the British South Sea Bubble imploded around the same time that John Law's speculative Mississippi Company foundered. A century and a half later, the crisis of 1873 came on the heels of simultaneous booms in Germany, Central Europe, and the United States. These turned to brutal busts, first in Austria-Hungary, then in the United States, and then throughout much of the rest of Europe. A little over a century later speculative booms in emerging economies throughout Asia that had been fueled with foreign investment went bad in quick succession, hammering South Korea, Thailand, Indonesia, and Malaysia. Again, this was a matter of shared vulnerabilities as much as simple contagion.

Many of the economies that collapsed in the recent crisis, not surprisingly, had similar vulnerabilities as the United States. The United States was hardly the only country, for one thing, with a housing bubble. Dubai, Australia, Ireland, New Zealand, Spain, Iceland, Vietnam, Estonia, Lithuania, Thailand, China, Latvia, South Africa, and Singapore all had recently seen housing values appreciate at relentless rates. In 2005 *The Economist* calculated that the total value of the residential properties in the world's developed economies had effectively doubled from 2000 to 2005. This gain, a stunning $40 trillion, was equivalent to the combined gross domestic products of *all* the countries in question. "It looks like the biggest bubble in history," the magazine observed.

Some of these increases were staggering. While *The Economist* noted that American home prices appreciated by 73 percent between 1997 and 2005, Australian prices rose 114 percent, and Spanish prices by 145 percent. In Dubai, locale of a massive real estate bubble, prices of villas rose a staggering 226 percent between 2003 and 2007 alone, according to real estate consultants Colliers International. Figures on housing price appreciation in Asia and Eastern Europe are less dependable, but anecdotal evidence suggests that these regions enjoyed comparable booms. The United States was bad, but it was hardly the worst offender, even if it may have generated more problem loans than any other country.

Whatever the rate of appreciation, the reasons for the boom were invariably the same. Most of these countries had pursued easy monetary policies, so that borrowing costs hit historic lows, a trend only reinforced by a global savings glut. By 2006, mortgage rates in every developed and developing economy had declined to single digits for the first time ever. And like the United States, most countries did little to regulate their mortgage and financial markets. The result was the same: as home prices went up, households in these countries felt wealthier; they spent more and saved less. The ensuing boom in residential investment boosted many of these countries' GDP.

But this masked a deeper problem, much as it did in the United States. Low savings and high investment rates implied that the current account balance—the difference between a country's total savings and its total investments—was veering into negative territory. Unlike countries that run a current account surplus, countries that run a deficit need savings from other countries to underwrite their investments. The latter was the situation with the United States and other countries with housing bubbles: they had grown increasingly dependent on foreign capital to bring their accounts into balance. This in turn led to inflated currencies and caused a further deterioration in these countries' current account balance.

When the housing bust hit the United States, all the other economies with housing bubbles underwent comparable, if not greater, declines. Contrary to conventional wisdom, their housing busts were not a direct consequence of the American subprime crisis. The American crash may have been the catalyst, but it was not the cause: most if not all of these countries with overheated housing markets were poised for crashes as well. All they needed was a push, which they got when the global economy plunged into a crisis and a widespread recession in 2008.

If the United States had company in hatching an enormous housing bubble, it had peers in other areas as well. Take, for example, the problem of leverage and risk taking. While American financial institutions were reckless, their counterparts around the world were no less guilty. For example, by June 2008, leverage ratios at European banks had hit new highs. Venerable Credit Suisse had levered up 33 to 1, while ING hit 49 to 1. Deutsche Bank was up to its eyeballs in debt at 53 to 1, and Barclay's was the most levered of all, at 61 to 1. By comparison, doomed Lehman Brothers was levered at a relatively modest 31 to 1, and Bank of America was even lower, at 11 to 1.

Many European banks had avidly joined in the frenzy of financing and securitizing mortgages and other kinds of loans. This left them holding toxic mortgage-backed securities and CDOs that eroded in value when the housing crisis hit the United States. As markets for these securities dried up, many European banks saw their potential losses rise to frightening levels. By the end of 2009, the European Central Bank raised estimates of write-downs to €550 billion, topping earlier estimates.

Not all these assets came from the United States. Many banks in Europe engaged in their own securitization party, slicing and dicing mortgages from homeowners in European countries, with Britain, Spain, and the Netherlands providing most of the loans. In 2007 alone, €496.7 billion worth of European loans became the basis of asset-backed securities, mortgage-backed securities, and CDOs. While the excesses of this market paled in comparison to those of the United States, standards remained lax. Even worse, many of the loans and securities that banks had in the securitization pipeline were parked in conduits and SIVs. When the crisis hit, banks had to bring them back onto their balance sheets, much as their American counterparts did.

Finally, many European banks made high-risk loans in emerging Europe, particularly Latvia, Hungary, Ukraine, and Bulgaria. When the crisis hit, many of these economies saw their currencies fall sharply, and partly as a result, they could no longer make good on their loans. Suddenly European banks—especially those in Austria, Italy, Belgium, Sweden, and Germany—found themselves taking massive losses on their loan portfolios. As one Danish analyst observed in early 2009, "the markets have decided that the [emerging] region is the subprime area of Europe and now everyone is running for the door." It wasn't the same subprime crisis that hit the United States, but it stemmed from the same underlying problem: too many high-risk loans.

Hence the United States was hardly the only developed economy to fall during the crisis. Indeed, many European institutions got into trouble in advance of their American counterparts. The French bank BNP Paribas was one of the first, suspending several hedge funds in the summer of 2007. The German bank IKB imploded at the same time, a victim of runs on its SIVs; another German bank, Sachsen LB, was bailed out later that summer. This was but the beginning: Iceland's entire banking system would eventually collapse, and most banks in the United Kingdom ended up nationalized.

Similar problems eventually surfaced in Ireland, Spain, and a host of other European nations. And the bust of the real estate bubble in Dubai eventually led Dubai World, the government-owned enterprise most involved in these risky real estate developments, to seek a bailout from Abu Dhabi in December 2009.

Throughout it all, the crisis was following a familiar path. Many economies, particularly those in Western Europe, could not avoid the crisis because they suffered from many of the same vulnerabilities: housing bubbles, an overreliance on easy money and leverage, and an enthusiastic embrace of high-risk assets and financial innovation.

This fact highlights a broader truth about crisis economics: similar crises emerge in different places with seeming synchronization because of shared weaknesses. Too often market watchers refer to financial crises as "pandemics" or some other disease metaphor without acknowledging an important underlying truth: disease spreads most readily and quickly among those who are weak and lack immunity. In the recent crisis, many economies in Europe shared the same vulnerabilities as the U.S. economy. It's no surprise, then, that when the United States sneezed, they caught the cold—or perhaps more accurately, the flu.

But not everyone got sick, and that too is revealing. Look, for example, at India's experience. Though buffeted by the meltdown, its economy proved remarkably resilient. In the years leading up to the crisis, its conservative central bankers had gone down a different road than most of the world. Indian policy makers had resisted attempts to deregulate the financial system, and banks were forced to maintain hefty reserves. Where other countries embraced the mantra of free markets, India kept a tight lid on its financial system. As a consequence, it was relatively immune to the "disease" emanating from the United States.

Sadly, the same cannot be said for the world's other emerging economies, many of which—particularly those in Central and Eastern Europe—followed a familiar boom-to-bust trajectory. Still, their fate was not purely a function of shared vulnerabilities; rather, the peculiar way that developed and less developed economies can become entangled in a mutually destructive relationship contributed to their fate.

Emerging Economies, Existing Problems

Emerging economies usually depend on capital from more developed nations. That dependency, though mutually beneficial to both parties when times are good, can end up looking like a suicide pact when things fall apart. In the crisis of 1825, British investors flooded into the newly independent nation of Mexico as well as several other Latin American states recently freed from Spanish control. In the first year of independence alone, some £150 million worth of funds flowed into the region, with much of the mania focused on gold and silver mining. As investors poured into these countries, the new nations flourished. So too did speculators back in London, as investors bid up the prices of the new nations' mining stocks and bonds. Unfortunately, many of the ventures proved to be failures or even outright frauds, and the market collapsed. Investors fled stocks and pulled their funds out of Peru, Colombia, and Chile. The Latin American nations proved unable to service their debt, and in 1826 Peru defaulted, causing what one observed called "considerable panic" in the City of London. The other countries soon followed.

In the nineteenth century the most crisis-prone of the emerging markets was none other than the United States. European investors, in particular the British, plowed enormous amounts of capital into the country, snapping up the bonds of state governments, canal and railroad securities, and a host of other assets. The influx of funds helped underwrite booms in the United States, as well as speculative bubbles back in Europe. Most of them eventually collapsed, and when they did, foreign investors abruptly divested themselves of "risky" American assets.

In every case the result was predictable: booms turned to busts on both sides of the Atlantic. Many of the American banks and businesses that had benefited from the surfeit of foreign capital collapsed; many of their counterparts in Europe suffered too. In the wake of the panic of 1837, foreign investors fled en masse. Hundreds of banks perished in the United States, and a quarter of the individual states defaulted on some portion of the debt they had issued; panic simultaneously seized the City of London. A similar flight took place in 1857, after which one commentator claimed—with some exaggeration—that the "distrust felt by nearly all foreigners in the future of the United States was so great that the larger portion of American securities . . . held in foreign countries, were returned for sale at almost any sacrifice." History repeated itself yet again in 1873, as the railroad boom collapsed, prompting European investors to run for the exits once more.

Other emerging markets have suffered similar fates. In the 1990s a new generation of emerging markets around the world were shaken by a series of crises: Mexico in 1994; South Korea, Thailand, Indonesia, and Malaysia in 1997; Russia, Brazil, Ecuador, Pakistan, and Ukraine in 1998 and 1999; Turkey and Argentina in 2001. After flooding these countries with capital, foreign investors got spooked and fled in droves, leaving behind currency crises, waves of failures in the banking and corporate sectors, and defaults on government debt. Only the timely intervention of the IMF and the world's central banks prevented a worldwide economic disaster.

Emerging-market crises also played a role in the recent crisis, though in a more muted and complicated way. The ones that conformed to the previous pattern included the economies of emerging Europe. Like their predecessors, they generally had one thing in common: large current account deficits. Sometimes these deficits were fueled by a housing boom and huge increases in consumer spending, along with a drop in private savings; other times it was a function of government deficits or even corporate borrowing. Whatever the reason for the deficits, these countries borrowed extensively from investors and banks in more developed nations. They borrowed an enormous amount: between 2002 and 2006, borrowing from foreign sources increased by 60 percent every year. Even worse, much of their debt was denominated in foreign currencies, a strategy that went awry when their own domestic currencies started to depreciate during the crisis.

Though the crisis hit countries as different as Romania, Bulgaria, Croatia, and Russia, it was the Baltic states—Latvia, Estonia, and Lithuania—as well as Hungary and Ukraine that suffered the most. All of them saw an abrupt reversal of capital flows, as skittish investors fled "risky" markets—in other words, emerging economies—and headed for safer havens. The results were predictable, if brutal. Hungary, Iceland, Belarus, Ukraine, and Latvia all went hat in hand to the IMF, begging for a bailout. All three Baltic countries saw spectacular rises in unemployment; all three saw their banking sectors edge toward a crisis. The

Baltics suffered the worst consequences, registering double-digit unemployment by the spring of 2009. Latvia, arguably the hardest hit of all, suffered riots, the downfall of the government, and the collapse of its credit rating.

These countries fit the classic pattern of emerging economies that boom with an influx of foreign capital, then collapse when investors head for the exits. But another group of emerging economies that were hammered in the bust did not fit the usual profile: they enjoyed current account surpluses. China was the most prominent member of this group, but Brazil and smaller countries in the Middle East, Asia, and Latin America fell into this category too.

Most countries with current account surpluses tend to see their currencies appreciate. But in the years leading up to the crisis, the governments in these countries intervened aggressively in the foreign exchange markets in order to keep their currencies undervalued. They did so because many of them depended on exports, and the cheaper their currencies remained, the more effectively they could compete in world markets. This kind of intervention helped underwrite exports, but it meant an accumulation of dollars and other currencies at home, fueling a growth in the money supply.

The abundance of easy money and low interest rates then contributed to inflation and to asset bubbles, particularly on domestic stock exchanges. At their peak, stocks in China and India hit price-to-equity ratios of 40 or even 50 late in 2007—definite bubble territory. Many of these economies overheated in advance of the American financial meltdown, making them extraordinarily fragile and susceptible to sudden shocks. To a certain degree, their vulnerabilities had evolved independently of the excesses in the United States. Their eventual downfall had little direct relationship to the American crisis; rather, it was a consequence of policies pursued in the years before the bust. They ended up casualties of the crisis, but to a remarkable extent, they were the architects of their own misfortune.

The Death of Decoupling

As the crisis gathered steam in early 2008, most policy makers outside the United States, despite all the historical and contemporary evidence suggesting that a global pandemic was imminent, dithered. Still smitten with the idea of decoupling, many worried that their economies might overheat, generating inflation. Then central bankers in a number of emerging economies raised interest rates in an attempt to tighten monetary policy. Their counterparts in the more advanced economies followed suit; and in mid-2008 the European Central Bank implemented an ill-fated and misguided increase in policy rates.

To make matters worse, European policy makers refused to adopt an aggressive stimulus policy. The European economies that could most readily afford such a program (Germany in particular) did relatively little initially, and those who needed it the most (Spain, Portugal, Italy, and Greece) lacked the money to implement one. These "Club Med" countries were already running big budget deficits and carried a large stock of public debt relative to the size of their economy; they had little room to maneuver.

These decisions ill prepared policy makers in both advanced and emerging economies to combat the effects of the unfolding crisis. It caught them by surprise, and thanks in no small part to their flawed analysis, the global economy sank into the worst recession since the 1930s. In the fourth quarter of 2008 and the first quarter of 2009, the global economy contracted at a rate that paralleled, in size and in depth, the collapse from 1929 to 1931 that began the Great Depression.

As for decoupling, the rest of the world actually suffered more than the United States that winter. While the U.S. economy contracted during those two quarters at an annual rate of 6 percent, the contraction elsewhere was far more brutal. Economies that were supposed to decouple did not; they "recoupled" with a vengeance. Japan, which many initially hailed as immune to the crisis, saw its economy contract at an annualized rate of 12.7 percent in the final quarter of 2008; South Korea saw an even bigger decline of 13.2 percent. China managed to avoid an outright recession, even if its growth dropped below sustainable levels. Most of the rest of the world was not so lucky. In the finger-pointing that followed, many market watchers focused on the collapse of Lehman Brothers, seeing in that catastrophe the cause of all the world's ills. Even now some consider this event the catalyst for the crisis.

This interpretation is comforting but wrong. By the time of Lehman's collapse in September 2008, the United States had been in a recession for ten months, and much of the rest of the world was already in the same boat. The global credit crunch had been in full swing for over a year, and global equity markets had been headed south for nearly the same length of time. The crisis in the United States, which had started a year and a half before Lehman's collapse, had already radiated to the rest of the world along a host of channels: the financial system, trade relations, commodities, and currencies.

It did not infect these other countries by accident. For years, many of them had played host to housing and equity bubbles, credit bubbles, and excessive leverage, risk taking, and overspending. Their vulnerabilities had been building for years, and even countries that had taken a more prudent course—China and much of the rest of Asia—depended far too much on exports for their continued survival. They too were vulnerable, if in a different way: their continued prosperity depended on bubbles halfway around the world, bubbles that had already popped in advance of Lehman's collapse.

But the collapse of that famous firm did more than anything else to focus the minds of policy makers on the reality that the risk of another Great Depression loomed. At the end of 2008 they looked into the abyss and got religion. They started deploying all the weapons in their arsenal. Some tactics, like cutting interest rates, came from the standard playbook. But many others seemed to come from another world, and in some cases another era. To the uninitiated, the names of these tactics—"quantitative easing," "capital injections," "central bank swap lines"—defy definition. But these and many other unorthodox weapons came off the shelf and were mustered into battle. Some had been tried before; others had not. Some worked; some did not.

Nonetheless, their collective effect arguably prevented the Great Recession from turning into another Great Depression. Whether the cure will turn out to be worse than the disease is another matter, and it is to that question—and the risks and rewards of using unconventional policy measures to deal with financial crises—that we turn next.

Chapter 6

The Last Resort

When the worst financial crisis in generations hit the United States in 2007, Ben Bernanke had just been appointed head of the Federal Reserve a year earlier. It was a remarkable coincidence, for Bernanke was not just any central banker; he was one of the world's leading authorities on the Great Depression. Far more than almost any living economist, Bernanke was acutely aware of the complicated dynamics behind this watershed event. Over the course of his academic career, he had written influential articles that helped untangle the causes and effects of the worst depression in the nation's history.

Bernanke self-consciously built on the pioneering work of monetarists Milton Friedman and Anna Jacobson Schwartz, whose writings he first encountered in grad school. As we saw in chapter 2, these two scholars had broken with earlier interpretations of the Great Depression by arguing that monetary policy—courtesy of the Federal Reserve—was to blame for the disaster. According to this interpretation, the Fed's inaction and ineptitude not only failed to prevent the unfolding disaster but even contributed to the problem. Bernanke elaborated on that thesis, showing how the consequent collapse of the financial system threw sand in the gears of the larger economy, dragging the nation into a brutal depression.

Bernanke's keen appreciation of the burdens of history and his debt to Friedman were evident when he attended the venerable economist's ninetieth birthday party in 2002. By then Bernanke was a governor on the board of the Federal Reserve, and when he stood up to give a speech, he famously turned to the elderly man and said, with regard to the Great Depression: "You're right, we did it. We're very sorry. But thanks to you, we won't do it again."

This was the man in charge of monetary policy when the crisis hit. Not surprisingly, he saw events through the prism of what had happened nearly eighty years earlier and acted accordingly. Rules would be broken, and new tools tried. There would be no repeat of the Great Depression. As he told a reporter in the summer of 2009, "I was not going to be the Federal Reserve chairman who presided over the second Great Depression."

To that end, Bernanke revolutionized monetary policy, directing a stunning series of interventions into the financial system that even today few people understand. Some of these moves Bernanke had anticipated making; others he developed as the months passed and the threat of deflation and even a depression increased. They ran the gamut from conventional monetary policy—slashing interest rates to zero, for example—to unprecedented measures heralding a massive expansion of the Federal Reserve's power over the economy.

These interventions probably did help avert a twenty-first-century Great Depression, but for the student of crisis economics they raise a host of unsettling issues. Aside from the difficulty of scaling back Bernanke's policies once they're in place, many of them may prove conducive to moral hazard on a grand scale. The Fed, in its rush to prop up the financial system, rescued both illiquid and insolvent financial institutions. That precedent may be hard to undo and, over the long run, may lead to a collapse of market discipline, which in turn may sow the seeds of bigger bubbles and even more destructive crises.

No less problematic is the fact that some of Bernanke's monetary policies infringe on the traditional fiscal powers of elected government—namely, the power to spend money. In the recent crisis, the Fed pushed the statutory envelope, assuming various powers, implied and otherwise, to swap safe government bonds for toxic assets and, more radical, to purchase toxic assets and hold them on its balance sheet. Such measures, even if they prove effective, amount to an end run around the legislative process.

Bernanke's response, orchestrated by himself and other central bankers, offers a glimpse of the unorthodox ways in which monetary policy can be used—and perhaps abused—to prevent a crisis from spiraling out of control.

Deflation and Its Discontents

Since the end of the Second World War, the American business cycle has followed a fairly predictable path. The economy would emerge from a recession, grow, and eventually boom; the Federal Reserve would then begin to bring the cycle to a close by hiking interest rates to keep inflation in check, and more broadly, to keep the economy from overheating. Inevitably, the economy would contract; a recession would ensue.

In some cases, most notably in 1973, 1979, and 1990, the recession was set off in part by what economists call an exogenous negative supply-side shock. All three times, a geopolitical crisis in the Middle East triggered a sudden rise in oil prices that sparked inflation. Here too, to control rising prices, the Fed moved interest rates higher, after which the economy started to contract.

Whatever their causes, these various contractions would inevitably moderate inflation, without eliminating it altogether. The fall in output or the gross domestic product—typically a single percentage point or two—led to unpleasant but tolerable increases in unemployment and the familiar hardships of a recession.

In some instances, the economy would grow again of its own accord; in others, policy makers facilitated a recovery by resorting to a time-honored tool: they would cut interest rates, effectively making it cheaper for households and firms to borrow money. This would nudge people to spend more, driving up demand for everything from houses to factory equipment. Cutting interest rates often had the added effect of driving down the value of the dollar, making exports more attractive, making imports more expensive, generating demand for domestic goods, and contributing to an eventual recovery. Fiscal stimulus was also used to restore growth.

The first ten recessions in the postwar United States largely followed this script. Most lasted less than a year, save for a nasty recession in the wake of the oil shock of 1973, which was triggered by the Yom Kippur War; and after a second oil shock in 1979 caused by the Iranian Islamic Revolution, the Federal Reserve used high interest rates to slay inflation, resulting in a far more unpleasant recession. While brutal, that campaign proved successful and set the stage for the much-celebrated Great Moderation. As a consequence, recessions in 1991 and 2001 lasted a mere eight months each, and while these downturns brought pain aplenty, they ended with renewed growth and optimism, thanks in part to varying doses of monetary easing, fiscal stimulus, and tax cuts.

The twelfth postwar recession, which took hold in the wake of the recent financial crisis, has been different. Prices not only moderated but in some cases registered declines for the first time in fifty or sixty years. This was deflation, a phenomenon that unnerved policy makers across the ideological spectrum. Its recurrence "gives economists chills," reported *The New York Times* in the fall of 2008. The following spring Bernanke explained, "We are currently being very aggressive because we are trying to avoid . . . deflation."

To the uninitiated, the fuss seemed a bit mystifying. After all, aren't falling prices a good thing? Consumer goods cost less; people can buy more with every dollar they own; what's not to like? In fact, in a handful of episodes small, steady rates of deflation have gone hand in hand with robust economic growth, as technological advances drove down the price of goods. Between 1869 and 1896, for example, the spread of railroads and new manufacturing techniques helped push down prices by some 2.9 percent a year. At the same time, despite recurrent crises, the economy grew at an average annual rate of 4.6 percent.

This episode remains something of a curiosity for economic historians because deflation is generally not compatible with economic growth. Why? In most cases, deflation isn't caused by a technological revolution; it's caused by a sharp fall of aggregate demand relative to the supply of goods and the productive capacity of the economy.

This more common kind of deflation can have all sorts of peculiar effects on the day-to-day functioning of the economy. It can deter consumers from spending on big-ticket items: buying a car or a house, for example, becomes a bit like catching a falling knife. Similarly, a factory contemplating some capital investments may prefer to remain on the sidelines until prices stop falling. Unfortunately, postponing spending, far from stimulating economic growth, does precisely the opposite.

A bout of deflation born of a financial crisis is of a different order altogether and may be far more dangerous and destructive. Such bouts were relatively common in the wake of the perennial crises of the nineteenth century, then became much rarer in the twentieth. While deflation accompanied the global depression of the 1930s, it largely disappeared after that watershed event. Only in the 1990s did it resurface, first after the collapse of Japan's asset bubble, and then during the brutal recession that hit Argentina in 1998–2001.

During the recent crisis, the prospect of this kind of deflation was what gave economists the chills. They knew well that its ill effects could ramify throughout the economy. Even if it doesn't end in an outright depression, deflation can suffocate growth for years, leading to a condition that might best be described as stag-deflation, in which economic stagnation and even recession are combined with deflation. In such a condition, the usual tools of monetary policy cease to have much effect.

Irving Fisher was one of the first economists to understand the dynamics of deflation. While Fisher remains infamous today for claiming, shortly before the market crashed in 1929, that stock prices would remain on a "permanently high plateau," he redeemed himself by subsequently articulating a compelling theory of the connection between financial crises, deflation, and depression, or what he called the "debt-deflation theory of great depressions." Put simply, Fisher believed that depressions became great because of two factors: too much debt in advance of a crisis, and too much deflation in its wake.

Fisher began by observing that some of the worst crises in American history—1837, 1857, 1893, and 1929—followed on the heels of an excessive accumulation of debt throughout the economy. When the shock came—the stock market crash of 1929, for example—margin calls led to frenzied attempts to pay down debt. Fisher believed that this rush to liquidate debt and stockpile liquid reserves, while rational, damaged the health of the larger economy. As he explained in 1933, "The very effort of individuals to lessen their burden of debts increases it, because of the mass effect of the stampede to liquidate . . . the more debtors pay, the more they owe." Fisher famously noted that from October 1929 to March 1933, while debtors frantically reduced the nominal value of their debt by 20 percent, deflation actually increased their remaining debt burden by 40 percent.

Why? The rush to liquidate assets at fire-sale prices, Fisher argued, would lead to falling prices for everything from securities to commodities. Supply would far outstrip demand, and prices would fall. At the same time, people would tap money deposited in banks in order to liquidate debts or as a precaution against bank failures. These withdrawals would lead to a reduction of what economists call "deposit currency" and, by extension, a contraction of the overall money supply. This contraction would depress prices still further. As prices continued to fall, the value of assets across the board would drift downward, triggering a commensurate decline in the net worth of banks and businesses holding those assets. More fire sales and more deflation would result, leading to less liquidity in the markets, more gloom and pessimism, more hoarding of cash, and more fire sales.

The resulting deflation would have perverse consequences. As borrowers moved to pay off their debts (and as aggregate demand for goods started to fall in a severe recession), the lowered prices of goods and services would paradoxically increase the purchasing power of the dollar, and by extension, the real burden of their remaining debt. In other words, deflation increases the real value of nominal debts. Instead of getting ahead of their debts, people fell behind. Fisher called this the "great paradox"—the more people pay, the more their debts weigh them down.

This is debt deflation. To understand it better, let's consider its counterpart, what might be called "debt inflation." Imagine that you are a firm or a household, and you take out a ten-year loan for $100,000 at an interest rate of 5 percent. At the time, inflation hovers around 3 percent. If inflation stays at this rate, you'll really be paying interest at 2 percent per year—that's what's left after inflation eats away at the nominal, or original, rate of interest. If inflation goes up to 5 percent a year, it will effectively wipe out the interest rate entirely, and you will have the equivalent of an interest-free loan. But if inflation runs out of control, hitting 10 percent, you're not only getting an interest-free loan; your principal is eroding as well. These examples show you how to calculate the "real interest rate"—the difference between the nominal interest rate and the inflation rate.

Confused? Let's think about a more extreme example. Imagine that you take out that same $100,000 loan—and inflation runs completely out of control. Prices and wages soar to astonishing levels. It used to cost a dollar to buy a loaf of bread; now it costs a thousand dollars. At the same time, a minimum-wage job that once paid peanuts now pays several million dollars a year; a "good" job pays a hundred million. Now go back to that $100,000 debt you incurred. It's still sitting there, denominated in those older, more valuable dollars. The amount of the principal has not changed with inflation. It's now much easier to pay off your loan. Heck, it's nothing more than a month's worth of groceries.

The key here is that the dollars you're using to pay off the debt are worth less than when you incurred the debt in the first place. For this simple reason, inflation is the debtor's friend: it effectively erodes the value of the original debt.

Deflation, however, is not the debtor's friend. Let's go back to our original example of a ten-year loan at an interest rate of 5 percent. Contrary to expectations, the economy experiences deflation of 2 percent. That means you're effectively paying 7 percent interest a year. If deflation hits 5 percent, your real borrowing costs have doubled to 10 percent a year. In other words, the dollars you're using to pay off your debt are worth more than they were when you incurred the debt in the first place. Unfortunately, even though each dollar is worth more, you now have fewer of them because your wages have declined.

The upshot of debt deflation is that debtors—households, firms, banks, and others—see their borrowing costs rise above and beyond what they originally anticipated. And during a major financial crisis—with rising unemployment, growing panic, and a general unwillingness to lend—anyone who owes money has much more difficulty making good on his debt or, alternatively, refinancing it on less onerous terms. Investors shun risky assets, seeking liquid and safe assets like cash and government bonds. People hoard cash and refuse to lend it, which only exacerbates the liquidity crunch. As credit dries up, more and more people default, feeding the original cycle of deflation, debt deflation, and further defaults.

The end result is a depression: a brutal economic collapse in which a nation's economy can contract by 10 percent or more. In the Great Depression that both traumatized and inspired Irving Fisher, the collapse was unprecedented. From peak to trough, the stock market lost 90 percent of its value, the economy contracted by close to 30 percent, and 40 percent of the nation's banks failed. Unemployment surged to close to 25 percent. And deflation? Prices fell off the cliff. A dozen eggs that cost $0.53 in 1929 cost $0.29 in 1933, a drop of some 45 percent. Comparable declines hit everything from people's wages to the price of gas.

It's no surprise that Fisher's vision was a dark one. As he wrote from the depths of the crisis in 1933, "Unless some counteracting cause comes along to prevent the fall in the price level, such a depression . . . tends to continue, going deeper, in a vicious spiral, for many years. There is then no tendency of the boat to stop tipping until it has capsized." While Fisher acknowledged that things might ultimately stabilize—after "almost universal bankruptcy"—he thought this to be "needless and cruel." Instead, he counseled that policy makers "reflate" prices up to precrash levels. As he put it, "If the debt-deflation theory of great depressions is essentially correct, the question of controlling the price level assumes a new importance; and those in the drivers' seats—the Federal Reserve Board and the Secretary of the Treasury—will in [the] future be held to a new accountability."

Those words likely haunted Ben Bernanke, Henry Paulson, and Timothy Geithner as they confronted what looked like a reprise of the Great Depression. Unfortunately, like almost everything else with financial crises, engineering a reflation—or to put it more baldly, creating inflation—is not as simple as it seems. Once a deflationary spiral has gained momentum, conventional monetary policy tends not to work. Nor does it work against other ills that accompany financial crises. Other weapons must be developed and thrown into battle.

The Liquidity Trap

When economists talk about the futility of ordinary monetary policy, they refer to a "liquidity trap." Policy makers dread this state of affairs, and to understand why, we must examine how central banks exercise control over the money supply, interest rates, and inflation.

In the United States, the Federal Reserve primarily controls the money supply through "open market operations": that is, it can wade into the secondary market and buy or sell short-term government debt. When it does so, it effectively adds or removes money from the nation's banking system. It thereby changes what is known as the "Federal funds rate," the interest rate banks charge each other for overnight loans for funds on deposit at the Federal Reserve. In normal times, the Federal funds rate is a proxy for the cost of borrowing at any number of levels of the economy, and manipulating it is one of the most effective tools at the disposal of the Fed.

Here's how it works. Let's say that the Fed is worried about inflation and wants to keep the economy from overheating. The Fed therefore goes out and sells $10 billion worth of short-term government debt. By doing so, it effectively removes money from the banking system. Why? Because the purchasers of the debt have to write checks drawn on their respective banks, which the Fed then cashes and keeps. The banking system and the larger economy are now out $10 billion. Moreover, because banks use every dollar on deposit to create many more dollars' worth of loans, the real hit to the banking system—and by extension, the money supply—is something approaching $25 billion or $30 billion.

In this way, the Fed has tightened the money supply and made credit harder to obtain: it has effectively raised the cost of borrowing. Money, like any other commodity, responds to the laws of supply and demand, and now that the supply is lower, borrowing money costs more. Interest rates, in other words, go up because lenders can now command a higher rate. Whenever the media report that the Federal Reserve has "raised" interest rates, it hasn't literally done so; rather, it has "targeted" a higher interest rate—the Federal funds rate—via these open market operations.

Now let's imagine that the Fed is no longer worried about inflation; in fact, it's worried about the fact that the economy, instead of overheating, is headed toward a recession. The Fed therefore sets a lower target for the Federal funds rate and floods the economy with money, buying up short-term government debt. Where does it get the money? It creates it out of thin air. The Federal Reserve effectively writes a check for $10 billion and gives it to the sellers of government debt. These sellers deposit the money they've received from the Fed in various banks. Now those banks can use it to make loans worth several times that amount. Money is suddenly more available, and as a consequence, credit is easier to obtain. More to the point, it's cheaper: the net effect of adding money to the economy is that the Federal funds rate will fall, as will interest rates generally.

This is what takes place during normal times. A liquidity trap, by contrast, is not normal. It's what happens when the Fed has exhausted the power of open market operations. That dreaded moment arrives when the Federal Reserve has driven the Federal funds rate down to zero. In normal times setting that rate would pump plenty of easy money and liquidity into the economy and spur wild growth. But in the wake of a financial crisis, cutting interest rates to zero may not be enough to restore confidence and compel banks to lend money to one another. The banks are so worried about their liquidity needs—and so mutually distrustful—that they will hoard any liquid cash rather than lend it out. In this climate of fear, the policy rate may be zero, but the actual market rates at which banks are willing to lend will be much, much higher, keeping the cost of borrowing expensive. Because it's almost impossible to drive policy rates below zero—you can't make banks lend money if they'll be penalized for doing so—policy makers find themselves in a serious quandary. They're in the dreaded liquidity trap.

During the recent crisis, central banks around the world found themselves in precisely this position. As the crisis worsened, they slashed interest rates, and by late 2008 and 2009 the Federal Reserve, the Bank of England, the Bank of Japan, the Swiss National Bank, the Bank of Israel, the Bank of Canada, and even the European Central Bank had pushed interest rates close to zero. Compared to previous financial crises, this exercise of monetary policy was remarkably swift and partially coordinated. But the collective cuts did little to stimulate loans, much less consumption, investment, or capital expenditures, as market rates remained very high given the fear and uncertainty that gripped banks, households, and firms. Nor did these cuts arrest the slide toward deflation. Conventional monetary policy ceased to have sway over the markets. The metaphor of choice was that exercising monetary policy was like "pushing on a string." It was useless.

The reason was simple: the cuts in the Federal funds rate (or its equivalent in other countries) did not percolate throughout the wider financial system. Banks had money, but they didn't want to lend it: uncertainty bred by the crisis, and concerns that many of their existing loans and investments would eventually sour, made them risk averse. This failure of conventional monetary policy nicely illustrated an old adage: you can lead a horse to water, but you can't make it drink. The Fed could pump plenty of water or liquidity into the banks, but it could not make them lend. If they did anything with their excess reserves, they sank them into the closest thing to cash: risk-free government debt.

We can glimpse the liquidity trap in the gap or "spread" between interest rates paid on supersafe or otherwise solid investments and those paid on riskier investments. There are many ways of measuring this spread. For example, the "TED spread" is the difference between the interest rate on the short-term government debt of the United States and the three-month LIBOR (see chapter 1), the interest rate that banks charge one another for three-month loans. During normal times, the TED spread hovers around 30 basis points, reflecting the fact that the market deems bank-to-bank loans as only slightly riskier than loans to the government.

At the height of the crisis, the TED spread hit 465 basis points, because banks no longer trusted one another enough to lend money on a three-month horizon, except at exorbitant rates. At the same time, risk-averse investors fled to the haven of the safest asset of all: the debt of the U.S. government. These forces conspired to simultaneously drive up the cost of borrowing for banks and drive down the cost of borrowing for the U.S. government. The widening spread was a reflection of this dynamic, and the higher the spread, the greater the stress in the markets. So while the Fed was willing to lend money at low rates, the actual market rates at which banks lent to one another—the LIBOR—remained very high. Worse, because the rates of many other kinds of short-term loans and of variable-rate mortgages are pegged in part to the LIBOR, borrowing remained very high for private firms and households.

Measurements like the TED spread are a bit like blood pressure readings: they reflect the underlying health of the economy's circulatory system. They reveal how readily money flows through the economy, or how "liquid" markets are at a given moment. When conditions are normal, markets are relatively liquid and trust rules; people lend money to one another with ease, and borrowing costs remain at normal levels. In a time of crisis, when the patient (the financial system) is very sick indeed, the lifeblood of the system (money) isn't flowing, despite the usual measures used to keep it healthy: namely, pursuing open market operations to achieve lower interest rates. Deflation becomes a very real possibility.

How does one deal with this sort of problem? Back in 2002, when Bernanke spoke about the perils of deflation, he alluded to a number of possible interventions. As he recognized at that time, these experimental measures carried significant risks, given "our relative lack of experience with such policies," as he rightly characterized it. The Japanese had experimented with some of these policies in the 1990s, but they remained highly controversial.

When the crisis hit, Bernanke instituted a series of such measures, aimed at cutting the spreads between the short-term—and subsequently, the long-term—rates set by the market and the short-term rates set by policy makers. To accomplish this feat, the Fed set up a series of new "liquidity" facilities that made low-cost loans available to anyone who needed them. In effect, the government jumped directly into the market, reaching far beyond the usual mechanisms of injecting liquidity—cutting the overnight Federal funds rate—and made loans directly to ailing financial institutions. It became the quintessential lender of last resort, making loans and liquidity available to an ever-widening cross section of the financial system.

Initially, the Fed aimed these maneuvers at institutions—depository institutions or banks—that already had some rights to borrow overnight funds directly from the Federal Reserve, from the "discount window" (the term refers to an earlier era, when cash-strapped banks would literally go to a teller window at the Fed). Few banks exercised this right, simply because in normal times the Fed imposed a penalty rate on anyone who approached the discount window. The window was designed to make small, emergency loans; it wasn't designed for a crisis. As conditions worsened, however, the Fed cut the borrowing penalty and allowed banks to obtain loans for longer periods of time. By March 2008, banks could borrow for up to ninety days from the discount window, with almost no penalty.

Yet the crisis worsened, whereupon the Fed then introduced new liquidity facilities. The Term Auction Facility (TAF) targeted depository institutions, giving them another means of securing ready cash for periods much longer than overnight. But it did little to stop the liquidity crunch or the ugly cycle of fire sales, forced liquidations, and declining asset prices that Fisher had predicted. The Fed had to adopt other tools aimed at the parts of the financial system that had no existing access to its resources.

Accordingly, the Federal Reserve established the Primary Dealer Credit Facility (PDCF), which made overnight loans to "primary dealers," the banks and broker dealers with whom the Fed trades when it conducts open market operations. Another facility, the Term Securities Lending Facility (TSLF), made loans of medium-term maturity to the same group, in exchange for illiquid securities held by such institutions. Thus, for the first time since the Great Depression, the Fed used its emergency powers to lend to nondepository institutions. From there the facilities multiplied, with acronyms to rival anything devised during the New Deal: the Commercial Paper Funding Facility (CPFF), the Money Market Investor Funding Facility (MMIFF), and most unpronounceable of all, the Asset-Backed Commercial Paper Money Market Mutual Fund Liquidity Fund (ABCPMMMFLF), better known simply as the AMLF.

This alphabet soup of lending facilities operated in a variety of different ways and had different objectives or targets. Sometimes the facilities permitted financial institutions to borrow directly from the Fed. In other cases, they enabled financial institutions to swap illiquid assets—higher-quality asset-backed securities, corporate bonds, commercial paper—for supersafe and liquid government debt. In still other cases, the facilities directly or indirectly financed the purchase of illiquid short-term debt. Whatever the mechanism, the objective was the same: inject liquidity into specific markets that showed signs of trouble and stress. This unprecedented intervention was not as indiscriminate as it might seem. The Federal Reserve did not accept junk bonds or other low-grade debt as collateral; it accepted only what was, in theory, higher-quality debt.

These efforts eventually bore some fruit: at the end of 2008, in the aftermath of the Lehman collapse, the Fed and other central banks flooded the financial markets with hundreds of billions of dollars' worth of liquidity, and the spreads between short-term market rates and safe government assets started to decline. As cumbersome and radical as these measures were, they successfully injected a measure of liquidity into the short-term credit markets.

Nonetheless, it was arguably a Pyrrhic victory. The Federal Reserve and other central banks that instituted comparable programs had gone from being lenders of last resort to lenders of first, last, and only resort. In the process, they crossed the proverbial Rubicon not once or twice but many times.

In normal times, the lender of last resort helps individual banks with liquidity problems. But in this particular crisis, central banks ended up providing support to virtually every bank. And they did so not simply in the form of overnight loans, as is usually the case; this time the liquidity crunch was so severe that the Fed lent money for weeks or even months. In addition, it lent to institutions that had never before been recipients of such aid: the primary dealers, which included many firms that weren't banks in any sense of the word, and the money market funds. The Fed even effectively lent money to corporations via the CPFF. It also provided "liquidity support"—special low-cost lines of credit—to a host of institutions considered too big to fail: AIG, Fannie Mae and Freddie Mac, and Citigroup. Central bankers in Europe adopted similar measures.

These interventions had little or no precedent in the history of central banking. They amounted to a massive expansion of government support of the financial system. But they were only the beginning.

Last Lender Standing

As a typical crisis gathers steam, runs against a nation's banks and other financial institutions take place. Depositors in Mexico demand their pesos back; investors in Japan demand the return of the yen they've lent out. It's an unpleasant scene, but the central bank in each of those nations can save the day because it can print money to meet the demands. The domestic currency is in demand, and to quell the panic, the central banks can provide it.

But when the liabilities of financial institutions, corporations, households, or even the government are denominated in a foreign currency, the situation can unravel. Emerging-market economies may end up getting much of their financing from banks and other financial institutions in other countries. The foreign currency in question is most often the dollar, but it could also be the euro or any number of different currencies.

If for some reason the creditors of an emerging-market economy decide not to roll over its debt when it comes due, then anyone who owes dollars has to pay off the debt. That puts debtors in a tight spot: they don't have the dollars. They can go to the central bank, but it is unlikely to have stockpiled massive foreign currency reserves, and it can't help out. Nor can it print dollars: that would be counterfeiting. So these debtors are extraordinarily vulnerable. Their predicament has been at the heart of a number of recent emerging-market crises: Mexico in 1994, East Asia in 1997 and 1998, Russia and Brazil in 1998, and Turkey and Argentina in 2001.

Enter the International Monetary Fund. The IMF was born at the end of World War II; one of its principal responsibilities has been to act as an international lender of last resort to governments and central banks who find themselves in the position so many countries did in the 1990s. The IMF was busy that decade, but in the 2000s the world's emergency-room doctor had little to do—until the crisis hit. Then the IMF once again became the world's lender of last resort to a host of emerging-market countries.

It gave this support in two forms. It extended the more traditional lifeline, a Stand-By Arrangement (SBA), to fourteen countries, with Hungary, Ukraine, and Pakistan among the biggest recipients. As with the support given to emerging markets in the 1990s, the IMF made these foreign-currency loans only if the recipients adopted economic reforms that would in theory put them on more stable ground in the future. Other more stable countries with a stronger track record of instituting financial reforms—Mexico, Poland, and Colombia—tapped unconditional lines of liquidity known as Flexible Credit Lines (FCLs). Unlike SBAs, FCLs served as precautionary or prophylactic lines of credit: the IMF effectively pledged to help out but did not immediately disburse any money.

The scale of all this lending was remarkable. By the summer of 2009, the IMF had authorized over $50 billion in SBAs and $78 billion in FCLs. Many of these lifelines overshadowed the rescue packages put together a decade earlier. In 1997, for example, South Korea received a loan of under $10 billion to tide it through the crisis that was then sweeping Asia.

By contrast, Ukraine, a country with an economy a fraction of the size of South Korea's, received a whopping $16.4 billion in 2008.

The IMF was not the only lender of last resort. In addition to its myriad domestic interventions, the Federal Reserve played this important international role, by providing "swap lines." Under these agreements, the Fed "swaps" dollars for some other central bank's currency. It thereby enables the central banks to lend out dollars to anyone needing them in their home countries. For example, in April 2009, Mexico activated a $30 billion swap line with the Fed. This infusion of money injected liquidity into the market for dollars and helped anyone who owed dollars to pay off or roll over his debt.

These actions alone were remarkable, but in one of the strange and unprecedented features of the recent crisis, even the most stable, advanced economies faced liquidity crises comparable to the ones suffered by emerging markets. Many financial institutions in Europe had borrowed enormous quantities of dollars in short-term loans to underwrite various speculations. When the interbank market froze up at the peak of the crisis, they were unable to roll over their dollar-denominated debts. Everyone needed dollars, and as a consequence, the value of the dollar went through the roof. This fact was terribly ironic: the country that was the ground zero of the financial crisis—the United States—saw its currency appreciate sharply in 2008.

Bernanke's solution was yet another bit of lender-of-last-resort legerdemain. The Federal Reserve can't lend directly to financial institutions outside the United States, but it can lend dollars to foreign central banks, who can in turn lend them to the financial institutions that need them so desperately. In return, the Fed gets an equivalent sum of whatever currency is the stock in trade of the central bank receiving the dollars. In this way, vast quantities of dollars traveled from the Federal Reserve to the European Central Bank, the Swiss National Bank, and the Bank of England, as well as the central banks of Sweden, Denmark, and Norway. In return, the Fed took custody of an equivalent amount of euros, pounds, francs, and other currencies. By late 2008 these swap lines totaled half a trillion dollars, and they started to decline only in the spring of 2009.

The crisis subsided because of these and many other extraordinary efforts undertaken to bring liquidity and stability back to the markets. But as policy makers found out, arresting the more immediate and dramatic crisis in short-term lending was one thing; getting banks to stop the larger drift toward deflation and depression was quite another.

Nuclear Options

One of the more remarkable weapons that the Fed and other central banks brought to bear on the crisis was "quantitative easing," though Ben Bernanke advocates calling it "credit easing"; economist Paul Krugman argues that it should be called "qualitative easing." Whatever its name, a modest version of this particular strategy had been tested in Japan in the 1990s. The basic idea is to have the central bank intervene in markets for long-term debt in the same way that it does in markets for short-term debt.

Why go down the path of credit easing? The measures adopted so far hadn't worked their magic. Thanks to cuts in the overnight Federal funds rate, banks had access to plenty of cash; and thanks to the host of new liquidity facilities, financial institutions of all stripes had access to cash as well, eventually driving down the cost of short-term borrowing, as measured by the LIBOR rate. Yet for all that largesse, banks continued to refuse to make longer-term loans to the many firms and businesses that needed credit to stay alive. Banks were getting no-interest loans from the Fed, but market rates for everyone else remained high. Financial institutions continued to hoard cash in anticipation of future losses, or they sank it into the safest investments around: government debt, or "agency debt," the obligations of Fannie Mae and Freddie Mac.

Banks' propensity to park money in government or agency debt—particularly long-term debt—was understandable. By borrowing money from the Fed at policy rates approaching zero, then plowing it into a ten-year or thirty-year Treasury bond paying 3 to 4 percent, they could make a reliable profit and steer clear of all the risky borrowers who were clamoring for loans. While this strategy did nothing to ease the credit crunch, it made eminent sense from the standpoint of self-preservation.

Using quantitative easing, the Federal Reserve would attack this problem on multiple fronts. It would wade into the financial system and start buying up long-term government debt: ten-year and thirty-year Treasury bonds. That would immediately inject massive amounts of liquidity into the market because the Fed would pay for those bonds by creating money out of thin air. As it purchased hundreds of billions of dollars' worth of bonds, cash would flow to the banks that sold them. Now the banks would have even more cash, and presumably, they would be tempted to lend it.

The Fed's actions were designed to have the additional positive consequence of reducing the attractiveness of those bonds as a future investment. Why? Because bond prices and bond yields move in opposite directions. If the price goes up, the yield goes down. When the government created a demand for the bonds by buying them up, their price went up, and their yield went down. That meant they became less attractive as a place for banks to park money. In theory, banks would therefore look for other places to sink their money and therefore would consider making loans to those starving for credit.

This policy, announced in March 2009, went hand in hand with massive purchases of other assets. On the same day the Fed announced that it would purchase upwards of $300 billion in long-term Treasury bonds, it also announced that it would buy a trillion dollars' worth of mortgage-backed securities and $55 billion worth of agency debt. As was the case with the proposed purchase of government bonds, the Federal Reserve had already made forays into these markets the previous fall. Still, the scale and scope of these interventions—particularly in the MBS market—was astonishing. So too was the announcement that the Fed would commit a trillion dollars to the Term Asset-Backed Securities Loan Facility (TALF), to support with Fed loans the private securitization of credit card debt and auto loans.

By broadening the range of assets it held, the Fed sought to prop up markets for various kinds of long-tem debt. Its intervention via the TALF program was a relatively modest attempt to revive the market for securitization. But by wading into the housing market, the Fed had bigger ambitions. Its purchases of mortgage-backed securities effectively gave Fannie Mae and Freddie Mac breathing room to guarantee more mortgages or bundles of mortgages. That strategy went hand in hand with the Fed's campaign to drive down the yield on ten- and thirty-year government bonds. Because long-term interest rates tend to move in tandem with one another, this intervention would have the effect of lowering mortgage rates, thereby jump-starting the mortgage market. It would also help drive down the costs of borrowing for corporations.

The Federal Reserve was not alone in its use of quantitative easing. In Britain, the Bank of England was caught in a liquidity trap as well. It had cut its benchmark rates close to zero, the lowest since it was founded in 1694, and it had created liquidity facilities similar to those devised in the United States. But these moves failed to halt the prospect of debt deflation, and so in March 2009, in a bit of quantitative easing of its own, the Bank of England pledged to buy some £150 billion worth of government debt and corporate bonds. The European Central Bank followed suit two months later, pledging €60 billion to purchase "covered bonds," a form of mortgage debt.

All these interventions constituted a dramatic shift in the role of central banks. In previous crises, central banks restricted their efforts to acting as lenders of last resort. This time, however, in a series of incremental steps, central banks around the world adopted a new role: as investor of last resort. They began by creating liquidity facilities that enabled financial institutions to swap toxic assets for supersafe government debt; they thereby effectively created an artificial market for unwanted assets. At the same time, when they made outright loans, they accepted a remarkable range of collateral, everything from corporate bonds to commercial real estate loans to commercial paper. This too helped prop up the value of a range of assets.

The policy of quantitative easing, adopted by the Fed and other central banks, marked the culmination of this process: outright purchases of long-term debt in the open market. As a consequence, the balance sheets of central banks underwent a profound transformation. In 2007, for example, the Federal Reserve held approximately $900 billion worth of assets, consisting almost entirely of its stock in trade: the debt of the U.S. government. By the summer of 2009, the Fed's balance sheet had ballooned to approximately $2.3 trillion or $2.4 trillion, the overwhelming majority of which consisted of assets accumulated during the crisis. Some of these assets, such as the debt of Fannie Mae and Freddie Mac, were somewhat safe. Others were less safe, particularly those derived from home mortgages, credit card debt, and auto loans.

Most dodgy of all were the collateralized debt obligations and other potentially toxic assets acquired during the bailout of Bear Stearns and AIG. These assets, Fed staffers reported in February 2009, represented "some of the most esoteric components of the Federal Reserve's balance sheet." It was a serious understatement. Unlike most of the assets it holds at this writing, the Fed "owns" these assets via its control of three limited-liability corporations known as Maiden Lane I, II, and III. Each is privately administered by BlackRock Financial Management. This highly unusual arrangement has attracted considerable criticism—and skepticism. It is also without precedent in the history of the Federal Reserve.

Taken together, all these actions constituted a massive and unprecedented intervention in the financial system, using conventional and unconventional monetary policy. Over the course of the crisis, Bernanke (and to a lesser extent, other central bankers) sought to counter the effects of the financial crisis with three kinds of tools. Most traditional was the provision of liquidity (lender-of-last-resort support) to a host of financial institutions, including banks, broker dealers, and even foreign central banks. Less conventional was the creation of the special facilities that purchased (or financed the purchase of) specific kinds of short-term debt—commercial paper, for example. Then the Fed began to play the role of investor of last resort, which culminated in the most radical programs of all: its commitment to intervene in markets for long-term debt (various asset-backed securities and long-term government debt).

While these measures are somewhat staggering to contemplate, they were not as crazy as some of the other options that had been contemplated during the crisis. For example, the Federal Reserve could have intervened directly in the stock markets, buying up unwanted equities. This tactic had been deployed during the Asian financial crisis of 1998, when monetary authorities in Hong Kong purchased 5 percent of the shares being traded on the local stock exchange. The measure was widely criticized at the time, but it managed to forestall a foreign exchange crisis by frustrating the attempts of some large hedge funds to pull off a "double play," shorting both the currency and the stock market. Indeed, the government went on to make a tidy profit from its investment. Likewise, the Bank of Japan adopted a similar policy in 2002, though its intervention paled in comparison to Hong Kong's and aimed merely to prop up the prices of certain bank stocks and, by extension, the banks themselves. In 2009, it repeated these measures for much the same reason.

The Fed did not go down this road, and with good reason: it would have raised the understandable concern that the government was manipulating markets in the world's biggest economy, thereby endangering its already fragile credibility. That same concern explains why the Fed set certain limits on its other interventions. It accepted only investment-grade assets as collateral for making loans and refused to purchase low-grade commercial paper when it waded into that particular market. There were limits to how far the Fed would go to stop the crisis.

Nor did the Fed ever deploy several other extremely controversial weapons. It might have used quantitative easing on a far more massive scale, manipulating the foreign exchange markets to weaken the value of the dollar, or even employed some version of a strategy half-seriously proposed by Milton Friedman: having the government print money and scatter it on the population from helicopters. Friedman never intended that policy makers actually distribute money like manna from heaven, but there were functional equivalents of doing this: giving people tax cuts financed entirely by printing money, for example. Bernanke embraced this idea back in 2002 but never pursued it during the crisis.

Nevertheless, Bernanke and other central bankers did employ some highly unconventional measures in their efforts to put a stop to the crisis. Unfortunately, a radical remedy administered in a crisis is bound to have unintended consequences. For starters, the Fed has sent a clear message to the financial markets that it will do almost anything and everything to prevent a financial crisis from spinning out of control. That's wonderfully reassuring, but it creates moral hazard on a grand scale. The next time a crisis hits, banks and other financial firms could be forgiven for believing that the Fed will rescue them once again. In fact, now that there's a precedent for setting up special liquidity facilities and extending lender-of-last-resort support to broad swaths of the global financial system, firms may reasonably expect them to be resurrected at the slightest sign of trouble down the line.

This is a problem. As Frank Borman, the chief of Eastern Airlines, said back in the early 1980s, "Capitalism without bankruptcy is like Christianity without hell." Unfortunately, the Fed's interventions have kept afloat both the illiquid and the insolvent; the major banks and financial firms have undergone precious few bankruptcies. Financial institutions that no amount of liquidity or regulatory forbearance can save remain in operation. Like the infamous zombie banks that became a symbol of Japan's Lost Decade, these firms must go bankrupt, and the sooner they do, the better.

But that will depend a great deal on another problem: how to unwind and dismantle the various special facilities that the Fed established in the midst of the crisis. As early as January 2009, Bernanke spoke confidently about the Fed's "exit strategy," and he clearly believes that as credit conditions improve, the financial system's dependence on easy money will subside. Perhaps. But the rescue effort that he and other central bankers oversaw is on a scale never before tried. Its extraordinarily large number of moving parts make it very difficult to know how attempts to wean one swath of the financial sector off easy money might affect other parts of the system. Bernanke has reassured anxious lawmakers that there is a plan, but we're in uncharted waters here: this level of intervention has no precedent.

The monetary policies pioneered by Bernanke have another, less noticed aspect: many of them are, strictly speaking, no longer purely a matter of managing the money supply. The Fed has instead stepped into the financial system and effectively subsidized its operations, potentially incurring losses that could ultimately fall on the shoulders of taxpayers. Put differently, it's engaging in monetary policies that bleed imperceptibly into the traditional domain of fiscal policy—namely, government's power to tax and spend. Those are prerogatives of the legislative branch, but in this crisis Bernanke's policies have blurred that line, turning the Federal Reserve's power to lend money into a means of spending money on the financial system. It has granted many subsidies to the financial system in its time of need, and it has purchased potentially risky asset-backed securities. Even its policy of purchasing long-term government debt may end up costing money: when the time comes to sell it, the Fed may well have to unload these bonds at a loss.

These encroachments on the terrain of fiscal policy, however, may have been inevitable. After all, proposals to allocate taxpayer dollars to rescue the financial system have encountered tremendous political resistance, from the first, failed attempt to secure money for the Troubled Assets Relief Program to the strong resistance to the stimulus package in the spring of 2009.

From the beginning of the crisis, there has been some resistance to using fiscal policy to combat the crisis.

That's unfortunate: the government's ability to tax and spend, while not always immediate in its effect, is one of the most powerful weapons in the arsenal of crisis economics. Still, its use carries plenty of serious risks, particularly in the recent crisis, when legislators disbursed taxpayer money not merely on the traditional objects of deficit spending but on bailouts, guarantees, and backstops of everything from banks to carmakers to the very homeowners whose troubles helped ignite the crisis in the first place.

Chapter 7

Spend More, Tax Less?

When President Herbert Hoover gave the annual State of the Union speech in 1930, the United States was one year into what would become an enormous economic catastrophe. But on that day he emphatically declared that "economic depression can not be cured by legislative action or executive pronouncement" and that "economic wounds must be healed by the action of the cells of the economic body—the producers and consumers themselves." Hoover counseled that "every individual should sustain faith and courage" and "each should maintain his self-reliance."

Thanks to words like these, Hoover remains the quintessential symbol of government apathy and inaction. The truth is actually much more complicated—and more interesting. In the very same speech, Hoover noted that spending on public works projects typically collapsed during economic downturns. This time, he proudly reported, national, state, and local governments had deliberately spent money on infrastructure improvements as a counterweight to the Depression. In fact, he bragged that "as a contribution to the situation the Federal Government is engaged upon the greatest program of waterway, harbor, flood control, public building, highway, and airway improvement in all our history." Under this "do-nothing" president, the federal government effectively doubled its spending on such projects.

Though Hoover supported such expenditures, he also believed in limits. "I can not emphasize too strongly the absolute necessity to defer any other plans for increase of Government expenditures," he proclaimed. Nothing less than "rigid economy" would keep the federal budget in balance. The message was clear: there would be no deficit spending on his watch.

Pity Hoover: he lived at a turning point in the history of crisis economics. His speech revealed a man trapped between two very different paradigms for handling the crisis. One, which looked to the past, prescribed patience and balanced budgets; the other, which became the wave of the future, prescribed deficit spending and massive public works projects. Hoover could see the future, but he was tethered to the past. He wanted to reconcile contradictory aims: to cultivate self-reliance, to provide government help in a time of crisis, and to maintain fiscal discipline. This was impossible.

Six years after Hoover stood before Congress, John Maynard Keynes articulated what would become the new orthodoxy: in future crises, the government would rely on fiscal policy to cushion the economy, to increase the demand for goods and services, and to revive the "animal spirits" necessary for capitalism's eventual resurgence. In other words, the government would aggressively spend money and, to a lesser extent, cut taxes, financing these measures with deficit spending. The old policy of letting the economy heal itself became tantamount to letting the patient suffer. In the succeeding decades, fiscal policy became the weapon of choice when dealing with economic downturns, whether caused by crises or not.

If Hoover stood at one watershed in the history of fiscal policy, we may be living at another. Keynes's toolkit has grown from a few trusty instruments to a bewildering array of devices that government uses to intervene in the economy. In the United States and many other countries, national governments spend money not only for public works but for other purposes, like guaranteeing bank loans, debts, and deposits. They have even used tax dollars to acquire significant ownership stakes in industrial behemoths and giant banks. Just as monetary policy has evolved in bewildering and complicated ways, fiscal policy has become a gigantic—and expensive—bag of tricks.

Contemporary policy makers now find themselves in a fix comparable to Hoover's. They may want to hand out tax cuts and spend money to prop up the labor market and increase demand and production, but many governments are already running massive budget deficits that are increasing public debt to unsustainable levels. They want to force Hoover's "producers and consumers" to help themselves, but they keep bailing them out at ever-greater expense. And while they want to hold the line on moral hazard, they keep providing households, financial institutions, and corporations with new incentives to behave in precisely the ways that contributed to this crisis in the first place.

In short, a bundle of contradictions lie at the heart of twenty-first-century fiscal policy. While our present predicament may not be as dire as it was in Hoover's day, the old way of doing things is no longer compatible with the new realities that loom on the horizon.

Conventional Fiscal Policy

John Maynard Keynes was the first major economist to propose that government should use its powers to tax and spend in order to ameliorate economic hardship. His analysis was simple and straightforward: in an economic downturn, the total demand for goods and services falls far below the supply, triggering unemployment and a drop in production. Writing in the shadow of the Great Depression, Keynes concluded that this cycle, if permitted to go unchecked, could feed on itself. If the crisis got bad enough, the "animal spirits" of the economy would perish, and fearful entrepreneurs and consumers would curtail spending more than was justified by weakened incomes and economic woes. Despite a surplus of desperate workers and idle factories, a vicious circle of ever-falling demand, employment, production, and prices would grip the economy in a deflationary spiral and result in a permanent state of stagnation.

Keynes believed that the economy would not emerge from the doldrums on its own. Only if the government stepped into the breach and directly or indirectly picked up the slack in demand relative to the glut of excess supply and idle capacity could the economy stabilize itself, let alone return to prosperity. That would require deficit spending, but it was better to spend money preventing a catastrophe from worsening, Keynes maintained; balancing the budget could wait until after the crisis passed. In fact, Keynes believed that a premature return to fiscal discipline would likely throttle any nascent recovery.

Though Keynes first published his ideas in 1936, government policies instituted earlier in the decade anticipated his recommendations. Beginning with Hoover's early experiments and culminating with Roosevelt's New Deal, public works projects large and small put people back to work and propped up the demand for goods and services. The amount of construction undertaken then remains impressive even today. The Public Works Administration, the Works Progress Administration, and the Civilian Conservation Corps built 24,000 miles of sewer lines, 480 airports, 78,000 bridges, 780 hospitals, 572,000 miles of highways, and upwards of 15,000 schools, courthouses, and other public buildings.

The results, though hardly miraculous, were dramatic: from 1933 to 1937, unemployment fell from approximately 25 percent to a little under 15 percent. In 1937 a renewed commitment to balancing the budget triggered a yearlong relapse into a severe recession, whereupon the Roosevelt administration resumed its earlier strategy of financing the New Deal with deficit spending. The outbreak of World War II, which necessitated government spending on an even more massive scale, helped the United States escape the lingering effects of the Great Depression and brought about a more sustained recovery of growth.

Keynes became the preeminent economist of the postwar era, and his prescriptions became the standard response not only to crises but to economic downturns large and small. Keynes eventually fell into disfavor in the 1970s. But in the early 1990s, after the collapse of the Japanese real estate bubble left that economy reeling, the Japanese government embraced his ideas once more, and in the succeeding decade, it instituted no fewer than ten separate stimulus packages that together cost more than a trillion dollars. These efforts raised Japan's deficit to record levels and left behind a mixed legacy: plenty of welcome improvements to infrastructure but also many wasteful and pointless projects in rural areas. Economists continue to argue ad nauseam as to whether any of it was useful. Many believe the policy's failure lay not with the idea of public works spending but with the choice of specific projects. Others maintain that the government spent too little, or pulled back too soon.

But this kind of fiscal stimulus is but one of several approaches available to policy makers. Aside from direct spending to stimulate demand, fiscal policy also encompasses tax cuts and rebates, which in theory encourage consumers to spend by providing them with more income. In other words, they stimulate spending—or so the theory goes. This strategy wasn't part of the playbook in the 1930s: Hoover raised taxes, and so did Roosevelt, even if the burden fell largely on the wealthy and the middle class. But in the postwar era, tax cuts and credits have become an integral part of fiscal policy in times of recession and crisis. Japan, for example, used tax cuts as part of its postcrisis response.

A third variant on fiscal policy is a "transfer payment," whereby the government sends money to particular cash-strapped groups (the poor, the unemployed) or to struggling state and local governments. Transfer payments have been a mainstay of fiscal policy since the 1930s, when many New Deal programs threw lifelines to these groups. Like tax cuts, they are part of the standard arsenal for dealing with economic crises and garden-variety recessions. Transfer payments can come in myriad forms, such as unemployment benefits, food stamps, and funds for job retraining.

The recent crisis saw a heavy reliance on all three conventional fiscal strategies. In January 2008 lawmakers fired the first of several shots by approving a $152 billion package of tax breaks aimed at individuals and businesses. The Economic Stimulus Act of 2008 was overshadowed by the American Recovery and Reinvestment Act of 2009. The total cost—a whopping $787 billion—aimed at every single target of fiscal policy. Government spending on goods and services got plenty, and straight-up spending on infrastructure and energy projects topped $140 billion; a miscellany of other spending projects—everything from fisheries to flood control systems—got billions more.

The legislation also dedicated plenty of money for tax credits and transfer payments. Indeed, tax credits took the lion's share of the package, as individuals received breaks worth some $237 billion. Some applied across the board to broad swaths of the population; others, like the tax credit for first-time homeowners and the one for the purchase of new fuel-efficient cars (cash for clunkers), targeted specific segments of the economy. Finally, the bill directed billions to the unemployed, the elderly, and other vulnerable populations. It also steered billions more to state and local governments.

Countries around the world adopted comparable, if less ambitious, fiscal stimulus packages. The European Economic Recovery Plan, adopted in the fall of 2008, earmarked some 200 billion euros to a variety of projects; individual countries followed with their own smaller plans. Japan initially planned a massive stimulus package, but it ran afoul of politics, and the government ultimately instituted a much more modest mix of tax cuts and spending measures. China's far more ambitious plan totaled $586 billion, the bulk of which went to public works: rail lines, roads, irrigation, and airports; some of the funds went to the earthquake-stricken region of Sichuan. Smaller countries as diverse as South Korea and Australia also adopted stimulus measures.

These fiscal interventions certainly helped arrest the slide toward depression, but a few words of caution are in order. For starters, fiscal policy isn't a free lunch: if a government increases spending and cuts taxes—and does so during a recession, when tax revenues decline—the budget deficit will soar. The government will have to issue more debt, which it will eventually have to pay. If it doesn't pay the debt, and its deficits grow larger every year, then it will have to entice investors to buy more debt by raising interest rates. Those higher returns will then compete with interest rates on other investments—mortgages, consumer credit, corporate bonds, and auto loans—and can drive up the cost of borrowing for everyone else, thus reducing debt-financed capital spending by firms and consumption spending by households.

Soaring public debt ultimately ties the hands of the government. Interest rates may go too high as fears of a possible default intensify. At that point, the government has limited options. It can opt to "cheat" and print money to pay the deficit, as long as the public debt is issued in local currency, a tactic known as "monetizing" the deficit. The mechanism is the same as quantitative easing, except that buying up debt has nothing to do with defeating deflation; it's about making debt disappear. As money chases goods and pushes their prices higher, inflation is the inevitable result. That means even higher interest rates all around, and even more private spending diverted into propping up the public sector.

There's some evidence that taxpayers may be mindful of the risks as well. In some countries that have implemented stimulus packages, consumers recognized that whatever the short-term benefits of such measures, the government would ultimately have to raise taxes. Knowing they had to save for that eventuality, consumers cut back on their spending in tandem with the introduction of a fiscal stimulus. They effectively anticipated the long-term costs of short-term spending and, in the process, nullified some of its benefits.

Tax cuts, the other main tool of fiscal policy, can also run into obstacles. Rather than going out and spending the money derived from tax rebates or permanent reductions in tax rates, households may save it or use it to pay off their debts. That's what happened in 2008 and 2009, when two rounds of income tax rebates largely went unspent—consumers parted with only 25 or 30 cents on every dollar they received from the government. The rest they plowed into improving household balance sheets. While that was all well and good, such prudence did nothing to prop up demand. It also shifted debt from one part of the economy to another: private debt went down, but public debt went up. This was less a stimulus than a sleight of hand.

Worse, certain kinds of fiscal measures can spur demand in the present at the cost of demand in the future. Many targeted tax cuts or subsidies that aim at enhancing specific forms of spending—automobiles, homes, capital improvements by the corporate sector—do nothing more than amplify demand beyond what's normal, then undercut it when the subsidies expire. In other words, they steal demand from the future. This seems to have happened with the various cash for clunkers programs adopted in many countries: car sales went through the roof, then fell back to earth, depressing future demand.

The idea of a flawless fiscal stimulus is a mirage, at least in most democracies. Unlike monetary policy, which can be implemented immediately by a central bank insulated from the pressures of voters, fiscal measures take time to initiate and come laden down with useless pork barrel projects, bridges to nowhere, and other inefficient allocations of resources. A perfect stimulus package would deliver a tremendous bang for the buck, rebuilding a nation's dilapidated infrastructure and contributing to future economic growth. But as Japan's experience and some of the more dubious projects funded by the American Recovery and Reinvestment Act suggest, that's easier said than done. It's perhaps instructive that China—an authoritarian state—implemented one of the more effective stimulus packages in the wake of the recent crisis. Mostly free of parochial political considerations, its government simply accelerated its existing, successful campaign to modernize its infrastructure. Even in that case, however, some of the spending may yet turn out to be wasteful and inefficient or may foster future bubbles.

In conventional fiscal policy, the government uses its powers to tax and spend in order to help the economy out of a crisis. But tax cuts and public works are just the beginning; government can deploy its fiscal powers against a financial crisis in many other ways, which are far more subtle, if expensive.

Let the Bailouts Begin

Government can spend money, but it can also *guarantee* other people's money. Because guarantees often end up costing taxpayers money, they qualify as a kind of fiscal policy. A number of guarantees old and new played an important role in quelling the recent crisis, even as they opened the door to the problem of moral hazard.

The most typical guarantee given by a government is that it will protect money that people have deposited in a bank from a run. Although the idea dates back to the nineteenth century, the United States lacked national deposit insurance until 1933. That wasn't for lack of trying: between 1866 and 1933, Congress considered some 150 proposals for deposit insurance. Some of them would have required banks to purchase surety bonds, a kind of third-party insurance; others called for the federal government to guarantee the deposits directly. Still others called for a common insurance fund out of which depositors' claims would be paid.

In the Great Depression, the United States finally adopted deposit insurance that combined features of an insurance fund with a federal guarantee. Conceived and born in the opening weeks of the New Deal, the institution that eventually came to be known as the Federal Deposit Insurance Corporation (FDIC) did not depend on taxpayer dollars; rather it operated by assessing fees on the commercial banks that were its members. Those assessments went into a fund that reimbursed depositors whose banks had failed. The government staffed and administered the FDIC, which also monitored the health of member banks and wound up insolvent institutions or arranged their takeover by better-capitalized banks. A similar institution, the Federal Savings and Loan Insurance Corporation (FSLIC), was founded in 1934 to protect deposits in savings and loans thrifts.

These two institutions operated without mishap until the 1980s, when the failure of more than a thousand savings and loans overwhelmed the FSLIC. Insolvent, it was subsequently taken over by the FDIC and recapitalized with taxpayer money to the tune of $153 billion. As this episode amply illustrates, a systemic crisis in the banking system can easily overwhelm funds set aside to meet the occasional failure. The federal government could have stood aside and let depositors lose their money, but it chose not to, as it had informally guaranteed the integrity of these funds and a bank run could have overwhelmed both solvent and insolvent banks.

But the episode summoned the specter of moral hazard. By bailing out the banks, the government signaled that it would likely rescue them again should the need arise. Bank managers didn't have to worry about angry depositors, and depositors didn't have to worry about losing their money: as long as a bank was insured by the FDIC, their money was safe. The FDIC effectively said as much, announcing that deposits under its protection were "backed by the full faith and credit of the United States Government."

That guarantee became an issue once again in 2008–9. Prior to the crisis, the FDIC insured deposits up to $100,000. Similar guarantees existed in other countries as well, though the "ceiling" varied from place to place. Unfortunately, the programs could not cover all deposits: many people's accounts exceeded the maximum. In the United States alone, upwards of 40 percent of the deposits remained uninsured and vulnerable, a point underscored by bank runs on Countrywide, IndyMac, and Washington Mutual.

The threat of more runs triggered a new round of government guarantees. In September 2008, Ireland had to increase its deposit insurance to

100,000 euros, then fully guarantee all the deposits of its six largest banks. In the United States, holding the line against moral hazard proved equally difficult. Shortly after Ireland issued its blanket assurance, the FDIC raised the ceiling for insured bank deposits to $250,000. Two days later Germany guaranteed all of its private bank accounts; the next day Sweden extended insurance to all deposits to the sum of 500,000 kronas, or approximately $75,000; the day after, the United Kingdom raised its ceiling to £50,000. A week later Italy announced that none of its banks would be allowed to fail and that no depositor would suffer any loss. The next month Switzerland increased its own ceiling on deposit insurance. Other countries followed with similar guarantees.

This dynamic was comparable to an arms race: Ireland announcing a blanket guarantee forced other countries to do the same or at least raise the ceiling. The reason was simple: depositors could readily shift their money out of countries with limited guarantees and place it in safer havens. As a result, governments could not hold the line against moral hazard. It was a race to the bottom.

Other kinds of deposits came under the umbrella of government insurance programs. In the United States, the National Credit Union Administration (NCUA), a kind of FDIC for credit unions, took over two beleaguered members—U.S. Central and WesCorp—and then pledged $80 billion to cover the losses on all deposits in all credit unions throughout the country.

Insuring depositors was just the beginning. Many banks in the United States and Europe borrowed massive amounts of money by issuing unsecured bonded debt. As this debt came to maturity at the height of the financial crisis, it became next to impossible to roll over, particularly after the collapse of Lehman Brothers. But since the inability to renew these debts would have destroyed banks as effectively as a run on their deposits, the European Union guaranteed its banks' bonded debt in October 2008. The same month the FDIC guaranteed the principal and the interest payments on debt issued by banks and bank holding companies up to a total of $1.5 trillion.

All of these guarantees came with a price tag. In the third quarter of 2009, the funds set aside by the FDIC dipped into negative territory. Almost inevitably taxpayers will be asked to shoulder the burden in the form of a bailout, much as they did in the wake of the savings and loan crisis. While that kind of support has plenty of precedent, a host of other measures sparked by the recent crisis also pledged unprecedented amounts of taxpayer dollars.

These outsize bailouts began with Fannie Mae and Freddie Mac. As the two mortgage giants came under government conservatorship, the Treasury Department pledged $400 billion to underwrite the takeover, though more may become necessary. In taking this fateful step, the federal government made explicit that the debt of these two enterprises was indeed guaranteed by its "full faith and credit."

Not for years will we know the full fiscal cost of the rescue of Fannie Mae and Freddie Mac. In moving them into conservatorship, the government has put itself on the line to cover some $5 trillion worth of obligations insured by the two institutions, along with another $1.5 trillion worth of debt that they issued. Obviously, the government won't be on the hook for anything approaching these sums. But if housing prices continue to decline and many more mortgages go into foreclosure, the government could end up sustaining considerable losses.

The same could be said of its efforts to prop up the housing market. The Housing and Economic Recovery Act, passed in July 2008, pledged some $320 billion to help struggling homeowners refinance into mortgages that were insured by the Federal Housing Administration. Though the initial program associated with this allocation failed, President Barack Obama tapped some of these funds when he announced his own $75 billion plan to prevent foreclosures. Needless to say, all these programs are works in progress, though one thing is certain: they will cost the taxpayers billions of dollars.

The biggest bailout of all is really a cluster of separate bailouts and guarantees funded by the Troubled Asset Relief Program (TARP). The original legislation in Congress allocated $700 billion to purchase toxic assets. Instead, the money has been used to prop up a host of alms-seekers, including the automakers General Motors and Chrysler and their financial arms, GMAC and Chrysler Financial. All told, these bailouts of the auto industry amounted to $80 billion. Some of this money was disbursed as loans; the rest of it was used by the government to purchase an ownership stake in the companies.

Unfortunately, car companies were but the beginning. A sizable portion of the TARP funds—some $340 billion—was funneled to nearly seven hundred different financial institutions, giants like Citigroup, Bank of America, and AIG as well as a host of smaller banks. For the most part, the money spent on these ailing institutions consisted of mysterious "capital injections," in which the government purchased preferred shares in a bank. These shares provided a potential ownership stake and a current steady dividend payment. This may seem like a straightforward expenditure of government money, but it marks a radical departure and takes fiscal policy in new and potentially disruptive directions.

A Capital Idea?

Banking is a business shrouded in mystery. Few people really understand how banks and other financial institutions work, largely because they don't understand how a bank's balance sheet works. So while some attempts to shore up the banking system are readily comprehensible—insuring deposits or enabling banks to access a lender of last resort—other measures like capital injections remain puzzling. To understand them, it's necessary to understand how a bank works.

Let's begin with a hypothetical bank's balance sheet. On the right side you have liabilities, and on the left you have assets. What are a bank's liabilities? Put very crudely, a bank accumulates liabilities when it takes money in order to do business. It gets this money in two main ways. The first way is to issue stock, which investors buy and thereby become the bank's shareholders. The bank doesn't "owe" the shareholders that money in return, but it does owe them a share of any profits. That's why the shares are considered liabilities: the shareholders have an equity claim on the bank.

The second way banks accumulate liabilities is by borrowing money, most obviously from people, other banks, and other financial institutions. For example, when you deposit money into a bank, you're loaning it money. Your deposit is a liability for the bank: you may decide you want your money back, and the bank has to give it to you. The same goes for loans that other banks have made to the bank: they're liabilities. The bank is merely borrowing that money. Banks borrow money in other ways too: by issuing bonds, for example. These too are liabilities, or loans to the bank. Most of these loans cost the bank: it pays interest on deposits, for example, and on bonds.

What does the bank do with all the money it has raised from shareholders and borrowed from lenders? It creates the other side of the balance sheet: its assets. For example, it loans money out to other banks, businesses, and homeowners. These loans are considered assets because they are investments that will, over the long run, give the bank a profit. That makes them worth something. The same goes for the other assets the bank accumulates. It may invest in government bonds or other securities, which are worth something. So are the remaining assets of the bank: the cash that's sitting in the vault, the building that houses the bank, and other tangible items. But these odds and ends are just a small portion of the total assets of the bank. They're also inert: they're not making the bank much money.

That, in brief, is how banks work. They raise money by issuing equity shares and borrowing money from a range of lenders. Having accumulated these liabilities, the bank then loans the money, accumulating assets. It's able to make a profit from moving all this money around because the rate at which it borrows is lower than the rate it charges when it lends. If all this sounds simple and straightforward, that's because it isn't rocket science, no matter what bankers might want you to think.

Now comes the important part. How much is the bank worth? That's pretty simple: it's the difference between the value of the assets and the value of the debt liabilities. Put differently, it's the amount by which a bank's assets exceed its debt liabilities. In banking parlance, that difference is the "net worth" of the bank. It's also known as its "capital" or equity. This capital belongs to someone: the bank's owners, or shareholders, who have a residual claim on the bank's assets. This is only right: the bank owes its existence in no small part to these shareholders, who put up money when the bank was first formed, or bought into the bank's equity when it issued additional shares. They get a share of whatever profits the bank makes—in the form of dividends—and they benefit when the bank's shares go up in value.

Now let's look at how banks can get into trouble in a financial crisis. So far we've focused on how things go awry with the liability side of the balance sheet, when a bank can no longer borrow money, or when the money it borrows is available only at exorbitant rates. That can happen if depositors panic and pull out their money, or if other banks refuse to renew loans, or if no one wants to buy the bank's bonds. During the recent crisis, the Fed found many ingenious ways to allow banks to borrow money, while simultaneously assuring anyone who lent to the banks that he would not lose his money. The government backstopped most components of the liability side of the balance sheet: it replenished equity claims with capital injections; it more widely guaranteed the deposit liabilities and fully guaranteed the unsecured debt of banks.

But what about the other side of the balance sheet, the assets? The Fed can do everything within its power to make it easy for the banks to borrow money, but if the bank's assets are worth less with every passing day, then the bank's capital or net worth declines too. When a bank's liabilities outstrip its assets, the bank's net worth sinks to zero. It is insolvent, or bankrupt.

As the recent financial crisis worsened, many of the assets that banks had on their balance sheets did start to lose their value. Some of those assets were loans that went bad; others consisted of the securities derived from mortgages and other loans. As homeowners defaulted on their mortgages and these losses rippled throughout the financial food chain, the value of everything from loans to local real estate developers to collateralized debt obligations started to fall. And as the value of these assets fell, the remaining capital withered away.

Banks in the United States and Europe therefore needed to raise more money, or capital. First they went hat in hand to government-owned sovereign wealth funds, which purchased newly issued "preferred shares." Their name notwithstanding, these shares did not give the investors any voting rights; they merely gave them a certain share in the banks' current and future profits. Money flowed into the banks' coffers and temporarily restored them to some measure of health. But asset values continued to decline, so banks raised more capital from private equity firms by issuing shares to them too. It wasn't enough. In the fall of 2008 the value of bank assets continued to fall, and no one was interested in pumping any more capital into banks.

At this point, policy makers had a number of options. They could have let the banks (and other nonbank financial institutions, such as bank holding companies and broker dealers) fail. Thereafter they would have been restructured in or out of court or through the FDIC receivership process. Typically, when that happens, some of a bank's unsecured creditors—its bondholders, for example—will agree to convert some of the money that the bank owes them into shares, or equity in the bank. These "debt-for-equity swaps" are not exactly a bargain for anyone the bank owes money, but they're better than nothing: those who have lent it money get a stake in it once it resumes operations. And it will be able to resume, because as its creditors forgive part of its debt, its liabilities decline relative to its assets. Voilà! Now the bank has some capital and can resume lending.

This approach is the equivalent of letting the markets sort things out. Bad banks fail, are restructured, and are reborn. The same result can be achieved by having the federal government unilaterally declare certain banks insolvent and then take them over, placing them in the custody of government-appointed trustees who sell off the good assets, dispose of the bad ones, and relaunch the bank. This was the "nationalization" option that Sweden used in its own banking crisis in the early 1990s, and the United States effectively used when it took over Continental Illinois, a big bank that fell in advance of the savings and loan crisis.

But in the recent crisis neither of these approaches got a serious hearing, and after the failure of Lehman Brothers, the notion of making bondholders shoulder any losses lost its appeal. Instead, the Treasury opted to use some of the $700 billion acquired under the TARP legislation to buy stakes in banks and thereby "inject" capital into them. The biggest beneficiaries included behemoths like Bank of America, Citigroup, JPMorgan Chase, Goldman Sachs, and AIG, all of which were given tens of billions of dollars. Hundreds of other, smaller banks lined up for government aid as well. In the process, the government—and by extension, the American taxpayers—became effective owners of huge swaths of the financial system.

It amounted to creeping, partial nationalization of the financial system. As with all the other bailouts, its long-term cost is next to impossible to calculate. Most of the biggest banks have already paid back the TARP funds at this writing, and the government has divested itself of those institutions. Others—including many of the smaller, regional banks—remain dependent on TARP and may never return the money, inflicting significant fiscal costs on future taxpayers.

For the banks that have yet to return the money, the core problem remains the same: troubled assets continue to lose value, casting a pall over their financial future. The government could keep enlarging its equity stake in the banks, but absent some fundamental change in the banks' asset base, that could turn out to be throwing good money after bad.

Toxic Waste

The question of what to do with the banks' bad assets has loomed over the crisis from the beginning. As long as loans continued to sour, and as long as securities derived from those loans continued to lose value, the banks would be unable or unwilling to lend. Rather than letting the banks continue to struggle with these toxic assets, policy makers floated a variety of proposals, all of which had the aim of extracting the assets and disposing of them, leaving the banks free to resume their business.

The most promising proposal called for banks to undergo radical surgery. This would entail taking a troubled bank and splitting it into two banks: a "good" bank that included all the solid assets, and a "bad" bank that contained everything else. The good bank could then go on to make loans, attract money and capital, and resume business. In exchange for ridding it of the toxic waste, the bank's shareholders and unsecured creditors would take a loss proportionate to the assets spun off into the bad bank. In turn, the bad bank would be run by private investors who hoped to profit from the orderly liquidation of its assets.

A version of this scenario was implemented in 1988, when the venerable Mellon Bank got itself into trouble after a host of its real estate and industrial loans went bad. Using financing from an investment bank, Mellon extracted its dubious assets and deposited them into something called the Grant Street National Bank. Private investors with an appetite for risk capitalized the new institution, whose employees then went to work collecting on the remaining bad loans, liquidating the assets, and maximizing the return on these bum investments. Unburdened of its bad assets, the newly reborn Mellon was back on its feet in short order; it attracted capital and began to make loans once again. Grant Street National Bank completed its work in 1995 and then shut its doors.

That's arguably the most effective way to deal with the problem. Another, less preferable option would have been for the government to buy the banks' toxic assets as in the original TARP plan. The price it paid would be set by a "reverse auction," in which the sellers would "bid" by posting the lowest possible price they would accept in exchange for ridding themselves of a specific asset. This is a bit like government contractors' bidding on completing a particular project: in theory, the competitive dynamic among bidders helps drive prices downward.

It's an interesting idea, but it's debatable whether this system would really price the assets fairly. The banks participating in the auction would have every reason to resist seeing prices plummet too far. They might even cooperate or collude with one another to make sure that this didn't happen. Moreover, many of these assets—particularly structured financial products—are rather unique, held by only a handful of banks. That seriously undercuts the reverse auction's pricing power. For all these reasons, the government would likely end up overpaying for these assets and taking a significant loss on its investment. It might end up being the functional equivalent of a bank bailout, subsidizing the bad investment decisions of the banks with taxpayer money.

Still another option would be for the government to form a kind of insurance partnership with the ailing banks. Let's say a bank has toxic assets originally worth some $50 billion. In effect, the bank would agree to pay a deductible—for example, it would take the first $3 billion in losses—and the government would cover most of any additional losses on the remaining $47 billion. In exchange for getting a guarantee that it would take a hit "up front" of only $3 billion, the bank would pay the government an insurance premium. Alternatively, the government could receive an equity stake in the bank equivalent to any losses above and beyond that first $3 billion.

A version of this approach has been widely adopted in the United Kingdom, and the U.S. government guaranteed several hundred billion dollars' worth of impaired assets held by Bank of America and Citigroup. Here's how it works in practice. In Bank of America's case, the pool of troubled assets totaled $118 billion, with a "deductible" of $10 billion. After taking that first hit, Bank of America was off the hook, though it had to pay "coinsurance" covering 10 percent of any additional losses; the government would cover the remaining 90 percent. In return, the government received a hefty amount of stock, giving it a significant equity stake in the bank.

While preferable to a reverse auction, this approach still runs the risk of making the government subsidize the losses incurred by private banks. In the Bank of America case, the government has assumed that it won't have to "insure" much of the losses above and beyond what Bank of America is going to pay. But if the cost of insuring those losses outstrips whatever revenue the government gains from entering into the deal, the end result will be the same as having the government overpay for some dud assets: the government will lose money on the deal and subsidize the bad decisions of private bankers. Taxpayers will foot the bill.

For now, the problem of dealing with bad assets seems to lie with another approach. The basic idea is to have the government subsidize the private investors who agree to purchase the toxic assets and thus remove them from troubled banks. This is the idea behind the Public-Private Investment Program (PPIP, better known as "Pee-Pip"), which went into operation in 2009. It's arguably one of the weakest ideas of the bunch. The trillion-dollar program gives low-interest loans to private investors who want to bid at auctions in which banks sell their toxic assets. The government sweetened the deal even more by offering to inject capital into institutions that take part in this process.

Unfortunately, these low-interest government loans are nonrecourse loans, meaning that in the event that things go badly, investors can walk away from them without penalty. In practice investors have every incentive to overbid; after all, the government is subsidizing the purchase of the assets. The government is also the one stuck with the asset if it turns out to be a bum investment. In effect, the private sector gets all the glory and the profits when things go well, while the government—or more accurately, the taxpayer—shoulders the fiscal burden when things go awry.

So far PPIP hasn't attracted many investors, largely because the government has effectively subsidized the banks in another way: by sanctioning the removal of regulations that would have forced them to value their toxic assets at something approaching real-world market value. Thanks to this intervention, banks have been able to pretend that their crappy assets are worth far more than any sane assessment would suggest. It's like putting lipstick on a pig, but as long as the assets can be overvalued for accounting purposes, banks have little interest in unloading them.

None of these approaches are perfect, but some are better than others, particularly the idea of splitting off dud assets into a "bad bank." This approach minimizes the cost to the government by leaving the problem in private hands. It also holds the line on moral hazard and gives reborn banks every incentive to lend again. But it requires that investors take a loss, with the pain felt now rather than later. At the present time, there's an unwillingness on the part of policy makers and politicians to deal with things up front. That's unfortunate: kicking the can down the road runs the risk of letting banks slowly sink into a financial coma, becoming zombies dependent on public credit.

In retrospect, that dependency reached astonishing levels. In the course of the crisis, governments threw lifeline after lifeline. They injected capital into banks and other financial firms and broadened the scope of deposit insurance. They even insured the debt of banks, preventing market forces from wreaking havoc on their creditors. These measures went hand in hand with central banks' stunning offer to buy up banks' illiquid assets for cash, or alternatively, to exchange them for safe government bonds. In the United States, the government went so far as to guarantee the toxic assets of some financial institutions and eventually implemented programs to directly or indirectly purchase those assets. All this amounted to a staggering, unprecedented intervention in the financial system. Unfortunately, for all the obstacles that policy makers encountered, rescuing the financial system may prove easier than fostering a genuine recovery.

The Aftermath

In the early 1930s a financial crisis spawned a relentless cycle of deflation and depression. Thousands of banks in the United States went under; three quarters of households with mortgages defaulted; unemployment soared. The help that arrived with FDR's New Deal was belated, and the economy stagnated. Many other countries followed a similar trajectory, limping through the rest of the 1930s until war ushered in recovery for some and destruction for others.

This time around, instead of letting things spiral out of control, the U.S. government unleashed a shock-and-awe campaign against the crisis. The directors of this campaign had cut their teeth studying the Great Depression, and the failures of their predecessors shaped their aggressive response. They threw everything they had at the problem, borrowing ideas from the past as well as tactics that had never seen the light of day.

They began with conventional monetary and fiscal policy, tossing all the usual weapons into the fight, from tax cuts to interest rate cuts. When those didn't work and deflation and depression became real possibilities, the Fed embraced its historic role as a lender of last resort, throwing lifelines of liquidity to one kind of financial institution after another, as well as to ordinary corporations that needed to roll over their commercial paper obligations. Other central banks followed suit, interpreting their statutory powers in expansive, even radical ways.

The scale of the rescue effort was without precedent. It transcended national boundaries, as the IMF stepped into the fray, and the Fed lent to other central banks, directing much-needed dollars to struggling banks and corporations around the world. It was the biggest financial rescue effort of modern times, if not all times.

And it was only the beginning. The government became a shareholder in a host of businesses, buying shares and injecting capital in exchange for an equity stake. The government also guaranteed deposits, money market funds, and even the bondholders of banks. As if that weren't enough, in several high-profile cases it covered prospective losses to investors, then instituted outright bailouts of individual banks, homeowners, and others. It even offered to subsidize the purchase of toxic assets, hoping this might restore faith.

Yet even that was not enough. To lend, to guarantee, and to absorb the losses were one thing; to restore faith to the markets was another. The Fed and other central banks eventually became investors of last resort, wading into government debt markets to inject still more liquidity into the system via quantitative easing. In their most radical interventions of all, central banks attempted to provide demand where demand had all but disappeared, purchasing mortgage-backed securities and other structured financial products backed by everything from auto loans to student loans.

Lawmakers in the United States and other countries did their part too, freeing up funds to underwrite these actions, offering help to distressed homeowners, and most important of all, approving trillions of dollars' worth of deficit spending to underwrite the classic strategy of a targeted fiscal stimulus aimed at infrastructure improvements and aid aimed at anyone floundering in the face of the crisis, from local governments to the unemployed.

All these monetary and fiscal measures fell into place over the course of over two years—unevenly, imperfectly, and accompanied by enormous controversy and skepticism. The response to the financial crisis had all the grace and beauty of a battlefield retreat, but in the end it seemed to work: capitalism did not collapse; the fate of particularly hard-hit Iceland was not the fate of the world at large. The measures adopted by central banks, governments, and legislatures effectively brought the crisis to a near end. Some semblance of calm returned to the financial markets, and many nations' economies, while wounded, managed to eke out better-than-expected performances as 2009 came to a close. What had seemed like the end of the world a year earlier now seemed like a very close call.

That's the good news. The bad news is that this stability has been purchased at tremendous cost. Thanks to all the bailouts, guarantees, stimulus plans, and other costs of managing the crisis, the public debt of the United States will effectively double as a share of the nation's gross domestic product, as deficits in the coming decade are expected to hit $9 trillion or more. Economists of a Keynesian bent tend to minimize these risks, pointing out that the United States ran enormous deficits during the New Deal and World War II and managed to pay them off without a problem. The total value of the public debt hit an all-time high in 1946, when it was equivalent to 122 percent of the nation's GDP. By contrast, current projections point to debt reaching 90 percent of the GDP in the near future, though it may certainly go higher.

That's a somewhat comforting comparison, but it's highly misleading. In 1946 the United States was at the peak of its power. Its manufacturing base, unscathed by the war, was the envy of the world, and its future competitors—Japan and Germany—were in ruins. The United States was the world's biggest creditor and net lender by running current account surpluses, and the dollar had just become the global reserve currency. Little wonder it was able to pay down its debt with ease. Whether the same can happen today is another question. Much of the country's manufacturing base is weak, and the United States has become the world's biggest debtor and net borrower as it runs large current account deficits, thanks in no small part to loans made by China, its apparent rival in the twenty-first century. The United States of today is not the country of 1946, and it's naïve to believe that it will be able to escape the shadow of the crisis by deficit spending alone.

The fiscal burden of the response is but the beginning of our problems. At many critical junctures in the crisis, governments opted for forbearance and bailouts over a more aggressive resolution of the problem. The United States did not nationalize problem banks; it gave them easy money, covered their losses, and otherwise kept them alive. Many of these banks were and remain insolvent, but the rescue efforts did not differentiate between the good and the bad. Stabilizing the financial system was the order of the day.

The same can be said of all the bailouts aimed at homeowners, automakers, and other beneficiaries of the government's largesse. So far the recent crisis has produced precious little of the creative destruction that Schumpeter saw as essential for capitalism's long-term health. Preventing this necessary adjustment via tax cuts, cash-for-clunkers incentives, and programs designed to prop up the housing market will only delay an inevitable reckoning. That's not to suggest that the middle of the financial crisis would have been the best time to stage that shakeout; doing so would only have fueled the crisis. But it will have to take place. Debt will have to be forgiven, banks will have to go under, automakers will have to shutter factories, and homeowners will have to leave homes they can no longer afford.

In a way, our response to the recent crisis has only been partly different from that of Herbert Hoover. True, we have been infinitely more effective in preventing the crisis from spinning out of control via aggressive fiscal stimulus, but we are still trying to reconcile the irreconcilable. We cannot have our cake and eat it too; we cannot rescue everyone who made bad decisions in advance of the crisis while simultaneously restoring our capitalist economy to its former vitality. That's an unpleasant truth, but one that has so far been avoided in the rush to save anyone and everyone from the effects of the crisis.

Nor will this indiscriminate approach solve the growing problem of moral hazard. In the past few decades, central bankers have moved aggressively to contain potential crises. Alan Greenspan led the way, intervening in markets after the crash of 1987, the savings and loan crisis, and September 11. The recent crisis occasionally tested this belief in the Greenspan (or Bernanke) "put"—most notably with the decision to let Lehman Brothers fail—but for the most part, faith in the omnipotence of central banks and governments was upheld. If anything, it seemed that there was nothing that governments wouldn't do to save the financial system.

That said, the cloud has a few silver linings. For example, many of the countries that sustained heavy hits to their balance sheets while managing the crisis began with relatively low levels of debt by historical standards, giving them some leeway to "break the bank" in allocating funds to combat the crisis. Moreover, had they not committed those funds—particularly the various stimulus packages enacted around the world— the long-term cost would arguably have been greater, thanks to a collapse in tax revenues and a need to cover huge portions of the population with unemployment benefits and other aid. While recent fiscal policies may weigh many countries down in the coming years, debt burdens are not yet at a breaking point for many of the advanced industrial nations, even if issues of public debt sustainability and risks of refinancing crises—if not outright default—are becoming sources of serious concerns for financial markets.

The larger problem of bailouts and moral hazard is a bit more complicated. Bailouts of reckless lenders and borrowers can easily lead to even more reckless behavior in the future. That in turn can lead to more bubbles and more crises. But it's important to keep things in perspective: holding the line on moral hazard in the midst of a crisis can inflict tremendous collateral damage. Why? Imagine that someone living in a huge apartment building has done something extraordinarily reckless and stupid, like smoking in bed. His apartment catches fire. Should he be bailed out? In other words, should the fire department come to rescue him? If the fire department doesn't, the entire building may go up in flames, taking the lives not only of the person who started the blaze but of hundreds of innocent people.

That's basically the predicament faced by central banks and governments in the midst of this crisis. Does some investment bank or insurance company that set fire to the global economy deserve to go under? Absolutely. But if the resulting conflagration devours the entire financial system, never mind destroys the lives of ordinary workers around the world, the lesson tends to be lost in the ensuing mayhem. While some fiscal actions were wasteful and some bailouts not warranted, the fiscal stimulus and the backstopping of the financial system prevented the Great Recession from turning into another Great Depression at a time when private demand was in free fall.

The time to address issues of moral hazard, and all the other weaknesses of the financial system, comes after the immediate crisis has passed. A financial crisis is a terrible thing to waste: it opens, however fleetingly, the possibility of real, enduring reforms of the global financial system. Just as the Great Depression swept away the contradictions embodied by Hoover and replaced them with the consistencies of Keynes, the Great Recession promises to usher in a new way of understanding and, above all, preventing crises. It is to that pressing matter that we turn next.

Chapter 8

First Steps

It's a truism that crises go hand in hand with regulation and reform of the financial system. The near-death experience of a financial crisis pushes many people to contemplate what government can and should do to prevent another disaster. As Harvard economist Jeffrey Frankel wryly observed at the onset of the recent crisis: "They say there are no atheists in foxholes. Perhaps, then, there are also no libertarians in [financial] crises."

Like so much else in crisis economics, this theme is recurrent. In 1826, the year after a speculative bubble collapsed in Britain, leaving behind scores of broken banks, Parliament passed legislation that overhauled the entire banking system. In the United States, the panic of 1907 left many lawmakers concerned about the nation's lack of a central bank, and prompted the formation of the Federal Reserve a few years later.

The mother of all financial crises—the chain of disasters known as the Great Depression—sparked radical reforms of financial systems internationally. In the United States, the Glass-Steagall Act of 1933 created federal deposit insurance and established a firewall between commercial and investment banking; subsequent legislation gave the Federal Reserve the power to regulate bank reserves. The government brought the stock market to heel as well: the Securities Act of 1933 required issuers of securities to register them and to publish a prospectus, and it made the investment banks that underwrote the sale criminally liable for any errors or misleading statements in the prospectus. The following year saw the creation of the Securities and Exchange Commission, which remains the agency charged with regulating the buying and selling of securities. Though many other countries adopted similar measures, the United States implemented one of the most comprehensive series of reforms.

In light of this history, we might reasonably expect the United States once again to take the lead in reforming the financial system. The financial turmoil revealed fundamental weaknesses in the operation of U.S. and European financial markets and serious flaws in the existing system of supervision and regulation. But over the course of 2010, the urgent calls for reform faded, and legislation that would radically overhaul regulation and supervision had yet to see the light of day. Just like soldiers in foxholes abandoning their pledges to lead a better life as soon as the firing stops, lawmakers and policy makers now seem happy with the status quo.

There's a perverse irony in all of this. Had policy makers failed to arrest the crisis, as they failed during the Depression, the calls for reform today would be deafening: there's nothing like ubiquitous breadlines and 25 percent unemployment to focus the minds of legislators. But because the disaster was handled more deftly this time, the impetus for deep, structural reforms of the financial system has faltered. Instead, the surviving banks are paying out record bonuses, despite the fact that they owe their lives to government largesse.

This absence of reform is profoundly unfortunate. We live at a dangerous time, when the structural problems that created the crisis remain, even as aftershocks continue to rattle countries and economies around the world. Massive intervention in the financial system has restored some confidence in the financial system, but we have yet to undertake the necessary reforms to preserve that confidence and prevent a crisis from recurring.

What reforms make the most sense? Many proposals are now lying on the table, from institutions at home and around the world: from the U.S. Treasury and the Federal Reserve; but also from the Financial Stability Board, the Financial Services Authority, and other policy bodies in the United Kingdom; and from the G-7, the Bank for International Settlements, and the IMF. Innumerable further proposals have emanated from think tanks, policy workshops, and academia.

Rather than assessing the merits of each proposal, it makes more sense to pinpoint the fundamental weaknesses and distortions that plague the world's financial systems, then pose some pragmatic solutions. We stress the word *fundamental*. There is plenty wrong with the financial system, but not all its problems are essential; many are merely superficial manifestations of a deeper rot.

Unfortunately, fundamental is not always synonymous with simple. Some of the subjects that follow—derivatives, capital requirements—may seem rather recondite. That's true, but getting to the bottom of this mess requires that we deal with such daunting concepts. As the crisis has amply shown, the devil lies in these details, and the discussion that follows should give the reader a genuine appreciation—as well as a clear comprehension—of the complex but core issues that need to be addressed to prevent future crises.

Curing Compensation

Whenever the question of compensation on Wall Street comes up, visceral anger toward the bankers tends to overwhelm more careful considerations of the underlying problem. Put differently, while torches and pitchforks may seem appropriate under the circumstances, it's wiser to step back and dispassionately evaluate the options.

First, contrary to conventional wisdom, the biggest problem with compensation is not the amount of money involved; it's the way this compensation is structured and delivered. Much research on corporate governance suggests that any corporate environment is apt to suffer from the principal-agent problem, which we discussed in chapter 3. That is, modern corporations are run not by the shareholders (the principals) but by managers (the agents). These two groups don't see eye to eye: the shareholders want to maximize their long-run returns from ownership of the company, but the managers want to maximize their short-term income, bonuses, and other forms of compensation.

As we have seen, if shareholders could monitor managers, all would be well. But it's difficult in any corporation and next to impossible in the financial institutions at the heart of the recent crisis. Why? Simply put, traders and bankers know much more about what's going on than the shareholders to whom they answer. All traders have their own profit-and-loss budget, and their own strategies for making money in the market. It's difficult for outside shareholders or a board of directors to know what's going on in one of these little cells; it's utterly impossible to know what's going on in several thousand of them, as in a large bank or financial firm. This predicament is known in corporate governance circles as the "asymmetric information problem," also discussed in chapter 3. Translation: one side knows more than the other.

Add to this problem what could be called "double agency conflict." In many financial firms, the shareholders (the principals) are themselves enmeshed in a principal-agent problem: they own shares via large institutional investors, such as pension funds. The managers of these funds are their agents, and just as it's hard for shareholders to monitor what traders are doing, it's equally difficult for shareholders to monitor the actions of their proxies. Worse, these institutional investors, not the ultimate shareholders, are often the ones who end up sitting on a firm's board of directors.

If this seems like a hall of mirrors, that's not far from the truth. The entire financial system was—and remains—riddled with these kinds of problems, in which one group delegates responsibility to another, which in turn delegates it to another group. Little wonder that no one knew—or cared—what was going on at all the trading desks.

Here's the upshot: absent any direct or indirect oversight from shareholders, traders and bankers have every incentive to do crazy things that maximize their short-term profits and bonuses (like rustling up a bunch of toxic CDOs and leaving them hanging on the bank's balance sheet). By the time the bank blows up, the traders and bankers have already spent the money on fast cars and that summer place in the Hamptons. And if recent history is any guide, it's easier to get money back from Bernie Madoff than it is to claw back a trader's bonus.

In an ideal world, shareholders and their representatives would be aware of this problem and create a system of compensation that's "incentive compatible," one that stops traders from taking on too much leverage and risk. In theory, this system would align their interests with those of the existing shareholders and make everyone work for the long-term interest of the bank. One incentive-compatible solution would be for firms to compensate the traders who work for them with restricted shares in the firm. (Restricted shares have to be held a certain amount of time before they vest.) That way, everyone would have the long-term health of the firm in mind.

If only it were so simple. In fact, at both Bear Stearns and Lehman Brothers, employees held upwards of 30 percent of the firm's shares. Yet both firms pursued suicidal trading strategies that led to their eventual destruction. This fact raises the unsettling possibility that the problem goes beyond a bunch of rogue traders subverting the will of shareholders. In fact, it points to a grim reality: there are times when the interests of shareholders and traders align to destructive effect.

Sometimes shareholders are more than happy to see traders take on leverage and risk. They're willing to let them do so because they don't actually have much skin in the game. They've put up some of the bank's capital, but not a whole lot of it, and while they don't want to lose their shirts, they're fine turning a blind eye when traders roll the dice. In fact, most of the money that the traders are playing with is borrowed; it belongs to someone else. If the traders win at the roulette table, the shareholders win too. If the traders lose, the burden falls on the fools who loaned the bank money—and, if the recent crisis is any indication, the government. Shareholders take only a minor hit.

This principle is true in good times and bad. When a boom is under way, banks are under pressure to deliver supercharged returns so as to maintain the loyalty of the pension funds, endowment managers, and others who give them money to invest. Even if managers and shareholders both think the trading strategies are risky, they know that if they don't pursue them, their investors will walk to other banks that promise higher returns. Former Citigroup CEO Chuck Prince summarized it best in 2007 when he observed, "As long as the music is playing, you've got to get up and dance."

When things go south, traders and shareholders don't necessarily retreat from risk. Instead, they may share a willingness to double down and bet the farm in the hopes of righting the sinking ship. In banking parlance, this strategy is known as "gambling for redemption," and while it's sometimes successful, it does nothing to curtail the culture of risk taking. This sort of behavior is fueled even further by the presumption that if things blow up, government will ride to the rescue—a belief that, though occasionally tested in the recent crisis, has been affirmed again and again.

At this point, the reader may be forgiven for wanting to put the entire financial system to the torch. On the one hand, if the shareholders of financial firms are virtuous and actually have the long-term interests of the firm at heart, they lack the ability to control the traders. And if they aren't virtuous (because they don't have much skin in the game or are simply seeking oversize returns), they're not going to do anything to stop the traders—which, as the principal-agent problem makes clear, would be impossible anyway. Either way, financial firms are apt to unleash behavior that is ruinous to the stability of the global financial system.

So what to do? This complex problem clearly has no easy solutions. But some very basic, commonsense approaches to dealing with this mess could tackle the problem at its core: the issue of compensation. That is where the problem originates, and it's where the solution should be focused.

For starters, when employees of financial firms are compensated with restricted stock, provisions should be in place that force them to hold these shares for an even longer period of time than is now customary. Currently, many vesting periods are limited to a few years; they should be extended. Employees should be restricted from selling the stock until their retirement, or at the very least, for well over a decade.

That's a good first step, but a small one. The bigger issue is the bonus culture of Wall Street, in which employees are compensated when their bets pay off, but are not penalized when those bets cost the firm money. This system encourages risk taking that generates oversize "alpha" returns in the short term, with little consideration of long-term consequences.

One way to fix this mess would be to create bonus pools that aren't calculated on short-term returns but are based on a longer time horizon—say, three years or so. Instead of rewarding its employees for making their particular canny bets, a firm averages their performance over the course of several years. Let's say a trader's risky bets yield outsize returns one year and equally outsize losses the next. Under the current system, that trader will get a nice bonus the first year and nothing the second. By contrast, under a longer time horizon, the losses would cancel out the profits, and the trader would get nothing at all.

A variant of bonus pooling has been proposed by Raghuram Rajan. In his scheme, traders would be compensated for their high returns, but their bonuses would be held in escrow for several years. Should a trader incur a loss in subsequent years, it would be *subtracted* from the existing bonus account. In this "bonus-malus" system, bonuses can be clawed back and nullified according to the ups and downs of a trader's long-term performance. The longer the bonuses are held in escrow, the more likely the traders will be to think more carefully about assuming risk at the expense of long-term revenue.

The bonus-malus system works best if applied on an individual level. Unfortunately, bonuses are often calculated on an institutional level, so that when bets pay off, everyone shares in the proceeds. Traders and bankers do not directly suffer the consequences of their bad decisions, which are borne by the pool at large. Still, collective clawbacks—the repossession of bonuses across the board—may nonetheless cast a pall of prudence over all those trading desks.

The problem of compensation has a more diabolical solution: to compensate traders and bankers not with money or with stock but with the very same esoteric securities that they're cooking up in their laboratories. Traders and bankers would get bonuses, but in a very specific form: a little slice of, say, that CDO that they had a hand in making. If traders cook up toxic securities, they get paid with the same. The thinking here is that if traders know that the proverbial chickens will come home to roost in their bonus package, they may be a little bit more careful about the eggs they lay.

A version of this plan is already operational. At the close of 2008, Credit Suisse announced that it was shifting some $5 billion worth of toxic assets off its own balance sheet and into a special fund. It then paid bonuses to employees out of this fund, replacing the usual form of compensation (shares of stock in the company) with shares of this fund. This raised some howls of protest; after all, many of those compensated had had nothing to do with the bad bets. Still, however imperfect, this is a good start.

Yet another kind of compensation scheme could draw from all of these proposals. For example, rather than retroactively saddling employees with the consequences of their bad bets (as the Credit Suisse scheme does), make it clear from the beginning that bonuses of bankers and traders will be paid in the securities they have a hand in creating. Better yet, put those securities-cum-bonuses in escrow for several years, letting enough time pass to determine whether they are toxic or not. Finally, forbid employees to hedge against any potential losses on these future bonuses. (They are traders, after all, and if there's one thing they're good at, it's making money regardless of where the market is moving.)

Whatever change in compensation is ultimately adopted should be implemented across the board. If one major financial firm adopts some version of the bonus-malus system but no one else does, employees from the more prudent firm will likely flock to high-rolling firms, where they'll be better compensated.

That means government must be involved. In the United States, only the federal government has the power to reform the compensation system in comprehensive fashion. It has plenty of justification for doing so: the government—or more to the point, the taxpaying public—has effectively bailed out and backstopped the entire financial system and has a cogent interest in making sure it doesn't have to do it again. Moreover, given the tangled web of principal-agent problems, shareholders cannot possibly be expected to reform compensation. But government could set across-the-board changes along the lines above.

Let's be clear: we're not suggesting that government cap compensation, though it would certainly be well within its rights to do so, particularly with banks still on government life support. What we're proposing is in a way more radical: that compensation be completely overhauled to reduce risky behavior, and by extension, the likelihood of another systemic collapse in the global financial system.

Those caveats aside, removing traders' incentives for taking on short-term risk (and creating disincentives, in the form of clawbacks) will probably cause compensation to decline. Is this a bad thing? No. In recent years, the financial services industry—and compensation within it—has undergone exorbitant and utterly unwarranted growth, driven by financial liberalization, financial innovation, elimination of capital controls, and the globalization of finance.

In the process, finance's "contribution"—if that's the word—to the U.S. gross domestic product has soared from 2.5 percent in 1947 to 4.4 percent in 1977 to 7.7 percent in 2005. By that time financial firms accounted for upwards of 40 percent of the earnings of the companies listed in the S&P 500, and these firms' share of the total S&P 500 market capitalization doubled to approximately 25 percent. Even more startling, the combined income of the nation's top twenty-five hedge fund managers exceeded the compensation of the combined income of the CEOs of *all* companies listed in the S&P 500. In 2008 no less than one in every thirteen dollars in compensation in the United States went to people working in finance. By contrast, after World War II a mere one in forty dollars in compensation went to finance workers.

This outsize and excessive growth of the financial system did little to create any "added value" for investors. While many hedge funds, investment banks, private equity funds, and other asset managers claimed that they could provide investors with superior "alpha" returns (in other words, bigger returns than those provided by more traditional asset managers), "schmalpha," not "alpha," became the norm. These high-flying asset managers often got higher returns, but investors saw little of it, because the managers charged higher fees for their allegedly superior services.

The various players in the financial system parted investors from their money in other ways too. Take securitization: at every step of the process, someone—a mortgage broker, an originating bank, a home appraiser, a broker dealer, a bond insurer, a ratings agency—charged high fees for its "services" and transferred the credit risk down the chain. But it was an oligopoly of investment banks that profited the most from this arrangement, exploiting the lack of transparency about these operations to extract profits from credulous investors, most of which ended up in the pockets of these firms' employees rather than those of the shareholders of the firms.

The cancerous growth of finance has arguably had significant social costs too, as innovation and creativity have fled from manufacturing and other old-fashioned industries in favor of Wall Street. Indeed, since the 1970s, as our colleague Thomas Philippon has revealed, finance has attracted an ever-growing number of intelligent, highly educated workers. As compensation soared, graduates of elite schools increasingly went to Wall Street. In fact, among Harvard seniors surveyed in 2007, a whopping 58 percent of the men joining the workforce were bound for jobs in finance or consulting. In a curious paradox, the United States now has too many financial engineers and not enough mechanical or computer engineers.

Not coincidentally, the last time the United States saw comparable growth in the financial sector was in the years leading up to . . . 1929. In the 1930s, compensation in the financial sector plummeted, a victim of regulatory crackdowns that made banking a boring, if more respectable, profession. Reforming today's warped compensation structure is a necessary first step toward making banking boring once more.

Making Better Sausage

Compensation is hardly the only problem that cries out for reform; the elaborate system of securitization that helped cause the recent crisis must be fixed as well. In the originate-and-distribute model of securitization (see chapter 3), a potentially risky asset—a subprime mortgage, for example—was pooled with similar assets and turned into securities that would be sold to investors better able and willing to tolerate the risk.

One obvious flaw with this system was that it reduced incentives for anyone to actually monitor the creditworthiness of the borrower. Instead, the various players in the securitization process pocketed a fee while transferring most, if not all, of the risk to someone else. Everyone was complicit in this chain: the mortgage broker who handled the initial loan; the home appraiser, who had every incentive to give inflated values; the bank that originated the mortgage and used it to make mortgage-backed securities; the investment bank that repackaged these securities into CDOs and far more esoteric investments; and the ratings agencies that bestowed coveted AAA ratings along the way; and the monolines that insured those toxic tranches.

Any solution to the problem of securitization must somehow force these different players to more carefully consider the risks involved. In other words, each player must somehow be encouraged to pay more attention to the quality of the underlying loans. One way to do so is to force intermediaries—the originating bank and the investment banks—to hold on to some of the MBSs or CDOs in question. Forcing them to retain some risk, the thinking goes, will induce them to do a better job of monitoring the creditworthiness of the original borrowers (and leaning on the mortgage brokers and others who serve as the first link in the chain).

A number of proposals in circulation push this idea. Some came out of international bodies, including working groups within the G-20; others are homegrown, such as the Credit Risk Retention Act, which passed in the House of Representatives in December 2009. This legislation proposes that banks involved in creating asset-backed securities (not only mortgages, but any number of loans) be forced to retain 5 percent of the securities they create; a separate proposal in the Senate would increase that figure to 10 percent. Both proposals wisely forbid the banks to hedge or transfer any risk that they incur by retaining these securities.

Unfortunately, these low amounts of retained risk may be insufficient to change behavior. In the recent crisis, many banks and other financial institutions maintained a significant exposure to the various securities that they had a hand in creating. Most of the AAA supersenior tranches of CDOs, for example, were retained rather than sold to investors. At the time of the crisis, in fact, approximately 34 percent of all the assets of major banks in the United States were real-estate-related; the figure for smaller banks was even higher, at roughly 44 percent. The originate-and-distribute model transferred some risk, but it certainly didn't transfer all of it; most financial institutions had plenty of skin in the game. Otherwise, they would not have sustained the losses they did.

Firms retained that risk because traders made money by doing so. For this reason, relying on retained risk or "skin in the game" as the principal method of reforming securitization is questionable. While it's a useful complement—and certainly will focus attention down the line on the risk incurred by holding such assets—it's unlikely to be a cure-all. Traders may gladly comply with requirements to retain risk, particularly if they can find a way of doing so that yields a bigger bonus. But a bigger bonus, as we've emphasized already, is no guarantee of stability.

Forcing firms to retain risk won't do much to resolve an even more pressing problem: the fact that securitization has, despite government subsidies, all but ceased. The reason it remains comatose is that even now, it's not really clear what went into the alphabet soup of securities that fed the boom. Indeed, securitization in the go-go years was a bit like sausage making before the creation of the Food and Drug Administration: no one knew what went into the sausage, much less the quality of the meat. And so it remains today: financial institutions can still churn out the sausage, but given what we know might (or might not) go into these things, is it any surprise that investors have lost their appetites?

Some people believe that securitization should be abolished. That's shortsighted: properly reformed, securitization can be a valuable tool that reduces rather than exacerbates systemic risk. But in order for it to work, it must operate in a far more transparent and standardized fashion than it does now. Absent this shift, accurately pricing these securities, much less reviving the market for securitization, is next to impossible. What we need are reforms that deliver the peace of mind that the FDA did when it was created.

Let's begin with standardization. At the present time, there is little standardization in the way asset-backed securities are put together. The "deal structures" (the fine print) can vary greatly from offering to offering. Monthly reports on deals ("monthly service performance reports") also vary greatly in level of detail provided. This information should be standardized and pooled in one place. It could be done through private channels or, better, under the auspices of the federal government. For example, the SEC could require anyone issuing asset-backed securities to disclose a range of standard information on everything from the assets or original loans to the amounts paid to the individuals or institutions that originated the security.

Precisely how this information is standardized doesn't matter, so long as it is done: we must have some way to compare these different kinds of securities so that they can be accurately priced. At the present time, we are stymied by a serious apples-and-oranges problem: the absence of standardization makes comparing them with any accuracy impossible. Put differently, the current system gives us no way to quantify risk; there's far too much uncertainty.

Standardization, once achieved, would inevitably create more liquid and transparent markets for these securities. That's well and good, but a few caveats also come to mind. First, bringing some transparency to plain-vanilla asset-backed securities is relatively easy; it's more difficult to do so with preposterously complicated securities like CDOs, much less chimerical creations like the CDO^2 and the CDO^3.

Think, for a moment, what goes into a typical CDO^2. Start with a thousand different individual loans, be they commercial mortgages, residential mortgages, auto loans, credit card receivables, small business loans, student loans, or corporate loans. Package them together into an asset-backed security (ABS). Take that ABS and combine it with ninety-nine other ABSs so that you have a hundred of them. That's your CDO. Now take that CDO and combine it with another ninety-nine different CDOs, each of which has its own unique mix of ABSs and underlying assets. Do the math: in theory, the purchaser of this CDO^2 is supposed to somehow get a handle on the health of ten million underlying loans. Is that going to happen? Of course not.

For that reason, securities like CDOs—which now go by the nickname of Chernobyl Death Obligations—must be heavily regulated if not banned. In their present incarnation, they are too estranged from the assets that give them value and are next to impossible to standardize. Thanks in large part to their individual complexity, they don't transfer risk so much as mask it under the cover of esoteric and ultimately misleading risk-management strategies.

In fact, the curious career of CDOs and other toxic securities brings to mind another, less celebrated acronym: GIGO, or "garbage in, garbage out." Or to return to the sausage-making metaphor: if you put rat meat and trichinosis-laced pig parts into your sausage, then combine it with lots of other kinds of sausage (each filled with equally nasty stuff), you haven't solved the problem; you still have some pretty sickening sausage.

The most important angle of securitization reform, then, is the quality of the ingredients. In the end, the problem with securitization is less that the ingredients were sliced and diced beyond recognition than that much of what went into these securities was never very good in the first place. Put differently, the problem with originate-and-distribute lies less with the distribution than with the origination. What matters most is the creditworthiness of the loans issued in the first place.

That's why reform should focus on the circumstances in which loans are originated. It's not as if the regulatory apparatus for doing so isn't in place. In the United States, the Federal Reserve, the FDIC, the Office of Thrift

Supervision, the Office of the Comptroller of the Currency, and the National Credit Union Administration all have jurisdiction to oversee and regulate the sorts of loans that end up in various kinds of asset-backed securities. The existing regulations and guidelines must be beefed up and given real teeth to ensure that what ends up in the securitization pipeline isn't toxic.

The Federal Reserve has already taken steps in that direction, proposing significant changes to Regulation Z (also known as Truth in Lending). These changes would make it significantly easier for potential borrowers to recognize the true costs of the mortgages they're assuming. It would also place restrictions on those originating the loans. Compensation of mortgage brokers and loan officers would no longer be linked to the interest rate of the loan, much less any of the other terms. Likewise, mortgage brokers and loan officers would be expressly forbidden to steer consumers to bigger or more expensive loans, simply to increase their compensation.

The changes would be sensible, but cleaning up securitization requires that policy makers consider another important aspect of sausage making: the meat inspectors who grade these products. Their financial equivalent would be the ratings agencies, and like their counterparts in the USDA, they haven't always lived up to their responsibilities.

Reforming Ratings

In the United States, three major private ratings agencies—Standard & Poor's, Moody's Investors Service, and Fitch Ratings—wield remarkable power, slapping grades on everything from mortgages to corporate bonds to the sovereign debt of entire nations. These grades reflect the likelihood that the borrower or borrowers will default on their debt, and they are central to how financial markets ascertain risk. In effect, ratings are a way to outsource due diligence: if Moody's says a particular CDO tranche is supersafe and gets an AAA rating, then it spares anyone else from having to pop the hood of the security and look at the underlying assets.

The ratings agencies' rise to power began in the 1930s. Their forerunners issued ratings that federal regulators used to assess the quality of bonds held by banks. This stamp of government approval helped cement their influence, and while their power waned in the immediate postwar era, it rose again in the 1970s, a time when bond defaults rose, and ratings became increasingly important to evaluating risk.

In 1975 the Securities and Exchange Commission created a category known as Nationally Recognized Statistical Rating Organization (NRSRO). Fitch, Standard & Poor's, and Moody's were among those granted this coveted designation. In effect, anyone selling debt had to get a rating from one of these specially designated agencies. While the SEC eventually recognized seven of these agencies, mergers reduced their ranks to the three familiar firms, though the SEC has recently given this designation to a handful of lesser-known companies.

Over the course of their careers, the ratings agencies have changed dramatically. In the early years, they made their money from investors, who paid them to evaluate potential investments. Over time this revenue model shifted, partly because some investors obtained ratings by photocopying their friends' rating manuals instead of paying for them. To get around that problem, the ratings agencies adopted a new business model: they would sell their services to issuers of debt rather than to investors. At the same time the SEC's reforms effectively put the onus of obtaining a rating on anyone who wanted to sell debt. By the 1980s the transition was complete: issuers of debt now paid for ratings.

This arrangement, however, created a massive conflict of interest. Banks looking to float some securities could shop around among the agencies to find the best rating. A ratings agency that looked at a proposed offering and slapped a subprime rating on it risked losing business. Increasingly, the ratings agencies had an interest in giving the customers what they wanted—and if a customer wanted a AAA rating for an MBS made up of subprime mortgages, there's a good chance that's what it got.

As if that weren't bad enough, the ratings agencies started to generate revenue from other, equally problematic sources. A bank putting together a structured financial product would go to one of the ratings agencies and pay for advice on how to engineer that product to attract the best possible rating from the very agency the bank would ultimately pay to rate its securities. This service was described as "consulting" or "modeling." Perhaps. In fact, it was a bit like a professor's accepting a fee in exchange for telling students how to get an A on an exam. That's not kosher.

How, then, might the ratings agencies be reformed? At a bare minimum, the agencies must be forbidden to offer any consulting or modeling services. They should exist for one purpose: to assign a rating to a debt instrument. That's it; anything more introduces a possible conflict of interest. While the SEC has issued rules that forbid the ratings agencies to consult with the companies they rate, this ban is extraordinarily difficult to enforce. Instead, the SEC should forbid the ratings agencies to consult or model for anyone.

It also makes sense to open up competition in this privileged realm. While this proposal might have been difficult to justify ten years ago, when the collective reputation of the big three was still intact, it's an easier sell now. Unfortunately, the SEC makes it very difficult for new companies to obtain that coveted NRSRO rating: newcomers must have been in business for several years and have many major clients. But it's hard to get major clients without first being inducted into the sacred circle. To address this problem, the SEC needs to lower the barriers to entry, so that more competition—free market competition, if you will—enters into this vitally important industry.

More radical still would be to take away the semiofficial role that the ratings agencies now enjoy. Everything from SEC regulations to Basel II capital requirements formally recognize the NRSROs as the only place from which ratings can be obtained. That recognition invests them with disproportionate, if not excessive, power. Taking that power away would be another way of opening up competition.

An even more comprehensive reform would be to force the ratings agencies to return to their original business model, in which investors in debt—not the issuers of it—pay for the ratings. Unfortunately, this is easier said than done. One reason is the "free rider problem": once a set of investors pays for a rating and makes a decision based on it, other investors can figure out the rating and make their own decision free of charge.

A solution would be to mandate that all institutional investors pay into a common pool that would be administered by regulators. For every new issuance of debt, this pool would be used to purchase ratings from a group of sanctioned agencies. This solution would require that all players in the financial system—even less-regulated entities like hedge funds—contribute to the pool.

This requirement would upend the economy of the ratings agencies, but that's precisely the point: the idea that the issuers of debt pay for their ratings is bizarre. To return to our earlier analogy, it's comparable to having students pay professors for their grade. Imagine that students have a choice of professors (just as debt issuers have some choice of ratings agencies). Those professors who hand out lots of Fs will soon find that their more easygoing colleagues—who hand out nothing but As—are attracting more students and more revenue. But all those As will be just as spurious as the AAA ratings handed out at the height of the housing bubble.

Make no mistake: reforming the ratings agencies will be no easy task; they occupy a unique place within the financial firmament. But unless some of the foregoing reforms are put in place, the conflicts of interest will almost certainly continue.

But let's assume for a moment that those conflicts can be made to disappear, and that ratings agencies henceforth bestow accurate ratings on things like mortgage-backed securities. Unfortunately, not even the ratings agencies will touch the opaque, mysterious, and often baffling instruments known as derivatives.

Dealing with Derivatives

In 2002 Warren Buffett penned a now-legendary annual report to investors in Berkshire Hathaway. He decried the growing use of derivatives, which he ominously described as "time bombs, both for the parties that deal in them and for the economic system." Buffett didn't pull any punches, characterizing derivatives as "financial weapons of mass destruction." They carry dangers, he warned, "that, while now latent, are potentially lethal." Most presciently of all, he warned that "the derivatives genie is now well out of the bottle, and these instruments will almost certainly multiply in variety and number until some event makes their toxicity clear."

Buffett was right, but the story is a bit more complex. Derivatives have been around for several centuries; not until recently did they assume forms that posed a significant danger to the global financial system. After all, a derivative is simply a bet on the outcome of some future event: a movement in interest rates, oil prices, corn prices, currency values, or any number of other variables. They go by various names—swaps, options, futures—and they've worked just fine for decades, enabling people to "hedge" against risk. In their original iteration, farmers could hedge against fluctuations in the prices of their crops in advance of a harvest, giving them peace of mind they would otherwise lack.

But in recent years derivatives have grown into something altogether different, thanks to the rise of several new varieties, such as the credit default swap (CDS). This instrument has been compared to an insurance contract but was in fact very different. It superficially did resemble insurance in that it allowed a buyer to purchase protection in the event that a debtor defaulted on his obligations. If that happened, the seller of the "insurance" would be on the hook to help the buyer recoup his losses. However, unlike the purchaser of an insurance contract, the purchaser of a CDS didn't have to actually own a chunk of the asset that was the subject of the bet. Worse, anyone who had placed a bet that someone would default had every incentive to make this happen. In these cases, purchasing a CDS was akin to buying homeowners' insurance on a house that you didn't actually own—and then trying to set fire to it.

The CDS market grew from next to nothing to astonishingly large. By the time the crisis broke in 2008, the notional value of CDSs (the amounts of money being insured) topped out at $60 trillion. Much of the credit—or blame—for their meteoric rise lies with free-market zealot Senator Phil Gramm, who from 1995 to 2000 presided over the Senate Banking Committee. In his final year he managed to insert a provision in the Commodity Futures Modernization Act that exempted CDSs and other "over-the-counter" derivatives from regulation by the Commodity Futures Trading Commission (CFTC).

The key phrase here is "over the counter" (OTC). It might seem to be the opposite of "under the table," but in fact "under the table" is as good a definition as any of an OTC transaction. OTC transactions are ones in which the derivative contract is signed by two private parties—typically a "bilateral contract," to which no one else is privy. The lack of transparency is complete: no one knows the extent of anyone else's exposure, much less where it's concentrated. The financial firms that created many of these instruments were all too happy to keep the details secret; after all, their trading strategies were proprietary information and their trading fees very high. But during the crisis this secrecy proved corrosive to investor confidence.

No less troubling was "counterparty risk": the chance that the institutions that had sold this "insurance" would be unable to make good on their promises, particularly during a systemic financial crisis. That's precisely what happened as the recent crisis gathered steam: major financial institutions, confident that they would never have to pay, didn't set aside the necessary reserves. This posed a risk to the entire financial system, particularly in the case of AIG, which had insured—via CDS transactions—over a half trillion dollars' worth of toxic CDO tranches. AIG was in no position to cover the losses on these tranches, and because its failure would have bankrupted the firms whose assets it insured, the U.S. government stepped in and bailed it out. In effect, counterparty risk created a financial system that was not only too big to fail, but too interconnected to fail.

Derivatives have been associated with a number of other infamous episodes in financial stress and crisis. For example, a kind of derivative known as portfolio insurance was implicated in the 1987 stock market crash, and in 1994 losses on derivative positions brought Orange County, California, to the brink of bankruptcy. Derivatives played a major role in the LTCM fiasco in 1998, and they aggravated the boom and bust in oil prices during 2008 and 2009. Derivatives can wreak havoc in other ways as well, hiding liabilities, avoiding taxes, frustrating attempts to restructure debt, and even serving as a means of purposely triggering defaults of banks, firms, and nations.

Given this rap sheet, banning derivatives may seem like a good idea. But it's not: most derivatives operate without ill effect. What we need to do is control the excesses that certain derivatives can cause. As with everything else in this mess, that's easier said than done; there is no panacea. But some sensible steps should be taken immediately.

First we must correct the problem of transparency. True, some derivatives have long been traded over the counter without problems—like plain-vanilla interest-rate swaps and currency swaps—and could reasonably remain that way. But CDSs are another story altogether. These must be brought into the light of day and subjected to rigorous regulation by the SEC and the CFTC. The Obama administration has already taken steps along these lines, and several proposals to make this regulation a reality are already on the table.

One school of thought advocates forcing credit derivatives onto the kind of central exchange similar to those where simpler derivatives are bought and sold. This idea makes perfect sense, as exchanges guarantee that derivatives will be cleared and settled in a straightforward, transparent fashion. Such a new institution could also ensure that the parties to derivatives have the necessary collateral to make good on their promises.

Unfortunately, while some of the existing credit derivatives could be standardized and traded on such a central exchange, not all of them can be: many of the OTC derivatives are next to impossible to standardize and are not traded in sufficient volumes; their price can't be consistently quantified like a stock or bond (or a common derivative).

These more esoteric credit derivatives should be registered in a central clearinghouse. Such institutions already exist for other, simpler kinds of derivatives: the Options Clearing Corporation, for example, handles a host of derivatives related to equities and commodities. Though a private organization, it has the imprimatur of both the SEC and the CFTC. Part of its job is to make certain that the parties to a derivatives contract have sufficient collateral to make good on their promises. (In other words, no financial firm could offer to "insure" against defaults without posting sufficient collateral.) In return, the clearinghouse would assume the burden of the contract in the event the counterparty failed. All this helps reduce the problem of counterparty risk.

While a clearinghouse is a good idea, a few caveats are in order. First, if the markets undergo a systemic meltdown, the clearinghouse may be unable to cover all the contracts, forcing it to default too. To some extent, that risk can be minimized by raising margin requirements. Nonetheless, as recent events have shown, it's easy to underestimate systemic risk, so such a clearinghouse would necessarily operate under the scrutiny of regulators, who would be charged with making sure that it had the necessary reserves to ride out a storm.

More problematic is the risk of regulatory arbitrage: if the clearinghouse handles only straightforward, standardized credit derivatives, financial engineers are likely to deliberately create exotic derivatives that the clearinghouse cannot accommodate, simply to evade regulation. Far better to have the clearinghouse handle all such derivatives.

This solution could go hand in hand with other reforms to increase transparency. For example, CDS transactions could be registered in a central database that would be accessible to the public. As our colleagues at New York University have suggested, that sort of data collection could be modeled on the Trade Reporting and Compliance Engine (TRACE), the database administered by the Financial Industry Regulatory Authority. Making these markets less opaque will have the added benefit of making pricing more competitive and cutting into the ability of firms to game the system, quoting higher prices than market conditions warrant.

In some cases, it's worth banning certain derivatives altogether, or severely restricting their use. For example, regulators should consider forbidding CDS contracts entirely. One of the cardinal rules of insurance holds that the party purchasing the policy must have an "insurable interest": a direct stake in the outcome. Most CDS contracts dispense with this custom. To return to an earlier analogy: CDS contracts effectively gave Wall Street "huge incentives to burn down your house," as one reporter for the *Financial Times* pithily put it.

If they cannot be banned outright, insurance companies should be barred from selling these guarantees. The only ones trafficking in these instruments should be hedge funds and other high-risk players in the financial markets. Moreover, they should be subject to rigorous margin and collateral requirements via a clearinghouse. If a hedge fund is going to get into the insurance business, it should be required to demonstrate beyond a shadow of a doubt that it will be able to make good on its obligations.

One final measure that would go a long way toward streamlining the regulation of derivatives would entail changing the relative responsibilities of the SEC and CFTC. These agencies regulate different slices of the derivatives market, effectively dividing regulatory authority. Consolidating the responsibility for overseeing all derivatives within a single agency would permit a more systematic approach to regulating and supervising derivatives and, more important, reducing the potential threat they pose to the stability of the international financial system.

These sorts of reforms would address several problems: counterparty risk, a lack of price transparency—even the outsize fees that are a feature of the mysterious market in over-the-counter derivatives and that enable insiders to reap enormous fees and fleece investors.

Nonetheless, these suggestions are not a cure-all. Derivatives are among the trickiest things to regulate and monitor, and their explosive growth over the last decade has only made that job harder. They have gone from being a means of hedging risk to a purely speculative instrument that permits often naïve investors—pension fund managers, for example—to assume massive amounts of leverage and risk. Increasingly exotic, opaque, and impenetrable to nonspecialists, they pose a very serious danger to the financial system that the foregoing reforms alone will not cure.

For this reason, the new generation of derivatives should be the subject of far more systematic and ruthless scrutiny by regulators. Put differently, this is not a situation where regulators need to fear that cracking down on these instruments will somehow imperil economic growth. Far from it: their continued existence poses a far greater danger to global economic stability, and the sooner legislators, policy makers, and regulators understand that, the better.

Unfortunately, that stability has to be shored up worldwide. That means reexamining some of the global guidelines that shape how banks do business too.

Basel and Beyond

The quaint Swiss city of Basel has many claims to fame: the oldest university in Switzerland, the country's first zoo, and, more recently, its tallest building. Basel's schools have been home to intellectual giants like Friedrich Nietzsche, and its storied chemical and pharmaceutical companies have given the world everything from Valium to LSD. And its banking community has given the world something a little less exciting but no less important: the Basel Committee on Banking Supervision.

Born in 1974, this little-understood institution draws its members from central banks of the advanced economies known as the G-10. Its mandate is to come up with better ways to regulate and supervise banks and other financial institutions. While its recommendations are nonbinding, it nonetheless carries a great deal of weight. Much of the financial system as it existed on the eve of the crisis was a creature of the Basel Committee's guidelines.

Those guidelines, or accords, have evolved over the years. The first accord, the Basel Capital Accord, known as Basel I, asked banks to differentiate between the various classes of assets they held in order to better assess the relative risk posed by holding them. This risk assessment would affect how much capital a bank had to hold.

Consider two hypothetical banks, each of which borrows a billion dollars from other sources and invests it. One invests in low-risk, supersafe U.S. Treasuries, the other in high-risk corporate junk bonds. Under the Basel I guidelines, the two banks would assign a different risk factor (a percentage) to these different assets. This risk factor would guide how much capital they had to hold relative to these risks. In practice the bank with the supersafe government debt didn't need to hold as much capital as the bank with its money in junk bonds.

Basel I had a few other stipulations. Banks that operated in multiple countries had to hold capital equivalent to 8 percent of their risk-weighted assets. In an additional wrinkle, the guidelines spelled out the form that this capital or equity could take: common shares, preferred shares, and other high-quality capital (called Tier 1 capital), and everything else (Tier 2 capital).

The first Basel accord went into effect in the 1980s, and by 1992 most of the G-10 had adopted its recommendations. Many emerging-market economies voluntarily adopted these guidelines too, as a demonstration of financial stability and prudence. Unfortunately, standards that made sense for advanced industrial economies proved more difficult for emerging economies to maintain, particularly in times of crisis, and proved their undoing.

No less troubling, bankers had found ways to hide risk that Basel I did not anticipate—for example, by securitizing assets. These sleights of hand gave bank balance sheets the appearance but not the reality of stability. Bankers had obeyed the letter but not the spirit of the Basel I guidelines.

These failures led to Basel II. While its predecessor had filled a mere thirty-seven pages, the new accord was almost ten times as long. It gave much more precise technical guidelines on weighing the relative risk of various assets; suggested methods for making these calculations; expanded the definition of risk to encompass other perils, such as the likelihood that assets might fall in value on the open market; sought to close various loopholes by which banks had hidden risk; urged regulators to move more aggressively to monitor compliance with capital reserve requirements; and spelled out terms by which banks would make their financial condition public. Though many European nations wanted Basel II to apply to all banks, the United States, Canada, and the United Kingdom successfully argued that it should apply only to large international banks.

The members of the G-10 hammered out a final version of Basel II in 2006. It then went to the individual nations for implementation, a process that was under way when the crisis hit. It immediately became apparent that for all its specificity, Basel II had serious flaws. Although many of the revisions were a response to the crises of the 1990s, Basel II did not protect large banks from the kind of disruptions that attend a major financial crisis. Simply stated, Basel II assumed that the world's financial system was more stable than it actually was. This was a serious mistake.

The crisis underscored several realities. One, banks needed higher-quality capital and more of it. Two, the "capital buffer" that many banks had established was nowhere near large enough to shelter them from the kind of shock delivered by the housing bust and the credit crisis. Three, the quality of the capital as defined by Tier 1 and Tier 2 could deteriorate significantly in a time of crisis.

Reforming Basel II will take years, but a few things stand out. For starters, the way Basel II defines and ranks capital should be changed. Rather than relying on the Tier I definition to calculate bank capital, it might use a narrower measure known as Tangible Common Equity (TCE). TCE counts only common shares in its calculation of capital; by contrast, Basel's Tier I capital definition includes both common and preferred shares. TCE is thus a more conservative estimate of the capital a bank has on hand. As such, it may be a more realistic way to assess a bank's health in the face of a crisis.

There's a deeper problem with the way that Basel II is structured. The methods it used to calculate capital had the perverse effect of exaggerating the amount of capital that banks had on hand during boom times while doing the opposite when the crisis hit, causing them to curtail their exposure to risk in excessive and disruptive ways. This happened because during boom times the price of assets held by the banks rose, simultaneously reducing their need for capital and encouraging them to take on more risk. In the crisis, the process went into reverse: asset prices fell, and suddenly the banks needed more capital just when it was most difficult to obtain.

In economics, this phenomenon is known as "procyclicality." The meaning of this unwieldy term is simple: something that's procyclical amplifies fluctuations in the economy at large—for example, a boom-and-bust cycle. When it comes to capital, that's obviously a problem; if anything, you want the guidelines not to amplify economic fluctuations but to shield banks from them. To avoid procyclicality, one could adopt a different way of calculating capital called "dynamic provisioning." Instead of forcing banks to hold a static amount of capital at all times—like the 8 percent imposed by the Basel accords—a dynamic system would allow it to vary over time. In boom years, capital requirements would go up. When things go sour, the capital requirements would decrease. A version of dynamic provisioning has already been used by Spanish banks, and while not a cure-all, its widespread adoption under a new Basel regime may be worth trying.

Another possible solution to the problem of procyclicality is the use of "contingent capital." This idea, which is gaining adherents, deserves a close look, though it's not without problems. Here's how it works: in good times, banks issue a special kind of debt known as "contingent convertible bonds." It differs from ordinary debt in that if a bank's balance sheet declines past a particular "trigger point," the debt will "convert" into shares or equity in the bank.

Contingent capital potentially provides several benefits. First, the bank gets more capital when it really needs it, enabling it to stay afloat. The ailing bank survives, but at a price: its former bondholders lose their money but end up with a significant ownership stake in it. This sudden influx of outside shareholders diminishes the power of the existing shareholders.

That's not in the interest of the original bondholders or shareholders. So both groups have an incentive to keep a closer eye on what the bank is doing so that it never finds itself at this unfortunate juncture. In theory, if the bondholders think the bank is headed in the wrong direction, they will impose market discipline in the form of higher borrowing costs. Likewise, the shareholders will rein in risky activity that might land the bank in trouble.

This idea may work better on paper than in practice. For it to work, after all, banks would have to issue enough contingent convertible bonds. Otherwise, the sort of self-discipline it's meant to encourage—never mind the capital it's supposed to provide—will be insufficient. Still, it's one of the better proposals on the table at the moment, and it may address one of the major failures of Basel II. A central conceit of that agreement was that if a bank's regulators, shareholders, and managers couldn't restrain risky behavior, its creditors might be encouraged to do so in their stead; purchasers of the bank's debt would impose "market discipline," jacking up borrowing costs on banks that took too many risks.

Unfortunately, when the recent crisis hit, there wasn't enough bank debt out there to impose meaningful market discipline. But even if there had been, governments around the world threw market discipline out the window when they decided to guarantee all that debt *and* make it easy for banks to borrow more. Contingent capital may be one way around that problem too, ensuring that debt gets converted into equity rather than guaranteed, backstopped, and bailed out. It might—perhaps—hold the line on moral hazard.

Another problem for the sages of Basel to consider is the peril associated with a lack of liquidity. As the recent crisis amply demonstrated, financial institutions—both traditional banks and members of the shadow banking system—are highly susceptible to a liquidity crunch. In the past, the Basel Committee paid little attention to this problem. That needs to change. As we've noted in previous chapters, the recent disaster was a banking crisis writ large, with financial firms of all stripes borrowing money on a short-term, liquid basis, then investing it in long-term, illiquid assets. When panic struck, banks and shadow banks couldn't renew their short-term loans. They became illiquid.

Therefore an essential element of future regulation of all financial institutions—banks and nonbanks—should be a greater emphasis on the management of liquidity risk. One way to manage it would be to require firms to avoid short-term borrowing—in other words, to significantly lengthen the maturity and duration of their liabilities. A bank that has to renew its borrowing once a year is less likely to suffer a liquidity crunch than one that renews loans every day. Again, this technique for managing liquidity risk won't solve everything: as the recent crisis demonstrated, even institutions that traffic almost exclusively in liquid investments—money market funds, for instance—can still get themselves in trouble by putting just a tiny bit of their money into less liquid assets.

Another flaw with the existing Basel regime is that it gives too much discretion to financial institutions to use their own internal models for assessing risk. The Value at Risk model (VaR) is one, a mathematical formula that purports to calculate the likelihood that a firm will suffer a loss on its assets; another is the Gaussian copula, a statistical tool that was used to price esoteric assets like CDOs. Both models disregarded the likelihood of crises and other disruptive events, leaving banks vulnerable when the crisis hit. Sadly, the solution is not simply to devise a better set of equations. Models are only as good as the people using them, and if individuals wish to jack up short-term profits by ignoring risk, they will be able to fiddle with any formula in order to get the answer they want.

So we must think about other ways to minimize risk. For starters, it's worth rethinking how financial institutions themselves manage risk. At present, the "silo" approach is dominant: each division or business line considers risk in isolation, never contemplating how its ventures might interact with those of other divisions. The classic example is AIG: a small branch of the company based in London with only 375 employees managed to insure enough toxic CDOs to bring down countless other divisions that employed more than a hundred thousand people.

No less troubling, many risk managers are marginalized; after all, they stand in the way of bigger profits. That makes it all the more difficult for them to be effective in controlling the traders with whom they work. For this reason, risk management in the future should dispense with the silo model and instead strive for a bird's-eye view of risk throughout the organization. That means appointing a more powerful chief risk officer who reports directly to the CEO and the board of directors, along with a staff capable of monitoring what's going on in multiple divisions of the bank and, more important, cracking down on risky behavior.

The Coming Crisis

Financial crises have a funny way of making radical reforms seem reasonable. Much of what we've described in this chapter would have seemed extreme and unnecessary in advance of the crisis that hit in 2008. That's no longer the case.

The reforms we've outlined would go a long way toward increasing accountability and transparency in the financial system by reforming compensation, regulating securitization, bringing derivatives under public scrutiny, and putting the putative guardians of the system—the ratings agencies—on a very short leash. These reforms would also ensure that banks and other financial firms have enough capital and, no less important, enough liquidity to weather a major financial crisis.

These reforms would also put an end to the potential abuses associated with having a small oligopoly of banks and investment banks controlling so much of the financial system. If derivatives and other financial instruments were more transparent, it would be much harder for these firms to charge their clients outsized fees and bid-ask spreads. These firms are understandably reluctant to see these instruments' trading moved from dealers' markets onto exchanges: doing so would deprive them of the ability to extract the kind of profits that come with having access to information their clients lack. Under the current system, firms can very easily charge high bid-ask spreads because there is no price transparency; they can effectively "front run" their clients, meaning that they can use information about their clients' investments to make money in other departments, such as in proprietary trading or even in the actual market-making and market-dealing activities. Greater transparency will frustrate those sorts of behaviors.

Skeptics might reasonably point out that if investors want to pay through the nose for the privilege of alpha—or schmalpha—returns, that's their business. But the rise of a small coterie of incredibly powerful, opaque financial firms has generated a far more unsettling problem. These firms now house a staggering assortment of financial functions: everything from securities origination and underwriting, market making and dealing, prop trading, private equity, hedge funds, and asset management to bread-and-butter banking. The interconnections among those various functions, never mind the interconnections among the handful of surviving firms, have created a system that is extraordinarily vulnerable to systemic risk.

Moving most trading from OTC markets that rely on market makers/dealers to exchanges would reduce these rent-extracting distortions but, more important, would radically reduce the counterparty risk that makes the financial institutions too interconnected to fail. Indeed, the more that transactions occur on exchanges, the less the system becomes interconnected as counterparty risk is significantly reduced. Not only do we need to reduce the TBTF problems by making each institution smaller, we also need to unbundle financial services within financial institutions to reduce the too-interconnected-to-fail problem: with exchanges, broker dealers would be involved only in the efficient execution of trades for clients, not in market making/dealing, which is rife with conflicts of interest, lack of price transparency, and large and systemic counterparty risk. So we need to go back to Glass-Steagall, and even beyond it, to a financial system in which both institutions and their activities are unbundled to make them less too big to fail and less too interconnected to fail.

In short, the concentration of financial power has created a system that is too interconnected to fail. The proposals outlined in this chapter represent the first steps toward curing these problems. But far more radical reforms must be implemented if the financial system is to achieve any semblance of stability in the coming years.

Chapter 9

Radical Remedies

In early January 2010, Ben Bernanke defended the Fed's handling of the recent financial crisis. The lesson he drew was straightforward and simple: better regulation could have prevented it. As he put it, "The lesson I take from this experience is not that financial regulation and supervision are ineffective for controlling emerging risks, but that their execution must be better and smarter."

This is correct. But how, precisely, might regulators do a "better and smarter" job of executing their responsibilities? In this chapter we consider some of the significant obstacles that stand in the way of this ambition. These obstacles include the intentional evasion of regulatory oversight, or what's known as regulatory arbitrage; the too-many-cooks-in-the-kitchen problem, in which an overabundance of regulators and a lack of coordination frustrate effective supervision of the financial system; and last but not least, the problem that regulations are only as good as the regulators who enforce them. The recent history of regulation shows that these problems have a way of derailing even the most rigorous and well-conceived rules and regulations.

Any successful reform of the regulation and supervision of the financial system will have to confront them.

That's a start. So too are the commonsense, middle-of-the-road recommendations laid out in the previous chapter. But sometimes it's not enough to impose new regulations on the status quo; sometimes a bit of regulatory "creative destruction" is in order. In this chapter, we take up some of the more radical changes that can and should be imposed in the coming years, including breaking up big banks and imposing a number of new firewalls in the financial system.

Finally, we weigh an entirely different but equally radical idea: the use of monetary policy to prevent speculative bubbles. Though it is relatively simple and straightforward, most economists and policy makers consider this idea heretical and dangerous. In fact, Bernanke explicitly ruled it out when he delivered his postmortem, arguing that better regulation and supervision offered a more "surgical" approach to addressing the problem.

We beg to differ. When used appropriately, monetary policy is one of the most effective and powerful ways to deal with asset bubbles and the crises they cause. Its effects are not surgical, but that's precisely the point: monetary policy can have a broader, systemic influence on the speculative climate that creates a bubble in the first place. It's therefore worth adding to the toolkit available to policy makers.

What follows is a glimpse of the possible future of finance—if and only if policy makers and politicians recognize that confronting crises requires some big-picture thinking and some radical reforms. Anything less would be tantamount to rearranging the deck chairs on the *Titanic*.

Avoiding Arbitrage

When people think of new financial regulation, they generally think of actual rules, guidelines, and laws that promise to end bad behavior, encourage stability, and otherwise prevent crises. That's all well and good, but bankers and traders have a funny way of dodging even the most carefully constructed regulations. Such regulatory arbitrage is one of the issues that policy makers must confront if reforms are going to have any effect.

In the years before the crisis, ordinary banks were reasonably well regulated, and in exchange, they had access to a government safety net: deposit insurance and explicit lender-of-last-resort support. This bargain was stifling for bankers who wanted more freedom to take risks. So they increasingly shifted banking activities to the shadow banks: institutions that looked and acted like banks but weren't regulated like them. This was regulatory arbitrage: the purposeful movement of financial activity from more regulated to less regulated venues.

In the wake of the crisis, the consensus holds that these nonbank financial institutions—the shadow banks—have to be regulated like ordinary banks. Most of them have received unprecedented levels of government support; now it's time for them to return the favor and submit to greater regulation. In addition, the recent crisis demonstrated that many of these firms are systemically important: their failure can send shock waves through the entire financial system—all the more reason that they should be regulated.

This all sounds good, right? Unfortunately, many policy makers are drawing the wrong lessons from history. They look at the monster shadow banks—institutions like AIG—and conclude that only the big fish deserve to be regulated. That's the philosophy embodied in some of the proposals now on the table. For example, the Obama administration's proposals for regulatory reform specifically target "systemically significant financial firms."

A selective application of regulations would be a profound mistake: it would simply open the door to more regulatory arbitrage. Next time around, financial intermediation would move from the bigger, newly regulated institutions to their less significant brethren. However small, these less regulated institutions would become increasingly important to the larger system in the aggregate, and their collective failure could be equally problematic. For example, during the savings and loan crisis about fourteen hundred such thrifts went bust; no single one of them was systemically important, but their collective poor loan underwriting and losses had systemic effects.

For this reason, any new regulations must be applied across the board to all institutions, not just to those deemed to pose a systemic risk. The same regulations governing everything from capital to liquidity ratios to compliance and disclosure standards should be imposed without exception, even if systemically important institutions should be more tightly regulated than smaller ones given their potential systemic effects. Financial engineers should have no place to run and hide; regulation should not be applied only here and there. Otherwise there will be more arbitrage—and more crises.

In all fairness, regulatory arbitrage was too easy a game to play in recent years, thanks to what was euphemistically called "self-regulation." This was the idea that regulators could establish general "principles" for financial institutions to follow, then request that the firms find some way to conform to them. Almost inevitably, this approach (also known as "soft-touch" regulation) bred more arbitrage. Charged with managing risk on their own terms, firms selected models that almost always underestimated the amount of capital needed to weather a crisis.

In dealing with the problem of self-regulation, regulators should be cautious about immediately issuing vast numbers of very specific rules governing each and every kind of structured financial product. This would be a fool's errand: such granular regulation will only generate another burst of regulatory arbitrage, as financial engineers figure out how to tweak products so as to evade the law.

Superspecific regulations would also be pointless on another level: the degree of financial innovation that has already taken place is staggering. One measure can be seen in the relentless expansion of a standard industry guide to derivatives. Originally a mere seven hundred pages long in 1989 (when it was called *Swap Financing*), the latest edition, published in 2006 (retitled *The Das Swaps & Financial Derivatives Library*), fills almost five thousand pages. It's astonishingly difficult to keep pace with financial innovation.

But this doesn't mean that regulators should throw up their hands, return to the old system of setting out "principles," and trust that the good traders and bankers at financial firms will abide by them. Rather, they should establish a robust set of simple rules governing key features of the financial system. For example, they should set clear caps on leverage—not on "risk-adjusted leverage" but on absolute leverage. The same specificity should apply to capital requirements and liquidity buffers. These can and should be absolute and should be applied across the board, to firms both large and small. Moreover, any discretion in interpreting them should lie not with the bankers, as has been the practice, but with the regulators.

That raises a somewhat vexing problem that transcends any particular set of reforms. How should regulations be administered? What official institutions should take the lead in administering them? And how should those institutions coordinate their efforts?

Enforcement and Coordination

In the United States, a bewildering array of regulatory bodies, at both the state and the federal levels, share responsibility for the financial system. These bodies have evolved haphazardly over the course of more than a century.

Let's begin on the state level. Over the course of the nineteenth and twentieth centuries, each of the fifty states created its own separate banking and insurance commissions. These bodies operate in different ways and have varying levels of experience monitoring the firms in their jurisdictions, which include both state-chartered banks and national banks with federal charters. Some states also have securities regulators, akin to the SEC, as well as credit union regulators. All of these regulatory authorities vary greatly in their funding, their sophistication, and the rules they are responsible for enforcing.

Atop this decentralized structure sits the federal regulatory edifice, sharing enforcement in some cases, superseding it in others. The number of federal regulatory bodies is staggering, ranging from the Office of the Comptroller of the Currency to the Federal Reserve to the Commodity Futures Trading Commission, along with many, many others. Many of these agencies patrol the same territory, or overlap in substantial ways. Finally, as if that weren't confusing enough, there are several government-sanctioned, private supervisory bodies that advise the government, set rules for financial firms, and even police their members—institutions like the Financial Accounting Standards Board (FASB).

Why this patchwork quilt? It's partly an outgrowth of the federal system of government, which purposely divides power between the states and the nation at large. And it partly reflects the regulatory agenda of the New

Deal, which, for all its radical expansion of government, divided regulatory authority among multiple institutions. The gaps and inefficiencies associated with this system only increased over the years with the rise of new kinds of financial firms and new financial instruments. Various "reforms" that deregulated the financial system in recent years created other gaps.

These problems notwithstanding, many policy makers have defended this overlapping, layered regulatory regime. Having so many different regulatory bodies, they argue, introduces beneficial "competition" that will lead to the wider adoption of the best, most effective regulatory practices. Unfortunately, financial firms aren't looking for the best regulation; they're looking for the least regulation, or regulation that doesn't restrict the activities that are at the core of the banks' business.

This wouldn't be a problem if banks had no choice over who regulates them. But under the present system, they do have a choice. It grows out of how they opt to incorporate themselves. A commercial bank, for example, could choose to charter itself under a particular state's law rather than under federal law. It would then need to choose whether to become a member of the Federal Reserve System. Those choices would effectively dictate whether it fell under the regulatory umbrella of the Office of the Comptroller of the Currency, the Federal Reserve, and the FDIC, not to mention selected state regulators.

Banks don't make these choices at random. There's considerable evidence that U.S. commercial banks, for example, change regulatory jurisdictions to take on more risk. This should come as no surprise: banks are looking to maximize returns, and they would have no reason to voluntarily submit to rules that put them at a competitive disadvantage. As a consequence, there's a "race to the bottom," as banks and other financial firms search for the regulator that will regulate them the least.

Regulators may have exacerbated the problem in recent years. Here's why: when banks choose their own regulators—and gravitate toward those that promise the least oversight—more rigorous regulatory agencies may see their domain erode. And a regulator with no one to regulate has no reason to exist. So regulators have every incentive to be lenient in order to attract more financial institutions into their regulatory nets. Here too we have a race to the bottom. Such is the paradox of choice or "regulatory shopping."

In 2009 the Obama administration proposed a serious overhaul of financial regulation. It included creating three new federal regulatory agencies: the Financial Services Oversight Council, which would serve as a kind of über-regulator, coordinating regulation across agencies, eliminating gaps, and working to identify institutions that might pose a systemic risk to the financial system; a National Bank Supervisor, which would oversee all banks with a federal charter; and an Office of National Insurance, which would take on responsibility for regulating insurers.

This is all well intentioned, and some version of it may receive legislative sanction in 2010. But it's worrisome that the proposals on the table do not address the underlying problem, the existence of a confusing patchwork of state and federal regulation. It would add regulators and consolidate others, but its net effect would be to leave the existing crazy quilt unchanged, even if it adds a "council" to oversee this mess.

Rest assured: maintaining the status quo would be very much in the interest of the financial services industries. If the past few decades have taught us—and them—anything, it's that firms thrive in the interstices of the regulatory structure. The existing system offers firms plenty of regulatory nooks and crannies where they can dodge effective oversight.

When pondering how to reform this system, it's worth considering the model offered by the United Kingdom's Financial Services Authority (FSA). This organization, born in 1997, effectively put a host of regulatory regimes under a single roof. The FSA handles the regulation of banks, insurers, securities, derivatives—even mortgages. Regulators in different departments ultimately answer to the same leadership, and in theory, this kind of centralization prevents the arbitrage and "cherry picking" that the more fragmented, decentralized U.S. system allows.

There's one fly in the ointment. By assuming such sweeping powers, the FSA has removed responsibility for regulating banks from Britain's central bank, the Bank of England. This is potentially problematic: given that central banks serve as lenders of last resort, they have historically retained regulatory authority over banks and other "systemically important" financial firms. If central banks are going to cede this authority along the lines of the FSA model, they and the new regulatory authority must coordinate their activities and maintain a proper exchange of information.

That said, the FSA model is superior to one where regulatory powers are dispersed among many different competing institutions. While nothing comparable will likely be adopted in the United States anytime soon—the long-standing tradition of power sharing between national and state governments rules that out—some significant consolidation and centralization is desirable and necessary. While it might not prevent the kind of regulatory arbitrage that helped create the recent crisis, it would certainly make it far more difficult.

Unfortunately, financial firms have another way to circumvent regulations. In this kind of "jurisdictional arbitrage," financial firms pick up and relocate to places that have fewer regulations and restrictions. In an era of financial globalization, mobile capital, and a lack of capital controls, firms can pull this off relatively easily. While some regulators may find it tempting to say good riddance and let some of the reckless firms responsible for the recent crisis depart for other, more hospitable climes, this will do little to prevent future disasters.

For that reason, regulators must coordinate any reforms with those under consideration in other countries. This is easier said than done: the infrastructure for such coordination is even less developed than what exists for dealing with other global problems like terrorism and climate change. Frustrated by the lack of coordination, some leaders have argued for the creation of a "global superregulator" that would serve, as German finance minister Peer Steinbrück put it, as "an international authority that will make the traffic rules for financial markets."

This idea sounds appealing but is hugely impractical. It's one thing for an international body like the Basel Committee to issue recommendations that national regulators implement; it's far more difficult to get all those regulators—and the legislators that created them—to relinquish some or all of their sovereignty to a single, all-powerful regulator. In fact, more modest versions of this idea have gone nowhere: attempts to make the European Central Bank the über-regulator for the member nations of the EU, for example, failed to gain traction. For now, responsibility for regulating European banks remains in the hands of the various nations' central banks.

Even if all the major advanced economies could agree on the creation of a global superregulator, it's probably not a good idea anyway. While the system in place in the United States—scores of regulatory authorities—isn't ideal, the opposite extreme carries its own risks. Putting all the regulatory eggs in one basket would place too much faith in a single body, whose über-regulators may or may not be up to the task before them.

That raises a final issue: the best, most coherent, and most comprehensive regulations mean nothing if they're poorly enforced. Put differently, regulations are only as good as the regulators who implement them. How should we deal with that?

Quis Custodiet Ipsos Custodes?

An old Latin phrase captures this most modern dilemma: *Quis custodiet ipsos custodes?* Or to paraphrase a little, "Who will regulate the regulators?" Who will ensure that those who are given the power to police society will perform their duties effectively and selflessly?

It's not a new problem. Plato acknowledged this predicament in the *Republic*, though he was talking about a society's guardians or stewards, not its financial regulators. (Derivatives were still a long way off.) Plato's solution was an intriguing one: the guardians—and the people generally—would be told a "noble lie," or useful myth, that the guardians were more virtuous than other people. Convinced of their own goodness, they would scorn private gain and instead look out for the welfare of the republic. The illusion of virtue would be its own reward.

This vision is apt to prompt snickers today, but it highlights an unsettling truth. Consider what happens if the guardians or regulators are not permitted to believe in their own superiority but are derided as incompetent and corrupt. This is a different kind of lie, but we've been encouraged to believe it in our own time. Until very recently, regulators have been told they're chumps for not going to work in the private sector. They're fools who can't compete with the financial geniuses on Wall Street. Worse, they're an impediment and an obstacle to the brave new world of financial innovation.

This lie, spread by fanatics of laissez-faire, deserves refutation. It has been challenged before: in the 1930s, the newly created SEC (as well as other regulatory agencies) attracted plenty of bright, capable, idealistic people who in a different era might have landed on Wall Street. Instead, they ended up regulating Wall Street and, not coincidentally, presiding over several decades of unprecedented financial stability, as well as steady, solid economic growth for the nation at large.

There's no reason that this can't happen again. But it would mean changing the reputation of regulators and regulation. That's a tall order, but that process can begin with the way the federal government recruits regulators. The people who staff these positions have the power and the responsibility to prevent another financial crisis. That's a pretty big responsibility, and it should be reflected in how the job is portrayed and sold to prospective employees. If that's a "noble lie," so be it. But without some change in our perception of careers in regulation, attracting the qualified people we need in these positions is going to be hard.

Regulators also deserve better compensation. Here we part ways with Plato; after all, you're reading a book written by economists, not by philosophers. And look at the facts: until relatively recently, the SEC was one of the worst-paid agencies in the entire federal government. Even today, it's hard to find an SEC employee who's paid over $100,000. While how much salaries can be raised is obviously limited—the secretary of the Treasury makes slightly less than $200,000—the people charged with overseeing the stability of the global financial system should reasonably be paid more than a receptionist at Goldman Sachs.

Some reformers have tried to address this problem by suggesting that regulators' compensation be pegged to their performance. In other words, the more fines they collect and the more insolvent banks they close, the more they get paid. This may sound like a good idea, but it's not. The potential for abuse is too high. Think of how well a police force would work if officers got paid by the number of arrests they made, or the number of traffic tickets they issued. Doubtless they would be more aggressive in enforcing the laws, but whether they would be fair or honest is another matter.

It's better to deal with the problem of recruitment in other ways. For starters, keep in mind that the federal government can offer something that Wall Street can't: job security. Given the number of unemployed former bankers and traders in the post-crisis years, the prospect of guaranteed employment may be particularly appealing. It will be especially appealing to the veteran traders and bankers who may be nearing retirement. These individuals have seen it all, and many of them are now collecting unemployment benefits. Let them finish out their careers working for the SEC and other regulatory agencies as rank-and-file regulators.

In suggesting that former traders join the government, we are by no means counseling a continuation of the high-level "revolving door" that connected some of the biggest financial firms with the regulatory establishment in Washington. Goldman Sachs is particularly infamous for this practice: several CEOs of that firm have held senior positions in the U.S. government, while scores of other Goldman executives have held high-level government jobs too. Creating countless conflicts of interest, these and other executives move seamlessly from the private sector to government, where they serve as allies rather than regulators of their former employers. Many of them then move back to the private sector and use their government connections to lobby in favor of looser regulation and more lax supervision of financial firms.

This problem, known as "regulatory capture," remains as troubling as ever. In the fall of 2009, for example, the SEC announced with great fanfare that it was hiring a managing executive for its newly created Division of Enforcement, which would necessarily keep an eye on big firms like Goldman Sachs. That hire was none other than a twenty-nine-year-old with limited experience, save for serving as an executive at Goldman Sachs.

There are ways to deal with regulatory capture and revolving-door appointments. One, the lobbying activities of former government employees, particularly those who serve in senior positions, should be significantly restricted. Reforms introduced by President Obama in early 2009 have banned government employees from lobbying activities for two years. That's a start, but the time frame should be extended to four or five years, if not longer.

It's also necessary to limit the lobbying power of financial firms. That's obviously a tall order. Politicians batten on the financial sector for the simple reason articulated by bank robber Willie Sutton: because "that's where the money is." They insulate the financial system from regulatory meddling and starve agencies of the taxpayer funds necessary to implement regulations.

In exchange, financial firms funnel massive amounts of money toward candidates—$311 million in 2008 alone.

It's hard to choke this flow off. It requires political will, and that's in short supply, if what happened in 2009 is any indication. Over the course of that year, many recipients of TARP money spent tens of millions of dollars successfully lobbying Congress against caps on executive compensation and all manner of tougher financial regulation, including rules governing derivatives. They also managed to persuade Congress to lean on the Financial Accounting Standards Board, which suspended so-called mark to market accounting rules. This enabled the banks to magically return to health—at least on paper. It also permitted them to begin returning TARP funds—but not before they lobbied Congress to cut the penalties for doing so.

As long as this incestuous relationship between finance and politics remains unbroken, the perverse exchange of favors that fosters deregulation, asset bubbles, crises, and moral-hazard-ridden bailouts will continue. Only significant restrictions on the ties between political institutions and financial firms will curtail this mutually destructive relationship. As it now stands, politicians have tremendous power over the scope of regulation as well as the regulators themselves. That is not a good thing. Legislatures hold the purse strings, and agencies that fail to do the politicians' bidding can be punished for their independence.

One proposed solution is to make regulators in the United States and elsewhere more independent. This independence can take different forms: regulators might be given more discretion over how they implement legislative directives. Alternatively, regulators can be given political and even budgetary independence.

There are different ways of doing so. In the United States, the Federal Reserve is largely independent of the executive and legislative branches of government and is "self-funded," meaning that it does not rely on taxpayer money. (Contrary to popular perception, the Fed is not part of the federal government. Rather, as the Fed itself announces on its Web site, it is "an independent entity within the government, having both public purposes and private aspects.")

Moving responsibility for regulation to the Fed would in theory make regulators more independent. Another model is the FSA in the UK. Though answerable to ministers in the government, it is operationally independent. And like a central bank, it takes no money from taxpayers; rather, it gets all of its funding from fees assessed on the firms under its aegis.

Like so many sweeping solutions, these have serious shortcomings. In fact, cutting regulation loose from direct government control does not alone guarantee better regulation. The FSA didn't do much to anticipate or forestall the recent crisis. In the United States, even the nominally independent Federal Reserve, responsible for regulating banks and even mortgages, failed to use its powers. It then had to compensate by serving as a lender of last resort on an unprecedented scale.

Moreover, the problem of regulatory capture doesn't disappear just because an agency has been removed from accountability to legislators. For example, significant power centers within the Fed—most notably, the board of directors of the Federal Reserve Bank of New York—are effectively controlled by banks on Wall Street. That political independence doesn't necessarily translate into regulatory independence is a point worth considering when contemplating sweeping structural reforms.

Given these flaws, it's probably better to approach the corrupt nexus of finance and politics from another direction. There's a very simple way to curtail the power of the big firms that helped cause the crisis: break them up.

Breaking Up Is Hard to Do

The recent crisis highlighted what's increasingly known as the "too-big-to-fail" problem. The collapse of Lehman Brothers and the resulting cardiac arrest of the global financial system revealed that many financial institutions had become so large, leveraged, and interconnected that their collapse could have systemic and catastrophic effects.

In the United States, when your garden-variety bank fails, the FDIC assumes control via a receivership process. But the ranks of too-big-to-fail institutions—the TBTF club—contain few such traditional banks. Instead, most TBTF institutions belong to another species: big broker dealers like Morgan Stanley and Goldman Sachs; AIG and other sprawling insurance companies; government-sponsored enterprises like Fannie Mae and Freddie Mac; and hedge funds like Long-Term Capital Management.

While the crisis left fewer such firms intact, those that remain are often larger, thanks to the waves of consolidation that followed the panic. JPMorgan Chase took over Bear Stearns and then Washington Mutual; Bank of America absorbed Countrywide and then Merrill Lynch. Finally, Wells Fargo and Citigroup fought over who would gobble up Wachovia, an enormous but otherwise insolvent bank. Why do such a thing? The cynical interpretation is that both firms recognized that whoever acquired Wachovia (Wells Fargo eventually triumphed) would be perceived as an even bigger risk to the financial system and could thus earn more bailouts and more forbearance.

We are now in the worst of all worlds, where many TBTF institutions have been bailed out and expect to be bailed out in any number of future crises. They have as yet faced no sustained regulatory scrutiny, and no system is in place to put them into insolvency should the need arise. Even worse, many of these institutions—starting with Goldman Sachs and JPMorgan Chase—are starting to engage once more in "proprietary trading strategies," which are complicated bets on stocks, bonds, commodities, and derivatives driven by algorithms devised by the firm's traders. Some of these "prop trading" strategies are risky, yet firms have resumed them while remaining under the protective umbrella of a dozen different government support programs.

Policy makers are tackling the TBTF problem in several ways. For example, they're looking at how to make the shock waves produced by the failure of these firms less disruptive and destructive to the rest of the financial system. During the recent crisis, the looming collapse of these firms prompted two equally problematic responses aimed at limiting this collateral damage: a full bailout of the creditors and counterparties of a large financial firm (as in the Bear Stearns and AIG cases) and a disorderly bankruptcy (as in the Lehman case). We need a third way that would provide government authorities with the powers to wind down these firms in an orderly fashion.

One way of achieving this would entail requiring TBTF firms to adopt "living wills" that would kick in should they find themselves incapacitated. Like a doctor fulfilling a dying patient's wishes, the government would step in and implement the terms of this legal document, making the firm's death throes a little less disruptive, painful, and expensive. That way a firm's demise would not play out in a disorderly, destructive fashion as it did in the case of Lehman Brothers. Call it death with dignity.

Another, related solution would entail the creation of a special bankruptcy regime for these sorts of firms. Rather than having them plunge into bankruptcy under Chapter 11 proceedings, which has proved disruptive, it may be appropriate to create an alternative mechanism for winding down these firms. One option would be some kind of conservatorship, comparable to what the federal government has used with Fannie Mae and Freddie Mac. Alternatively, a government entity endowed with the power to place a firm in receivership—much like the powers possessed by the FDIC—might be preferable. Both ideas would replace the chaos that comes with a Chapter 11 filing, shifting the action from a federal court to a more powerful federal body. In contrast with a bankruptcy trustee, a federal receiver or conservator would have greater powers to determine how the liquidation of a firm would proceed, could curtail disruptive litigation, and could take other measures to prevent liquidation from becoming too disruptive.

There are some shortcomings in these ideas. As critics of the living will concept have pointed out, various interested parties may not permit such a death to happen. Like some irate family member who refuses to let a DNR (Do Not Resuscitate) order be carried out, bank executives and politicians who have a vested interest in the continued survival of a bank in question might interfere with this process. Tens of thousands of jobs in someone's congressional district might be at stake, as would be generous donations to political campaigns.

Both ideas also have the drawback of putting the government in the role of deciding how much to pay the bondholders as it winds up the concern. Paying too much would send the message to the markets that moral hazard is going out the window. On the other hand, paying too little—or more accurately, less than what the markets expect—could trigger more panic throughout the financial system. These institutions are not small: the kind of losses or "haircuts" that bondholders take will have systemic effects. When that happens, even the most artfully designed protocol for winding down these firms may unravel, increasing the temptation to take the path of least resistance—a bailout.

Finally, some policy makers want to adopt a concerted international approach to supervising TBTF institutions. An international college of supervisors made up of regulators could monitor firms operating on a global scale. These individuals would confer on the status of these mega-institutions and basically keep an eye on them. It's a nice idea, and we have no objections to it. But it's not clear whether this kind of tracking would do a whole lot to prevent a crisis: it's hard enough for shareholders and senior management to anticipate fatal flaws in their firm; it may be even harder for a small band of regulators charged with monitoring the world's financial behemoths.

Indeed, these sorts of solutions avoid acknowledging the elephant in the room: not only are such firms too big to fail; they're too big to exist, and too complex to be managed properly. Frankly, they shouldn't exist—at the very least, they should be pushed to break themselves up.

One way of doing this would be to impose higher "capital adequacy ratios," which is a fancy way of saying that these institutions should be forced to hold enough capital relative to all the risks posed by their different units. This requirement would reduce leverage and, by extension, profits. Ideally, sending the message that bigger isn't better would lead these firms to break themselves up.

In order for this to happen, capital ratios—like the one established by Basel II—would have to be increased substantially. By just how much is hard to know. For example, Switzerland recently tried to deal with the TBTF problem by unilaterally doubling the Basel capital ratio from 8 to 16 percent for two of its biggest firms, UBS and Credit Suisse. So far, these firms have managed to raise their ratios without shedding any units. That suggests that capital ratios may have to be increased even higher, perhaps to 20 percent or more. Only such draconian measures would force them to fragment into smaller, less dangerous entities—or so we hope.

Such aggressive action will prompt howls of protest from the TBTF firms, which consider themselves essential to the day-to-day operation of the world economy. Thanks to their scale, we're told, they offer "synergies" and "efficiencies" and other benefits. The global economy can't function without us, they'll say. In fact, without the kind of one-stop shopping that financial supermarkets like Citigroup provide—well, without them, the global economy would suffer terribly.

This is preposterous. For starters, the financial supermarket model has been a failure. Institutions like Citigroup became gargantuan monsters under the leadership of empire builders like Sanford Weill. No CEO, no matter how adept and visionary, can manage a global financial institution that provides thousands of kinds of financial services. The complexity of these firms, never mind the exotic financial instruments they handle, makes it mission impossible for CEOs—much less shareholders or boards of directors—to keep tabs on what's going on across every division and at every trader's desk. That's hard enough to do with any bank; it's impossible with a firm like Citigroup, which at its height employed more than 300,000 people.

Others will argue that only the big financial conglomerates can offer the kind of one-stop shopping that big corporations need to operate in the twenty-first century. This too is risible. No corporation does business with only one firm. For example, corporations issuing bonds on the international market usually rely on a dozen or more banks in several countries to underwrite these offerings. It's clear that a global system of smaller, more specialized financial institutions can more than meet the needs of even the largest, most sophisticated firms.

But let's assume for the sake of argument that gigantic conglomerates like Citigroup, ING, and other megabanks do manage to provide services a bit more efficiently than smaller firms. Even if that were true—which it isn't—are those minor efficiencies really worth holding the global financial system hostage to giant firms whose failure can have catastrophic effects? By that logic, one might build a gigantic nuclear power plant that's a hundred times the size of Chernobyl, simply to gain some minor economies of scale. That's nice—until there's a meltdown.

Another reason to contemplate breaking up the TBTF firms is that many of them wouldn't even exist were it not for heavy helpings of government largesse. Take Citigroup. Over the course of the last eighty years, this bank has repeatedly overextended itself and teetered on the brink of insolvency, only to bounce back thanks to government forbearance, rescues, and bailouts. It has arguably happened four times: during the Great Depression; in the wake of Mexico's default on debts owed the bank in the early 1980s; after the commercial real estate bust a decade later; and now in the wake of the recent financial crisis. Any bank that needs that much help doesn't deserve to exist, and while it's now in the process of breaking itself up, the bits and pieces that emerge from the wreckage may be TBTF too.

Citigroup is hardly the only TBTF firm that should be dismembered. Even nominally "healthy" firms like Goldman Sachs pose a threat by virtue of their continued existence. Not that you would know it listening to the firm's CEO, Lloyd Blankfein, who in early 2010 defended handing out record bonuses by claiming, "We're very important. We help companies to grow by helping them to raise capital. Companies that grow create wealth. This, in turn, allows people to have jobs that create more growth and more wealth. We have a social purpose."

Spare us. Like other broker dealers, Goldman Sachs has a long history of reckless bets and obscene leverage. It was at the center of the investment trust debacle that exploded in 1929, ushering in the Great Depression. It learned from that mistake and spent the succeeding decades operating in a relatively prudent fashion, following a strategy that scorned short-term profits in favor of long-term revenue for its increasingly wealthy partners.

The turning point came in the late 1990s, when Goldman, following the lead of other investment banks, went public. This fateful switch moved the firm from a revenue model where the partners had "skin in the game" to one in which shareholders had little ability or incentive to monitor what was going on inside the famous firm. From this point onward, Goldman helped inflate a host of speculative bubbles, ranging from tech stocks to housing to oil. After the SEC eliminated leverage restrictions for investment banks, Goldman's leverage ratios soared to all-time highs, making it extraordinarily vulnerable when the crisis hit Wall Street. In Wall Street circles the running joke was that Goldman Sachs was just a hedge fund—in fact, the most highly leveraged of all hedge funds.

Like its competitors, Goldman was up to its neck in risky securitization, and while it's true that it saw the subprime bust coming earlier than others, its survival has little to do with its savvy traders. In the end, it lived through the crisis because the federal government propped it up again and again. Like the other broker dealers, it benefited from the bailout of the counterparties of Bear Stearns in the spring of 2008, and from the Fed's decision to provide broker dealers with lender-of-last-resort support. Likewise, it was saved during the bailout of AIG, netting a cool $12 billion from taxpayers. (No surprise there:

Goldman was heavily involved in discussions about the AIG bailout during the run-up to the rescue of the ailing firm.) It netted $10 billion more after the Fed guaranteed the senior unsecured debt of banks and bank holding companies. Then there's all the indirect aid: the low interest rates that slashed Goldman's borrowing costs; and the Fed's decision to purchase $1.8 trillion in Treasury debt, mortgage-backed securities, and other instruments, propping up prices and indirectly helping the firm. All told, Goldman probably took upwards of $60 billion in direct and indirect help, then took even more after converting to a bank holding company, when it got access to TARP funds.

Goldman would be bust without this help. That it would likely have been the last of the investment banks to perish simply because it placed better bets than most doesn't alter that fact. Yet its close brush with annihilation doesn't seem to have left its ringleaders chastened—and no wonder. They now belong to the TBTF club, which apparently gives them license to do whatever they want. There seems to be no means of stopping them: they've wriggled free of restrictions on compensation by returning the TARP funds. Now they're back in business as the world's biggest hedge fund, pursuing their high-risk prop trading strategies. That's bad enough, but unlike any normal hedge fund, they've got lender-of-last-resort support from the Fed, plenty of easy money, and even the option of FDIC-insured deposits, all of which give it an unfair competitive advantage. For all these reasons, Goldman should be broken up. Or at the very least, its broker-dealer activities should be split off from the parts of the firm involved in proprietary trading, hedge funds, private equity, and other risky investment strategies.

Plenty of other TBTF firms deserve to be nudged to break up as well: Bank of America, UBS, Wells Fargo, ING, Royal Bank of Scotland, Dexia, JPMorgan Chase, BNP Paribas, and others. But despite the grave danger that these TBTF firms pose, policy makers in Europe and the United States strenuously resist the idea of dismantling them. The genie is out of the bottle, the thinking goes; there's no way to go back to a more decentralized banking system. Massive, somewhat monopolistic financial firms are here to stay, despite the dangers they pose to the financial system.

If you believe this, we have some CDOs to sell you. Big firms have been dismantled many times before, typically by court order. In the United States, antitrust laws offer the most obvious means for doing so. In the early twentieth century, Presidents Roosevelt and Taft oversaw the dismemberment of Standard Oil and other trusts; more recently, in 1982, the Department of Justice succeeded in breaking up AT&T. A similar campaign could be launched against the TBTF institutions, which increasingly control broad swaths of the financial system.

An even better solution would be to pass legislation granting regulators the authority to break up banks and other financial institutions that are so large, leveraged, and interconnected that their collapse would pose a danger to the entire financial system. Unlike antitrust actions, this approach would make a breakup contingent on whether the bank in question is too big to fail, as opposed to monopolistic. Indeed, plenty of firms may not merit an antitrust proceeding but still pose a dire threat to the stability of the global economy.

Even these approaches, however, may not yield the sort of sweeping transformation of finance that's necessary. Some firms might be broken up, while others might successfully ward off efforts to do so. This would be an imperfect solution. That's why the approaches we've discussed may work best when combined with another equally radical strategy: breaking up all the big banks.

Initially the Obama administration showed little inclination to do so. But thanks to some nudging from Paul Volcker, there are signs that senior policy makers will implement rules that may limit the potential size of the TBTF firms. If they do, they might also consider the following proposal. While radical, it would go a long way toward taming the various Brobdingnagian banks that have become too interconnected, too important, and too big to fail.

Glass-Steagall on Steroids

In the wake of the recent crisis, distinguished thinkers like former Fed chairman Paul Volcker have argued for some kind of return to the Glass-Steagall legislation of 1933, which separated commercial banking from investment banking. This firewall eroded in the 1980s and 1990s, finally disappearing altogether with the Gramm-Leach-Bliley Act of 1999. The result was the current system, where a firm like Citigroup or JPMorgan Chase can be a commercial bank, a broker dealer, a prop trader, an insurance company, an asset manager, a hedge fund, and a private equity fund all rolled into one sprawling institution.

The breakdown of barriers meant that banks with access to deposit insurance and lender-of-last-resort support pursued high-risk activities that resembled gambling more closely than banking. This was bad for the financial system and for the economy at large. As Keynes rightly observed in 1936, "When the capital development of a country becomes a by-product of the activities of a casino, the job is likely to be ill-done."

Many reformers have understandably counseled a return to Glass-Steagall, and as of early 2010, there are bills in Congress that would restore it in some way or another. Thanks to Volcker's lobbying, the Obama administration was considering whether to prohibit bank holding companies—which now include firms like Goldman Sachs and other major financial players—from pursuing proprietary trading, private equity deals, and any hedge-fund activity. But industry lobbying is likely to prevent the restrictions from being implemented.

These proposals are good but not good enough. What we need is a twenty-first-century version of that historic legislation that would create a number of new firewalls. It would move beyond a simple separation between commercial and investment banking and create a system that can accommodate—and separate—the many different kinds of financial firms now in existence, as well as curtail the sort of short-term lending that made the financial system "too interconnected to fail."

Accordingly, commercial banks that take deposits and make loans to households and firms would belong in one category; investment banks (broker dealers) would belong in another. In order to avoid any entanglements between the two kinds of banks, investment banks would be forbidden to borrow from insured commercial banks via the short-term, overnight "repo financing" that proved so fragile during the recent crisis. The divide between these two types of banks would thus be institutional as well as relational.

That's a start. Given that so many of the shadow banks got themselves into trouble by borrowing on liquid, short-term bases and then sinking that money into long-term, illiquid investments, regulators must restrict their ability to do it even further. That means banning investment banks and broker dealers from doing any kind of short-term borrowing. If they're going to make long-term investments in illiquid assets, they'll have to raise money by issuing stock or long-term debt. This reform would make the financial system less interconnected, and therefore less prone to the kind of systemic chain reactions that lead to widespread failures.

In order to stabilize the system even further, all banks—including investment banks—should be forbidden to practice any kind of risky proprietary trading. Nor should they be permitted to act like hedge funds and private equity firms. Instead, they should confine themselves to doing what they've done historically: raising capital and underwriting offerings of securities. The kind of proprietary trading that many investment banks now do, never mind hedge fund operations, should be the franchise of hedge funds alone. But like the investment banks, hedge funds would not be permitted to engage in large-scale short-term borrowing from banks and other financial institutions. They would have to turn to long-term funding instead.

Insurance companies and private equity firms would fall into additional categories. Neither type of institution would be permitted to branch out into kinds of financial intermediation beyond their core activities. Insurers could not engage in proprietary trading; nor would any commercial bank, investment bank, or hedge fund be permitted to venture into insurance. Private equity would remain the province of private equity firms. A firm belonging to one category could not venture onto the turf occupied by firms in any other category. This would help eliminate the too-interconnected-to-fail problem; it would also rid these firms of the twisted conflicts of interest that invariably arise by having different units pursuing contradictory ends.

One final note: only commercial banks would have access to deposit insurance and a government safety net. Everyone else—investment banks, broker dealers, hedge funds, insurance companies, and private equity firms—would be on their own. Some of these institutions would eventually fail. But they would not pose a systemic risk: they would not be as large or as interconnected as they are today. Finally, because they would not be permitted to act like banks—borrowing short and lending long—their demise would be unlikely to trigger the kind of panic that seized the shadow banks at the height of the recent crisis.

The financial system we're describing is compartmentalized, sanitized—

and boring. And that's precisely the point. It could be made more boring by forcing banks to become "narrow banks," which can only take deposits and invest them in safe, short-term debt. Unfortunately, this kind of draconian restriction would simply chase financial intermediation into the shadows—precisely the problem that originally created the crisis.

For that reason, it's better to preserve different kinds of financial institutions in their present forms but pursue the regulatory equivalent of divide and conquer. By unbundling the financial services now combined under one roof, we can steer the financial system away from an excessive reliance on too-big-to-fail—and too-interconnected-to-fail—firms. By returning to a beefed-up version of Glass-Steagall, and by adopting reforms aimed at moving financial activity away from opaque trading strategies and onto transparent exchanges, we can create a safer, saner financial system, with the added benefit of robbing firms of their ability to extract disproportionate profits from deluded investors.

Financial firms will howl at this prospect. Let them. For all their whining, one fact remains indisputable: these firms' reckless appetite for risk helped create a crisis that has inflicted widespread suffering around the world. They are complicit in that wider disaster, and in the future they should be kept on a very short leash.

Let's not forget one final point. The financial firms could have been stopped from going down this destructive path. The most obvious way would have been better regulation and supervision. Sometimes, though, even that is not enough; a more systemic solution is needed, like using the power of central banks to prevent bubbles from forming in the first place.

Banishing Bubbles

In 1996 Alan Greenspan gave a speech that warned of the dangers of "irrational exuberance." Market watchers who dissected Greenspan's every utterance immediately concluded that he was on the verge of raising rates, and global stock markets plunged. Chastened, Greenspan never again issued any public warnings as the tech bubble grew to monstrous proportions. Aside from a token interest rate hike of one quarter of one percent in 1997, he did not raise interest rates again until the middle of 1999; following the LTCM near collapse, the Fed actually cut the Federal funds rate by 75 basis points, thus further inflating the tech bubble.

The bubble eventually burst in 2000, and Greenspan's Fed responded by slashing interest rates by 5.5 percentage points—from 6.5 percent to 1 percent—between 2001 and 2004. The rising tide of easy money helped cushion the bursting of the tech bubble, but it fed another bigger bubble in housing. Here too the Fed stood by and did nothing. Despite mounting evidence that the market was spinning out of control, Greenspan and then Bernanke kept interest rates low, raising them too slowly and only when it was far too late. The bubble burst shortly thereafter, and the result was the financial catastrophe of 2007–8. This prompted yet another round of dramatic rate cuts, bringing borrowing costs close to zero.

There's a familiar pattern here: the Fed stands by and does nothing as bubbles form and asset prices go through the roof; then when the bubble bursts, it tries every trick in the book to alleviate the damage done. This approach is wrongheaded and wasteful. Central bankers do not seem to buy the old adage that an ounce of prevention is worth a pound of cure. Like a doctor who will do nothing to stop a patient from smoking but will aggressively treat him for lung cancer many years later, central banks have taken a halfhearted, "asymmetric" approach to dealing with bubbles.

In all fairness, the reluctance of central banks to prevent bubbles from forming reflects the fact that the idea remains controversial in academic and policy circles. Unfortunately, much of that controversy emanates from the writings and speeches of Alan Greenspan and Ben Bernanke, who along with a handful of other economists have argued that central banks cannot do much to control bubbles; they can only clean up in the aftermath. As Greenspan argued in 2004 in reference to the tech bubble, "Instead of trying to contain a putative bubble by drastic actions with largely unpredictable consequences, we chose . . . to focus on policies 'to mitigate the fallout when it occurs and, hopefully, ease the transition to the next expansion.'"

This strategy is strange. For starters, it generates moral hazard on a grand scale. Watching the Fed over the past two-plus decades, investors now have every reason to conclude that central banks will do nothing to stop a speculative bubble from forming and growing—and in fact may even encourage it, becoming cheerleaders for the "new economy" or the virtues of home ownership—but will do everything in their power to limit the damage. This is extraordinarily problematic. If investors believe the Fed will save them, they'll take even more risks the next time around. Likewise, they'll know that when the other shoe finally drops, the Fed will slash interest rates to rock-bottom levels, creating opportunities to speculate in some even bigger bubble.

Bernanke and other apologists for the status quo have countered by arguing that central banks can't possibly intervene against rising asset prices because of "uncertainty." This is nonsense: all monetary policy decisions are plagued by uncertainty. Uncertainty doesn't stop central bankers from targeting inflation; it shouldn't stop them from countering bubbles either. Moreover, policy makers have available certain tools that can at least give some measure of whether asset prices are spiraling out of control. And let's face it: models aside, there's always common sense, an asset in short supply among policy makers in recent years. If central bankers look at share prices of tech stocks doubling and tripling within the space of a few months and still can't see a bubble—well, perhaps they should consider another line of work.

Other arguments often get trotted out in favor of central bank passivity in the face of asset bubbles. Some economists claim that bubbles aren't bad for the economy; therefore central banks shouldn't mess with them. This claim is patently ridiculous: a vast body of historical evidence amassed over centuries shows that when bubbles burst, the larger economy suffers tremendous collateral damage that can linger for years.

Yet another argument holds that any hike in interest rates meant to prick an asset bubble risks triggering a massive recession. In other words, the risks outweigh the potential benefits. By that logic, it's better to do nothing at all. Proponents of this point of view believe the Fed's decision to raise interest rates in 1929 caused the crash, much as the Bank of Japan's attempt to control that country's asset and real estate bubble caused the crash in 1990. These and other examples provided by the "prick-the-bubble-crash-the-economy" pessimists conveniently ignore the fact that in both cases the central bank aided and abetted speculation in the bubble's critical earlier stages, taking away the proverbial punch bowl long after the party had gotten out of control.

We don't mean to suggest that policy makers should impose drastic interest rate hikes to curtail bubbles. That would be dangerous. But a moderate, preemptive approach is appropriate, and far preferable to the current policy of doing nothing as bubbles grow, and then pulling out the stops when they finally pop. In a way, it's especially unfortunate that Greenspan became most associated with this do-nothing, do-everything strategy. He was clearly worried about rising share prices when he delivered that famous speech in 1996, and as he spoke of the dangers of asset bubbles, he argued that "evaluating shifts in balance sheets generally, and in asset prices particularly, must be an integral part of the development of monetary policy." But he then abandoned this strategy, fearing, perhaps, that factoring asset prices into monetary policy would have a disproportionate, destructive effect on the markets.

In reality, the danger of using monetary policy to control bubbles is not that it will be too effective but that it won't be effective enough. Had the Fed tried to control "irrational exuberance" in the 1990s by hiking policy rates by 100 or 150 basis points, this would have been insufficient in a climate where investors expected that share prices would double every year. Similarly, a decade later, comparable rate hikes might have had a limited effect among homeowners who believed that housing prices would go up 20 percent a year in perpetuity.

At such times, monetary policy alone may not be enough to control a credit or asset bubble; central banks may have to deploy other powers at their disposal. The Fed has power under Regulation T, for example, to alter "margin requirements," the amount of money that investors can borrow to purchase securities. Though the Fed periodically changed these requirements in the early years of its existence, it has left them steady at 50 percent since 1974. Raising these requirements would have done a great deal to control the excesses of the tech bubble, when growing numbers of speculators bought shares on margin. Its failure to do so allowed the bubble to grow still larger.

The Fed has other "credit policy" tools that it could use to control the expansion of credit and the consequent growth of an asset bubble. Regulation D permits it to alter the reserve ratio of member banks. In other words, the Fed can alter how much money a bank has to hold in reserve against certain kinds of deposits, or liabilities; this in turn can constrain credit creation. Other statutory powers give the Fed other kinds of indirect control over the availability of credit and, by extension, speculative bubbles.

Still more tools could be placed at the Fed's disposal. One proposal under consideration is to give banks the power to set Asset-Based Reserve Requirements (ABRRs). In one variation of this idea, central banks could unilaterally raise reserve requirements for certain assets. Had the Fed possessed this power in the years leading up to the current crisis, it could have raised reserve requirements for any assets rooted in real estate. This kind of precision would allow it to target asset prices in a particular sector, while leaving other parts of the financial system unscathed.

But new powers mean nothing if the Fed won't use them. For years, the Fed has adopted a laissez-faire approach to asset bubbles. That alone would be bad enough, but the Fed's behavior has arguably been worse. Far from "taking away the punch bowl," it has served as a cheerleader, flooding the system with easy money and refusing to exercise its regulatory authority over integral parts of the financial system—mortgage lending, for example. That has to change. The Fed is only as effective as the people running it. In the coming years, its leaders will need more than the power to pop asset bubbles; they will need to be willing to use that power.

They will also need to know that there are limits to their power in the global monetary system. For over sixty years, the United States and its dollar have reigned supreme. Those days may be coming to an end, and how we manage that difficult transition will be integral to determining the prevalence of crises in the coming years. This is the subject of the following, final chapter.

Chapter 10

Fault Lines

The financial crisis that crept onto the radar late in 2007 and reached gale-force intensity in 2008 has come and gone. We live in its aftermath, and like the survivors of a hurricane, we're mopping up the damage and picking up the pieces. At this point, it's tempting to assume the worst is behind us. Unemployment may continue to climb and housing prices could resume their downward slide, but a consensus holds that we've weathered the storm.

But crises of other kinds loom on the horizon, crises of countries and currencies, in which nations default on their debt or see their monetary system collapse. Such crises were largely absent in 2007 and 2008: nations didn't default on their debt, nor did monetary systems break apart at the seams, even if currencies fluctuated wildly. Only Iceland came close to total collapse.

Sadly, Iceland may soon have some company. In the past, speculative booms and busts often triggered a wave of sovereign debt defaults. This time around, as a consequence of bailouts and stimulus programs, many of the world's advanced economies are now running record fiscal deficits. The risk is growing that these countries—call them the risky rich—will no longer be able to finance these deficits, raising the alarming possibility that they might default on their sovereign debt or wipe it out with high inflation.

Not even the United States is immune to this possibility. Its deficits are soaring, thanks to foolish tax cuts and the cost of bailing out everyone from banks to car companies to homeowners. As the United States continues to borrow more and more money from abroad, its creditors have started to whisper the unthinkable: that the United States might resort to the time-honored way of making debts disappear, by cranking up the printing press and flooding the world with depreciated dollars.

It may or may not happen, but that such a scenario even merits serious discussion portends a major geopolitical shift. For many decades the United States enjoyed international political and economic hegemony, thanks in part to the dollar's role as a reserve currency for the rest of the world. But over the last twenty years the United States has increasingly spent more than it has produced and earned, and imported more than it exports. As it went from being the world's biggest creditor to being its largest debtor, its power has weakened. So too has the dollar, which conceivably may one day be replaced by, say, the Chinese renminbi.

In this chapter we look at the origins of this disquieting development, about which a remarkable amount of confusion and misinformation reigns. How might these problems resolve themselves in the coming years? We will assess different options for managing the difficult transition from the American Century to what may well become the Chinese Century.

This tectonic shift may well take place in a disruptive, disorderly fashion; only time will tell. But if it does happen suddenly, it won't be pretty. Sovereign debt defaults, high inflation, and currency crashes are bad enough when smaller, emerging markets crumble and fall, commonly spawning widespread bank runs, devastating inflation, exploding unemployment, and widespread political and social unrest. If the world's largest and most powerful economy—the United States—were to fall prey to that kind of crisis, one can only imagine the effects. Such a calamity would give "too big to fail" a whole new and scary meaning.

Accounting for the Current Account

In order to better grasp what may lie ahead for China and the United States, we must understand an important measure of a country's economic health: the current account.

A country's current account is its "external balance," a measure of how its economy compares with those of other countries at any given time. The current account balance comes in two flavors: a current account *surplus* and a current account *deficit*. While it's theoretically possible for a country to have a current account of zero, that doesn't really happen; it would be like a corporation that reported neither a profit nor a loss.

That said, countries aren't really like corporations; they have bigger and more complicated balance sheets. One ingredient of a country's current account is the tally of its imports and exports. The difference between them yields either a negative or a positive number. Some countries, like the United States, run a trade deficit, meaning that they import more goods and services than they export. That's a negative number. Other countries, like China and Japan, run a trade surplus, exporting more goods and services than they import. That's a positive number.

That number is one part of a country's current account. But the current account also takes stock of the country's foreign assets and foreign liabilities. Let's begin with assets. If the United States owns equities, bonds, or even real estate in another country, these holdings generate income in the form of dividends, interest, and rent; it all flows into the United States. That's a positive number. On the other hand, if companies in the United States have issued equities or debt that is owned by nonresidents, or if the United States itself has issued government debt owned by nonresidents, these are liabilities: they cause money—in the form of dividends or interest payments—to flow out of the country. That's a negative number.

The current account adds together the difference between exports and imports (the balance of trade) and the difference between income earned on foreign assets and payments made toward foreign liabilities (what economists call "net factor payments"). Additionally, the current account has a third component: one-sided transfers of money across national boundaries, such as foreign aid and migrant worker remittances back home. Such transfers tend to be relatively minor, except in certain countries that receive a lot of aid (in sub-Saharan Africa, for example) or that have a lot of their citizens working abroad (the Philippines and some Central American economies), so let's leave that figure aside for now. In any case, if the number derived from adding all three components together is negative, the country is running a current account deficit. If that number is positive, it's running a surplus.

As a measure of a country's overall health, the current account can be misleading. Japan, for example, is now running a current account surplus. That may seem strange, since Japan's government has issued an astonishing amount of debt; one might expect it to be running a current account deficit. But it isn't, because Japan exports far more than it imports. In addition, most Japanese government debt is purchased by Japanese citizens, so it doesn't show up as a debt owed to other countries. That helps give Japan—a country not known recently for its robust economy—a current account surplus.

Now consider the United States, which is running a significant trade deficit. In addition, its government is issuing more and more debt, much of which is financed by investors overseas. Finally, until recently consumers spent far in excess of their income. That spending too was heavily financed by overseas investors, who snapped up securities derived from American mortgages and credit card debt. All these imbalances help contribute to what is now the biggest current account deficit in the world.

By contrast, China has the world's biggest current account surplus. Plenty of money flows into China as payments for all the goods that it makes and exports. Moreover, China has relatively little debt of its own, and foreigners don't own much of it. But it owns lots of debt issued in other countries, most obviously American mortgages and government bonds. China's massive current account surplus thus leads to an accumulation of foreign assets, like U.S. Treasury bonds. In this way, money flows from countries that run current account surpluses (China) to those that run current account deficits (the United States).

A country's current account balance also represents the difference between its "national savings" and its "national investment." This distinction is key. Let's start with national savings. Both the public sector (government) and the private sector (households and businesses) bring in income, in the form of taxes, wages, salaries, or other revenue. Different sectors of the economy then spend some or all of that income on things, which qualifies as consumption: the government purchases military supplies, a household buys food, or a manufacturer procures raw materials. After all that consumption, the aggregate amount left over is known as the "national savings." It is the "money in the pocket" of the nation at large.

Let's imagine that a country's national savings is a positive number: the government runs budget surpluses, and households and businesses have money left over after their consumption too. This money now must be invested somewhere. It can be invested at home: underwriting the construction of a new factory, for example, or going toward other capital improvements. The sum total of the various investments made at home is the national investment. If some savings are still left over after all that national investment, then the country is said to be running a current account surplus. The current account is the difference between national savings and national investment; when that difference is a positive number, as it is in this case, then the extra savings end up flowing out of the country.

This example is very simplistic: more typically, a country's government will run a deficit, even when its households and businesses are running an even bigger surplus. But a country with a positive national savings isn't necessarily running a current account surplus. Not at all. Let's say it plows all of its savings into investments at home, but that doesn't exhaust the demand for investments. (Emerging-market economies, for example, often have a demand for investments that domestic savings alone can't fill.) When that happens, the country is likely to attract investment from abroad, in which case borrowed money flows into the country. The country ends up running a current account deficit.

Clearly there are many ways of looking at current account surpluses and current account deficits. In itself, a surplus or a deficit is neither a good thing nor a bad thing; it's merely a reflection of a more complicated underlying reality. Soaring government budget deficits can fuel a current account deficit, but so can a boom in investment. A fall in private savings because people are consuming too much—particularly goods from abroad—can drive a current account deficit as well. All these different factors can come together either in a deficit or in a surplus.

Let's say a country is running a current account deficit, with excesses in spending over income, investment over savings, and imports over exports. How does it finance these various excesses? Usually other countries will lend the country money by buying up its debt or by investing in its economy by purchasing stocks, or buying real estate, or by directly investing in, acquiring, or creating productive firms (as Japanese and European automakers have built factories in the United States). Alternatively, a country may finance its current account deficit if its central bank sells off its holdings of foreign currency or if domestic investors sell off their assets overseas. Thus the sum of the current account balance and what economists call the "capital account"—the change in the country's private foreign assets minus its foreign liabilities—is equal to the change in the reserves of the central bank.

Normally some countries run deficits and others run surpluses. But in recent years these imbalances have became ever more, well, imbalanced. Up to 2007, when the recent financial crisis hit, the United States and a few other countries ran ever larger current account deficits. How did this happen?

Lessons from Emerging-Market Crises

Economic theory holds that for the most part emerging economies will run current account deficits while more advanced economies run current account surpluses. Theoretically, advanced economies, having a surplus of savings above and beyond their own capital investments, will invest in emerging markets, where capital investment opportunities exceed domestic savings. Investors from advanced economies can buy up debt, equities, and real estate in emerging economies, as well as make foreign direct investments, all in the hope of earning high returns. When they make such investments, sometimes both sides ultimately benefit. At other times, crises are the consequence.

For centuries, as we have seen, crises have followed a pretty predictable path. Foreign investment flows into a country and helps fuel an asset bubble of one sort or another. In the process, as private consumption rises and investment booms, the country's current account deficit widens. Large fiscal deficits may emerge—and debt and leverage accumulate. At some point the bubble bursts, and various sectors of the economy suffer: households, corporations, financial firms, and the government. Eventually the country defaults on its debt; or its currency collapses; or both happen at once.

In recent years emerging markets around the world have endured some version of this rags-to-riches-to-rags story. The reasons vary greatly. A typical culprit is a current account deficit driven largely by growing fiscal deficits. Fiscal deficits aren't bad in themselves; a country may be issuing debt abroad in order to finance improvements in its infrastructure, which eventually will enable the country to be more competitive, producing and exporting more goods and services, and ultimately turning that current account deficit into a surplus.

Unfortunately, government spending can also be the road to ruin, especially if it ends up going toward the salaries of government officials rather than toward investments in, say, infrastructure. In various ways countries may run large fiscal deficits and issue too much debt. Eventually foreign investors balk at renewing the debt, or refuse to purchase new debt. The result is a "sovereign debt crisis." That's precisely what happened in Latin America in the early 1980s, as well as Russia in 1998, Ecuador in 1999, and Argentina in 2001 and 2002. These countries effectively defaulted on the sovereign debt held by their own citizens and by foreigners, and their currencies collapsed. In each case foreign investors fled, and the domestic economy plunged into a severe recession. In Argentina, for example, consumer prices rose 40 percent in a single year, and unemployment approached 25 percent. Other countries—Ukraine and Pakistan in 1999, and Uruguay in 2002—avoided outright default but sustained significant damage nonetheless. Most of these countries experienced currency crises as well.

A current account deficit, as we've said, need not degenerate into a sovereign debt default or a currency crisis. An emerging market may be borrowing heavily from foreigners in order to finance investments in its economy: for example, in new factories that may become future sources of income. Ideally, these investments will enable the country to produce more goods and services that it can export abroad, enabling it to repay its debts and, it is hoped, run a current account surplus.

But a current account deficit driven by foreign investment can also go awry, as happened in Indonesia, South Korea, Thailand, and Malaysia in the 1990s. None of these countries were running significant fiscal deficits; rather, their current account deficits derived almost entirely from an excess of capital spending relative to private saving, with foreign investors making up the difference. Yet their current account deficit swelled to unmanageable levels, and eventually these economies crashed. Why?

For starters, much of the borrowing from foreign investors was denominated in foreign currencies: the dollar and the yen. These countries were willing to borrow in foreign currency partly because their central banks were buying and selling foreign currencies in order to maintain a somewhat inflated value for the local currency. They could then borrow even more from foreign creditors, adding to the amount of their foreign debt denominated in foreign currency.

When one of these countries' current account deficits reached extreme levels, some investors finally lost their nerve and fled. The central bank tried to maintain the old rate of exchange, but to no avail. More foreign investors cashed out at the fixed exchange rate, draining the central bank of reserves and undercutting its ability to prop up its own currency. Eventually, the old exchange-rate regime collapsed, as did the currency.

As the value of the local currency plunged, the real value of the debt denominated in foreign currency soared. Borrowers who exported goods had no problem with such debt: they earned foreign currency when they sold their wares and could repay their own debts. But for those whose investments in real estate and local services generated only local currency, the currency collapse was a disaster. They could no longer pay their debts, and many went under.

Other forces conspired to make these countries particularly vulnerable. Most of the foreign investment in these countries arrived in the form of loans rather than equity investment. With equity financing, profits and dividends can decline when times get tough and rise once conditions improve. Debt financing, by contrast, allows much less flexibility: interest and principal on bank loans and bonds have to be paid both in good times and in bad. When a crisis hits, that commitment can be tough to maintain.

For many of these countries it was particularly tough, because their obligations consisted of short-term debt, which had to be rolled over on a regular basis. That effectively gave foreign investors plenty of opportunities to pull out, which they did when they got spooked. They declined to renew their loans and asked the debtors to pay in full. Many of the latter lacked sufficient liquid assets, such as central bank foreign currency reserves, or could not convert their assets into liquid funds, and defaulted.

Most of the emerging markets that succumbed to crisis ended up going hat in hand to the IMF. The IMF deemed Russia, Argentina, and Ecuador effectively insolvent and pulled the plug, letting them default on some of their sovereign debt. It deemed other countries illiquid but not insolvent and rescued them by offering loans (bailouts) or by brokering agreements in which private creditors agreed to give them some breathing room by rolling over their debt obligations, or by participating in a formal debt restructuring (a "bail-in"). None of this prevented defaults on privately issued debt, and eventually huge numbers of banks and nonfinancial corporations defaulted on debts denominated in foreign currencies.

The string of emerging-market crises that began in the 1980s and continued for the next two decades left an indelible impression on policy makers in many countries, who concluded that a current account deficit was a bad thing: it had, after all, left economies vulnerable when the flows of foreign capital ("hot money") stopped and shifted into reverse. They also concluded that their countries had to prepare for future crises by accumulating war chests of foreign currency reserves that could be used to provide liquidity where needed. Accordingly, they cut their budget deficits and private spending, thereby reducing their foreign borrowing. Having put their financial houses in order, these countries then started to run current account surpluses—and accumulated massive amounts of foreign currency reserves to shield themselves from future crises.

For many of these economies, this accumulation of reserves had another, complementary purpose. A country that runs a current account surplus is likely to see its currency appreciate. For economies that depend on exports, an appreciating currency reduces their products' competitiveness on the global markets. So these economies deliberately bought up foreign currencies on the foreign exchange market, propping up the foreign currencies' value while simultaneously undercutting that of their own. China, home to the world's biggest current account surplus and possessor of one of the world's most undervalued currencies, has honed this dual strategy to perfection.

That current accounts in most emerging economies in Asia and Latin America went from deficit to surplus surprised most economists. So did the fact that a number of advanced economies—Ireland, Spain, Iceland, Australia, the United Kingdom, New Zealand, and, most important, the United States—went from running surpluses to running deficits.

In fact, these advanced economies started to resemble the emerging economies of a decade earlier: they played host to asset booms financed from abroad. Much of the U.S. housing bubble, for example, was financed by nonresidents—during the boom years they purchased more than half the mortgage-backed securities and collateralized debt obligations. This helped housing prices soar, and Americans felt richer, saved less, and spent more, further exacerbating the country's current account deficit. Residents of other advanced economies did the same. After the financial crisis, these current account deficits narrowed, but none of these countries is likely to run a surplus in the foreseeable future.

These developments ran counter to the conventional wisdom, as well as to historical precedent. Ordinarily advanced economies run surpluses and emerging markets run deficits; a surplus of savings accumulated in advanced economies ends up invested in emerging economies, not the other way around. But we now live in a world where the opposite is increasingly true—a world turned upside down.

Rashomon

The debate over current account imbalances resembles Akira Kurosawa's classic film *Rashomon*. In that saga a terrible crime has occurred in the forest, and various characters concede that something bad has occurred, but each gives a different explanation of what happened and who is to blame.

Likewise, no one disputes the facts of the current economic "crime": global account imbalances are very large and until recently were growing larger. The United States and a few other advanced economies live beyond their means, while most of the rest of the world—China, Japan, emerging Asia, various oil exporters, and much of Latin America, as well as Germany and a handful of other countries in Europe—do precisely the opposite. But as for who is to blame—and who should be punished—there's very little consensus.

Why? For one thing, within economic circles there are multiple accounts of this "crime," multiple accusations and alibis. While some of them contain shadings of truth, misinformation also abounds. So we must clear the air by addressing a few key questions: Why have these imbalances materialized in recent years? Are they sustainable? And if not, who should address them, and what policies should they pursue?

One of the more specious attempts to account for the current account deficit is the "dark matter" explanation. Proponents of this fairy tale—the economists Ricardo Hausmann and Federico Sturzenegger, among others—deny that the current account deficit is really as big as official figures suggest; if it were, they argue, the United States couldn't possibly be borrowing from the rest of the world at such low rates. They point to the fact that the United States is getting a better return on its foreign investments than foreigners are getting on their U.S. investments, which is hard to explain in the context of a massive current account deficit.

But their explanation is simple: there is no current account deficit. It is, they explain, "just a confusion caused by an unnatural set of accounting rules." Instead, there is "dark matter" out there that the existing accounting has failed to capture. This valuable dark matter is difficult to price because it consists of intangibles that the United States provides: things like insurance, liquidity, and knowledge. The authors put particular emphasis on knowledge, arguing that superior "know-how deployed abroad by U.S. corporations" isn't captured in the statistics, and that all this talk about a current account deficit is nonsense.

This argument has been challenged on a number of points. One, that foreigners investing in the United States have earned less than the United States earns overseas is not surprising: many of them invest in the United States for reasons other than turning a profit. China, for example, has sunk hundreds of billions of dollars into low-yield U.S. Treasury bonds in order to keep its currency cheap and its exports affordable. Moreover, economists at the Fed have collected data suggesting that the returns realized by the United States abroad and those realized by foreigners investing in the United States are actually the same. That too seriously undercuts the argument.

A more serious explanation of the current account balance is the "global savings glut" hypothesis. Ben Bernanke came up with this one; it effectively deflects the blame for the U.S. current account deficit onto other countries. The problem isn't that Americans aren't saving enough, says this hypothesis, or that the U.S. government is running massive deficits. Rather, the problem is that China and other Asian countries are saving *too much*.

At first glance this argument seems counterintuitive. But many advanced industrial economies in Europe, Bernanke points out, are saving a great deal in anticipation of an aging workforce. Without sufficiently attractive investment opportunities at home, they have sunk those savings into the United States. Even more central to his hypothesis is the idea that frugal citizens of various Asian countries, particularly China, are saving too much and spending too little.

This argument has some superficial truth. Savings rates in China are very high, and consumer spending is relatively low. That's partly due to structural constraints: China has no social safety net and lacks a sound consumer credit system; it's hard to borrow money there to buy a house. So China and other emerging economies have accumulated surplus savings for a reason. Moreover, in an age of financial globalization, money can flow easily across national borders and into the United States, making current account deficits more sustainable than in previous eras.

That said, this line of reasoning has a serious problem: it subtly shifts blame for the massive current account deficit onto foreigners. By that logic, the U.S. consumer shouldn't be blamed for the housing bubble; it's the fault of all those penny-pinching Chinese who sent us their surplus funds. Blaming them is like blaming drug lords in Bolivia for the coke habits of some Americans: there's some truth to the allegation, but the story is far more complicated.

In fact, other forces played a far bigger role in the rising current account deficit, particularly since 2001. Thanks to a recession and the enormous tax cuts that George W. Bush rammed through Congress, fiscal deficits soared. After having taken the trouble to put its fiscal house in order in the 1990s, the United States once again started to issue lots of debt, which the Chinese and other emerging-market economies purchased. Their only crime was purchasing that debt; American policy makers' crime was consciously pursuing policies that exacerbated the U.S. current account deficit.

The Federal Reserve played a role too, making plenty of easy money available after 2001 and doing little to supervise and regulate the financial system. These policies, more than any "global savings glut," helped create the housing boom, leading to an increase in residential investment and a decline in savings. Yes, much of the investment was financed with savings from other countries, but the Fed helped create the unsustainable boom that attracted these savings in the first place.

Looking back, it's clear that different factors at different points in time have driven today's global account imbalances. In the 1990s the tech boom and the corresponding rise in the stock market attracted an influx of foreign capital and thereby drove the rising current account deficit. That led many Americans to save less and consume more, further fueling the current account deficit. After the bubble's collapse, the deficit should have declined, but it didn't: instead, reckless fiscal policies enacted by the Bush administration sent it soaring.

The current account deficit increased even more after 2004, thanks in part to a dubious housing boom enabled by lax federal regulators. Savings rates fell, and foreign investors snapped up securities derived from the growing number of mortgages. Only after 2007 did the current account deficit finally decline, as the housing bubble burst, imports fell, and households started to save more. A drop in oil prices contributed to the decline as well.

So unlike Kurosawa's *Rashomon*, the tale of the current account deficit "crime" has an obvious culprit. To paraphrase Pogo, "We have met the enemy, and he is US"—the United States.

That's not to say that the United States didn't have help: everything from surplus savings from China to financial globalization enabled the country to run a current account deficit. But enabling is not the same as coercing. So the ultimate responsibility for this mess rests with the United States, which for a decade pursued policies that sent its current accounts deficit soaring. With its reckless tax cuts and its unwillingness to rein in the housing boom, the United States has dug itself deep into a hole.

Dangers and Dilemmas

Economists of a Panglossian bent use several arguments to dismiss concerns about the American current account deficit. Emerging-market economies, they say, will happily finance the deficit for the foreseeable future: they need to keep their currencies cheap, and one way to do that is to buy up U.S. equities and debt. Others point to the fact that the United States enjoys what Valéry Giscard d'Estaing, the French minister of finance in the early 1960s, called the "exorbitant privilege" of having the world's reserve currency. Surely, the reasoning goes, this will forestall the sort of currency crises that plague less fortunate countries. Given these advantages, the United States should be able to keep running massive current account deficits for many years.

That's absurd. The status quo is unsustainable and dangerous, and absent some difficult reforms it will ultimately unravel. Indeed, if the United States doesn't get its fiscal house in order and start saving more, it's headed for a nasty reckoning. When that reckoning will come is anyone's guess, but the notion that it might be put off for decades is delusional. Indeed, some signs suggest that the tide is already beginning to turn. Back in the 1990s the current account deficit was financed in no small part by foreign investment in U.S. equities, which by its peak in 2000 topped $300 billion. After the tech bubble burst, foreign investment collapsed, and while it has rebounded some, it has not returned to previous levels. Yet during that same period the current account deficit grew ever larger. This was made possible by foreign purchases of debt. The government issued some of that debt; plenty more was issued on the backs of private mortgages and other assets.

Foreign central banks and sovereign wealth funds purchased most of it. In fact, nonresidents now hold about half of the outstanding U.S. Treasury bills and bonds (outside of those held by the Federal Reserve), and two-thirds of these are held by central banks and sovereign wealth funds. In other words, it's not private investors who have financed the lion's share of the current account deficit. They're not stupid: they know the dollar might depreciate and have no interest in putting their money at risk. But governments and their proxies, as we've discussed, have other motives for buying up this debt.

But they too have their limits. As evidence of foreigners' growing unease, they're not holding on to U.S. debt as long as they once did. A decade ago the average maturity of U.S. public debt was close to sixty months. By 2009 that figure shrank to below fifty months, which reflects growing worry that the dollar will decline in value, whether by chance or by design. Indeed, as the United States accumulates ever more staggering loads of debt, some of its creditors fear that it may try to deliberately depreciate the dollar by "monetizing" the deficit, effectively printing money out of thin air. But then, it's already doing that via quantitative easing.

If the United States were an emerging market, it would have long ago suffered a collapse of confidence in its debt and its currency. That it hasn't reflects the fact that the United States is still regarded as a country that raises taxes and cuts spending when necessary, putting its fiscal house in order. It did so in the early 1990s after a decade of soaring deficits; there's no reason it can't do so again. Moreover, unlike many emerging economies, the United States has never defaulted on its public debt. That goes a long way toward reassuring investors. Finally, and most important, the United States borrows from abroad in its own currency. The potential depreciation of the dollar doesn't increase U.S. liabilities. Instead, that currency risk is transferred to foreign creditors.

That's a key difference. But it doesn't mean foreign creditors will keep piling up hundreds of billions of low-yield government bonds forever. At some point they're going to demand real assets—ownership stakes in American companies. So far the United States has resisted foreign ownership of its most important corporations. In 2005 public outcry stopped the China National Offshore Oil Corporation from purchasing an ownership stake in Unocal, and the following year a similar reaction prevented a state-owned company in Dubai (Dubai Ports World) from assuming management control of a number of key U.S. ports.

These skirmishes reflect a kind of "asset protectionism," in which the United States tries to tell its increasingly powerful creditors where to direct their money. Asset protectionism continued during the financial crisis, when several of the nation's biggest banks went hat in hand to sovereign wealth funds in the Middle East and Asia but refused to cede any significant control to these investors. Many of those investors got burned, which makes it highly unlikely that they'll be content to sit in the backseat next time they're tapped to prop up the financial system.

Many politicians and policy makers seem blithely unaware of how little leverage the United States has with the countries financing our twin fiscal and current account deficits. They tell China it can't buy up American companies, and they threaten to take protectionist measures if China doesn't revalue its currency. That's very quaint—and foolish. In effect, China is underwriting U.S. wars in Afghanistan and Iraq, never mind the bailout of the financial system and any costs associated with reforming health care. Biting the hand that feeds us may play well with voters at home, but with China it has its limits.

Is China's path to global hegemony free of obstacles? No. Only 36 percent of China's gross domestic product comes from consumption. In the United States that figure is upward of 70 percent. While U.S. domestic consumption is too high, China's remains far too low. For now, its continued survival and growth depend heavily on cheap exports to the United States, which are in turn financed by the sale of debt to China. This perverse symbiosis ("They give us poisoned products, we give them worthless paper," explains Paul Krugman) poses a threat to China's long-term interests.

China has other problems too. Undeniably it has staggering reserves, and it has plowed some of its sizable war chest into a massive stimulus program aimed at improving the nation's infrastructure and at forcing state-controlled banks to make loans to various state-owned enterprises. That may work in the short term, but it's not sustainable in the long run. Loaning money to build more factories in a global economy that's already drowning in overcapacity isn't the road to salvation. All it may do is foster a speculative bubble in China that will ultimately leave the nation's banks with a bunch of nonperforming loans.

As of 2010, China and the United States remain locked in what economist Lawrence Summers has described as a "balance of financial terror." Neither side can make a move without upsetting that balance. China can't stop buying U.S. debt, or its biggest market will collapse. Conversely, the United

States can't throw up protectionist barriers, or China will stop financing its profligate ways.

To get out of this bind, both countries need to take simultaneous steps to bring their current accounts into some semblance of equilibrium. The United States must tackle its twin savings deficits: its ballooning federal budget deficit and its low level of private savings. As its first step on the road to redemption, it will have to repeal the misguided tax cuts that the Bush administration pushed through earlier in the decade. If Americans think they can enjoy European-style social spending—universal health care, for example—while maintaining low tax rates, they are wrong. It won't work, and betting that the Chinese will forever foot the bill is wishful thinking.

For their part, China and other emerging economies in Asia need to let their currencies appreciate. They also need to adopt structural reforms to discourage saving, so that more of what China produces gets consumed at home. They must take concrete steps to promote the growth of consumer credit: at present, most Chinese continue to purchase their homes in cash, rather than relying on mortgages. And they must institute the sort of safety nets common in advanced economies, like unemployment insurance and affordable health care. These very basic steps would give China's citizens some assurance that they don't need to save every penny—or renminbi—for a rainy day. Absent these reforms, China will have a hard time stopping its famously frugal citizens from indirectly subsidizing the United States.

The rest of the world can help by trying to trim their own surpluses. More mature economies like Germany, France, and Japan need to accelerate structural reforms that will increase investment, productivity, and growth and (it is hoped) shrink their current account surpluses. Oil exporters like Saudi Arabia need to let their currencies appreciate and start spending more on domestic consumption and on investment in infrastructures and in the exploration and production of more oil.

All these measures would foster an orderly rebalancing of international current accounts. Unfortunately, none of the players in this drama seem to be taking the necessary steps. Everyone seems to be hoping that the status quo—soaring surpluses on one side, widening deficits on the other—is somehow sustainable. It's not. Unless things change, the pressure will continue to build until it can no longer be contained. Then it will snap, with unpredictable effects. The resulting crisis would be very different from the garden-variety booms and busts we discussed in chapter 1. It would be less a function of capitalism's inherent instability than a deep ebb and flow of geopolitical power. If ordinary financial crises are minor tremblors, the abrupt unraveling of global imbalances—never mind the associated sovereign debt defaults and currency crashes—would constitute an earthquake.

So far, we have felt only tremors. The financial crisis wounded a number of advanced economies, raising doubts about the long-term creditworthiness of Greece, Ireland, Italy, Portugal, Spain, and even the United Kingdom. Some of these nations—particularly the so-called Club Med countries of Greece, Italy, Portugal, and Spain—may default sooner rather than later, threatening the European Union and potentially plunging these regions into the sort of chaos that touched Argentina in 2002 and Iceland in 2008.

These tremblors will shake the global economy. But they're minor compared with the "big one"—a rapid, disorderly decline of the dollar.

The Decline of the Dollar

In the late 1950s the United States was at the peak of its power. It ran a current account surplus, and the dollar served as the international reserve currency. Under the famed Bretton Woods agreement, signed shortly before the end of World War II, other nations made their currencies convertible into dollars at certain fixed rates, and the United States pledged to convert those same dollars into gold.

Most economists of the day—particularly American economists—thought Bretton Woods was a good idea, but Robert Triffin, a Belgian-born economist, begged to differ. In 1960 he spoke against the idea of having one nation's currency simultaneously serve as an international reserve currency. Such an arrangement, he warned, contained the seeds of its own destruction. Triffin observed that nations that issue reserve currencies—Britain in the nineteenth century, the United States in the twentieth—generally maintain current account surpluses. In the case of the United States, that meant that more dollars flowed into the country than flowed out.

So far, so good. But other countries, Triffin pointed out, would need to hold the reserve currency. The resulting demand for dollars would create a countervailing force, causing dollars to flow out of the United States. Those pressures, Triffin argued, would eventually create a current account deficit, which would eventually undercut the economic standing of the United States and, by extension, the dollar. In effect, Triffin pointed out that the needs of the United States would collide with the needs of the rest of the world, paving the way for the decline of the dollar. That was precisely what happened in 1971, when President Nixon reneged on the pledge to convert dollars into gold.

Triffin's Dilemma remains relevant today. The dollar is no longer convertible into gold, but it remains the world's de facto reserve currency, even as that demand contributes to ever-greater global imbalances. Some economists have claimed that this arrangement—the so-called "Bretton Woods II" system—can persist for the foreseeable future, as dollars flow out of the United States and pile up in the vaults of central banks in Asia and the Middle East.

In fact, this uneasy arrangement shows serious signs of strain. Back in 2001 dollars made up a little over 70 percent of the currency reserves held overseas. Over the succeeding decade, as the fiscal deficits and current account deficit of the United States spiraled out of control, that percentage declined, reaching 63 percent in 2008. In the second half of 2009 foreign central banks displayed a pronounced aversion to the dollar and a strong preference for the euro and the yen; in the third quarter of 2009, dollars constituted only 37 percent of newly acquired reserves—a far cry from the average 67 percent a decade earlier. Gold and even some emerging-market currencies constitute a growing percentage of these reserves.

The ongoing effort to diversify away from the dollar is all the more apparent in the world's sovereign wealth funds. These state-owned investment funds—organizations like the China Investment Corporation—have started to avoid the U.S. Treasury debt that has long been a staple of central bank reserves, focusing instead on higher-yield investments, in everything from hedge funds to mineral rights.

That trend is likely to continue in the coming years. With any luck, the transition will be a gradual process, not a sudden, disorderly collapse. Possibly the United States may follow in the footsteps of Britain, whose power—and currency—ebbed over many decades. Indeed, though the United States surpassed Britain as the world's biggest economy sometime around 1872, the pound sterling remained the world's premier currency for two more generations. Only after World War I, when Britain went from being a net creditor to a net debtor, did the pound sterling seriously slip, and other countries began diversifying their currency holdings, though as late as 1928 the world's currency reserves still contained twice as many pounds as dollars. After Britain abandoned the gold standard in 1931, the dollar did displace the pound. The Bretton Woods agreement helped cement the dollar's supremacy, though only with the Suez Crisis of 1956—and the further collapse of the pound sterling—did the dollar become the world's unrivaled reserve currency.

The fall of the pound took three-quarters of a century, and we may reasonably hope that the dollar's decline will also proceed at such a leisurely pace. But this sort of historical analogy shouldn't be taken too far. China, which occupies roughly the same position that the United States did a century ago, is climbing the global economic ladder far more quickly than any other nation in history. It will likely surpass Japan as the world's second-largest economy in 2010 or 2011, and it may dethrone the United States from the top spot sooner rather than later. All of this has happened with astonishing speed. While the United States took a century to rise to power, China has managed to go from second-rate status to global power in only twenty years.

That raises the unnerving prospect that the dollar's days may be numbered in years rather than decades. How such an abrupt and disorderly decline might play out is difficult to know. Historically, currencies had some relationship to gold or silver; only in the 1970s was this connection severed entirely. The world's monetary system now rests not on gold but on a fiat currency—a currency that has no intrinsic value, is not backed by precious metals, and is in no way fixed in value. In a way, the dollar occupies the role that gold once did, and its collapse would be no less calamitous than if the regents and bankers of centuries past had opened their vaults one day to find that their precious piles of coin had turned to dust.

That may happen one day if the United States keeps running spiraling deficits. While China will likely continue to purchase debt, other, smaller countries may start to edge toward the exit. That may eventually prompt a stampede that even China would be tempted to join. Whatever the advantages of the present system for China, at some point the costs will outweigh the benefits.

The United States stands at a crossroads. If it doesn't get its fiscal house in order and increase its private savings, such a seismic event will only become more likely. It's all too easy to imagine a scenario where this plays out, particularly if a political stalemate develops: Republicans veto tax increases, Democrats veto spending cuts, and monetizing the deficits—printing money—becomes the path of least resistance. The resulting inflation will erode the dollar value of the public and private debt held around the world. Faced with such an "inflation tax," investors around the world dump their dollars, moving them into the currency of a country with a far better reputation for fiscal responsibility.

Should that take place, the United States would pay the price. Up to now, we have been able to issue debt in our own currency rather than a foreign one, shifting the losses of a fall in the value of the dollar to our creditors. If other countries effectively revoked this "exorbitant privilege," the burden would fall back on us, and our borrowing costs would shoot upward, dragging down consumption, investment, and ultimately economic growth. The price of imports—everything from cheap plastic toys from China to barrels of oil from Saudi Arabia—would rise, crimping a standard of living that Americans have come to consider their birthright. In the process, the dollar would become just another currency in the crowd.

But that invites a question: what would take its place?

The Almighty Renminbi?

At first glance, the Chinese currency—the renminbi or the yuan—seems the obvious candidate to follow in the footsteps of the American dollar. Few other currencies pose serious competition. The British pound, the Japanese yen, and the Swiss franc remain minor reserve currencies. They may offer temporary refuge from an eroding dollar, but they're the currencies of countries in decline. The same could be said, on a larger scale, of the euro, whose continued survival depends on the unity of a fractious group of countries, many of which shoulder staggering deficits, aging populations, and growing competition from emerging markets.

Far less feasible is a return to gold. For all its recent luster, the idea of making gold the basis of the monetary system remains what Keynes rightly called a "barbarous relic." While it may provide a temporary sanctuary from a collapsing dollar, its rising value is largely a function of fear and anxiety about the future. Gold is a place to hide, not a foundation for a new monetary order. It has few practical uses, is difficult to store, and exists in minute quantities relative to the present size of the global economy. None of these features make it a good candidate for a reserve currency.

That said, if governments resort to monetizing their deficits, triggering higher inflation, gold could rise sharply in price. But should that happen, central banks would probably not try to corner scarce supplies of gold. More likely they would invest more in oil and other commodities as a hedge against inflation. In other words, they would rush into real assets as they fled fiat currencies like the dollar.

That leaves the renminbi as the long-term alternative to the dollar. China looks much like the United States did when it came to power: it runs large current account surpluses, has become the world's biggest exporter, has a relatively small budget deficit, and carries much less debt relative to other countries. It has already taken subtle steps to challenge the dollar. For example, it has permitted financial institutions in Hong Kong to issue Chinese public debt denominated in the yuan, a crucial step in creating a regional market in the debt and, by extension, the currency. The Chinese finance ministry tellingly described this move as an effort to "promote the renminbi in neighboring countries and improve the yuan's international status."

China has taken other steps to bolster its monetary power. It has set up currency swaps with several countries, including Argentina, Brazil, Belarus, and Indonesia. It has also pushed some of its trading partners to use the yuan to settle accounts—that is, to denominate their invoices in yuan. This may seem like a small matter, but it's not: at present, much invoicing in international trade uses the dollar as the "unit of account," even when the trade doesn't involve the United States. This deference—similar to the respect accorded the pound sterling a century ago—reflects the dollar's real and symbolic status as the international reserve currency. If the yuan gains widespread acceptance in the world's account books, the dollar will see its reserve-currency status usurped.

For now, however, the renminbi faces an uphill battle to become the world's premier currency. Even the Chinese may not want it to happen too quickly. The exchange rate would have to become more flexible, allowing the renminbi to appreciate far more than it has already, and making China's exports less affordable to other countries. In addition, China would need to implement reforms it may not wish to take: easing restrictions on money entering and leaving the country, for example, and making its currency fully convertible for such capital transactions. China would also need to accelerate domestic financial reforms and start issuing much greater quantities of yuan-denominated debt.

Though the Chinese clearly want a greater role for the renminbi, they don't seem eager for it to become the world's reserve currency anytime soon. In 2009 Zhou Xiaochuan, governor of the People's Bank of China, proposed something very different: a new, supra-sovereign currency that would compete with the dollar. Zhou suggested a revision of the Special Drawing Rights (SDR), a quasi-currency created in 1969 under the auspices of the IMF, that can't pass from hand to hand the way a paper dollar or euro does but is purely a unit of account used by the IMF. It derives its value from four underlying currencies that are weighted in different ways: the dollar is the predominant ingredient, followed by the euro, the yen, and the pound. Anyone holding SDRs has a claim on the various currencies contained in the underlying "basket." The instruments can be used for a variety of purposes, like discharging debts owed to the IMF.

The relative quantities of the currencies in the basket get recalculated every five years, and Zhou's broadside made it clear that China expects its currency will be included. But wanting to sit at the table is not the same as wanting to run the show. In fact, Zhou cited Triffin's Dilemma in forcefully arguing for the creation of "an international reserve currency that is disconnected from individual nations and is able to remain stable in the long run, thus removing the inherent deficiencies caused by using credit-based national currencies."

In framing this proposal, Zhou looked back to the Bretton Woods

Conference of 1944. That year John Maynard Keynes pushed the attendees to contemplate the creation of a global supercurrency, called the "bancor," that would derive its value from a basket of some thirty underlying commodities. The Americans rejected the idea and pushed for the dollar to become the world's reserve currency. Zhou criticized that fateful step as misguided. Keynes, he claimed, had been "far-sighted," and the SDR might be a way of resurrecting his ideas.

For now, the idea of turning the SDR into a global reserve currency remains fanciful. A significant number of private and public parties would have to use it as a unit of account, and so far there's no sign of that happening; the SDR remains a creature of the IMF. Nonetheless, the growing interest in expanding its role highlights the degree to which China and many other emerging markets want to replace the dollar with something a bit more stable and resistant to crisis and collapse.

But that's not going to happen without international cooperation. So one of the other institutions that emerged from that fateful 1944 conference will have to be reformed: the IMF.

Global Governance

The swift rise of the economically powerful BRICs—Brazil, Russia, India, and China—and other emerging market economies has underscored the need to reform global economic governance. The original G-7—the United States, Japan, Germany, France, the United Kingdom, Canada, and Italy—cannot possibly claim to speak for the rest of the world. In order to resolve global imbalances, other players must sit at the table. To some extent they already are: in the past few years, the G-20 has started to supplant its more selective sibling, bringing Brazil, Indonesia, South Africa, Saudi Arabia, and other countries into the fold.

While more may be merrier, the G-20 is unlikely to make substantive changes in the global economy and the international monetary system. The G-7 has had enough trouble doing that; more than doubling the number of members may make it impossible, absent a more formal framework for discussing and implementing policy—and most of the world's economies would still have no voice.

The IMF may be more representative, but it has its own problems. Much of the IMF's decision making takes place via its executive board, which has twenty-four directors, each of whom represents a different global constituency. Unfortunately, European nations are overrepresented, while emerging economies in Asia and Africa are underrepresented. A similar problem bedevils the way the IMF calculates "shares"—the votes each country receives by virtue of its contributions to the IMF. One recent study found that in 2000 and 2001, the collective voting power of China, India, and Brazil was 19 percent less than that of Belgium, Italy, and the Netherlands, despite the fact that by one measure the former cluster of countries had a GDP four times the size—and a population twenty-nine times the size—of the latter.

So far the Europeans have been unwilling to cede power. That's foolish: if the IMF is to have any credibility in the coming years, its allocation of chairs and shares will have to reflect the interests and input of the emerging-market economies. That's true at the very top of the organization too. An informal precedent dictates that an American heads the World Bank while a European leads the IMF. So far, calls to dump this antiquated practice have fallen on deaf ears, further threatening the organization's legitimacy.

The IMF needs to be reformed in other ways too. While it has leverage over its members, this leverage applies only during times of crisis, and only to smaller countries that have trouble meeting payments on their debt. China, Japan, and Germany, nations that act as creditors to the rest of the world, can ignore the IMF. So can the United States, which runs current account deficits but gets to borrow in its own currency. In effect, the IMF can do nothing to force China, Europe, and the United States to change their ways. Worse, it has been reluctant to use the bully pulpit, failing to name and shame countries whose actions threaten the stability of the global economy.

That doesn't mean the IMF should be abandoned. Even with its limited resources, it can tackle one problem in particular: current account imbalances. As we have seen, emerging economies came away from the crises of the 1990s with two lessons: avoid running current account deficits, and amass a war chest of foreign currencies in anticipation of an international liquidity crunch. These strategies paid off during the recent crisis: countries in

Asia and Latin America that had surpluses and substantial foreign currency reserves aggressively intervened to prop up their own currencies, reassuring foreign investors that they could deal with a liquidity crisis without having to beg for support from the IMF.

However commendable, independence from the IMF has come at a serious price. Not only do these strategies contribute to unsustainable balances, but the real cost of such self-insurance—trillions of dollars stuck in low-yield assets—is high. Moreover, if left unattended, these reserves can help fuel asset bubbles in the countries that amass them. While governments sometimes deal with this problem by selling government bonds to soak up or "sterilize" the surplus cash, they end up paying high rates of interest on these new obligations—yet another cost to bear.

The IMF can address these problems, at the very least providing more liquidity in times of crisis. Until recently IMF loans came with strings attached: countries that accepted them had to agree to undertake economic reforms that the IMF deemed necessary. But not every country that suffers from a liquidity crunch needs to overhaul its economy. So during the recent crisis, the IMF offered a so-called Flexible Credit Line to qualifying countries. This is a good start. In the future, precautionary lines of credit should be made available to a greater range of countries as soon as signs of a crisis appear.

The IMF can also expand its issue of SDRs, particularly in times of crisis. In 2009 it obtained the right to issue $250 billion worth of SDRs, some of which went to emerging-market economies. That program should be expanded, especially through the issuance of international bonds denominated in SDRs. Central banks could purchase them to bulk out their reserves without contributing to the potential instability that conventional currency purchases cause (because the SDRs effectively spread the burden among several currencies rather than targeting a single one). Here the IMF should attach some strings: any recipients of SDRs should be forced to reduce their current account surpluses and otherwise reduce their accumulation of foreign currency reserves.

These modest proposals may go a long way toward weaning the global economy off the kinds of imbalances that played a role in the recent crisis. But if the world is going to move away from an obsolescent monetary system dependent on the declining dollar, much more will have to be done. A greater reliance on SDRs is a good first step but only a small one.

Addressing these challenges will require a level of international cooperation that has been noticeably absent in recent years. Whether the world's major economies will cooperate for the common good is an open question. If the United States and China continue to focus on short-term national interests, imbalances will continue to pile up, and an already-fragile international monetary system may fall victim to accumulated strain and stress.

In fact, the historical record would suggest that we live at a particularly vulnerable moment in financial history. In the past, international banking crises like the recent one have often been a prelude to waves of sovereign debt defaults and currency crashes. Economies damaged by the effects of asset bubbles gone bust and the consequent banking crises may limp along for a little while, but many will ultimately succumb, victims of accumulated injuries. That's going to be especially likely if the sorts of current account balances that preceded the recent crisis continue to spiral out of control. If they unravel, what happened to Iceland may be a harbinger of things to come in the world at large.

The Road Ahead

In chapters 8 and 9 we laid out ways that nations might reform their financial systems, imposing regulations on the banks and other firms that played a role in precipitating the recent crisis. But the push for reform can't end there: in the coming years policy makers will have to address the kinds of imbalances that can eventually cause national, regional, and even global financial crises. Every economy will have to do its share rather than try to free-ride on the system, using imbalances for its own advantage.

These reforms can approach the problem on the demand side and on the supply side; so far reforms on both fronts have been woefully insufficient. On the demand side, the excessive demand for foreign reserves by emerging-market economies has seriously exacerbated global imbalances. This problem needs to be addressed by the presence of a more stable and reliable international lender of last resort in order to avoid the risk of international liquidity crises. Only then will these economies' need for reserves start to diminish.

On the supply side, the menu of international reserve assets should be expanded beyond the U.S. dollar and a few other currencies: over time the SDR can and should play a greater role. Likewise, in the coming years, central banks and sovereign wealth funds may start to hold currencies of emerging-market economies as part of their reserves. In the short term, this won't threaten the role of the dollar as the major reserve currency; the U.S. dollar has no clear alternatives. But if the United States keeps running large twin deficits—or worse, starts to monetize its fiscal deficit—the resulting high inflation will accelerate the decline of the U.S. dollar as a major reserve currency, with unpredictable results.

Let's assume that the United States doesn't go down that road, and that the reforms we've described can bring about an orderly adjustment of global imbalances. There's one more piece of the puzzle. A substantial change in the institutions of global economic governance is necessary and desirable within both the G-20 and the IMF. The needed changes would provide more formal and effective power to emerging-market economies and ease the transfer of economic power from one part of the globe to another.

Will the world's major economies truly cooperate for the common global good? Or will they keep on following their national interests, eventually destabilizing the global economy and the global financial system? The question remains open, but both China and the United States in particular need to contemplate it in the coming years. Neither country stands to win from a continuation of the status quo, and everyone—emerging and advanced economies alike—stands to lose.

Conclusion

Throughout most of 2009, Goldman Sachs CEO Lloyd Blankfein repeatedly tried to quash calls for sweeping regulation of the financial system. In speeches and in testimony before Congress, he begged his listeners to keep financial innovation alive and "resist a response that is solely designed to protect us against the 100-year storm."

That's ridiculous. What we've just experienced wasn't some crazy once-in-a-century event. Since its founding, the United States has suffered from brutal banking crises and other financial disasters on a regular basis. Throughout the nineteenth and early twentieth centuries, crippling panics and depressions hit the nation again and again.

Financial crises disappeared only after the Great Depression, a period that coincided with the rise of the United States as a global superpower. At the same time the U.S. government reined in financial institutions with legislation like the Glass-Steagall Act and shored them up by creating agencies like the SEC and FDIC. The dollar became the ballast of an extraordinarily stable international monetary system, and crises came to seem like things of the past. Though serious cracks started to appear in the facade after the 1970s, economists in developed nations kept the faith, worshipping at the altar of the Great Moderation.

The recent cataclysm marks the beginning of the end of this dangerous illusion. It also marks the end of the financial stability ushered in by the Pax Americana. As American power erodes in the coming years, crises may become more frequent and virulent, absent a strong superpower that can cooperate with other emerging powers to bring the same stability to the global economy. Far from being a once-in-a-century event, the recent financial disaster may be a taste of things to come.

A new era demands new ways of thinking. We should jettison bankrupt ideas about the inherent stability, efficiency, and resilience of unregulated markets, and we should let crises take their rightful place in economics and finance. Sadly, many otherwise intelligent people cling to the belief that the recent crisis was an unpredictable, unheralded event. No one could have seen it coming, they say, and we'll never see the likes of it again—at least not in our lifetimes.

We can wait for a new financial calamity to deal a coup de grâce to this continuing complacency. Or we can embrace understanding a new economics: crisis economics.

Tragedy and Farce

Crises, as we have seen, are as old and ubiquitous as capitalism itself. They arose hand in hand with capitalism in the early seventeenth century, and like the plays that Shakespeare first staged at this time, they have remained with us ever since, in much the same form. The staging changes, as do the audiences, but everything else—the cast of characters, the order of the acts, and even the lines—remains remarkably consistent from crisis to crisis, century to century.

Almost all crises begin the same way: modestly. Subtle developments set the stage for the real drama down the line. This scene setting can take years, even decades, as numerous forces create conditions hospitable to a boom-and-bust cycle.

The crisis that exploded in 2007 was no exception. Decades of free-market fundamentalism laid the foundation for the meltdown, as so-called reformers swept aside banking regulations established in the Great Depression, and as Wall Street firms found ways to evade the rules that remained. In the process, a vast shadow banking system grew up outside regulatory oversight.

Over the same period banks increasingly adopted compensation schemes like bonuses that encouraged high-risk, short-term leveraged betting, even though such bets would undercut a financial firm's long-term stability. They effectively shifted negative consequences away from traders and bankers and onto the backs of the firm's shareholders and other creditors. Such problems, part of a larger epidemic of moral hazard, had been percolating throughout the U.S. financial system long before the crisis finally broke. The Federal Reserve played an instrumental role, rescuing the financial system in its time of need and giving rise to the famed "Greenspan put."

But setting the stage is not the same thing as creating a bubble. A bubble requires a catalyst. In previous financial crises the catalyst was a shortage of some coveted commodity or the opening of a new market overseas. Or a technological innovation stirred investors to believe that the old rules of valuation no longer applied. Fresh ways of doing things could originate in the financial system itself: a new way to package investments, or a new way of managing risk.

Unfortunately, the recent financial crisis fell into this final category, as financial institutions embraced securitization on a massive scale, giving us an alphabet soup of increasingly complex structured financial products. While securitization had been around for many years, it exploded in importance in the years immediately preceding the bubble. "Originate and distribute" became a vehicle for originating junk mortgages, slicing, dicing, and recombining them into toxic mortgage-backed securities, and then selling them as if they were AAA gold.

Another axiom of crisis economics is the straightforward observation that a bubble can grow only if investors have a source of easy credit. It might come courtesy of a central bank, or from private lenders—or from both, especially if unwary regulators allow the credit bubble to grow and fester. Easy credit might even come from an unexpected source of surplus cash sloshing around the global economy in search of an investment.

Here too the recent crisis followed a predictable plot. Greenspan slashed interest rates after September 11 and kept them too low for too long. Banks and shadow banks leveraged themselves to the hilt, loaning out money as if risk had been banished. Regulators and supervisors, captivated by industry and by an ideology of laissez-faire self-regulation, failed to do their jobs. And plenty of savings flowed into the United States, courtesy of savers in emerging economies around the world.

At a certain point bubbles become self-sustaining. Banks and other financial institutions eager to cash in on rising prices make even more credit available. Every asset that investors purchase can then become collateral for yet more borrowing and more investing. Using the magic of leverage, growing numbers of investors build soaring towers of debt—a sure sign that a bubble is brewing. And that's precisely what happened in the bubble that reached remarkable proportions by 2005. Vaulting ambition and utter greed kept pushing this process forward, as developers built innumerable tract homes, speculators snapped them up, and bankers packaged the resulting mortgages into increasingly fragile financial instruments.

In every such drama, a new character arrives onstage around this time: the self-proclaimed visionaries who spring up to explain why this boom will continue to yield perpetual profits—why "this time is different" or why the old economic rules no longer apply. The appearance of these boosters and their empty claims are a sure sign that things have started to spin out of control.

The recent housing bubble attracted hordes of such charlatans, all of whom disregarded history and common sense to claim that housing was a safe investment whose value would only increase. Their numbers included everyone from shills for the real estate industry to investment bankers who packaged dubious mortgages into AAA securities labeled as no riskier than supersafe government bonds.

These mountebanks may dominate the drama, but they do not go unchallenged. Inevitably, a handful of people who can see through the bogus claims speak up. Hardheaded realists, they point to accumulating weaknesses, but their warnings often go unheeded. One of the authors of this book played that role in the recent crisis, warning early on of a coming crash with remarkable specificity. Other prominent economists and analysts also pointed to the writing on the wall, but to no avail.

Like all bubbles, this one eventually stopped growing. And as in most bubbles, the end began with a whimper, not with a bang. Prices moved sideways; a strange sort of stasis came over the markets. The bubble boosters insisted this lapse was momentary; prices would rise again soon. But they did not. At this point in the drama, they rarely collapse overnight. They simply stall.

Then they collapse, a few institutions at first, then many. The effects reverberate throughout the financial system. Fear and uncertainty grip the markets, and while the price of the bubbly asset crumbles, the real action lies in the financial institutions that provided the credit behind the bubble. Deleveraging begins, and faced with overwhelming uncertainty, investors flee toward safer, more liquid assets.

The recent crisis stuck to this script. At first a few big mortgage lenders went under, stirring anxiety. Then came a series of higher-profile collapses, each one bigger than the last. Some big hedge funds failed. Eventually, other leading parts of the shadow banking system crumbled too. While many of these institutions didn't look like banks, their death throes would have been instantly recognizable to anyone familiar with financial crises from the seventeenth century onward. Like countless financial institutions before them, these twenty-first-century shadow banks swiftly succumbed to a crisis of liquidity and, in many cases, insolvency.

Rarely do the banks collapse all at once. In fact, one dramatic bank collapse may be succeeded by an interlude of relative peace, as a superficial calm returns to the markets, inducing a sucker's rally. But things continue to deteriorate beneath the surface, setting the stage for even more dramatic failures, and panic grows. The recent crisis displayed precisely these sorts of fluctuations, worsening, as in previous disasters, with each high-profile failure. The biggest crises have another defining characteristic: they rarely respect national boundaries. They can begin anywhere in the world, but they have a habit of going global, as problems in one country surface elsewhere, or problems in one country spread via channels—commodities, currencies, investments, derivatives, and trade—to other countries. When it comes to financial crises, all the world's a stage.

Though the recent crisis first surfaced in the United States, other countries soon exhibited the same symptoms. And no wonder: like Greenspan, central bankers around the world had adopted easy-money policies, fostering numerous housing bubbles. Banks overseas showed the same reckless appetite for risk displayed by their counterparts in the United States. With a few exceptions, they took on plenty of leverage and drank from the same poisoned chalice, investing in billions of dollars of the same bum assets generated by the magic of "financial innovation."

Crises often climax in one failure so spectacular that it overshadows all the rest. In the recent crisis, the calamitous collapse of Lehman Brothers played this role, making it seem that this one event was to blame for the tragedy that engulfed the global economy. As with earlier crises, explaining this one by a single high-profile failure is a simplistic way of looking at things that obscures more than it reveals. Lehman caused tremendous damage to the global financial system, but its failure was less a cause than a consequence.

Lehman's failure coincided with a scene commonly glimpsed in the final act: banks begging some lender of last resort—a central bank or some government entity—to step into the breach and prop up the financial system. Such requests invariably spark a debate: Should floundering banks be saved, fostering moral hazard? Or should the market be left to its own devices, leaving ailing patients to minister to themselves?

That debate played out in stark terms in the recent crisis, and in the end Ben Bernanke threw lifeline after lifeline to the deserving and undeserving alike on an unprecedented scale. Like some colossal deus ex machina, the Federal Reserve and other central banks brought the crisis to a rather abrupt, if somewhat unsatisfying, close, leaving plenty of questions unanswered and problems unresolved.

Indeed, when the dramatic phase of a crisis comes to an end, other troubles invariably begin, as the effects of the financial meltdown echo through the rest of the economy. The damage runs deep, and the wounds take a long time to heal—not months, but years. While all manner of palliative measures can be taken—stimulus packages, for example—the road to recovery can be rough, as households, banks, other financial firms, and corporate firms need to deleverage. Countries wounded by a financial crisis may falter, weighed down by debts accumulated in better times and by the socialization of private losses during the crisis. Eventually some countries will default on their debt or wipe it out with high inflation and suffer a currency crash.

This is the point where we find ourselves now. In the aftermath of previous crises, chastened politicians have enacted sweeping reforms of the financial system. We too have that opportunity. We must seize it. If we fail to do so, we may find, as many have before us, that what's past is prologue.

The Road to Redemption

For the past half century, academic economists, Wall Street traders, and everyone in between have been led astray by fairy tales about the wonders of unregulated markets, and the limitless benefits of financial innovation. The crisis dealt a body blow to that belief system, but nothing has yet replaced it.

That's all too evident in the timid reform proposals currently being considered in the United States and other advanced economies. Even though they have suffered the worst financial crisis in generations, many countries have shown a remarkable reluctance to inaugurate the sort of wholesale reform necessary to bring the financial system to heel. Instead, people talk of tinkering with the financial system, as if what just happened was caused by a few bad mortgages.

That's preposterous. As we've made clear throughout this book, the crisis was less a function of subprime mortgages than of a subprime financial system. Thanks to everything from warped compensation structures to corrupt ratings agencies, the global financial system rotted from the inside out. The financial crisis merely ripped the sleek and shiny skin off what had become, over the years, a gangrenous mess.

The road to recovery will be a long one. The first steps will entail undertaking the reforms outlined in chapters 8 and 9. For starters, traders and bankers must be compensated in ways that bring their interests into alignment with those of shareholders. That doesn't necessarily mean less compensation, even if that's desirable for other reasons; it merely means that employees of financial firms should be paid in ways that encourage them to look out for the long-term interests of the firms.

Securitization must be overhauled as well. Simplistic solutions like asking banks to retain some of the risk won't be enough; far more radical reforms will be necessary. Securitization must have far greater transparency and standardization, and the products of the securitization pipeline must be heavily regulated. Most important of all, the loans going into the securitization pipeline must be subject to far greater scrutiny. The mortgages and other loans must be high quality, or if not, they must be very clearly identified as less than prime and therefore risky.

Equally comprehensive reforms must be imposed on the kinds of deadly derivatives that blew up in the recent crisis. So-called over-the-counter derivatives—better described as under-the-table—must be hauled into the light of day, put on central clearinghouses and exchanges, and registered in databases; their use must be appropriately restricted. Moreover, the regulation of derivatives should be consolidated under a single regulator.

The rating agencies must also be collared and forced to change their business model. That they now derive their revenue from the firms they rate has created a massive conflict of interest. Investors should be paying for ratings on debt, not the institutions that issue the debt. Nor should the rating agencies be permitted to sell "consulting" services on the side to issuers of debt; that creates another conflict of interest. Finally, the business of rating debt should be thrown open to far more competition. At the present time, a handful of firms have far too much power.

Even more radical reforms must be implemented as well. Certain institutions considered too big to fail must be broken up, including Goldman Sachs and Citigroup. But many other, less visible firms deserve to be dismantled as well. Moreover, Congress should resurrect the Glass-Steagall banking legislation that it repealed a decade ago but also go further, updating it to reflect the far greater challenges posed not only by banks but by the shadow banking system.

These reforms are sensible, but even the most carefully conceived regulations can go awry. Financial firms habitually engage in arbitrage, moving their operations from a well-regulated domain to one outside government purview. The fragmented, decentralized state of regulation in the United

States has exacerbated this problem. So has the fact that the profession of financial regulator has, until very recently, been considered a dead-end, poorly paid job.

Most of these problems can be addressed. Regulations can be carefully crafted with an eye toward the future, closing loopholes before they open. That means resisting the understandable impulse to apply regulations only to a select class of firms—the too-big-to-fail institutions, for example—and instead imposing them across the board, in order to prevent financial intermediation from moving to smaller, less regulated firms. Likewise, regulation can and should be consolidated in the hands of fewer, more powerful regulators. And most important of all, regulators can be compensated in a manner befitting the key role they play in safeguarding our financial security.

Central banks arguably have the most power—and the most responsibility—to protect the financial system. In recent years, they have performed poorly. They have failed to enforce their own regulations, and worse, they have done nothing to prevent speculative manias from spinning out of control. If anything, they have fed those bubbles, and then, as if to compensate, done everything in their power to save the victims of the inevitable crash. That's inexcusable. In the future, central banks must proactively use monetary policy and credit policy to rein in and tame speculative bubbles.

Central banks alone can't handle the challenges facing the global economy. Large and destabilizing global current account imbalances threaten long-term economic stability, as does the risk of a rapidly depreciating dollar; addressing both problems requires a new commitment to international economic governance. The IMF must be strengthened and given the power to supply the makings of a new international reserve currency. And how the IMF governs itself must be seriously reformed. For too long, a handful of smaller, aging economies have dominated IMF governance. Emerging economies must be given their rightful place at the table, a move reinforced by the rising power and influence of the G-20 group.

All of these reforms will help reduce the incidence of crises, but they will not drive them to extinction. As the economist Hyman Minsky once observed, "There is no possibility that we can ever set things right once and for all; instability, put to rest by one set of reforms, will, after time, emerge in a new guise." Crises cannot be abolished; like hurricanes, they can only be managed and mitigated.

Paradoxically, this unsettling truth should give us hope. In the depths of the Great Depression, politicians and policy makers embraced reforms of the financial system that laid the foundation for nearly eighty years of stability and security. It inevitably unraveled, but eighty years is a long time—a lifetime.

As we contemplate the future of finance from the mire of our own recent Great Recession, we would do well to try to emulate that achievement. Nothing lasts forever, and crises will always return. But they need not loom so large; they need not overshadow our economic existence. If we strengthen the levees that surround our financial system, we can weather crises in the coming years. Though the waters may rise, we will remain dry. But if we fail to prepare for the inevitable hurricanes—if we delude ourselves, thinking that our antiquated defenses will never be breached again—we face the prospect of many future floods.

Outlook

During the global financial crisis of 2007–8, the world looked into the abyss. In the fourth quarter of 2008 and first quarter of 2009, global economic activity plummeted at rates last seen at the onset of the Great Depression.

Only swift, radical policy measures in a number of countries stanched the bleeding. Though not always coordinated or careful, this collective response successfully prevented another depression, and economies around the world stopped their free fall. The dangers of deflation faded, and the world started to recover. Emerging economies turned around first, and by the third quarter of 2009 most advanced economies stopped contracting too.

But while the global economy has started to rebound, its risks and vulnerabilities may lead to renewed crises in the coming years. One possible outcome is that exploding fiscal deficits may prompt some countries to default on their debt, or to resort to the printing press to mitigate it, triggering the sort of high inflation last seen in the 1970s.

Other troubles may emerge as well. Extremely loose monetary policies and quantitative easing—combined with a growing reliance on the carry trade in the dollar—may foster an even bigger bubble than the one that just burst. Should it deflate suddenly, the value of risky assets and global wealth would fall sharply, with the danger of a double-dip global recession.

Other equally frightening events might occur. The European Monetary Union could break up. Or Japan might return to deflation and near depression, triggering a major sovereign debt crisis. Even China faces growing risks: its investment-led recovery could lose steam, possibly triggering a rise in nonperforming loans and, ultimately, a banking crisis. All of these scenarios could lead to a backlash against globalization.

Much rides on how the global economy recovers—or falters—in the next few years. Here, then, is a glimpse of the near-term dangers facing us. (For a far more detailed analysis, please visit Roubini Global Economics at www.roubini.com.)

V, U, or W?

Recoveries come in different forms, reflecting their relative vigor or sustainability. A V-shaped recovery is swift and vigorous; a U-shaped recovery is slow and underwhelming; and a W-shaped recovery is a double dip, in which the economy experiences a fleeting recovery, then plunges downward again. The most likely scenario at present is a U-shaped recovery in advanced economies, featuring weak, below-trend growth for a number of years. Here's why.

First, labor market conditions remain weak. In 2010 the U.S. unemployment rate reached 10 percent. (A more comprehensive measure that accounts for partially employed workers and discouraged workers topped 17 percent.) Many jobs in real estate, construction, and the financial sector have disappeared forever. Likewise, many manufacturing and service-sector jobs that have been outsourced offshore will not return.

Even workers who have kept their jobs have seen their income decline. Many firms, as a way of "sharing the pain," asked their employees to work fewer hours or accept furloughs or even wage cuts. The fall in hours worked was equivalent to the loss of another 3 million full-time jobs, on top of the 8.4 million jobs formally lost by the end of 2009. Those losses may continue: a recent study by Alan Blinder suggests that up to one-quarter of all U.S. jobs could be eventually outsourced. Therefore the unemployment rate may continue to rise for a while, and when it finally falls, it will do so very slowly.

Moreover, the current recession is different from previous ones. This recent crisis was born of excessive debt and leverage in the household sector, the financial system, and even the corporate sector. The recession wasn't driven by monetary tightening; it was a "balance sheet" recession driven by a staggering accumulation of debt. Recent research by Carmen Reinhart and Kenneth Rogoff suggests that a "balance sheet" recession can lead to a weak recovery, as every sector of the economy "deleverages" and cuts down its debt.

This will take a while. Households in the United States and the United Kingdom have saved too little and spent too much. Though U.S. savings rates rose above 4 percent by the end of 2009, studies done by the IMF and other scholars suggest that this rate needs to rise to 8 percent or higher in the next few years. That will mean lower growth rates of consumption. But since consumption is 70 percent of GDP in the United States (and very high in other countries that have also seen declining savings rates), reduced consumption growth may undercut economic growth.

Other indicators point toward a U-shaped recovery. In a typical V-shaped recovery, the corporate sector plows money into capital expenditures—better known as "capex"—contributing to a rapid rebound. Unfortunately, in this recovery, capex spending will be anemic because much of the economy's capacity (factories, machines, computers, and other fixed assets) sits unused. Indeed, capacity bottomed out at a much lower number (67 percent) than in previous recessions (75 to 80 percent). Even by the end of 2009, 30 percent of capacity remained idle in the United States and Europe. Why, in this climate, would firms want to undertake new capex spending?

In addition, for all the government support that the financial system received, vast swaths of it have been damaged. As of this writing, in the United States alone the FDIC shut down more than 130 banks and placed 500 or more on a watch list. More important, much of the shadow banking system has collapsed or been irreparably damaged; much of it has become a ward of the state. Despite public subsidies, securitization is a shadow of its former self, and even private equity firms continue to struggle with the consequences of having taken on too much leverage.

The financial system will take a long time to mend. The damaged financial system's ability to finance future residential investment, construction activity, capex spending, and consumption of durable goods will be seriously constrained. We will not return to the kind of growth we saw during the go-go years of 2003–7, financed by an unsustainable credit bubble

Other factors suggest the likelihood of a U-shaped recovery. The policies that helped the economy recover—especially the fiscal stimulus—cannot last forever. When it's withdrawn, slower growth will follow. If it's not withdrawn—if policy makers resort to even bigger deficits to pay for tax cuts and spending increases—then we'll simply set ourselves up for a bigger fiscal train wreck. Continued stimulus spending will also lead to fears that countries will default on their debt or inflate it away, pushing long-term interest rates higher and crowding out the economic recovery.

Finally, persistent global current account imbalances imply slower global growth in the next few years. During the last decade the United States—as well as countries like the United Kingdom, Ireland, Iceland, Spain, Dubai, Australia, New Zealand, the Baltic states, and other central European economies—functioned as the world's consumer of first and last resort, spending more than its income and running current account deficits. Conversely, China, emerging Asia, most of Latin America, Japan, Germany, and a few other Eurozone economies served as the producers of first and last resort, spending less than their income and running current account surpluses.

The first group of countries is retrenching by saving more and importing less, but the second group is not compensating by saving less and consuming more. This necessarily means a net decline in the global demand for goods. Given that our world already has a glut of industrial capacity, the recovery of global aggregate demand will be weak at best.

All of these factors point toward a slow U-shaped recovery in the United States and in other spendthrift advanced economies. The recovery may not appear to be U-shaped at first: indeed, U.S. growth for the fourth quarter of 2009 was 5.9 percent, the strongest in six years. But most of that figure can be explained by the direct and indirect effects of the fiscal stimulus as well as by the fact that in the final months of 2009 companies replenished inventories.

These forces may boost growth to 3 percent or higher in the first half of

2010. So too may the lingering effects of the cash-for-clunkers programs and tax credits for first-time home buyers. The U.S. Census will hire almost a million temporary workers, which will help sustain growth for a brief period. But growth will stall in the second half of 2010 as the effects of these temporary factors fizzle out. At that point growth will slump well below par until the necessary increase in saving and the deleveraging of the private and public sectors have occurred.

Europe on the Edge

As bad as things look in the United States, the medium-term prospects of the Eurozone and of Japan may be equally bad, if not more so. In both regions the recovery will be U-shaped for many reasons.

First, the potential growth rate of the Eurozone and Japan (around 2 percent) is lower than that of the United States. Second, these countries will have a harder time using fiscal policy to counter the effects of the crisis: even before 2007 they ran large fiscal deficits and had large stocks of public debt relative to their GDP (in many cases close to or above 100 percent). Third, these countries face serious challenges over both the short term and the long term: poor productivity growth and aging populations. None of these problems can be easily addressed.

Moreover, a group of Eurozone countries known as the PIGS—Portugal, Italy, Greece, and Spain—are in grave trouble. In recent years their debts have soared and their competitiveness has declined. The reasons are complicated. The adoption of the euro enabled them to borrow more and consume more than they would have otherwise. The ensuing credit boom supported consumption but also led to rising wages. This made their exports less competitive. At the same time, excessive bureaucracy and other structural impediments discouraged investment in high-skill sectors, even though wages in these countries trailed behind the average for the European Union.

The resulting noxious mix of large current account deficits and budget deficits left the PIGS countries heavily indebted to banks elsewhere in Europe. All are highly leveraged, making them a likely source of financial contagion. Worse, the dramatic appreciation of the euro in 2008–9 has increased the loss of competitiveness, leaving them even more vulnerable to default and threatening to burden the wealthier, healthier members of the European Union.

This wasn't supposed to happen. The European Monetary Union was designed to bring stability and unity to Europe. When member states joined, they ceded control over monetary policy to the European Central Bank; they also joined the Stability and Growth Pact, which imposed restrictions on the size of their fiscal deficits. In theory their membership would force these countries to undertake structural reforms and force a convergence of economic performance among all member states. Instead, the opposite happened. Germany and a few other countries spent a decade reducing their fiscal imbalances and improving their competitiveness via corporate restructuring. But the opposite occurred in Italy, Spain, Greece, and Portugal, where fiscal imbalances remained high and labor costs rose above productivity growth. As a consequence, we now have two Europes instead of one.

Other factors have aggravated the divergence. Labor mobility within the union is only modest, as language and culture hamper migration. So a rise in unemployment on the periphery of the union will not lead workers to migrate to more prosperous regions as much as they otherwise might. As a consequence, labor markets in the European Union are much less flexible than those in the United States. Equally troubling, the individual nations of the EU do not share the fiscal burden of government, as states do in the United States. The fact that fiscal policy is left in the hands of the individual countries limits the degree to which one nation can help another.

If these economic divergences persist and widen, the European Monetary Union could break up. For example, suppose Greece resorts to financial engineering and fiscal fudges to deal with its problems. If it continues to do so, Greece could lose access to debt markets sometime in 2010. It would then have to go hat in hand, begging for direct loans from other member states, the European Central Bank, the European Commission, or the IMF.

These players might bail out Greece for the sake of the survival of the Monetary Union. But if similar trouble spreads to Spain, Italy, Portugal, or other member states, the willingness and ability of the European Central Bank, much less the French and German taxpayers, to bail out other member states would reach a limit. Greece would then have to exit the Monetary Union and adopt a new, devalued currency like the drachma to replace the euro.

This twin scenario—default and devaluation—could have terrible consequences. By adopting a new, depreciated drachma, Greece would necessarily default on public—and most likely private—debts denominated in euros.

Something like that happened in Argentina in 2001. Its exit from a currency board and a sharp devaluation of the peso triggered a massive default on public and private debts denominated in U.S. dollars. It also led to the forced conversion of dollar-denominated domestic debt into peso liabilities with a much lower value, a process known as "pesification." Likewise, a devaluation and default by Greece or Italy would lead to a "drachmatization" or "lira-lization" of domestically issued euro liabilities, effectively imposing massive losses on anyone holding these claims, mostly other European banks.

No currency union has ever survived without a fiscal and political union as well. Should such defaults and devaluations take place, the contrast between the Eurozone and the United States would become ever starker. California and many other states in the United States face budget crises, but a strong tradition of fiscal federalism—as well as provisions in the bankruptcy code—makes it possible to solve some of these local problems at a national level. The Eurozone lacks such burden-sharing mechanisms.

A breakup of the Monetary Union could even lead to the partial destruction of the European Union itself. Any member nation that exits the Monetary Union and defaults on debts held by other member nations may ultimately be expelled from the EU. That fate, inconceivable a few years ago, has become a very real possibility for authorities in Athens, Rome, Madrid, and Lisbon. Years of economic divergence and an erosion of economic competitiveness in these countries have made such an outcome far more likely than ever before.

Whither Japan?

Japan is in as much trouble as the Eurozone. As we have seen, the bursting of its real estate and equity bubble in the early 1990s led to a Lost Decade of economic stagnation—punctuated by four recessions—as well as serious deflation. In the wake of the bubble, Japan made many policy mistakes: it adopted monetary easing and fiscal stimulus too late, then abandoned them too early. It kept zombie banks alive for too long, recapitalizing only late in the decade. A double-dip recession in 2000 only exacerbated the twin problems of deflation and stagnation. Japan returned to a potential growth of 2 percent only after 2004.

During the recent crisis the contraction was more severe in Japan than in the United States, despite the fact that most of Japan's financial institutions had little exposure to toxic mortgages or structured financial products. Instead, Japan proved vulnerable on account of its heavy dependence on foreign trade, which was itself dependent on a weak yen. When global growth and trade collapsed in 2008–9, exports collapsed. The yen-based carry trade unraveled, driving the yen to appreciate. Its recovery since then has been anemic at best.

Japan faces a host of long-term problems. Its aging population, combined with its reluctance to welcome immigrants, has put its economy in a demographic vise that will reduce growth. An inefficient, somewhat ossified service sector with low productivity has proven resistant to change, as have rigid economic and social conventions like lifetime employment. The political system is equally rigid, showing no will to undertake the structural reforms necessary to break free of these restraints. Japan's position as the world's second-largest economy is probably no longer secure: China is likely to supplant it in the coming years.

More worrisome, Japan's high public deficits, weak growth, and persistent deflation point to a possible fiscal crisis. So far that fate has been avoided, thanks in part to high private savings rates. In addition, Japan's large current account surpluses have led both the private sector and the central bank to accumulate foreign assets, providing a buffer of savings that could be eventually used to service the growing domestic debt. For this reason Japan's government can still borrow at relatively low rates, even though it now shoulders a gross public debt equivalent to almost 200 percent of GDP.

Still, in the recent crisis the household savings rate fell sharply as income-strapped households had to spend more to maintain their standard of living; even the current account surplus shrank, as rising budget deficits and falling private savings overwhelmed the fall in private investment. Should these trends continue, Japan may be headed for a serious fiscal crisis, as continuing deflation, anemic growth, soaring deficits, and a strong yen conspire to drive down confidence in its economy.

In fact, some rating agencies have put Japan on a possible sovereign downgrade watch. If Japanese households lost confidence in the government's ability to tackle the deficit and public debt, they might dump domestic assets (starting with government bonds) and resume yen-based carry trades, sharply pushing down the value of the yen and sending long-term government bond yields upward. This could eventually trigger a public debt crisis.

Unfortunately, the Japanese political system's ability to deliver the kind of fiscal adjustments and structural reforms necessary to turn things around is limited. In 2009 the opposition Democratic Party of Japan (DPJ) finally ousted the dominant Liberal Democratic Party (LDP), which had maintained a virtual monopoly on power for over fifty years. This political shift suggested that Japan might be on the road to reform, but events soon suggested otherwise.

Upon assuming office, the DPJ's new leader, Yukio Hatoyama, made ambitious but contradictory promises. Acknowledging the constraints on Japan's budget, he and his party promised to cut inefficient and wasteful state spending. At the same time, he called for "an economy of the people" that depended on significant state subsidies, as well as a budget that required record borrowing. Equally troubling, Hatoyama then announced plans to halt the privatization of Japan Post Bank. This enormous enterprise, which holds more than $3 trillion in assets, has helped finance state spending for decades, and the move made it clear that Hatoyama expects to continue this tradition.

These policies will likely increase debt and keep growth at subpar levels. Unfortunately, Hatoyama's ability to pursue these goals has few political checks: in recent years, the DPJ built a strong single-party majority in the lower house while joining forces with coalition partners to dominate the upper house. Hatoyama also faces fewer institutional obstacles, analogous to the filibuster of the U.S. system, to setting and pushing a political agenda.

At the same time Hatoyama is unlikely to reform the larger economy. Prior to the DPJ's ascent to power, business elites worked with an LDP-dominated bureaucracy to frame legislation. Suddenly, the business elite has seen the one-party system shift to a no-party system; indeed, the new ruling coalition has far fewer connections in the business world. That means it has few opportunities for the kind of compromises necessary to achieve the sorts of structural reforms that would ensure higher growth in the coming years.

That may eventually leave Japan in a very dangerous position, as soaring deficits and a sclerotic economy bring about the unthinkable: a sovereign debt crisis or a surge in inflation and a decisive fall from grace for a country once considered likely to dominate the global economy.

BIC? BRIC? BRICK?

On paper, most emerging economies can reasonably expect robust medium-term growth ranging between 5 and 8 percent, depending on the country. This growth rate is much higher than the 2 or 3 percent that most advanced economies expect in the coming years.

Their strength has much to do with the advantages they possessed going into the recent crisis. Except for parts of central and eastern Europe, emerging markets lacked the leverage in the financial and household sectors that became the Achilles' heel of many advanced economies. Moreover, having endured financial crises in recent decades, these countries cleaned up their financial systems, followed sound fiscal policies, and insulated central banks from political pressure so that they might better provide price stability.

These strengths and lessons learned enabled the emerging economies to weather the crisis well. They implemented effective monetary and fiscal policies to restore demand and growth, setting themselves up for a quick recovery. In fact, most of them will grow at a healthy clip, should they stick with the market-oriented reforms and policies adopted before the crisis.

That's the best-case scenario. But we should keep a few caveats in mind. First, these economies aren't self-sufficient; they have extensive trading and financial ties to more advanced economies and cannot fully decouple from their problems. An anemic recovery in the United States will inevitably act as a drag on even the most dynamic emerging markets.

The emerging economies include dozens of nations. The BRICs—Brazil,

Russia, India, and China—are the biggest of the bunch, and China is the undisputed king. But China faces serious challenges. While it has weathered the crisis, its all-too-effective response may set it up for problems in the medium term.

For example, China has reacted to the crisis with state-directed credit growth. State-owned banks have been told to provide massive amounts of credit and loans to state-owned enterprises in order to induce them to hire more workers, produce more goods, stockpile more commodities, and increase capacity. Every province now induces banks to lend recklessly to state-owned enterprises in order to increase capacity in steel, cement, aluminum, car making, and other heavy industries. But China already has a glut of capacity in these areas.

Thanks to the boom in public and private investment, China now has an infrastructure that outstrips its level of development: it has plenty of empty new airports and highways with very few cars. It also has a staggering increase in real estate development that will inevitably lead to a glut in commercial and residential properties. While economic growth and urbanization will eventually make use of these improvements and properties, the supply is starting to outstrip the demand. Unfortunately, some of these distortions are a function of the fact that land is not properly priced at a market rate; the state continues to control the supply.

Some of the credit now flooding through the Chinese economy is going toward other, equally unproductive uses, including speculative, leveraged purchases of commodities, equities, and real estate. This has the potential to become a dangerous bubble, eventually leading to a significant downward correction in asset prices. The authorities recognize this possibility, and rising prices in energy, food, and real estate have prompted them to contract the money supply and credit in the hopes of engineering a soft landing.

China occupies a paradoxical position in 2010. While stimulus programs instituted the previous year pushed growth back up into the 9 percent range, its economy still hasn't made the necessary shift from an emphasis on exports to a reliance on private consumption. Consumption in China remains stuck at a paltry 36 percent of GDP, compared with 70 percent of GDP in the United States. There's certainly a happy medium between these numbers, but so far China hasn't done much to move toward it.

Other problems may bedevil China in the coming years. The country itself is growing at two different rates: coastal, urban areas that depend on exports are advancing more quickly than rural areas in the central and western parts. Moreover, economic growth in all regions has been pursued with a reckless disregard of the environment, leading to pollution that disfigures the landscape and causes significant health problems for millions of Chinese. Finally, an authoritarian political system that seems unable to tolerate any dissent, as well as the growing restlessness of ethnic minorities, may also spell trouble down the line.

The other members of the BRIC elite face a different set of challenges. Compared with China, India has a vibrant democracy, a stronger rule of law, and greater protection of property rights. But democracy is a mixed blessing: weak coalition governments in India have slowed down necessary structural economic reforms. These reforms include reducing budget deficits at the central and state levels, cutting inefficient government spending, and reforming the tax system.

Other liberal reforms must be instituted as well. Government intervention in the economy must be restrained; red tape and a bloated bureaucracy must be cut back. Labor markets remain too rigid and must be liberalized; so should trade and restrictions on foreign direct investment. Entrepreneurship should receive more encouragement, as should investment in human capital and skills. While India has made some progress on these fronts, the risk remains that these reforms will occur too slowly, increasing the gap between the Chinese hare and the Indian tortoise.

Brazil's situation is different still. It's a dynamic economy with plenty of natural resources, a sophisticated financial system, and an advanced manufacturing sector that could maintain robust growth for a long time. But even in the best of all times—the years between 2004 and 2007, when average growth in the other BRICs topped 8 or even 10 percent—Brazilian growth lagged far behind at 4 percent.

The Luiz Inácio Lula da Silva administration deserves credit for having followed sound macroeconomic policies—a low budget deficit and an independent central bank committed to low inflation—but more must be done. In order to get growth above 6 percent, the next president will have to deal with unfunded pension liabilities; reduce government spending and taxes that can badly warp economic decision making; increase the skills of the labor force by investing in education and training; and improve and expand infrastructures via private and public partnerships—all the while maintaining socially progressive policies that gradually reduce income and wealth inequalities.

The recent economic crisis exposed the remaining BRIC as a potential imposter. The weakness of the Russian economy—in particular, its highly leveraged banks and corporations—had been masked by the windfall generated by spiking oil and gas prices. After growing 8 percent in 2008, Russia's economy contracted by an equally stunning 8 percent the following year.

In effect, Russia's economy consists of one somewhat healthy sector—oil and gas—that fluctuates with the price of these commodities. It needs to diversify, but that would require the privatization of state-owned enterprises, the liberalization of the economy, a reduction in the kind of red tape that hampers the creation of new firms, and a serious crackdown on the corruption that permeates the private sector. Even the energy sector has to be liberalized. Unfortunately, foreign investors remain reluctant to sink money into facilities that might eventually be expropriated or nationalized.

Russia has plenty of other problems that should disqualify it from BRIC status. It has a decaying infrastructure and a dysfunctional, corrupt political system. Its population is rapidly shrinking, and serious health problems—alcoholism, most obviously—have driven down life expectancy to worrisome levels. While Russia retains the world's largest nuclear arsenal, and maintains a permanent seat on the UN Security Council, it is "more sick than BRIC."

In fact, several other countries probably have a better claim to BRIC status, even if that means adding some letters to the acronym. Given its potential, the case is far stronger for including South Korea in the BRIC—or BRICK—club. South Korea is a sophisticated high-tech economic power: innovative, dynamic, and home to a skilled labor force. Its only major problem is the danger that North Korea will collapse and inundate it with hungry refugees.

Turkey too deserves to be included in the inner circle. It has a robust banking sector, a thriving domestic market, a large and growing population, a savvy entrepreneurial sector, and a comparative advantage in labor-intensive manufacturing. It has ties to Europe (NATO and European Union membership candidacy), to the Middle East, and to Central Asia.

Indonesia may be the strongest candidate of the bunch. The world's largest Muslim state, it boasts a rapidly expanding middle class, stable and increasingly democratic politics, and an economy that outshone much of Asia despite the damage done by the global recession. From the perspective of the United States, Indonesia presents a rather attractive alternative to Russia, which increasingly vies with Venezuela for leadership of the "America in decline" cheering section.

Indonesia has displayed resilience not only as an economy but also as a nation. It has a remarkably diverse and far-flung population, attributes that might cast doubt on its ability to make the transition to a world-class economy. Yet the country has left behind the legacy of a military dictatorship and has recovered from multiple setbacks. Though the Asian financial crisis in 1997, the tsunami in 2004, and the emergence of radical Islam have all done damage, Indonesia continues to move forward at an impressive rate.

While Indonesia's per capita GDP remains low compared with that of other aspirants to BRIC status, it has remarkable potential. It depends far less on exports than do its Asian peers (never mind Russia), and its markets in timber, palm oil, coal, and other assets have attracted major foreign investment. The government in Jakarta, meanwhile, has taken a strong stand against corruption and has moved to address structural problems. Even demographic trends favor Indonesia, which, with 230 million people, is already the fourth-largest country in the world by population, equivalent to Germany and Russia combined.

The hype about the BRICs—or BIICs or BRICKs—reflects an important long-term trend: the rise of a broader range of emerging-market economies with economic, financial, and trading power. A few years ago Lawrence Summers argued that the integration of China and India into the global economy—with close to 2.2 billion "Chindians" joining the global labor force and the global markets—was the most significant event in the last thousand years of human history, after the Italian Renaissance and the Industrial Revolution.

How that plays out remains to be seen. China, India, and the other leading emerging economies all face their share of challenges and will need to pursue very specific reforms to move to the next stage. But in all likelihood, most will end up playing an increasingly central role in the global economy in the coming years.

A New Bubble?

Since March 2009 a range of risky global assets have undergone a massive rally. Stock markets rebounded in the United States; energy and commodity prices started to climb back upward; and stocks, bonds, and currencies in emerging markets shot skyward. As they regain their appetite for risk, investors have moved away from U.S. government bonds and the dollar, which has sent bond yields gently up and the value of the dollar down.

While this recovery in asset prices is driven in part by better economic and financial fundamentals, prices have shot up too fast too soon. Why? The most obvious reason is that the central banks of the advanced economies have used superlow interest rates and quantitative easing to create a "wall of liquidity" that has managed to surmount the "wall of worry" left behind after the crisis. And that's helping to fuel a massive rally in risky assets.

But something else is also fueling this global asset bubble: the carry trade in the dollar. In a carry trade, investors borrow in one currency and invest it in places where it will yield a higher return. Thanks to near-zero interest rates in the United States, investors can borrow dollars and sink them into any number of risky assets around the world. As the prices of these assets go up, the investors make a tidy profit, which they can then use to pay back those borrowed dollars, which by this point have depreciated, making it even easier to return the loan. In practice, that means investors aren't borrowing at zero percent interest rates; they're borrowing at negative interest rates, negative 10 or 20 percent, depending on how much the dollar depreciates. In this climate, it's pretty easy to make a profit: 50 to 70 percent since March 2009.

The Fed has inadvertently kept this game going. By buying up a range of asset classes—U.S. government bonds, mortgage-backed securities, and the debt of Fannie Mae and Freddie Mac—the Fed has reduced volatility in the markets. That only makes the carry trade more appealing, minimizing people's sense of risk and drawing more and more investors into a bubble. These measures, when combined with the Fed's policy of keeping interest rates near zero, have made the world safe for the "mother of all carry trades" and the mother of all asset bubbles.

The growing weakness of the dollar has put central banks in Asia and

Latin America in a difficult position. If they fail to intervene in foreign exchange markets, their currencies will appreciate relative to the dollar, making it even more attractive to borrow in dollars. If they do intervene to prevent this appreciation, buying up foreign currencies like the dollar, the resulting foreign reserves can easily feed asset bubbles in these economies. Either way the outcome is the same: a global asset bubble that grows bigger by the day.

Eventually the carry trade will unravel. The Fed will end its program of purchasing assets, effectively restoring some volatility to the markets; and at some point the dollar will stabilize, as it can't keep declining indefinitely. When it stabilizes, the cost of borrowing in dollars will no longer be negative; it will merely be close to zero. That's bad news for anyone who has bet that the dollar will continue to decline, and it will force these speculators to suddenly retrench and "cover their shorts."

That process may be especially violent if the dollar starts to appreciate quickly. Any number of things could cause it to do so: increased investors' risk aversion or military confrontations and other geopolitical tensions could suddenly send investors fleeing for safer havens. Whatever the reason, if the dollar appreciates suddenly—just as the yen did when the carry trade in that currency unraveled—a stampede will ensue. Investors who went long on risky global assets and short on the dollar will suddenly reverse course. The bubble will then burst.

This unraveling may not occur immediately. The wall of liquidity and the Fed's suppression of volatility can keep the game going a bit longer. But that means the asset bubble will only get bigger and bigger, setting the stage for a serious meltdown.

Defaulting on Debt

Until very recently, the idea that an advanced economy might default on its sovereign debt would have seemed outlandish. Emerging markets were the ones that defaulted. In the past decade alone, Russia, Argentina, and Ecuador defaulted on their public debt, while Pakistan, Ukraine, and Uruguay came close. This same pattern has held through the centuries: emerging economies occasionally default on their debt, then eventually "graduate" to a more respectable, reliable place in the global economy.

We seem to have come full circle. In recent years, with a few exceptions in central and eastern Europe, emerging-market economies have put their fiscal houses in order. The threat of default now looms over advanced economies. In 2009 rating agencies downgraded the debt of several advanced countries, and debt auctions in the United Kingdom, Greece, Ireland, and Spain found far fewer buyers than anticipated. It was a less-than-friendly reminder that unless advanced economies start to put their fiscal houses in order, the rating agencies—and in particular, the dreaded "bond vigilantes"—will bring them to heel.

That prospect puts many advanced economies in a bind. The recent crisis and the ensuing recession have led to a serious erosion in their fiscal position. Stimulus spending programs and lower tax revenues have hit hard. So has the decision to socialize the losses in the financial sector, effectively shifting them onto taxpayers' backs. In the coming years, an underwhelming recovery and an aging population may worsen the debt burden of the United States, the United Kingdom, Japan, and a handful of countries in the Eurozone.

Some countries have already taken measures to consolidate their fiscal position, including Iceland, Ireland, and the United Kingdom, as well as Spain, Portugal, and, to a lesser extent, Greece. These measures will hurt in the short term, but they will be the only thing that can prevent a loss of credibility and the inevitable spike in borrowing costs. Unfortunately, while putting one's fiscal house in order may play well with foreign investors, it could also sabotage a fledgling recovery. On the whole, however, these countries are better off taking the pain now rather than running the risk of defaulting on their debt.

Though the United States and Japan will likely avoid the bond market vigilantes for some time to come, they too may one day incur their wrath. The United States continues to run unsustainable current account deficits and has an aging population and plenty of unfunded entitlement spending on Social Security and health care. Japan has an even bigger aging population and has already racked up significant debts. Both countries may soon face growing scrutiny of their fiscal position, a prospect that poses particular dangers for the United States, which until now has been able to borrow in its own currency.

Unfortunately, it has another, less honest option. The United States (as well as the United Kingdom and Japan) issues its public debt in its own currency. That means it need not formally default on its debt if it proves unable to raise taxes or cut government spending. Instead, central banks can print new currency—or its digital equivalent—and monetize the debt. This time-honored method would send inflation soaring, wiping out the real value of the debt and transferring wealth from creditors to the government. While the so-called inflation tax avoids an outright default, it achieves the same end.

Proponents of the inflation solution argue that it kills two birds with one stone. First and most obviously, a moderate rate of inflation helps erode the real value of public debt, reducing the burden. At the same time, it resolves the problem of debt deflation, reducing the real value of private liabilities—fixed-rate mortgages, for example—while increasing the nominal value of homes and other assets. This is a win-win: the public and private sectors both get to wriggle free of their debts.

It sounds smart, but it's not. If inflation rose from near-zero levels to the low single digits—let alone double digits—central banks could lose control of inflation expectations. Once the inflation genie gets out of the bottle, it's hard to control. In the process, central banks would destroy their hard-won credibility. While Paul Volcker's success in fighting inflation in the early 1980s confirms that this credibility can be regained, doing so comes at the considerable cost of a severe recession.

Moreover, while inflation can reduce the real value of nominal debt at fixed interest rates, much of the debt in the United States and other advanced economies consists of short-term obligations with variable interest rates. These include bank deposits, variable-rate mortgages, short-term government debt, and other short-term liabilities of households, corporations, and financial institutions. Expectations of rising inflation would mean that these liabilities would be rolled over at higher interest rates. The rates would effectively keep pace with inflation. In the case of short-term and variable-rate debt, the inflation solution would be ineffective: you can't fool all of the people all of the time.

Needless to say, trying to use inflation to erode the real value of private and public debt would carry other risks. Foreign creditors of the United States would not sit back and accept a sharp reduction in the real value of their dollar-denominated assets. The resulting rush toward the exits—as investors dumped dollars—could lead to the collapse of the currency, a spike in long-term interest rates, and a severe double-dip recession. The United States would not have the sway that it did the last time inflation started to rage, in the 1970s. Back then the country was still running current account surpluses.

That's no longer the case: the United States has become the world's biggest debtor, owing a whopping $3 trillion to the rest of the world. Its current account deficits—$400 billion a year—have become the stuff of legend. As its creditors become increasingly leery of holding long-term debt, it will have to resort to borrowing on a shorter time frame to finance its various deficits. That makes it increasingly vulnerable to the kind of crises that hit emerging markets in the 1990s, with the sudden collapse of the dollar more likely.

The Chinese and other U.S. creditors—Russia, Japan, Brazil, and the oil exporters in the Gulf—would not accept such a loss on their dollar assets. Convincing China to accept such a financial levy would require some rather unpleasant negotiations. China might ask the United States for some other form of compensation, such as giving up on its defense of Taiwan. Such trade-offs would be likely in a world where the great powers on both sides of large financial imbalances vie for geopolitical leadership.

This "balance of financial terror" would seem to rule out the possibility that China would simply stop financing the U.S. fiscal and current account deficits. For China to halt its interventions in the foreign exchange markets, much less dump its stock of dollar assets, would severely damage the competitiveness of its exports. But should political tensions rise, and the United States begin actively to debase its own currency, China may well walk away from the table, even if its interests suffer in the short term. This outcome may be as unlikely as a nuclear exchange at the height of the Cold War, but it is not inconceivable.

Given these risks, U.S. authorities will likely not resort to the printing press to deal with the country's debt, even if the temptation to use inflation—just a little bit—to depreciate the debt will remain strong. But prudent policy makers should know that the costs and the collateral damage of such a solution would be significant, if not catastrophic.

All That Glitters

Through 2009 the price of gold rose sharply, reflecting fears that the United States might purposely debase and devalue its currency in order to resolve its debt problems. In 2009 gold prices breached the $1,000 barrier and rose to $1,200 by the end of the year, before falling once more. Some goldbugs forecast that in the next couple of years gold prices could reach a level above $2,000. Is that possible? Is the recent rise of gold prices justified by fundamentals, or is it evidence of a bubble?

Typically, gold prices rise sharply in one of two situations: one, when inflation starts to rage out of control, at which point gold becomes a hedge against inflation; two, when a near depression seems increasingly likely and investors become concerned that even their bank deposits may not be safe. The history of the last two years fits both situations.

First, gold prices started to rise sharply in the first six months of 2008 as emerging markets began to overheat, commodity prices skyrocketed, and fears of inflation in these markets increased. Oil prices hit record highs. Then the bubble burst, commodity prices fell, and gold prices fell too.

The second spike in gold prices occurred at the time of the Lehman collapse in 2008. Then the rush to gold was not driven by concerns about inflation; indeed, deflation had become a problem around the world. Rather, once the Lehman collapse triggered a global financial cardiac arrest, investors became sufficiently scared about the security of their financial assets—including bank deposits—that some preferred the safety of gold.

The G-7 contained that depression scare by widely insuring deposits and bailing out and backstopping the financial system. The price of gold then drifted downward, as the near depression gripping the global economy undercut commercial and industrial demand for gold, as well as the consumer demand for it as a luxury object.

But gold bounced back, spiking above $1,000 in the early spring of 2009 as concerns about the solvency of the financial system in the United States and Europe peaked once again. Fears grew that governments could not bail out the entire financial system—that something once considered "too big to fail" was now "too big to save." At that point growing concerns about an economic and financial Armageddon triggered another spike in gold prices. That's hardly surprising: when you begin to worry that your government cannot credibly guarantee bank deposits, it's time to buy a gun, ammo, canned food, and gold bars, and hunker down in a remote log cabin in hopes of surviving a global meltdown. But once again that panic subsided—and gold prices drifted downward again later that spring, as additional policy measures and the gradual bottoming-out of the global economy helped dispel fears.

The pattern is clear: gold prices spike in response to concerns about either inflation or depression. In both cases, gold makes a good hedge against risk, particularly extreme events that signal a total systemic collapse. When those threats ease, gold prices generally drift downward.

How might gold fare going forward? Any number of forces may propel gold prices higher, though it's unlikely to hit $2,000 per ounce. For example, growing concerns that governments might try to monetize their deficits could stoke fears of inflation, sending prices higher. Likewise, massive amounts of liquidity sloshing around the financial system could send any number of asset prices higher, including gold. In addition, carry trades funded by dollars have pushed the value of the dollar sharply downward. There's an inverse relationship between the relative value of the dollar and the dollar price of commodities: as the dollar goes lower, prices of a range of commodities, including gold, increase.

Other factors may fuel demand for gold. Central banks in India, China, and other countries have increased their holdings of gold. Private investors who have lingering fears of low-probability events—high inflation or a crippling double-dip global recession—may also fuel demand. Given the inelastic supply of gold, central banks and private investors need make only a small shift toward gold in their portfolios to increase its price significantly. A single event—a sovereign debt default, for example—can serve as a catalyst for gold prices to move upward into bubble territory. So-called herd behavior and momentum trading would only inflate the bubble still further.

Nonetheless, a downward correction in gold prices carries significant risks. The dollar carry trade will likely unravel at some point, and central banks will eventually exit quantitative easing and abandon near-zero policy rates. Both these developments will put downward pressure on commodity prices, including gold.

More generally, anyone who has blind faith in gold as a hedge against risk should understand that crises don't always drive people toward gold. The prospect of sovereign debt defaults in smaller countries may drive investors toward dollars, not gold. The same goes for any kind of crisis. So long as the dollar itself is not the focus of a crisis, gold prices do not automatically spiral higher simply because bad things are afoot.

For the sake of argument, let's assume that the global economy plunges into a near depression, and investors steer clear of dollars. Should they therefore put all their money into gold? Not necessarily. Unlike other commodities, gold has little intrinsic value. You can't eat it, heat your house with it, or put it to good use. It is what Keynes called a "barbaric relic." While you could exchange gold for something more useful, it might make more sense to stock up on commodity futures or, if you can stomach it, cans of Spam.

Investors should remain wary of gold. The recent swings in its price— up 10 percent one month, down 10 percent the next—underscore the fact that its price movements are often a function of irrational beliefs and bubbles. Holding some gold as a hedge against inflation may make some sense, particularly if governments start to monetize their debt. But holding lots of gold makes no sense, particularly given the likelihood that inflation will remain in check.

Inflation or Deflation?

At the height of the recent crisis, concerns about deflation drove many governments to take drastic measures to prevent prices from falling. Zero interest rates and quantitative easing would normally trigger a round of inflation, but that did not happen in 2009. Deflation crept into the United States, the Eurozone, Japan, and even some emerging-market economies. The reason was simple: banks held most of their excess liquidity in the form of reserves rather than loaning it out.

Deflationary pressures will persist in the short term in most advanced economies and even some emerging-market economies. In most places, demand for goods and labor remains slack, putting downward pressure on prices and wages. Inventories of unsold goods get liquidated at low prices, and workers facing record unemployment rates have little bargaining power, even accepting cuts in wages in exchange for job security.

Inflation has shown some signs of reappearing in emerging economies, which have enjoyed a swifter recovery from the financial crisis. At the end of 2009 oil, food, and real estate prices were rising in China and India. For these economies, which may soon overheat, inflation could become a problem, far more so than in advanced economies.

Still, advanced economies may see a return of inflation starting in 2012. It could happen for one of three reasons. One, if governments opt to monetize their deficits, expectations that inflation will soar, prompting a vicious cycle of falling currencies and rising prices and wages. Two, the glut of easy money unleashed in response to the crisis may end up fueling an asset bubble in commodities, prompting a return of inflation. Three, if the dollar continues to weaken, the price of commodities in the United States might go up: as we've seen, there's a negative relationship between the value of the dollar and the dollar price of commodities. Oil producers, for example, will raise the dollar price of a barrel of oil if the dollar weakens. Otherwise, they will see a decline in the purchasing power of the dollar they receive in revenue.

In all likelihood, neither deflation nor inflation is likely to be pronounced in the next year or so. Absent a severe double-dip recession, deflation will likely remain in check, but inflation might start to gain momentum under certain circumstances.

Globalization and Its Discontents

In the last few decades the world has become increasingly "globalized." Trade in goods and services has become increasingly international in scope, as has the migration of workers and the diffusion of information. Globalization has gone hand in hand with technological innovation, each reinforcing the other. For example, financial capital now moves around the world at a much faster pace thanks to the widespread adoption of information technology.

As a result, countries can now provide services to other countries on the other side of the world: think of India's call centers, for example, and the outsourcing of U.S. white-collar jobs. Likewise, China has been able to join complicated supply chains that stretch around the globe. Increasingly, countries on the economic periphery are connected to advanced economies and vice versa.

Globalization has brought a sharp increase in the standard of living in emerging economies. Hundreds of millions of Chinese, Indians, Russians, Brazilians, and other citizens of emerging-market economies have been lifted out of poverty. They have obtained higher-paying blue-collar jobs, or even middle-class salaries, gaining far greater access to necessities and luxuries alike. In turn, citizens of advanced economies have seen the prices of goods and services become ever more affordable.

But globalization and innovation are not without risks. Take, for example, the daunting challenge of adding billions of people to the global labor supply. China and India contain nearly 2.5 billion people, and other emerging economies have another 2 billion. Botching this integration could cause a backlash against globalization and free trade in advanced economies. Unfortunately, this sort of transition will not likely be smooth. Many stress points in the global economy—current account imbalances, for example, and the growing prevalence of financial crises—are in no small part a function of the complex integration of emerging markets in the global economy.

Globalization has also been associated with growing inequalities of income and wealth in advanced economies and emerging-market economies alike. Debate simmers over why this has happened. Some economists point out that technological progress has left some workers out of growing global prosperity (for example, if you don't know how to use a computer, you can't improve your situation). Others point to the rising comparativer, advantage of China and other emerging markets in the manufacture of labor-intensive goods.

Whatever its causes, this increased inequality has caused a growing malaise and concerns about globalization and free trade. It began with blue-collar workers, for understandable reasons, but has spread to white-collar workers, as outsourcing enables firms to shift service jobs from advanced economies like the United States to emerging economies like India. In time, entire industries may shift from one part of the globe to another, causing serious disruption. This kind of "creative destruction" may be inevitable, but it will cause considerable strife unless properly managed.

Finally, globalization may well usher in far more frequent and virulent crises. The speed with which financial capital and hot money can move in and out of specific markets and economies has increased the volatility of asset prices and the virulence of financial crises. Unfortunately, while finance has gone global, its regulation remains a national affair. All of this increases the likelihood of future crises that could assume global proportions.

The recent crisis has made it clear that the "Great Instability" may be a better description of the coming era than the "Great Moderation." Asset bubbles and busts may occur more frequently, and crises once thought to occur only once or twice a century may hammer the global economy far more often. Black swans may become white swans.

That would be unfortunate: as financial crises grow in frequency and severity, they will inflict social and political instability and ultimately breed a backlash against globalization. The backlash could take many forms: protectionist trade policies; financial protectionism, with restrictions on foreign direct investment; capital controls; and a broader rejection of any policies that promote free markets.

How to prevent such a backlash? First, it's essential for governments to adopt policies that reduce the frequency and virulence of asset booms and busts. This will entail reforming the financial system and monetary system along the lines described earlier in this book. But it will also require the construction of a much broader government safety net. If workers have to be flexible enough to switch jobs and careers frequently, they will need more government support to navigate the increasingly uncertain employment terrain. This approach—dubbed "flexicurity"—will mean greater investments in education, job skills, and retraining; a safety net of unemployment benefits; and portable health care plans and pension benefits. In the United States, it will also mean a more progressive tax system in order to pay for these benefits.

Paradoxically, making free markets function better, and enabling workers to be more flexible and mobile in a global economy where "creative destruction" will be the norm, requires more, not less, government. Government can use monetary policy and increased regulation to keep booms and busts from occurring. It can provide a broad social safety net to help make workers more productive and flexible. It can implement tax systems that will reduce inequalities of wealth and income. Finally, government will need to take a bigger role in more closely coordinating their economic policies so as not to create the kind of imbalances that produce crises in the first place. Crises may be here to stay, but governments can limit their incidence and severity.

In the shadow of the worst financial meltdown since the Great Depression, many policy makers and pundits have observed that "a crisis is a terrible thing to waste." This is true. We will plant the seeds of an even more destructive crisis if we squander the opportunity this crisis has presented us to implement necessary reforms. That opportunity would be a terrible—indeed, a tragic—thing to waste.

AFTERWORD

Two Paths to Recovery

Since *Crisis Economics* was first published in the spring of 2010, the world's advanced economies recovered in much the way we predicted in the "Outlook" section of that edition of this book. At the time, we warned that the typical recovery from a financial crisis resembles a U—in other words, several years of anemic growth. This is unavoidable: repairing gaping holes in the balance sheets of banks, corporations, and households is a time-consuming process, and this process of "deleveraging" helps keep the economy in the doldrums for some time.

This is where we find ourselves a year later as the first paperback edition goes to press. In the United States, the Eurozone, the United Kingdom, and Japan, the recovery has followed a predictable, if disappointing, path. In most of these nations, lower spending and higher savings rates may reduce the debt accumulated before the crisis, but it is unlikely to lay the foundation for a robust recovery until balance sheets are well repaired. In fact, the only advanced economies that have recovered a bit more quickly—Canada, Sweden, Norway, Finland, Australia, and Israel—never displayed the same enthusiasm for debt and leverage as countries like the United States.

The recovery was far more robust and V-shaped in most of the world's emerging markets, few of which had committed the same sins as the world's biggest mature economies. China and India rebounded quickly, as did Latin

America, led by Brazil, Peru, and Chile. (Most of the Middle East bounced back quickly as well, helped in part by rising oil and energy prices, which were a product of a strong recovery in economies like China.) Even traditional laggards like the countries of Sub-Saharan Africa recovered relatively fast, thanks to better governance, economic reform, and growing political stability.

Not every emerging economy followed this script, though the exceptions tend to prove the rule that any economy which accumulates too much debt in advance of a crisis is unlikely to recover quickly. Thus, most of the emerging economies burdened by too much private and public sector debt in Europe—particularly Latvia, Hungary, Romania, Bulgaria, and Ukraine—faltered, as have emerging economies that "drank the Kool-Aid" during the real estate bubble (Dubai comes to mind here). A handful of other emerging economies—Pakistan, for example—also failed to recover, weighed down by ineffective governments and political instability.

Still, the countries that enjoyed a V-shaped recovery have run into other troubles. In developing nations like China, there has been growing concern that the economy recovered too quickly, falling victim to rising inflation, soaring commodity prices, and asset and credit bubbles. While policy makers in these countries have been mindful of the risks that the economy might overheat, they've been reluctant to adopt tighter monetary policies, fearful that doing so would strengthen their currencies and undercut the competitiveness of their exports.

By contrast, advanced economies mired in a U-shaped recovery have not been constrained by such worries. Much as we warned in the previous edition, inflation has remained low and continues to be too low in the United States, Japan, and the Eurozone. In response, the United States and Japan have been aggressive in adopting fiscal policies aimed at jump-starting the economy as well as monetary policies—so-called quantitative easing—aimed at reducing interest rates and boosting growth.

The United Kingdom and the Eurozone have not been so blessed. Though inflation is little in evidence, borrowing rates for countries on the margins of Europe have soared amid growing fears that nations like Greece will default on their debt. This has in turn led to brutal bouts of fiscal belt-tightening that have helped to curtail inflation and will likely continue to do so for the foreseeable future. While the Bank of England has vowed to apply quantitative easing if the fiscal retrenchment proves too debilitating, the European Central Bank has so far refused to go down this road. But if the events of the last year are any indication, the ECB—and by extension, the entire Eurozone—has a far bigger problem on its plate: soaring levels of public debt.

As we noted in the previous edition, private sector debt accumulated before a crisis often morphs into public sector debt. This process, which eerily resembles the way that toxic chemicals move up the food chain, concentrates debt in ever larger players in the economy. In effect, debt moves from households and corporations to banks and other financial institutions, and eventually to national governments, if not international institutions like the European Central Bank and the IMF.

This has occurred in ways both subtle and obvious. In some cases, governments in the United States and Europe have bailed out corporations and banks with borrowed money. In other instances, policy makers and politicians have launched programs aimed at subsidizing and supporting debt-burdened consumers and others. In this way, debt either moves up the economic food chain, or governments take on new debt to cushion the burdens of existing debt. Whatever the mechanism, the effect is effectively the same: unsustainable levels of sovereign debt.

The Eurozone Crisis

In the first edition of this book, we warned of trouble ahead for the Eurozone, beginning with Greece. Unfortunately, our fears have been fulfilled: after years of fiscal recklessness, Greece could no longer borrow at affordable rates in 2010 and was ultimately forced to accept a bailout package underwritten by the IMF and the European Union. Ireland was next. After the collapse of Ireland's housing bubble and its banking system, the government effectively assumed these losses. It, too, saw its borrowing costs skyrocket, and like Greece, it "agreed" to a bailout package (with plenty of strings attached) from the IMF and the European Union. The crisis has since spread to Portugal and Spain. As we write, the latter is in the unenviable position of being both too big to fail and too big to save.

As a consequence, the European Monetary Union now faces a profound threat to its continued existence. Though it has always been a monetary union, with member states ceding control over monetary policy and exchange rates, the member nations never embraced a true fiscal or political union. It is true that member nations relinquished a good deal of fiscal autonomy under the terms of the Growth and Stability Pact, which formally constrained budget deficits and debt. This was supposed to lead to a "convergence" among the individual members, but the reality turned out to be different: some countries dodged the rules governing budget deficits using accounting gimmicks, or put off promised structural reforms. Then, in the heat of the crisis, many nations moved private losses onto the backs of national governments.

Three possible fates await the Eurozone. The first is a continuation of the status quo in which the member countries muddle through by relying on the current approach of "lend and pray," with financing provided to ailing member states in exchange for promises of fiscal discipline and future structural reforms. This approach reflects the misguided belief that distressed countries like Greece, Ireland, Portugal, and Spain are suffering from an irrational crisis of confidence in the financial markets. In other words, these countries are illiquid, not insolvent.

Should Europe's leaders continue to subscribe to this naive belief and otherwise kick the can down the road, they will increase the likelihood of a second, more unsettling scenario where a country on the European periphery exits the euro, precipitating a disorderly restructuring of debt. Such an event would send shock waves through global financial markets. If several countries exited the euro, the effects would be exponentially larger and would cast doubt on the decades-old campaign to forge a common European Union.

That said, it is conceivable that the Eurozone might survive and even thrive with some significant changes in policy. Most obviously, the Europeans need more official resources to deal with the threats to its continued existence. Thanks to a series of ad-hoc pledges (most of them from Germany) the Eurozone has enough resources to bail out Greece, Ireland, and Portugal. But it lacks the funds to arrest a crisis of confidence in Spain's finances, much less a larger, continent-wide crisis. This is true even if these countries adopt all the necessary fiscal and structural reforms: if investors sense that the Eurozone hasn't enough reserves to back its members, panic could easily spread.

How could Europe strengthen its hand? Ideally, its leaders would move beyond a mere monetary union and adopt a genuine fiscal union: a new, centralized body that could levy taxes and set budgets in every Eurozone country and, by extension, could bail out troubled countries. Unfortunately, there's no political will to drive such a radical reformation of Europe's government. There are, however, other ways for Europe to create a facsimile of a fiscal union. It could market more Eurozone bonds along the lines of those already issued by the European Financial Stability Facility, or EFSF. The European Central Bank could also take a much more visible role, making long-term bond purchases and offering more liquidity to troubled banks. None of this will happen without German support, and Europe's spendthrifts must make credible commitments to fiscal discipline in exchange for this assistance.

But resources alone cannot solve Europe's problems. Nor will any amount of budget cutting and austerity solve the problems of Greece, Ireland, and possibly Portugal and Spain. Many banks in these countries are arguably insolvent. That means all unsecured creditors of these institutions must be forced to accept losses—otherwise known as "haircuts"—on their claims. This should happen sooner rather than later, with the necessary regime put in place immediately. Otherwise, countries may be tempted to follow Ireland's lead and "socialize" the debt by moving it up the food chain to government balance sheets and thus ending up breaking the back of the sovereign.

The Eurozone must also impose a haircut on the holders of bonds in Greece and Ireland, if not in Portugal and Spain as well. Unfortunately, Europe is dragging its heels, pledging to hold off on restructuring debt until 2013. This is foolish. European policy makers should take the initiative and make unsecured private creditors of the sovereigns an offer they can't refuse, offering to restructure the existing debt by extending the maturity of the loans at more favorable interest rates. In exchange, creditors would avoid an outright default on the debt and minimize their losses.

Finally, Europe needs to take steps to make countries on the Eurozone's periphery more competitive, putting them on the path to growth. Without growth, debt levels won't stabilize, and will likely increase. And absent significant growth, it will be politically impossible for these countries to impose much-needed structural reforms, never mind the austerity measures demanded by creditors. The European Central Bank should therefore make money more freely available in order to jump-start growth and weaken the euro. In addition, Germany should delay its own fiscal consolidation. Rather than tighten its belt like the countries on the periphery, it should cut taxes for a couple years to boost its own growth and, via trade, the growth of countries on the periphery.

Long before the crisis in 2001, Romano Prodi, president of the European Commission, noted that "I am sure the euro will oblige us to introduce a new set of economic policy instruments. It is politically impossible to propose that now. But someday there will be a crisis and new instruments will be created." For good or for ill, the European Union is now at the juncture that Prodi foresaw a decade ago. Whether it will adopt the measures Prodi considered inevitable remains to be seen, but make no mistake: the future of Europe's monetary union is hanging in the balance.

Currency Wars and Trade Tensions

Throughout much of 2010, countries around the world tried to devalue their own currencies or, at the very least, prevent them from appreciating. This dynamic was a direct response to the fact that the global economy had become extraordinarily imbalanced in the years leading up to the crisis. Some countries—most notably the United States, the United Kingdom, and other advanced economies—spent too much, saved too little, and ran dangerously large current account deficits. These same countries exported too little and imported too much. Countries like Germany, Japan, and China sat on the other side of the equation. These nations saved too much, spent too little, and accumulated high current account surpluses. They also exported too much and imported too little.

In the wake of the crisis, these imbalances became the source of greater instability. In 2010, countries in the first group tried to undercut the value of their currencies. Doing so would make their exports cheaper and hence more competitive, driving down their trade deficits and bringing the world into a better balance. Unfortunately, currency wars are a zero-sum game. If one currency gets weaker, another gets stronger; if one country exports more, another country can end up exporting less.

This isn't a problem if, say, China is willing to replace its dependence on cheap currency and plentiful exports with growing domestic demand. But that's not what happened. In the wake of the crisis, China continued to intervene in the foreign exchange market in order to keep the value of the renminbi low, preserving its competitive edge in exports. As China began buying up Japanese yen and South Korean won, it sent the value of these currencies higher. Neither of these countries—or other emerging markets in Asia—could afford to see their exports get more expensive, and they retaliated in kind. This in turn put upward pressure on the euro, effectively increasing the debt burden of countries on Europe's periphery.

Currency wars are hard to stop once they start, and this one looks to be no exception. Countries around the world accelerated their interventions in the final months of 2010, with the United States and, to a lesser extent, Japan, adopting more "quantitative easing." In the United States, policy makers defended their actions, claiming it would boost growth. Though they made no mention that this action was aimed at weakening the dollar, this was precisely the idea, and it seems to have worked. Unfortunately, this stirred alarm in a host of other countries who wanted to see their own currencies weaken against the dollar.

But it is China where the conflict could turn especially ugly. So far, China has shown no interest in letting its currency appreciate at a more robust pace. It has taken minor, token measures aimed at letting its currency float, but these are cosmetic changes, not real attempts to grapple with underlying imbalances. If it continues down this path, China and other countries that run trade and current account surpluses around the world will force the United States to take more extreme measures. In fact, with Chinese growth close to 10 percent at the very moment when American unemployment is hovering around the same level, it is almost inevitable that the ongoing currency war will lead to a trade war. This could be calamitous for all parties: like currency wars, trade wars are difficult to win and cause a great deal of collateral damage.

Looking ahead, the scenario of a currency war degenerating into a trade war is not at all farfetched. A similar thing happened in the early 1930s, and while conditions are different today, the end result back then—a prolonged period of global instability, deflationary pressures, and defaults on debt both public and private—remains a very real possibility.

The Downside . . . and the Upside

Aside from the Eurozone crisis and the potential for currency wars, the outlook for the near future is decidedly mixed. In spite of expectations of stronger economic growth, many risks remain for the United States. Unemployment remains stubbornly high, and even the most optimistic growth projections will put only a minor dent in those figures. The housing market is equally troubled, and after rising briefly in the spring of 2010 (thanks to a tax credit and a foreclosure moratorium, both of which have since expired) it is now headed south again. If housing prices fall a mere 5 percent, this will bring the number of households underwater on their mortgage up to 20 million, putting a serious damper on economic growth. And plenty of financial institutions are still struggling with bad loans, and over nine hundred banks (mostly small ones) remain in critical condition, with regulators poised to shut them down. The ongoing retrenchment in the financial sector, while long overdue, has also shut plenty of households and small and medium sized firms out of the credit markets. This, too, will be a drag on growth.

But the biggest obstacle to recovery in the United States may well be the dire condition of individual states' finances. This is no minor matter. In the Eurozone, the fiscal woes of Greece—a member state that contributes only 3 percent to the region's GDP—has unleashed a crisis yet to be contained. Compare that to California, a state responsible for 13 percent of the nation's GDP. If Greece was too big to fail, the same is almost certainly true of California. And California is hardly alone: states as various as Nevada, Illinois, New York, and Florida are all struggling. So, too, are countless municipalities. As a consequence, the risk of defaults on the state and local level are at levels not seen since the 1930s.

In theory, the federal government could step into the breach and bail out the states. But this theory ignores the fact that the debt load of the United States is already approaching dangerous levels. Even if there is a recovery next year, thanks in part to the extension of the tax cuts, we must not forget that was "paid for" by issuing new debt. Absent any fiscal readjustment, the United States is expected to run trillion dollar deficits every year over the next decade. Some economists believe that such deficits aren't worrisome, and they point to the fact that the "bond vigilantes"—investors who impose discipline in the form of higher borrowing costs—have yet to materialize. Perhaps, but the latest debt-financed borrowing binge did spark a rise in the interest rate charged the United States. That may be a harbinger of things to come, particularly if policy makers succumb to the temptation to "inflate" their way out of debt.

Nonetheless, the most obvious challenger to American hegemony has problems of its own. China has been slow to raise interest rates and rein in its money supply, and like other emerging economies, it is attracting enormous inflows of capital. This may make an already bad situation worse, spurring runaway inflation and fostering ever larger credit and asset bubbles. Should these continue to grow—as will almost certainly happen if policy makers don't move soon—they will burst with unpleasant consequences. Managing these crises will pose a serious challenge to the legitimacy of governments in emerging economies, and nowhere is that more true than in China.

In fact, the United States and Europe may do better than expected, at least in the short term. The U.S. corporate sector is strong and profitable, thanks to its "lean and mean" strategy of shedding workers. Flush with cash and with strong balance sheets, corporations are well positioned to make capital investments and hire new workers. Moreover, after years of declining savings rates, American households have started to put their own balance sheets in order, cutting debt and saving more. These positive developments, when combined with quantitative easing and the recent tax legislation, could conceivably set the United States on the path to solid growth so long as the myriad other threats to the recovery—the Eurozone crisis, currency and trade wars, and soaring levels of state and federal debt—don't derail it.

In looking toward the future, it's useful to keep in mind the words of economist Arthur Pigou, who warned about the perils of extrapolating too readily from current events. "Prosperity ends in a crisis," he wrote. "The error of optimism dies in the crisis, but in dying it gives birth to an error of pessimism. This new error is born not an infant, but a giant." Pigou warned that this giant would make business "unduly depressed" and a recovery seem unfathomable. But as he recognized, all crises do end; time does heal all wounds. We may not escape the aftermath of the worst financial crisis since the Great Depression in the next year, or even in the next several years. Eventually, though, optimism will regain its former power, growth will resume, and prosperity will return, even as it sets the stage for future crises.

ACKNOWLEDGMENTS

Speaking as one, we want to thank Eamon Dolan, our editor at The Penguin Press. Eamon's unerring editorial instincts have proven invaluable in getting two professors to write for an audience beyond the confines of academia. Unflappable and whip smart, he has been instrumental in shepherding this book every step of the way. Many thanks as well to the rest of the staff at Penguin: Janet Biehl, Bruce Giffords, Nicole Hughes, and last but not least, Ann Godoff. We also want to extend our appreciation to those who read the manuscript with an eye toward clarification, especially Jane Cavolina, Dan Kaufman, and Richard Sylla. A special thanks goes to Wes Neff of the Leigh Bureau, who first proposed this project and brought us together with Eamon, Ann, and The Penguin Press.

Personal Acknowledgments

I would like to thank my collaborators at Roubini Global Economics—Christian Menegatti, Arnab Das, Elisa Parisi-Capone, Rachel Ziemba, Bertrand Delgado, Sandra Navidi, and many others—who have been my daily intellectual colleagues for the last few years. Parul Walia was helpful with a chronology of the crisis. Brad Setser, a former colleague in many different venues and the coauthor of my previous book on financial crises in emerging market economies, was always a great sounding board for ideas.

My colleagues at the Stern School of Business at New York University—starting with Richard Sylla, David Backus, Tom Cooley, Paul Wachtel, Matt Richardson, Viral Acharya, and others—provided me with intellectual rigor and opportunities for discussion and debate. Academic colleagues who have influenced my thoughts on international macroeconomics and financial crises include—among many others—Jeff Sachs, Paul Krugman, Ken Rogoff, Carmen Reinhart, Nassim Taleb, Raghu Rajan, Jeffrey Frankel, Richard Portes, Joe Stiglitz, Niall Ferguson, Robert Shiller, Hyun Shin, Barry Eichengreen, Willem Buiter, Simon Johnson, Bob Mundell, Joseph Mason, members of the International Finance and Macroeconomics Program at the National Bureau of Economic Research, and members of the International Macroeconomics group at the Centre for Economic and Policy Research. Giancarlo Corsetti, Paolo Pesenti, Bernardo Guimarães, Paolo Manasse, Vittorio Grilli, and Fabrizio Perri have been among my coauthors of academic research on international macroeconomics and financial crises; I have learned much from them.

Market practitioners, analysts, and other thinkers with whom I've had a productive dialogue include Martin Wolf, Steve Roach, David Rosenberg, Mark Zandi, Jim O'Neill, Luis Oganes, Joyce Chang, Lewis Alexander, Don Hanna, Stephen King, Manu Kumar, Jens Nystedt, Robert Kahn, Chris Whalen, Joshua Rosner, Barry Ritholtz, Yves Smith, Wolfgang Munchau, Gillian Tett, Ian Bremmer, Michael Pettis, Steve Drobny, Satyajit Das, Katerina Alexandraki, Daniel Alpert, Charles Morris, Richard Bookstaber, Edward Chancellor, and Walter Molano. Former policy makers and other policy think-tank scholars with whom I've interacted include Alex Pollock, Desmond Lachman, Ted Truman, Fred Bergsten, Morris Goldstein, Adam Posen, and Benn Steil. Marc Uzan has been a dynamo in organizing policy conferences via his Reinventing Bretton Woods Committee.

A number of former and current policy makers—some of them colleagues of mine while I worked at the Council of Economic Advisers and at the U.S. Treasury during 1998–2000—have shaped my views over the years. Without implicating any of them in any way or form with my views, I want to thank Larry Summers, Tim Geithner, Stan Fischer, David Lipton, Mary Goodman, Anna Gelpern, Dan Tarullo, Janet Yellen, John Lipsky, Bill White, Olivier Blanchard, Federico Sturzenegger, Andrés Velasco, Felipe

Larraín, and Hans-Helmut Kotz. I also have learned a great deal about financial crises from many colleagues at the International Monetary Fund, where I have had many stints as a visiting scholar over the years.

George Soros kindly hosted me in his summer home while I wrote parts of this book and has always been for me a model of a "Renaissance man." I also benefited from discussions with other investors interested in macroeconomics and economics policy issues, such as John Paulson, Louis Bacon, Bill Janeway, Ron Perelman, Steve Eisman, Daniel Loeb, Avi Tiomkin, Harry Lefrak, Stylianos Zavvos, Charles Krusen, and Jim Coleman. My friend Shai Baitel also supported my intellectual ventures. I thank Klaus Schwab and many folks at the World Economic Forum for a great venue to present and discuss my views.

Numerous bloggers—some top-notch academic economists and many accomplished veterans of Wall Street—provided me with real-time insights about the financial crisis. These include Yves Smith of "Naked Capitalism"; "Calculated Risk," home to Bill McBride and the much-missed Doris Dungey; the anonymous bloggers at Zero Hedge; Brad DeLong at "Grasping Reality with Both Hands"; Barry Ritholtz at "The Big Picture"; Mark Thoma at "Economist's View"; Jim Hamilton at "Econbrowser"; Paul Krugman at "The Conscience of a Liberal"; Mike Shedlock at "Mish's Global Economic Trend Analysis"; Tyler Cowen and Alex Tabarrok at "Marginal Revolution"; *The Wall Street Journal*'s "Real Time Economics"; Dave Altig and the other economists at the Atlanta Fed who contribute to "macroblog"; Dean Baker at "Beat the Press"; Greg Mankiw on his blog; and many, many others who have played such an instrumental role in covering the financial crisis.

Finally, I want to thank my agent, Wesley Neff, for first suggesting the idea of a book and helping me develop this project.

—Nouriel Roubini

I first met Nouriel Roubini while profiling him for a feature in *The New York Times Magazine*, and many of the ideas behind this book first surfaced in the course of that assignment. I want to thank my editor there, Jamie Ryerson, as well as Alex Star, Gerald Marzorati, Adam Moss, and Jack Rosenthal, all of whom have played key roles in fostering my work at the *Times*. Thanks as well to Steve Heuser at *The Boston Globe* for letting me air some of the ideas that ultimately shaped this book. I also owe a special debt of gratitude to Henry

Grunwald and Sarah Lewis, each of whom played an early but indispensable role in encouraging my forays into writing for a wider audience.

My colleagues at the University of Georgia deserve special acknowledgment too, beginning with the members of the Workshop in the Cultural History of Capitalism; Allan Kulikoff has been especially helpful in so many ways. I'm also grateful to Paul Sutter, Robert Pratt, and Garnett Stokes, who provided a course release so that I would have more time to work on this book. Other colleagues at the University of Georgia have provided moral support, constructive criticism, or simply a much-needed respite from work: Stephen Berry, Kathleen Clark, Jim Cobb, Rachel Gabara, Shane Hamilton, John Inscoe, Michael Kwass, Chana Kai Lee, Laura Mason, Bethany Moreton, Bob Pratt, Reinaldo Román, Susan Rosenbaum, Julie Rothschild, Claudio Saunt, George Selgin, Steve Soper, Paul Sutter, Pamela Voekel, and Chloe Wigston Smith. Thanks as well to those friends who put me up in New York City while I worked on this book, especially Michael Lacombe, as well as David Sampliner and Rachel Shuman.

Several economists, policy makers, and individuals with hands-on experience in the financial markets have fielded endless queries from me. David Dean, David Forquer, Michael Laskawy, Benjamin Schneider, Patricia Schneider, and Robert Wright have all provided insights on various esoteric financial matters. Finally, I owe a particular debt to Richard Sylla of New York University. I have known Dick since graduate school, and he has been an unfailing source of insight on the convergence of economics and history.

Particular thanks go to my agent, Tina Bennett, who has been an indispensable guide throughout this process from start to finish. She and the staff at Janklow & Nesbit—including Svetlana Katz—deserve special thanks for representing me throughout this process. A special thanks as well to Joyce Seltzer of Harvard University Press, who kindly gave me leave from another project so that I could complete this book.

I have great gratitude for those who have helped out on the home front. Richard and John Mihm contributed significantly toward child care; Kathy Mihm effectively shouldered the burden of taking care of the kids during one particularly stressful weekend; so too did my niece Alisa Dunning and my in-laws, Kathleen and Jamie Reason. Likewise, Sheridan Smith has done a heroic job of coralling my children while I work—no easy task. Jing Cui and Mary Elizabeth Nuttall have also lent a hand at critical junctures. So too did Martha Clinkscales and her family, helping out at a particularly critical time.

Last, but certainly not least, I want to thank my family. My wife, Akela Reason, has been a source of unwavering support throughout the process of writing the book: her patience, advice, and love have kept me going throughout the past year. A special thanks goes to my three sons: Silas, Asher, and Linus. They have provided comic relief as well as a constant reminder that however much the collapse of the global financial system demands my attention, it cannot compete with the more mundane—but more readily remedied—crises of dirty diapers, empty baby bottles, and bad dreams.

—Stephen Mihm

NOTES

Introduction

1 **"Nobody anywhere was smart enough . . .":** Dick Cheney, interview by Deb Riechmann, Associated Press, January 8, 2009.

1 **the most famous prediction:** Nouriel Roubini, lecture and discussion, International Monetary Fund, Washington, D.C., September 7, 2006, transcript.

2 **elaborated on his pessimistic vision:** Nouriel Roubini, "The Rising Risk of a Systemic Financial Meltdown: The Twelve Steps to Financial Disaster," February 5, 2008, online at http://www.roubini.com/analysis/44763.php; Stephen Mihm, "Dr. Doom," *New York Times Magazine*, August 15, 2008.

3 **Robert Shiller:** Robert Shiller, *Irrational Exuberance* (Princeton, N.J.: Princeton University Press, 2000); Karl E. Case and Robert J. Shiller, "Is There a Bubble in the Housing Market?" *Brookings Papers on Economic Activity* 2 (2003), 299–362.

3 **Raghuram Rajan:** Raghuram G. Rajan, "Has Financial Development Made the World Riskier?" speech delivered at Federal Reserve Bank of Kansas City symposium, "The Greenspan Era: Lessons for the Future," Jackson Hole, Wyo., August 27, 2005.

3 **"the greatest of all credit bubbles":** Justin Lahart, "NASDAQ: Five Years after the Peak," *Wall Street Journal*, March 7, 2005.

3 **William White:** Beat Balzli and Michaela Schiessl, "The Man Nobody Wanted to Hear," *Der Spiegel*, July 8, 2009.

3 **Maurice Obstfeld and Kenneth Rogoff:** Maurice Obstfeld and Kenneth Rogoff, "The Unsustainable US Current Account Position Revisited," National Bureau of Economic Research Working Paper no. 10869, November 2004.

3 **Stephen Roach:** Brett Arends, "Economic 'Armageddon' Predicted," *Boston Herald*, November 23, 2004.

5 **"animal spirits":** John Maynard Keynes, *The General Theory of Employment, Interest, and Money* (New York: Harcourt, Brace, and World, 1936), 161.

5 **"the ideas of economists . . .":** Ibid., 383.

11 **"The decadent international . . .":** John Maynard Keynes, "National Self-Sufficiency," *Yale Review* 22 (1933): 760–61.

Chapter 1: The White Swan

14 **on the eve of the Great Depression:** The single best account of the crash remains John Kenneth Galbraith, *The Great Crash, 1929* (Boston: Houghton Mifflin, 1954).

15 **"At this juncture . . .":** Ben S. Bernanke, "Economic Outlook," testimony before the Joint Economic Committee, U.S. Congress, March 28, 2007; online at http://www.federalreserve.gov/newsevents/testimony/bernanke20070328a.htm.

15 **"I don't think it poses . . .":** Paulson quoted in Kevin Carmichael and Peter Cook, "Paulson Says Subprime Rout Doesn't Affect Economy," Bloomberg.com, July 26, 2007, online at http://www.bloomberg.com/apps/news?pid=20601087&sid=aBvlvvm.ISfo&refer=home.

16 **"Looking forward . . .":** Henry M. Paulson, Jr., remarks to the *Washington Post* 200 Lunch, Washington, D.C., May 16, 2008, online at http://www.ustreas.gov/press/releases/hp981.htm.

16 **"Sure . . . there are trouble spots . . .":** Donald Luskin, "Quit Doling Out That Bad-Economy Line," *Washington Post*, September 14, 2008.

16 **"black swan":** Nassim Nicholas Taleb, *The Black Swan: The Impact of the Highly Improbable* (New York: Random House, 2007).

18 **households used their homes as collateral:** Karl E. Case, John M. Quigley, and Robert J. Shiller, "Comparing Wealth Effects: The Stock Market versus the Housing Market," *Advances in Macroeconomics* 5 (2005): 1–34.

18 **home equity withdrawals:** See Gene Sperling, "Housing Bust Meets the Equity Blues," Bloomberg.com, April 19, 2007, online at http://www.bloomberg.com/apps/news?pid=20601039&sid=a.mcWxg9aJ_E; Alan Greenspan and James Kennedy, "Sources and Uses of Equity Extracted from Homes," Working Paper no. 2007-20, Finance and Economics Discussion Series, Federal Reserve Board, online at http://www.federalreserve.gov/pubs/feds/2007/200720/200720pap.pdf.

18 **"This time is different":** Carmen M. Reinhart and Kenneth S. Rogoff, *This Time Is Different: Eight Centuries of Financial Folly* (Princeton, N.J.: Princeton University Press, 2009).

20 **Before the rise of capitalism:** Reinhart and Rogoff, *This Time Is Different*, 86–89, 101–11, 174–81.

20 **The Chinese pioneered:** Peter Bernholz, *Monetary Regimes and Inflation: History, Economic and Political Relationships* (Cheltenham, U.K.: Edward Elgar, 2003), 53.

20 **"tulip mania":** See, for example, Peter M. Garber, "Tulipmania," *Journal of Political Economy* 97 (1989): 535–60; Anne Goldgar, *Tulipmania: Money, Honor, and Knowledge in the Dutch Golden Age* (Chicago: University of Chicago Press, 2007).

20 **John Law's Mississippi Company:** John Law, *A Full and Impartial Account of the Company of Mississippi* (London, 1720); Antoin E. Murphy, *John Law: Economic Theorist and Policy-Maker* (Oxford: Clarendon Press, 2007).

21 **South Sea Company:** Rik G. P. Frehen, William N. Goetzmann, and K. Geert Rouwenhorst, "New Evidence on the First Financial Bubble," National Bureau of Economic Research Working Paper no. 15332, September 2009.

21 **the panic of 1825:** Larry Neal, "The Financial Crisis of 1825 and the Restructuring of the British Financial System," *Federal Reserve Bank of St. Louis Review*, May–June 1998, 53–76; Michael Bordo, "Commentary," *Federal Reserve Bank of St. Louis Review*, May–June 1998, 77–82.

21 **"a period of frantic . . .":** Walter Bagehot, *Lombard Street: A Description of the Money Market* (New York: E. P. Dutton, 1920), 190.

21 **the panic of 1857:** G. W. Van Vleck, *The Panic of 1857: An Analytical Study* (New York: Columbia University Press, 1943); Charles W. Calomiris and Larry Schweikart, "The Panic of 1857: Origins, Transmission, and Containment," *Journal of Economic History* 51 (1991): 807–34.

22 **Countries around the world:** Charles P. Kindleberger, *Manias, Panics, and Crashes: A History of Financial Crises* (New York: Basic Books, 1978), 129–30.

22 **the crisis of 1873:** Ibid., 132–133; Michael Bordo, "Discussion: The Panic of 1873 and Financial Market Volatility and Panics Before 1914," in Eugene White, ed., *Crashes and Panics: The Lessons from History* (Homewood, Ill.: Business One Irwin, 1990), 126–32.

23 **The crisis of 1907:** Robert F. Bruner and Sean D. Carr, *The Panic of 1907: Lessons Learned from the Market's Perfect Storm* (Hoboken, N.J.: John Wiley and Sons, 2009).

23 **the money supply sharply contracted:** Milton Friedman and Anna J. Schwartz, *A Monetary History of the United States, 1867–1960* (Princeton, N.J.: Princeton University Press, 1963), 299–419.

23 **"leave-it-alone liquidationist":** Hoover quoted in Kindleberger, *Manias, Panics, Crashes*, 139–40.

24 **the worst depression in its history:** David M. Kennedy, *Freedom from Fear: The American People in Depression and War, 1929–1945* (New York: Oxford University Press, 1999).

24 **Many nations in Europe:** Charles P. Kindleberger, *The World in Depression, 1929–1939* (Berkeley: University of California Press, 1986); Reinhart and Rogoff, *This Time Is Different*, 71–73, 111.

24 **Bretton Woods:** Michael D. Bordo and Barry J. Eichengreen, eds., *A Retrospective on the Bretton Woods System: Lessons for International Monetary Reform* (Chicago: University of Chicago Press, 1993), 3–108.

25 **All good things:** Peter M. Garber, "The Collapse of the Bretton Woods Fixed Exchange Rate System," ibid., 461–494.

25 **Every silver lining:** Timothy Curry, "The LDC Debt Crisis," in FDIC Division of Research and Statistics, *History of the Eighties: Lessons for the Future* (Washington: FDIC, 1997), 1:191–210.

26 **the Great Moderation:** James H. Stock and Mark W. Watson, "Has the Business Cycle Changed and Why?" *NBER Macroeconomics Annual 2002* 17 (2003): 159–218.

26 **What accounted for the Great Moderation:** The literature on the Great Moderation is extensive. See, for example, Shaghil Ahmed, Andrew Levin, and Beth Anne Wilson, "Recent U.S. Macroeconomic Stability: Good, Policies, Good Practices, or Good Luck?" *Review of Economics and Statistics* 86 (August 2004): 824–32; James Kahn, Margaret McConnell, and Gabriel Perez-Quiros, "On the Causes of the Increased Stability of the U.S. Economy," Federal Reserve Bank of New York, *Economic Policy Review* 8 (2002): 183–202; Jordi Gali and Luca Gambetti, "On the Sources of the Great Moderation," *American Economic Journal: Macroeconomics* 1 (2009): 26–57.

27 **"optimistic for the future":** Ben S. Bernanke, "The Great Moderation," remarks to the Eastern Economic Association, Washington, D.C., February 20, 2004, online at http://www.federalreserve.gov/boarddocs/speeches/2004/20040220/default.htm.

27 **Japan in the 1980s:** Paul Krugman, *The Return of Depression Economics* (New York: W.W. Norton, 1999), 60–82; Takatoshi Ito, "Retrospective on the Bubble Period and Its Relationship to Developments in the 1990s," *World Economy* 26 (2003): 283–300; Mitsuhiro Fukao, "Japan's Lost Decade and Its Financial System," *World Economy* 26 (2003): 365–84.

28 **a financial crisis engulfed Norway:** Harald A. Benink and David T. Llewellyn, "Fragile Banking in Norway, Sweden and Finland: An Empirical Analysis," *Journal of International Financial Markets, Institutions and Money* 4 (1994): 5–19.

28 **savings and loan associations:** Timothy Curry and Lynn Shibut, "The Cost of the Savings and Loan Crisis: Truth and Consequences," *FDIC Banking Review* 13 (2000): 26–35.

28 **countries in Latin America and Asia:** Nouriel Roubini and Brad Setser, *Bailouts or Bail-Ins? Responding to Financial Crises in Emerging Economies* (Washington, D.C.: Institute for International Economics, 2004).

29 **Long-Term Capital Management:** Roger Lowenstein, *When Genius Failed: The Rise and Fall of Long-Term Capital Management* (New York: Random House, 2000).

29 **Crises continued to materialize:** Roubini and Setser, *Bailouts or Bail-Ins*, 61–70.

31 **"There is no national housing bubble":** Daniela Deane, "In Real Estate Fever, More Signs of Sickness," *Washington Post*, April 17, 2005.

31 **"the charm of history . . .":** Aldous Huxley, *The Devils of Loudun* (London: Chatto and Windus, 1952), 259.

31 **greed:** See, for example, Ruth Gledhill, "Rowan Williams Says 'Human Greed' to Blame for Financial Crisis," *Times* (London), October 15, 2008.

33 **"we should be quite cautious . . .":** Alan Greenspan, "Consumer Credit and Financial Modernization," remarks to Economic Development Conference of the Greenlining Institute, San Francisco, Calif., October 11, 1997, online at http://www.federalreserve.gov/boarddocs/speeches/1997/19971011.htm.

33 **"lenders are now able . . .":** Alan Greenspan, remarks to the Federal Reserve System's Fourth Annual Community Affairs Research Conference, Washington, D.C., April 8, 2005, online at http://www.federalreserve.gov/boarddocs/speeches/2005/20050408/default.htm.

33 **slashing the rate:** Jean Claude Trichet, "Activism and Alertness in Monetary Policy," lecture to "Central Banks in the 21st Century" conference, Madrid, June 8, 2006, online at http://www.ecb.int/press/key/date/2006/html/sp060608_1.en.html.

Chapter 2: Crisis Economists

39 **"Practical men, who believe . . .":** Keynes, *General Theory*, 383.

40 **"invisible hand":** Adam Smith, *An Inquiry into the Nature and Causes of the Wealth of Nations* (London: Charles Knight, 1835), 3:112; Robert L. Heilbroner and Lester C. Thurow, *Economics Explained* (New York: Touchstone, 1987), 25–31.

40 **economists refined and reworked:** Denis P. O'Brien, "Classical Economics," in Warren J. Samuels, Jeff E. Biddle, and John B. Davis, eds., *A Companion to the History of Economic Thought* (Oxford: Blackwell, 2003), 112–29; Alessandro Roncaglia, *The Wealth of Ideas: A History of Economic Thought* (Cambridge, U.K.: Cambridge University Press, 2005), 179–243, 278–96, 322–83.

40 **Louis Bachelier:** Louis Bachelier, "Théorie de la spéculation," in *Annales Scientifiques de l'École Normale Supérieure* 3 (1900): 21–86; Justin Fox, *The Myth of the Rational Market: A History of Risk, Reward, and Delusion on Wall Street* (New York: Harper Business, 2009), 6–8.

40 **"The consensus of judgment . . .":** Lawrence quoted in John Kenneth Galbraith, *The Great Crash, 1929* (Boston: Houghton Mifflin, 1954), 75.

41 **postwar academic departments:** Fox, *Myth of the Rational Market*, 89–107.

41 **"random walk" theory:** Burton G. Malkiel, *A Random Walk Down Wall Street* (New York: W.W. Norton, 1973).

41 **"Don't bother . . .":** Andrew W. Lo and A. Craig MacKinlay, *A Non-Random Walk Down Wall Street* (Princeton, N.J.: Princeton University Press, 1999), 6.

41 **Yale economist Robert Shiller:** Robert J. Shiller, "Consumption, Asset Markets and Macroeconomic Fluctuations," *Carnegie-Rochester Conference Series on Public Policy* 17 (1982): 203–38.

42 **"While markets are not totally crazy . . .":** Robert J. Shiller, "From Efficient Markets Theory to Behavioral Finance," *Journal of Economic Perspectives* 17 (2003): 90.

42 **"models of human psychology . . .":** Ibid.

42 **recent research in behavioral finance:** Ibid.; Fox, *Myth of the Rational Market*, 175–210, 247–64.

42 **"fundamental parameters . . .":** Shiller, "From Efficient Markets Theory," 94.

42 **"biased self-attribution":** Kent Daniel, David Hirshleifer, and Avanidhar Subramanyam, "Investor Psychology and Security Market Under- and Overreactions," *Journal of Finance* 53 (1998): 1839–85.

43 **"some accident . . . sets speculation . . .":** John Stuart Mill, *Principles of Political Economy* (London: Longmans Green, 1909): 527–29.

45 **William Stanley Jevons:** Sandra J. Peart, "Sunspots and Expectations: W. S. Jevons's Theory of Economic Fluctuations," *Journal of the History of Economic Thought* 13 (1991): 243–65.

45 **Karl Marx:** Robert L. Heilbroner, *The Worldly Philosophers: The Lives, Times, and Ideas of the Great Economic Thinkers* (New York: Touchstone, 1999), 136–69; Roncaglia, *Wealth of Ideas*, 244–77.

45 **"Modern bourgeois society . . .":** Karl Marx and Friedrich Engels, *The Communist Manifesto* (New York: Penguin, 2002), 225–26.

47 **John Maynard Keynes:** Heilbroner, *Worldly Philosophers*, 248–87; Roncaglia, *Wealth of Ideas*, 384–88.

47 **no ordinary economist:** Heilbroner and Thurow, *Economics Explained*, 38–39.

47 **"I believe myself to be writing . . .":** Keynes quoted in Hyman P. Minsky, *John Maynard Keynes* (New York: Columbia University Press, 1975), 3.

48 **"paradox of thrift":** Keynes, *General Theory*, 84.

48 **"animal spirits":** Ibid., 162.

49 **"We Are All Keynesians Now":** "The Economy: We Are All Keynesians Now," *Time*, December 31, 1965.

49 **Friedman and his coauthor:** Milton Friedman and Anna J. Schwartz, *A Monetary History of the United States, 1867–1960* (Princeton, N.J.: Princeton University Press, 1963), 299–419.

49 **most notably Peter Temin:** Peter Temin, *Did Monetary Forces Cause the Great Depression?* (New York: W.W. Norton, 1976).

50 **"bastard Keynesianism":** Joan Robinson, *What Are the Questions? And Other Essays: Further Contributions to Modern Economics* (Armonk, N.Y.: M. E. Sharpe, 1980), 34.

50 **"Instability . . . is an inherent . . .":** Hyman Minsky, *Stabilizing an Unstable* Economy (New York: McGraw-Hill, 2008), 134.

50 **"Implicit in [Keynes's] analysis . . .":** Minsky, *John Maynard Keynes*, 11–12.

51 **"The interposition of this veil . . .":** John Maynard Keynes, *Essays in Persuasion* (New York: W.W. Norton, 1963), 169.

51 **Financial Instability Hypothesis:** Hyman Minsky, "The Financial Instability Hypothesis: An Interpretation of Keynes and an Alternative to 'Standard' Theory," and "The Financial Instability Hypothesis: A Restatement," both in Minsky, *Can "It" Happen Again? Essays on Instability and Finance* (Armonk, N.Y.: M. E. Sharpe, 1982), 59–70, 90–116.

52 **Irving Fisher:** Irving Fisher, "The Debt-Deflation Theory of Great Depressions," *Econometrica* 1 (1933): 346.

54 **The Austrian School:** See Steven Horwitz, "The Austrian Marginalists: Menger, Böhm-Bawerk, and Wieser," and Peter J. Boettke and Peter T. Leeson, "The Austrian School of Economics: 1950–2000," both in Samuel, Biddle, and Davis, eds., *Companion to History of Economic Thought*, 262–77, 445–53.

54 **Schumpeter's worldview:** Joseph Alois Schumpeter, *Capitalism, Socialism, and Democracy* (London: Routledge, 2006), 81–86.

55 **According to some Austrian economists:** See, for example, Murray Rothbard, *America's Great Depression* (New York: New York University Press, 1973).

56 **"Greenspan put":** Peronet Despeignes, "Greenspan Put May Be Encouraging Complacency," *Financial Times*, December 8, 2000; Marcus Miller, Paul Weller, and Lei Zhang, "Moral Hazard and the US Stock Market: Analysing the 'Greenspan Put,'" *Economic Journal* 112 (2002): C171–86.

57 **the road that Japan paved in the 1990s:** See, for example, Benjamin Powell, "Explaining Japan's Recession," *Quarterly Journal of Austrian Economics* 5 (2002): 35–50.

57 **Economists who swear fealty to Keynes:** Krugman, *Return of Depression Economics*, 74–77; Charles Yuji Horioka, "The Causes of Japan's 'Lost Decade': The Role of Household Consumption," *Japan and the World Economy* 18 (2006): 378–400.

59 **"economists set themselves . . .":** John Maynard Keynes, *A Tract on Monetary Reform* (London: Macmillan, 1923), 80.

59 **"Well, . . . this is probably a change . . .":** Conor Clarke, "An Interview with Paul Samuelson, Part Two," *Atlantic*, June 18, 2009, online at http://correspondents.theatlantic.com/conor_clarke/2009/06/an_interview_with_paul_samuelson_part_two.php.

60 **Scottish journalist:** Charles Mackay, *Memoirs of Extraordinary Popular Delusions and the Madness of Crowds* (London: National Illustrated Library, 1852). This expanded edition replaced the original work published in 1841.

Chapter 3: Plate Tectonics

62 **In the 1840s Great Britain:** C. N. Ward-Perkins, "The Commercial Crisis of 1847," *Oxford Economic Papers* 2 (1950): 75–94; H. M. Boot, *The Commercial Crisis of 1847*, Occasional Papers in Economic and Social History, no. 11 (Hull, U.K.: Hull University Press, 1984).

63 **The same argument could be made:** The single best argument for the positive effects of bubbles is Daniel Gross, *Pop! Why Bubbles Are Great for the Economy* (New York: Harper Business, 2007).

63 **Financial innovation changed that:** The account that follows draws heavily on Gillian Tett, *Fool's Gold: How the Bold Dream of a Small Tribe at J. P. Morgan Was Corrupted by Wall Street Greed and Unleashed a Catastrophe* (New York: Free Press, 2009), 51–56; Mark Zandi, *Financial Shock: A 360° Look at the Subprime Mortgage Implosion, and How to Avoid the Next Financial Crisis* (Upper Saddle River, N.J.: Financial Times Press, 2008), 111–19.

63 **the Government National Mortgage Association:** Cameron L. Cowan, American Securitization Forum, statement before the both the Subcommittee on Housing and Community Opportunity and the Subcommittee on Financial Institutions and Consumer Credit, Committee on Financial Services, U.S. House of Representatives, November 5, 2003.

65 **passed down the line like a hot potato:** On the erosion of due diligence, see Amiyatosh K. Purnanandam, "Originate-to-Distribute Model and the Sub-Prime Mortgage Crisis," paper presented at the American Finance Association Annual Meeting, September 18, 2009, Atlanta, Ga.

65 **As securitization became increasingly commonplace:** See, for example, Vinod Kothari, *Securitization: The Financial Instrument of the Future* (Hoboken, N.J.: John Wiley and Sons, 2006).

66 **new, exotic, and complicated:** Douglas J. Lucas, Laurie S. Goodman, and Frank J. Fabozzi, "Collateralized Debt Obligations and Credit Risk Transfer," *Journal of Financial Transformation* 20 (2007): 47–59.

66 **an elegant solution: the CDO:** Zandi, *Financial Shock*, 117–19. See also Janet Tavakoli, *Collateralized Debt Obligations and Structured Finance: New Developments in Cash and Synthetic Securitization* (Hoboken, N.J.: John Wiley and Sons, 2003).

68 **Moral hazard played a significant role:** See, for example, Kevin Dowd, "Moral Hazard and the Financial Crisis." *Cato Journal* 29 (2009): 141–66.

68 **the way these firms provided compensation:** Much of the discussion in this section is drawn from Gian Luca Clementi, Thomas F. Cooley, Matthew Richardson, and Ingo Walter, "Rethinking Compensation in Financial Firms," and Viral V. Acharya et al., "Corporate Governance in the Modern Financial Sector," both in Viral V. Archaya and Matthew Richardson, eds., *Restoring Financial Stability: How to Repair a Failed System* (Hoboken, N.J.: John Wiley and Sons, 2009).

68 **a system of annual bonuses:** Raghuram Rajan, "Bankers' Pay Is Deeply Flawed," *Financial Times*, January 8, 2008; Gian Luca Clementi and Thomas Cooley, "Executive Compensation: Facts," New York University, Stern School of Business, Working Paper, November 10, 2009, online at http://pages.stern.nyu.edu/~gclement/Papers/facts.pdf.

69 **paid ever more staggering sums:** Christine Harper, "Bonuses at Wall Street Big-Five Surge to $36 Billion," Bloomberg.com, November 6, 2006, online at http://www.bloomberg.com/apps/news?pid=20601087&refer=home&sid=atEk12XYMerk.

72 **as the career of Alan Greenspan amply suggests:** Alan Greenspan, *The Age of Turbulence: Adventures in a New World* (New York: Penguin Press, 2007).

72 **"In a crisis environment . . . we shouldn't . . .":** Greenspan quoted in John M. Berry, "Black Monday for Greenspan: A Race to Forestall a Liquidity Crisis," *Washington Post*, October 19, 1997.

73 **"take away the punch bowl . . .":** Martin quoted in Kenneth T. Jackson, Karen Markoe, and Arnie Markoe, eds., *The Scribner Encyclopedia of American Lives*, vol. 5 (New York: Charles Scribner's Sons, 2002),

73 **"irrational exuberance":** Alan Greenspan, "The Challenge of Central Banking in a Democratic Society," Francis Boyer Lecture of the American Enterprise Institute, December 5, 1996, online at http://www.federalreserve.gov/boarddocs/speeches/1996/19961205.htm.

73 **it created a Greenspan put:** Miller, Weller, and Zhang, "Moral Hazard and the US Stock Market."

73 **"For us to go in and audit . . .":** Greenspan quoted in Greg Ip, "Did Greenspan Add to Subprime Woes?" *Wall Street Journal*, June 9, 2007; Edmund L. Andrews, "Fed Shrugged as Subprime Crisis Spread," *New York Times*, December 18, 2007.

74 **"led to rapid growth in subprime . . .":** Alan Greenspan, remarks to the Federal Reserve System's Fourth Annual Community Affairs Research Conference, Washington, D.C., April 8, 2005, online at http://www.federalreserve.gov/boarddocs/speeches/2005/20050408/default.htm.

74 **The most notable casualty:** James R. Barth, R. Dan Brumbaugh, Jr., and James A. Wilcox. "Policy Watch: The Repeal of Glass-Steagall and the Advent of Broad Banking," *Journal of Economic Perspectives* 14, no. 2 (Spring 2000): 191–204; and Jill M. Hendrickson. "The Long and Bumpy Road to Glass-Steagall Reform: A Historical and Evolutionary Analysis of Banking Legislation," *American Journal of Economics and Sociology* 60 (2001): 849–79.

75 **"We've said these are the big guys":** Quoted in Stephen Labaton, "Agency's '04 Rule Let Banks Pile Up New Debt," *New York Times*, October 2, 2008.

75 **Community Reinvestment Act of 1977:** See, for example, Peter J. Wallison, "Cause and Effect: Government Policies and the Financial Crisis," *Critical Review* 21 (2009): 365–76.

76 **legislation passed in the 1990s:** Carol D. Leonnig, "How HUD Mortgage Policy Fed the Crisis," *Washington Post*, June 10, 2008.

77 **"shadow banking system":** Having coined the term at the Fed conference at Jackson Hole in 2007, McCulley elaborated on it in a newsletter for PIMCO. See Paul McCulley, "The Shadow Banking System and Hyman Minsky's Economic Journey," *Global Central Bank Focus*, PIMCO, May 2009. See also James Crotty, "Structural Causes of the Global Financial Crisis: A Critical Assessment of the 'New Financial Architecture,'" *Cambridge Journal of Economics* 33 (2009): 563–80.

77 **"You're thinking of this place . . .":** *It's a Wonderful Life*, complete film script, online at http://www.imdb.com/scripts/It%27s-a-Wonderful-Life.html.

78 **Federal Deposit Insurance Corporation:** Federal Deposit Insurance Corporation, *A Brief History of Deposit Insurance in the United States* (Washington, D.C.: FDIC, 1998), 20–44.

79 **3-6-3 rule:** John R. Walter, "The 3-6-3 Rule: An Urban Myth?" *Federal Reserve Bank of Richmond Economic Quarterly* 92 (2006): 51–78.

79 **Basel Committee:** Basel Committee on Banking Supervision, "History of the Basel Committee and Its Membership," Bank for International Settlements, August 2009, online at http://www.bis.org/bcbs/history.pdf?noframes=1.

79 **"Weaknesses in the banking system . . .":** Basel Committee on Banking Supervision, "Core Principles for Effective Banking Supervision," September 1997, online at http://www.bis.org/publ/bcbs30a.pdf.

80 **"whole alphabet soup . . .":** Paul McCulley, "Teton Reflections," Global Central Bank Focus, PIMCO, August–September 2007.

81 **"bond market conundrum":** Alan Greenspan, testimony before the Committee on Banking, Housing, and Urban Affairs, U.S. Senate, February 16, 2005, online at http://www.federalreserve.gov/boarddocs/ hh/2005/february/testimony.htm.

81 **determined in global markets:** See, for example, Tao Wu, "Globalization's Effects on Interest Rates and the Yield Curve," *Economic Letter*, Federal Reserve Bank of Dallas, September 2006, 1–8; online at http://www.dallasfed.org/research/eclett/2006/el0609.pdf.

82 **Leverage has been on the increase:** Minsky, *Stabilizing an Unstable Economy*, 265; Martin Wolf, "Seeds of Its Own Destruction," *Financial Times*, March 8, 2009; Susan Webber, "No Leverage," *Conference Board Review*, May–June 2009, 61–65.

83 **Leverage comes in many flavors:** See, for example, Charles R. Morris, *The Trillion Dollar Meltdown: Easy Money, High Rollers, and the Great Credit Crash* (New York: Public Affairs, 2008), 147–49; Katia D'Hulster, "The Leverage Ratio," World Bank Crisis Response Note no. 11, December 2009, online at http://rru.worldbank.org/documents/CrisisResponse/Note11.pdf.

Chapter 4: Things Fall Apart

86 **"are imprudent in so carefully . . .":** Bagehot, *Lombard Street*, 249–50.

87 **"We are in a minefield . . .":** Quoted in Ralph Atkins, Michael Mackenzie, and Paul J. Davies, "ECB Chief Fails to Reassure Markets," *Financial Times*, August 14, 2007.

87 **"advance it most freely . . .":** Bagehot, *Lombard Street*, 51–52.

88 **"Cassandra-like warnings . . .":** Minsky, *Stabilizing an Unstable* Economy, 237.

88 **"fashionable printouts":** Ibid.

88 **"stock prices have reached . . .":** Fisher quoted in "Fisher Sees Stocks Permanently High," *New York Times*, October 16, 1929; "Realtors Group Says Home Sales Will Slip in 2006," *Wall Street Journal*, December 13, 2005.

89 **cracks appeared in the facade:** This chapter draws heavily from Nouriel Roubini's blog postings, which are now available to subscribers at http://www.roubini.com. Also helpful in retelling this story have been Zandi, *Financial Shock*, and Tett, *Fool's Gold*.

90 **Bernanke fell into this trap:** Ben S. Bernanke, testimony before the Joint Economic Committee, U.S. Congress, March 28, 2007, online at http://www.federalreserve.gov/newsevents/testimony/bernanke20070328a.htm.

90 **"visibility and transparency":** Quoted in Grace Wong, "Behind Wall Street Subprime Fear Index," online at http://money.cnn.com/galleries/2007/news/0711/gallery.abx_index/index.html.

91 **A sudden aversion to risk:** Kindleberger, *Manias, Panics, and Crashes*,19–20; Justin Lahart, "In Time of Tumult, Obscure Economist Gains Currency," *Wall Street Journal*, August 18, 2007.

94 **Frank H. Knight's now famous distinction:** Frank H. Knight, *Risk, Uncertainty, and Profit* (Boston: Houghton Mifflin, 1921); Nouriel Roubini, "Current Market Turmoil: Non-Priceable Knightian 'Uncertainty' Rather Than Priceable Market 'Risk,'" August 15, 2007, available to subscribers at http://www.roubini.com.

95 **"twenty-five standard deviation events":** Peter Thal Larsen, "Goldman Pays the Price for Being Big," *Financial Times*, August 13, 2007.

95 **"every day, as a panic grows . . .":** Bagehot, *Lombard Street*, 49.

96 **On August 9 the European Central Bank:** Jeremy W. Peters and Wayne Arnold, "U.S. Stocks Recover Some Ground after Global Sell-off," *New York Times*, August 10, 2007.

97 **"We are certainly not going to protect . . .":** Quoted in Tett, *Fool's Gold*, 187.

98 **"Any aid to a present . . .":** Bagehot, *Lombard Street*, 100–101.

99 **"I'm at the age where . . .":** E. Scott Reckard and Annette Haddad, "A Rush to Pull Out Cash," *Los Angeles Times*, August 17, 2007.

99 **"I don't think the bank . . .":** Julia Werdigier, "Official Assurances Fail to Stem Rush of Withdrawals at British Bank," *New York Times*, September 18, 2007.

100 **"we have been passing through. . .":** Herbert Hoover, address to the Chamber of Commerce of the United States, May 1, 1930, online at http://www.presidency.ucsb.edu/ws/?pid=22185.

101 **"The worst is likely to be . . .":** Henry M. Paulson, Jr., remarks to the *Washington Post* 200 Lunch, Washington, D.C., May 16, 2008, online at http://www.ustreas.gov/press/releases/hp981.htm.

101 **Many crises follow this pattern:** H. M. Boot, *The Commercial Crisis of 1847*, Occasional Papers in Economic and Social History, no. 11 (Hull, U.K.: Hull University Press, 1984); R. Ray McCartney, *The Crisis of 1873* (Minneapolis: Burgess, 1935); Kindleberger, *World in Depression*.

102 **the LIBOR-OIS spread:** Liz Capo McCormick, "Interest-Rate Contracts May Be Best Gauge of Fed Plan," Bloomberg.com, December 17, 2007, online at http://www.bloomberg.com/apps/news?pid=20601083&sid=aP.BgxqgrJjE.

102 **"I'm optimistic . . .":** George W. Bush, press conference, January 8, 2008, online at http://georgewbush-whitehouse.archives.gov/news/releases/2008/01/20080108-5.html.

104 **banks found themselves stuck:** Greg Morcroft, "Banks Have Sold Off About Half of Hung Loans," Marketwatch.com, May 7, 2008, online at http://www.marketwatch.com/story/correctbanks-have-sold-off-about-half-of-hung-loans.

109 **a hero, the banker J. P. Morgan:** Bruner and Carr, *Panic of 1907*.

110 **Morgan had locked:** Ibid., 121–25.

110 **"Everybody is exposed":** Paulson quoted in Deborah Solomon, Dennis K. Berman, Susanne Craig, and Carrick Mollenkamp, "Ultimatum by Paulson Sparked Frantic End," *Wall Street Journal*, September 15, 2008.

Chapter 5: Global Pandemics

116 **"The financial crisis is above all . . .":** Noah Barkin, "U.S. Will Lose Financial Superpower Status," Reuters, September 25, 2008, online at http://www.reuters.com/article/idUSTRE48O2L020080925; "We Were All Staring into the Abyss," *Der Spiegel*, September 29, 2008, online at http://www.spiegel.de/international/business/0,1518,581201,00.html.

117 **catch the proverbial cold:** The academic literature on contagion has expanded to address the recent crisis. See, for example, Thijs Markwat, Erik Kole, and Dick van Dijk, "Contagion as a Domino Effect in Global Stock Markets," *Journal of Banking and Finance* 33 (2009): 1996–2012; and Philippe Jorion and Gaiyan Zhang, "Credit Contagion from Counterparty Risk," *Journal of Finance* 64 (2009): 2053–87. For historical parallels, see Graciela L. Kaminsky, Carmen M. Reinhart, and Carlos A. Vegh, "The Unholy Trinity of Financial Contagion," *Journal of Economic Perspectives* 17(2003): 51–74.

117 **"It must be a very long time . . .":** *Times* (London), June 3, 1837, quoted in Jessica Lepler, "The Pressure of 1836: Interpreting Atlantic Bank Wars," unpublished ms. in authors' possession.

118 **collapse of some venerable firm:** Robert Sobel, *Panic on Wall Street: A History of America's Financial Disasters* (New York: Collier, 1968), 154–96; Kindleberger, *World in Depression*, 144–47; Aurel Schubert, *The Credit-Anstalt Crisis of 1931* (Cambridge, U.K.: Cambridge University Press, 1991).

118 **"Lehman Shock":** Daniel Gross, "The Lehman Shock," *Newsweek*, September 14, 2009.

120 **"The whole world has become . . .":** Quoted in Kindleberger, *Manias, Panics, and Crashes*, 133.

121 **"There's all kinds of stuff . . .":** John Greenwood, "Grain Piles up in Ports," *Financial Post*, October 8, 2008.

122 **The collapse of global trade:** Richard Baldwin and Daria Taglioni, "The Great Trade Collapse and Trade Imbalances," VoxEu.org, November 27, 2009, online at http://www.voxeu.com/index.php?q=node/4301; Li Yanping, "China Trade Surplus Plunges as Exports Fall by Record," Bloomberg.com, March 10, 2009, online at http://www.bloomberg.com/apps/news?pid=20601087&refer=home&sid=a9Ih4pDxaIK4; Roslan Rahman, "East Asia: Exports in Decline," March 3, 2009, available to subscribers at http://www.stratfor.com.

122 **"The Great Synchronization":** Sónia Araújo and Joaquim Oliveira Martins, "The Great Synchronisation," online at http://www.voxeu.org/index.php?q=node/3751.

122 **In some Central American countries:** Dovelyn Agunias, "Remittance Trends in Central America," Migration Policy Institute, April 2006, online at http://www.migrationinformation.org/USfocus/display.cfm?ID=393.

123 **a range of commodity prices:** Kindleberger, *World in Depression*, 71–87, 136–41.

123 **commodity exporters:** Clifford Krauss, "Commodity Prices Tumble," *New York Times*, October 13, 2008; "Fall Copper Prices Hurt Chile," December 10, 2008, online at http://www.forbes.com/2008/12/09/chile-copper-budget-cx_1210oxford.html.

124 **seek safe havens:** Robert N. McCauley and Patrick McGuire, "Dollar Appreciation in 2008: Safe Haven, Carry Trades, Dollar Shortage and Overhedging," *BIS Quarterly Review*, December 2009, 85–93, online at http://www.bis.org/publ/qtrpdf/r_qt0912i.pdf.

124 **a pattern established by crises past:** Much of this discussion derives from Kindleberger, *Manias, Panics, and Crashes*, 116–37.

125 **"two nations . . . the most commercial . . .":** Martin Van Buren, address to Special Session of Congress, September 4, 1837, online at http://www.presidency.ucsb.edu/ws/index.php?pid=67234.

125 **"reckless extension . . .":** John Crosby Brown, *A Hundred Years of Merchant Banking: A History of Brown Brothers and Company* (New York: n.p., 1909), 79.

126 **"It looks like the biggest bubble . . .":** "In Come the Waves," *Economist*, June 16, 2005.

127 **leverage ratios:** Daniel Gross and Stefano Micossi, "The Beginning of the End Game," VoxEu.org, September 20, 2008, online at http://www.voxeu.org/index.php?q=node/1669.

128 **the European Central Bank raised estimates:** Ralph Atkins, "ECB Raises Estimate on Bank Writedowns," *Financial Times*, December 18, 2009, online at http://www.ft.com/cms/s/0/31f38b8c-ebdd-11de-930c-00144feab49a.html.

128 **In 2007 alone, €496.7 billion worth:** European Securitisation Forum Data Report, Winter 2008, online at http://www.europeansecuritisation.com/Market_Standard/ESF%20Data%20Report%20Winter%202008.pdf.

128 **"the markets have decided that . . .":** Marc Champion, Joanna Slater, and Carrick Mollenkamp, "Banks Reel On Eastern Europe's Bad News," *Wall Street Journal*, February 18, 2009, online at http://online.wsj.com/article/SB123489966805902405.html.

129 **similar crises emerge in different places:** For work that complicates the usual contagion model, see Andrew K. Rose and Mark Spiegel, "Cross-Country Causes and Consequences of the 2008 Crisis: International Linkages and American Exposure," Centre for Economic Policy Research Discussion Paper no. 7466, online at http://www.cepr.org/pubs/dps/DP7466.asp.

129 **India kept a tight lid:** See, for example, Vikas Bajaj, "In India, Central Banker Played It Safe," *New York Times*, June 25, 2009.

130 **In the crisis of 1825, British investors flooded:** Carlos Marichal, *A Century of Debt Crises in Latin America: From Independence to the Great Depression, 1820–1930* (Princeton, N.J.: Princeton University Press, 1989), 12–67.

130 **"considerable panic":** Frank Griffith Dawson, *The First Latin American Debt Crisis: The City of London and the 1822–1825 Loan Bubble* (New Haven, Conn.: Yale University Press, 1990), 125.

130 **In the wake of the panic of 1837:** Jessica Lepler, "The Pressure of 1836: Interpreting Atlantic Bank Wars." On the panic generally, see Peter Temin, *The Jacksonian Economy* (New York: W.W. Norton, 1969).

130 **a similar flight took place in 1857:** Mira Wilkins, *The History of Foreign Investment in the United States to 1914* (Cambridge, Mass.: Harvard University Press, 1989), 90–140.

131 **In the 1990s a new generation:** Roubini and Setser, *Bailouts or Bail-Ins?*

133 **the global economy contracted:** Barry Eichengreen and Kevin H. O'Rourke, "A Tale of Two Depressions," VoxEU.org, September 1, 2009, and original column of April 6, 2009, both online at http://www.voxeu.org/index.php?q=node/3421.

133 **"recoupled" with a vengeance:** Michael P. Dooley and Michael M. Hutchison, "Transmission of the U.S. Subprime Crisis to Emerging Markets: Evidence on the Decoupling-Recoupling Hypothesis," National Bureau of Economic Research Working Paper no. 15120, June 2009.

Chapter 6: The Last Resort

135 **Bernanke elaborated on that thesis:** See, for example, Ben Bernanke, "Nonmonetary Effects of the Financial Crisis in the Propagation of the Great Depression," *American Economic Review* 73 (1983): 257–76.

136 **"You're right, we did it . . .":** Ben S. Bernanke, remarks at the conference to honor Milton Friedman, University of Chicago, November 8, 2002, online at http://www.federalreserve.gov/boarddocs/speeches/2002/20021108/default.htm.

136 **"I was not going to be . . .":** Shamim Adam and Liza Lin, "Krugman Says Bernanke Should Be Reappointed to Fed," Bloomberg.com, August 10, 2009, online at http://www.bloomberg.com/apps/news?pid=20601110&sid=aK3wlrRdMC38.

138 **"gives economists chills":** Peter Goodman, "Fear of Deflation Lurks as Global Demand Drops," *New York Times*, October 31, 2008.

138 **robust economic growth:** Michael D. Bordo and Andrew J. Filardo, "Deflation in a Historical Perspective," Bank for International Settlements Working Paper no. 186, November 2005, online at http://www.bis.org/publ/work186.pdf?noframes=1.

139 **"debt-deflation theory of great depressions":** Irving Fisher, "The Debt-Deflation Theory of Great Depressions," *Econometrica* 1 (1933).

140 **"The very effort of individuals . . .":** Ibid., 344, 346.

140 **"great paradox":** Ibid., 344.

142 **brutal economic collapse:** Peter Temin, "The Great Depression," in Stanley L. Engerman and Robert E. Gallman, eds., *The Cambridge Economic History of the United States* (Cambridge, U.K.: Cambridge University Press, 2000), 3:301–10. On prices of specific commodities, see the chart at http://www.visualizingeconomics.com /2009/08/02/prices-inflation-and-deflation-great-depression-vs-great-recession/.

142 **"Unless some counteracting cause . . .":** Fisher, "Debt-Deflation Theory," 346, 347.

143 **"open market operations":** A useful introduction is M. A. Akhtar, *Understanding Open Market Operations* (New York: Federal Reserve Bank of New York, 1997).

146 **"our relative lack of experience . . .":** Ben S. Bernanke, "Deflation: Making Sure 'It' Doesn't Happen Here," remarks to the National Economists Club, Washington, D.C., November 21, 2002, online at http://www.federalreserve.gov/boarddocs/speeches/2002/ 20021121/default.htm.

146 **a series of new "liquidity" facilities:** The following section draws heavily from Viral V. Acharya, Thomas Philippon, Matthew Richardson, and Nouriel Roubini, "A Bird's-Eye View," in Viral V. Archaya and Matthew Richardson, eds., *Restoring Financial Stability: How to Repair a Failed System* (Hoboken, N.J.: John Wiley and Sons, 2008), 36–40; and on Federal Reserve Bank of New York, "Forms of Federal Reserve Lending," July 2009, online at http://www.newyorkfed.org/markets/Forms_of_Fed_Lending.pdf.

149 **recent emerging-market crises:** Roubini and Setser, *Bailouts or Bail-Ins?* 33–36.

149 **It gave this support:** Data in this section are derived from the IMF Web site, particularly the following documents: Fact Sheet, "IMF Stand-By Arrangement," November 2009, http://www.imf.org/external/np/exr/facts/pdf/sba.pdf; Fact Sheet, "A Changing IMF—Responding to the Crisis," September 2009, http://www.imf.org/external/np/exr/facts/changing.htm; and "IMF Lending: IMF Implements Major Lending Policy Improvements," March 24, 2009, http://www.imf.org/ external/np/pdr/fac/2009/032409.htm. For country-by-country data, see the interactive map at https://www.imf.org/external/np/exr/map/lending/index.htm.

150 **"swap lines":** Maurice Obstfeld, Jay C. Shambaugh, and Alan M. Taylor, "Financial Instability, Reserves, and Central Bank Swap Lines in the Panic of 2008," National Bureau of Economic Research Working Paper no. 14826, March 2009.

151 **"quantitative easing":** Ben S. Bernanke, "The Crisis and the Policy Response," Stamp Lecture, London School of Economics, London, January 13, 2009, online at http://www.federalreserve.gov/newsevents/speech/bernanke20090113a.htm; Volker Wieland, "Quantitative Easing: A Rationale and Some Evidence from Japan," National Bureau of Economic Research Working Paper no. 15565, December 2009; Paul Krugman, "Fiscal Aspects of Quantitative Easing (Wonkish)," online at http://krugman.blogs.nytimes.com/ 2009/03/20/fiscal-aspects-of-quantitative-easing-wonkish/; and Chris Giles, Cynthia O'Murchu, Steve Bernard, and Jeremy Lemer, "Quantitative Easing Explained," *Financial Times*, February 5, 2009, online at http://www.ft.com/cms/s/0/8ada2ad4-f3b9-11dd-9c4b-0000779fd2ac.html.

154 **"some of the most esoteric components . . .":** John Carlson, Joseph G. Haubrich, Kent Cherny, and Sarah Wakefield, "Credit Easing: A Policy for a Time of Financial Crisis," Federal Reserve Bank of Cleveland, February 11, 2009, online at http://www.clevelandfed.org/research/trends/2009/0209/02monpol.cfm.

154 **the Asian financial crisis of 1998:** See, for example, Scott Lanman, "Greenspan Says Hong Kong's Yam Was Right to Buy Stocks in 1998," Bloomberg.com, May 19, 2009, online at http://www.bloomberg.com/apps/news?pid=20601087&sid=aTDcelSOTQU4&refer=home; "Bank of Japan to Spend £8bn Buying Shares Held by Banks," *Telegraph*, February 3, 2009.

155 **from helicopters:** Milton Friedman, *Money Mischief: Episodes in Monetary History* (New York: Harcourt Brace, 1992), 27–37.

155 **Bernanke embraced this idea:** Ben S. Bernanke, "The Crisis and the Policy Response," Stamp Lecture, London School of Economics, London, January 13, 2009, online at http://www.federalreserve.gov/newsevents/speech/bernanke20090113a.htm.

155 **"Capitalism without bankruptcy . . .":** Borman quoted in J. Madeleine Nash, Bruce Van Voorst, and Alexander L. Taylor III, "The Growing Bankruptcy Brigade," *Time*, October 18, 1982.

156 **"exit strategy":** Ben S. Bernanke, "The Crisis and the Policy Response," Stamp Lecture, London School of Economics, London, January 13, 2009, online at http://www.federalreserve.gov/newsevents/speech/bernanke20090113a.htm.

Chapter 7: Spend More, Tax Less?

158 **"economic depression can not be . . .":** Herbert Hoover, annual message to the Congress on the State of the Union, December 2, 1930, online at http://www.presidency.ucsb.edu/ws/index.php?pid=22458.

161 **amount of construction:** Jason Scott Smith, *Building New Deal Liberalism: The Political Economy of Public Works, 1933–1956* (New York: Cambridge University Press, 2006).

161 **from 1933 to 1937, unemployment fell:** Peter Temin, "The Great Depression," in Stanley L. Engerman and Robert E. Gallman, eds., *The Cambridge Economic History of the United States* (Cambridge, U.K.: Cambridge University Press, 2000), 3:301–10. On the lessons drawn by the Obama adminstration—and a useful overview of the Great Depression—see Christina D. Romer, "Lessons from the Great Depression for Economic Recovery in 2009," speech to the Brookings Institution, March 9, 2009, online at http://www.brookings.edu/~/media/Files/events/2009/0309_lessons/0309_lessons_romer.pdf.

161 **Japanese government embraced his ideas:** Toshihiro Ihori, Toru Nakazato, and Masumi Kawade, "Japan's Fiscal Policies in the 1990s," *World Economy* 26, no. 3 (March 2003): 325–38; Martin Fackler, "Japan's Big-Works Stimulus Is Lesson," *New York Times*, February 5, 2009.

161 **Economists continue to argue:** See, for example, Kenneth N. Kuttner and Adam S. Posen, "The Great Recession: Lessons for Macroeconomic Policy from Japan," *Brookings Papers on Economic Activity* 2 (2001): 93–160; Sanjay Kalra, "Fiscal Policy: An Evaluation of Its Effectiveness," in Tim Callen and Jonathan D. Ostry, eds., *Japan's Lost Decade: Policies for Economic Revival* (Washington, D.C.: International Monetary Fund, 2003), 164–78.

162 **Hoover raised taxes, and so did Roosevelt:** Paul Studenski and Herman E. Krooss, *Financial History of the United States* (New York: McGraw-Hill, 1963), 361–64, 419–25.

162 **Economic Stimulus Act of 2008:** The text of the act is online at http://www.govtrack.us/congress/billtext.xpd?bill=h110-5140. For a detailed account of the American Recovery and Reinvestment Act of 2009, see http://www.recovery.gov/Pages/home.aspx.

164 **only 25 or 30 cents:** See, for example, http://www.federalreserve.gov/Pubs/Feds/2009/200945/200945pap.pdf.

165 **between 1866 and 1933:** Federal Deposit Insurance Corporation, *A Brief History of Deposit Insurance in the United States* (Washington, D.C.: FDIC, 1998), 17.

166 **overwhelmed the FSLIC:** Timothy Curry and Lynn Shibut, "The Cost of the Savings and Loan Crisis: Truth and Consequences," *FDIC Banking Review* 13 (2000): 26–35.

166 **"backed by the full faith and credit . . .":** See http://www.fdic.gov/regulations/laws/rules/4000-2660.html.

166 **upwards of 40 percent of the deposits:** See, for example, Mike Shedlock, "How Many Uninsured Deposits Are at Risk?" July 15, 2008, online at http://globaleconomicanalysis.blogspot.com/2008/07/how-much-uninsured-deposits-are-at-risk.html. Raising the ceiling on insured deposits did not mean that all deposits were covered. See Felix Salmon, "Are Uninsured Bank Depositors in Danger?" February 14, 2009, online at http://seekingalpha.com/article/120608-are-uninsured-bank-depositors-in-danger.

166 **new round of government guarantees:** New York Federal Reserve Bank, "International Responses to the Crisis Timeline," chart updated monthly, online at http://www.ny.frb.org/research/global_economy/IRCTimelinePublic.pdf.

167 **National Credit Union Administration:** Mark Maremont, "U.S. Moves to Bail Out Credit Union Network," *Wall Street Journal*, January 29, 2009.

167 **European Union guaranteed:** Mark Landler and Kartin Bennhold, "Bold Pledges from Leaders, but Investors Await Details," *New York Times*, October 12, 2008; and Mark Landler, "U.S. Investing $250 Billion in Banks," *New York Times*, October 14, 2008.

168 **The biggest bailout of all:** Detailed information on recipients of TARP funds can be found online at http://online.wsj.com/public/resources/documents/st_TARPREPAYMENTS0906_20090609.html.

173 **A version of this scenario:** Max Holmes, "Good Bank, Bad Bank; Good Plan, Better Plan," *New York Times*, January 31, 2009, online at http://www.nytimes.com/2009/02/01/opinion/01holmes.html; Dominic Barton, Robert Newel, and Gregory Wilson, "Managing Successful Bank Restructuring: The Mellon Bank Story," McKinsey and Company, November 2003.

174 **Bank of America's case:** Binyamin Appelbaum and Neil Irwin, "Bank of America Gets New Round of U.S. Aid," *Washington Post*, January 16, 2009.

175 **PPIP:** See http://www.financialstability.gov/roadtostability/publicprivatefund.html.

178 **hit an all-time high in 1946:** Simon Johnson and James Kwak, "National Debt for Beginners," National Public Radio, February 4, 2009, online at http://www.npr.org/templates/story/story.php?storyId=99927343.

Chapter 8: First Steps

182 **"They say there are no atheists in foxholes . . .":** Jeffrey Frankel, "Responding to Crises," *Cato Journal* 27 (2007): 165.

182 **radical reforms of financial systems:** Eugene N. White, "Banking and Finance in the Twentieth Century," in Stanley L. Engerman and Robert E. Gallman, eds., *The Cambridge Economic History of the United States* (Cambridge, U.K.: Cambridge University Press, 2000), 3:764–73.

185 **incentive to do crazy things:** Gian Luca Clementi, Thomas F. Cooley, Matthew Richardson, and Ingo Walter, "Rethinking Compensation in Financial Firms," in Viral V. Acharya and Matthew Richardson, eds., *Restoring Financial Stability: How to Repair a Failed System* (Hoboken, N.J.: John Wiley and Sons, 2008), 198–201.

186 **"As long as the music is playing . . .":** Michiyo Nakamoto and David Wighton, "Citigroup Chief Stays Bullish on Buy-Outs," *Financial Times*, July 9, 2007.

187 **"gambling for redemption":** Nouriel Roubini, "Ten Fundamental Issues in Reforming Financial Regulation and Supervision in a World of Financial Innovation and Globalization," March 31, 2008, online at www.roubini.com/analysis/pdf/Ten_Fundamental_Issues_in_Reforming.pdf.

187 **no easy solutions:** See, for example, Eli Ofek and David Yermack, "Taking Stock: Equity-Based Compensation and the Evolution of Managerial Ownership," *Journal of Finance* 55 (2000): 1367–84.

188 **"bonus-malus"**: Raghuram Rajan, "Bankers' Pay Is Deeply Flawed," *Financial Times*, January 8, 2008.

188 **Credit Suisse:** Aaron Lucchetti, "Bankers Beat Odds in Toxic Pay Plan," *Wall Street Journal*, August 7, 2009; Graham Bowley, "Credit Suisse Overhauls Compensation," *New York Times*, October 20, 2009.

189 **forbid employees to hedge:** On these difficulties, see, for example, William A. Sahlman, "Management and the Financial Crisis (We have met the enemy and he is us . . .)," Harvard Business School Working Paper no. 10-033, 2009.

189 **exorbitant and utterly unwarranted growth:** David Wessel, "The Source of Our Bubble Trouble," *Wall Street Journal*, January 17, 2008; and Mercedes Rule, "Flocking to Finance," *Harvard Magazine*, May–June 2008, 18–19. The discussion in this section owes a great deal to Thomas Philippon and Ariell Reshef, "Skill Biased Financial Development: Education, Wages and Occupations in the U.S. Financial Sector," National Bureau of Economic Research Working Paper no. 13437, 2007; and to Thomas Philippon and Ariell Reshef, "Wages and Human Capital in the U.S. Financial Industry: 1909–2006," National Bureau of Economic Research Working Paper no. 14644, January 2009.

191 **elaborate system of securitization:** An excellent introduction can be found in Dwight Jaffee, Anthony W. Lynch, Matthew Richardson, and Stijn Van Nieuwerburgh, "Mortgage Origination and Securitization in the Financial Crisis," in Viral V. Acharya and Matthew Richardson, eds., *Restoring Financial Stability: How to Repair a Failed System* (Hoboken, N.J.: John Wiley and Sons, 2008).

192 **Credit Risk Retention Act**: See http://www.govtrack.us/congress/bill.xpd?bill=h111-1731. For an analysis of this legislation, see Cadwalader, Wickersham & Taft LLP, "Securitization Reform Proposals: The Credit Risk Retention Act of 2009 and the Restoring American Financial Stability Act of 2009," *Clients & Friends Memo*, December 17, 2009, online at http://www.cadwalader.com/assets/client_friend/121709SecuritizationReformProposals.pdf.

192 **approximately 34 percent of all the assets of major banks:** See "Statistical Supplement to the Federal Reserve Bulletin," December 2008. The data for 2007 on large and small domestically chartered commercial banks is at http://www.federalreserve.gov/Pubs/supplement/2008/12/table1_26d.htm and http://www.federalreserve.gov/Pubs/supplement/2008/12/table1_26c2.htm.

195 **Regulation Z:** See the Board of Governors of the Federal Reserve, press release, July 23, 2009, online at http://www.federalreserve.gov/newsevents/press/bcreg/20090723a.htm.

195 **ratings agencies' rise:** The following account relies heavily on Richard Sylla, "An Historical Primer on the Business of Credit Ratings," in Richard M. Levich, Carmen Reinhart, and Giovanni Majnoni, eds., *Ratings, Rating Agencies, and the Global Financial System* (Boston: Kluwer, 2002); Matthew Richardson and Lawrence J. White, "The Rating Agencies: Is Regulation the Answer?" in Viral V. Acharya and Matthew Richardson, eds., *Restoring Financial Stability: How to Repair a Failed System* (Hoboken, N.J.: John Wiley and Sons, 2008); and Patrick Bolton, Xavier Freixas, and Joel Shapiro, "The Credit Ratings Game," National Bureau of Economic Research Working Paper no. 14712, February 2009.

198 **"time bombs, both for the parties . . .":** Berkshire Hathaway Annual Report for 2002, p. 13, online at http://www.berkshirehathaway.com/2002ar/2002ar.pdf.

199 **Senator Phil Gramm:** Eric Lipton and Stephen Labaton, "A Deregulator Looks Back, Unswayed," *New York Times*, November 16, 2008.

200 **infamous episodes:** An excellent overview of their checkered history can be found in Lynn A. Stout, "Why We Need Derivatives Regulation," *New York Times*, October 7, 2009, online at http://dealbook.blogs.nytimes.com/2009/10/07/dealbook-dialogue-lynn-stout/; also Satyajit Das, *Traders, Guns, and Money: Knowns and Unknowns in the Dazzling World of Derivatives* (Upper Saddle River, N.J.: Financial Times Press, 2006).

200 **some sensible steps:** Some of the following proposals echo those found in Viral A. Acharya et al., "Derivatives: The Ultimate Financial Innovation," in Acharya and Richardson, eds., *Restoring*

Financial Stability; and Rym Ayadi and Patrick Behr, "On the Necessity to Regulate Credit Derivatives Markets," *Journal of Banking Regulation* 10 (2009): 179–201.

204 **Basel Committee on Banking Supervision:** For basic information on the Basel Committee, see "The New Basel Capital Accord: An Explanatory Note," Bank for International Settlements, 2001, online at http://www.bis.org/publ/bcbsca01.pdf; see also Bryan J. Balin, "Basel I, Basel II, and Emerging Markets: A Nontechnical Analysis," Johns Hopkins University School of Advanced International Studies, May 10, 2008, online via Johns Hopkins University Library; and "History of the Basel Committee and Its Membership," Bank for International Settlements, August 2009, online at http://www.bis.org/bcbs/history.pdf.

206 **"dynamic provisioning":** Jesús Saurina, "Dynamic Provisioning: The Case of Spain," World Bank Crisis Response Note no. 7, July 2009, online at http://rru.worldbank.org/documents/CrisisResponse/Note7.pdf.

206 **"contingent capital":** Nicholas Paisner and Hugo Dixon, "Newfangled Bank Capital," *New York Times*, November 12, 2009, online at http://www.nytimes.com/2009/11/13/business/13views.html.

Chapter 9: Radical Remedies

211 **"The lesson I take from this experience . . .":** Ben S. Bernanke, "Monetary Policy and the Housing Bubble," speech to annual meeting of the American Economic Association, January 3, 2010, http://www.federalreserve.gov/newsevents/speech/bernanke20100103a.pdf.

214 **standard industry guide to derivatives:** Satyajit Das, *The Das Swaps & Financial Derivatives Library* (Hoboken, N.J.: John Wiley and Sons, 2006).

215 **a bewildering array of regulatory bodies:** See Richard H. K. Vietor, "Government Regulation of Business," in Stanley L. Engerman and Robert E. Gallman, eds., *The Cambridge Economic History of the United States* (Cambridge, U.K.: Cambridge University Press, 2000), 3:969–1012, particularly the chart on 3:980; also Andreas Busch, *Banking Regulation and Globalization* (New York: Oxford University Press, 2009), 33–66.

216 **beneficial "competition":** See, for example, Richard J. Rosen, "Is Three a Crowd? Competition Among Regulators in Banking," *Journal of Money, Credit, and Banking* 35 (2003): 967–98; Richard J. Rosen, "Switching Primary Federal Regulators: Is It Beneficial for U.S. Banks?" *Federal Reserve Bank of Chicago Economic Perspectives* 29 (2005): 16–33.

216 **every incentive to be lenient:** Ann B. Matasar and Deborah D. Pavelka, "Federal Banking Regulators' Competition in Laxity: Evidence from CRA Audits," *International Advances in Economics Research* 4 (1998): 56–69.

216 **"regulatory shopping":** "Regulator Shopping," *New York Times*, May 20, 2009, online at http://www.nytimes.com/2009/05/21/opinion/21thu1.html; Busch, *Banking Regulation*, 53.

217 **a serious overhaul:** U.S. Treasury, *Financial Regulatory Reform. A New Foundation: Rebuilding Financial Supervision and Regulation* (Washington, D.C., 2009), online at http://www.financialstability.gov/docs/regs/FinalReport_web.pdf.

218 **"global superregulator":** Leigh Phillips, "Germany and UK Want Global Financial Regulator," *EuObserver*, September 22, 2008, online at http://euobserver.com/9/26784.

219 ***Quis custodiet ipsos custodes?*:** Charles Stocker, ed., *The Satires of Juvenal and Persius* (London: Longman, Orme and Company, 1839), 141.

219 **"noble lie":** See Malcolm Schofield, "The Noble Lie," in G. R. F. Ferrari, ed., *The Cambridge Companion to Plato's Republic* (Cambridge, U.K.: Cambridge University Press, 2007), 138–64.

220 **one of the worst-paid agencies:** David Simons, "The High Price of Low Salaries at the SEC," Forbes.com, March 27, 2002, online at http://www.forbes.com/2002/03/27/0327simons.html; Andrew Ross Sorkin, "What If Watchdogs Got Bonuses?" *New York Times*, February 2, 2009, online at http://www.nytimes.com/2009/02/03/business/03sorkin.html.

221 **"revolving door":** Julie Creswell and Ben White, "The Guys from 'Government Sachs,'" *New York Times*, October 17, 2008; Marcus Baram, "Government Sachs: Goldman's Close

Ties to Washington Arouse Envy, Raise Questions," *Huffington Post*, June 2, 2009, online at http://www.huffingtonpost.com/2009/06/02/government-sachs-goldmans_n_210561.html.

221 **hiring a managing executive:** "Adam Storch Named Managing Executive of SEC's Enforcement Division," SEC press release, October 16, 2009, online at http://www.sec.gov/news/press/2009/2009-220.htm.

221 **banned government employees:** Sheryl Gay Stolberg, "On First Day, Obama Quickly Sets New Tone," *New York Times*, January 21, 2009.

222 **funnel massive amounts:** See statistics in Americans for Campaign Reform, "Wall Street Money in Politics," August 25, 2009, online at http://youstreet.org/sites/default/files/Fact%20Sheet%20%20Wall%20Street%20Money%20in%20Politics.pdf.

222 **make regulators . . . more independent:** Marc Quintyn and Michael W. Taylor, "Should Financial Sector Regulators Be Independent?" International Monetary Fund, Economic Issues no. 32, March 8, 2004, online at http://www.imf.org/external/pubs/ft/issues/issues32/index.htm.

224 **"living wills":** Noam Scheiber, "Can We Fix Too Big to Fail Without Shrinkage?" *New Republic*, October 28, 2009, online at http://www.tnr.com/blog/the-stash/can-we-fix-too-big-to-fail-without-shrinkage; David Wessel, "Three Theories on Solving the 'Too Big to Fail' Problem," *Wall Street Journal*, October 29, 2009; Mike Konczal, "Fixing Too Big to Fail," *Nation*, November 6, 2009, online at http://www.thenation.com/doc/20091123/konczal.

225 **some kind of conservatorship:** See, for example, "The FDIC's Role as Receiver," in FDIC, Resolutions Handbook (Washington, D.C.: FDIC, 2003), online at http://www.fdic.gov/bank/historical/reshandbook/.

226 **supervising TBTF institutions:** See, for example, William Buiter, "Too Big to Fail Is Too Big," *Financial Times*, June 24, 2009, online at http://blogs.ft.com/maverecon/2009/06/too-big-to-fail-is-too-big/; Wessel, "Three Theories"; Daniel K. Tarullo, "Confronting 'Too Big to Fail,'" speech to Exchequer Club, Washington, D.C., October 21, 2009, online at http://www.bis.org/review/r091023e.pdf.

226 **unilaterally doubling the Basel capital ratio:** Christine Seib, "UBS Unveils £2bn Capital Raising and Warns of Second-Quarter Loss," *Times* (London), June 26, 2009, online at http://business.timesonline.co.uk/tol/business/industry_sectors/banking_and_finance/article6580096.ece. Both UBS and Credit Suisse seem capable of meeting these demands without a breakup. See Sven Egenter, "Swiss Should Tighten Rules on UBS, CS Further—OECD," Reuters, January 15, 2010, online at http://blogs.reuters.com/financial-regulatory-forum/2010/01/15/swiss-should-tighten-rules-on-ubs-cs-further-oecd/.

227 **Take Citigroup:** Binyamin Applebaum, "Citi's Long History of Overreach, Then Rescue," *Washington Post*, March 11, 2009; Andrew Martin and Gretchen Morgenson, "Can Citigroup Carry Its Own Weight?" *New York Times*, November 1, 2009.

228 **"We're very important . . .":** Blankfein quoted in John Arlidge, "I'm Doing 'God's Work.' Meet Mr Goldman Sachs," *Times* (London), November 8, 2009, online at http://www.timesonline.co.uk/tol/news/world/us_and_americas/article6907681.ece.

228 **reckless bets and obscene leverage:** Kenneth Galbraith, *The Great Crash, 1929* (Boston: Houghton Mifflin, 1954), 65–70; Matt Taibbi, "Inside the Great American Bubble Machine," *Rolling Stone*, July 2, 2009.

231 **"When the capital development of a country . . .":** Keynes, *General Theory*, 159.

233 **Banishing Bubbles:** This section relies heavily on information contained in Nouriel Roubini, "Why Central Banks Should Burst Bubbles," *International Finance* 9 (2006): 87–107.

234 **writings . . . of Alan Greenspan and Ben Bernanke:** See, for example, Ben S. Bernanke and Mark Gertler, "Should Central Banks Respond to Movements in Asset Prices?" *American Economic Review* 91 (2001): 253–57; Alan Greenspan, "Risk and Uncertainty in Monetary Policy," speech to the annual meeting of the American Economic Association, San Diego, Calif., January 3, 2004, online at http://www.federalreserve.gov/boarddocs/speeches/2004/20040103/default.htm.

236 **Regulation T:** Peter Fortune, "Margin Requirements, Margin Loans, and Margin Rates: Practice and Principles," *Federal Reserve Bank of Boston New England Economic Review* (2000): 19–44.

237 **Asset-Based Reserve Requirements:** Thomas I. Palley, "Asset-Based Reserve Requirements: Reasserting Domestic Monetary Control in an Era of Financial Innovation and Instability," *Review of Political Economy* 16 (2004): 43–58; Michael Holz, "Asset-Based Reserve Requirements: A New Monetary Policy Instrument for Targeting Diverging Real Estate Prices in the Euro Area," *Intervention* 4 (2007): 331–51.

Chapter 10: Fault Lines

243 **ran ever larger current account deficits:** Nouriel Roubini and Brad Setser, "The US as a Net Debtor: The Sustainability of the US External Imbalances," August 2004, online at http://pages.stern.nyu.edu/~nroubini/papers/Roubini-Setser-US-External-Imbalances.pdf.

244 **"sovereign debt crisis":** Roubini and Setser, *Bailouts or Bail-Ins?*

247 **The debate over current account imbalances:** Nouriel Roubini, "Global Imbalances: A Contemporary 'Rashomon' Saga," November 2006, online at http://www.centrecournot.org/pdf/conference9/Nouriel%20ROUBINI.pdf. This section draws on this paper.

248 **"dark matter" explanation:** Ricardo Hausmann and Federico Sturzenegger, "U.S. and Global Imbalances: Can Dark Matter Prevent a Big Bang?" November 13, 2005, online at http://www.cid.harvard.edu/cidpublications/darkmatter_051130.pdf.

248 **This argument has been challenged:** Roubini, "Global Imbalances: A Contemporary 'Rashomon' Saga," November 2006. See also Barry Eichengreen, "Global Imbalances: The New Economy, the Dark Matter, the Savvy Investor, and the Standard Analysis," March 2006, online at http://www.econ.berkeley.edu/~eichengr/matter.pdf.

249 **"global savings glut":** Ben S. Bernanke, "The Global Savings Glut and the U.S. Current Account Deficit," Homer Jones Lecture, St. Louis, Mo., April 14, 2005, online at http://www.federalreserve.gov/boarddocs/speeches/2005/20050414/default.htm.

251 **"exorbitant privilege":** Giscard d'Estaing quoted in Richard A. Iley and Mervyn Lewis, *Untangling the U.S. Deficit: Evaluating Causes, Cures and Global Imbalances* (Northampton, Mass.: Edward Elgar, 2007), 106.

251 **foreign investment in U.S. equities:** James K. Jackson, "Foreign Direct Investment in the United States: An Economic Analysis," CRS Report for Congress, August 15, 2008, online at http://www.fas.org/sgp/crs/misc/RS21857.pdf.

251 **nonresidents now hold about half:** Justin Murray and Marc Labonte, "Foreign Holdings of Federal Debt," CRS Report for Congress, November 28, 2005, online at http://www.house.gov/berry/crs/RS22331.pdf; Financial Management Service, *Treasury Bulletin*, December 2009, online at http://www.fms.treas.gov/bulletin/b2009_4.pdf.

253 **Only 36 percent of China's gross domestic product:** Richard Dobbs, Andrew Grant, and Jonathan Woetzel, "Unleashing the Chinese Consumer," *Newsweek*, September 5, 2009, online at http://www.newsweek.com/id/215024.

253 **"balance of financial terror":** Lawrence H. Summers, "The United States and the Global Adjustment Process," Third Annual Stavros S. Niarchos Lecture, Institute for International Economics, Washington, D.C., March 23, 2004.

255 **Robert Triffin:** See Robert Triffin, *Gold and the Dollar Crisis: The Future of Convertibility* (New Haven, Conn.: Yale University Press, 1960).

256 **"Bretton Woods II":** See, for example, Michael Dooley, David Folkerts-Landau, and Peter Garber, "An Essay on the Revised Bretton Woods System," National Bureau of Economic Research Working Paper no. 9971, September 2003.

256 **this uneasy arrangement:** See http://www.ustreas.gov/offices/international-affairs/economic-exchange-rates/pdf/Appendix%201.pdf; and Ye Xie and Anchalee Worrachate, "Dollar

Reaches Breaking Point as Banks Shift Reserves," Bloomberg.com, October 12, 2009, online at http://www.bloomberg.com/apps/news?pid=20601087&sid=a4x9dIJsPn4U.

257 **footsteps of Britain:** Avinash Persaud, "When Currency Empires Fall," lecture at Gresham College, London, October 7, 2004, online at http://www.321gold.com/editorials/persaud/persaud101204.html; Barry Eichengreen, "Sterling's Past, Dollar's Future: Historical Perspectives on Reserve Currency Competition," Tawney Lecture, Economic History Society, Leicester, U.K., April 10, 2005, online at http://www.econ.berkeley.edu/~eichengr/research/tawney_lecture2apr29-05.pdf.

258 **The Almighty Renminbi?:** See Nouriel Roubini, "The Almighty Renminbi," *New York Times*, May 13, 2009.

258 **the renminbi or the yuan:** The Chinese currency is called the renminbi, but the unit used for accounting purposes is called the yuan. For a concise explanation of the difference, see Paul Krugman, "What's in a Name?" online at http://krugman.blogs.nytimes.com/2009/10/23/whats-in-a-name-3/.

260 **Zhou Xiaochuan:** See Zhou Xiaochuan, "Statement on Reforming the International Monetary System," Council on Foreign Relations, March 23, 2009, online at http://www.cfr.org/publication/18916/.

261 **"bancor":** John Williamson, "Bancor and the Developing Countries: How Much Difference Would It Have Made?" in A. P. Thirlwall, ed., *Keynes and Economic Development: The Seventh Keynes Seminar Held at the University of Kent at Canterbury, 1985* (New York: St. Martin's Press, 1987).

262 **The IMF has . . . its own problems:** Edwin M. Truman, "Rearranging IMF Chairs and Shares: The Sine Qua Non of IMF Reform," in Edwin M. Truman, ed., *Reforming the IMF for the 21st Century* (Washington, D.C.: Institute for International Economics, 2006), 201–32.

Conclusion

266 **"resist a response . . .":** See, for example, Lloyd C. Blankfein, remarks to the Council of Institutional Investors, April 2009, online at http://www2.goldmansachs.com/ideas/public-policy/l-compensation/lcb-speech-to-cii.html.

269 **"this time is different":** Reinhart and Rogoff, *This Time Is Different.*

274 **"There is no possibility . . .":** Minsky, *Stabilizing an Unstable Economy*, 370.

Outlook

278 **recent study by Alan Blinder:** Alan Blinder, "How Many U.S. Jobs Might Be Offshorable?" Centre for European Policy Studies Working Paper no. 142, March 2007, online at http://www.princeton.edu/~ceps/workingpapers/142blinder.pdf.

278 **savings rates rose above 4 percent:** Evan Tanner and Yasser Abdih, "Rebuilding U.S. Wealth," *Finance and Development* 46, no. 4 (December 2009): 23–35, online at http://www.imf.org/external/pubs/ft/fandd/2009/12/tanner.htm.

280 **large stocks of public debt relative to their GDP:** See, for example, charts at http://www.visualeconomics.com/gdp-vs-national-debt-by-country/.

282 **"pesification":** Roubini and Setser, *Bailouts or Bail-Ins?* 271–75.

283 **shoulders a gross public debt:** See, for example, Organisation for Economic Co-Operation and Development, "Economic Survey of Japan 2009," September 30, 2009, online at http://www.oecd.org/document/37/0,3343,en_2649_34595_43783525_1_1_1_1,00.html.

284 **"an economy of the people":** Ian Bremmer and Nouriel Roubini, "Why Japan Needs a Hatobama," *Wall Street Journal*, December 30, 2009, online at http://online.wsj.com/article/SB10001424052748704779704574553491570666698.html.

285 **robust medium-term growth:** International Monetary Fund, *World Economic Outlook*, July 8, 2009, online at http://www.imf.org/external/pubs/ft/weo/2009/update/02/index.htm.

285 **The BRICs—Brazil, Russia, India, and China:** Nouriel Roubini, "Another BRIC in the Wall?" Project Syndicate, October 15, 2009, online at http://www.project-syndicate.org/commentary/roubini18/English.

290 **"mother of all carry trades":** Nouriel Roubini, "Mother of All Carry Trades Faces an Inevitable Bust," *Financial Times*, November 1, 2009.

292 **The threat of default now looms over advanced economies:** Nouriel Roubini, "The Risky Rich," Project Syndicate, January 18, 2010, online at http://www.project-syndicate.org/commentary/roubini21/English.

SELECT BIBLIOGRAPHY

The literature on financial crises is vast. This bibliography of works covering various facets is not intended to be comprehensive, but many of the following books, articles, working papers, and speeches informed the writing of this book.

Acharya, Viral V., and Matthew Richardson, eds. *Restoring Financial Stability: How to Repair a Failed System*. New York: John Wiley and Sons, 2009. Summaries available online at http://whitepapers.stern.nyu.edu/home.html.

Acharya, Viral V., and Philipp Schnabl. "Do Global Banks Spread Global Imbalances? The Case of Asset-Backed Commercial Paper During the Financial Crisis of 2007–09." Paper presented at the Tenth Annual Jacques Polak Research Conference, Washington, D.C., November 5–6, 2009. Online at http://www.imf.org/external/np/res/seminars/2009/arc/pdf/acharya.pdf.

Acharya, Viral V., Thomas Cooley, Matthew Richardson, and Ingo Walter, eds. *Real Time Solutions for Financial Reform: An NYU Stern Working Group on Financial Reform*, December 2009. Online at http://govtpolicyrecs.stern.nyu.edu/docs/whitepapers_ebook_full.pdf.

Adrian, Tobias, and Hyun Song Shin. "Financial Intermediaries and Monetary Economics." Federal Reserve Bank of New York Staff Report no. 398, October 2009. Online at http://www.newyorkfed.org/research/staff_reports/sr398.pdf.

____. "Liquidity and Leverage." Federal Reserve Bank of New York Staff Report no. 328, May 2008. Online at http://www.newyorkfed.org/research/ staff_reports/sr328.pdf.

____. "The Shadow Banking System: Implications for Financial Regulation." Federal Reserve Bank of New York Staff Report no. 382, July 2009. Online at http://www.newyorkfed.org/research/staff_reports/sr382.pdf.

Ahamed, Liaquat. *Lords of Finance: The Bankers Who Broke the World*. New York: Penguin Press, 2009.

Akerlof, George A., and Robert J. Shiller. *Animal Spirits: How Human Psychology Drives the Economy, and Why It Matters for Global Capitalism*. Princeton, N.J.: Princeton University Press, 2009.

Almunia, Miguel, Agustín S. Bénétrix, Barry Eichengreen, Kevin H. O'Rourke, and Gisela Rua. "From Great Depression to Great Credit Crisis: Similarities, Differences and Lessons." Paper presented at Fiftieth Economic Policy Panel Meeting, Tilburg, Netherlands, October 23–24, 2009. Online at http://www.econ.berkeley.edu/~eichengr/great_dep_great_cred_11-09.pdf.

Bagehot, Walter. *Lombard Street: A Description of the Money Market*. New York: E. P. Dutton, 1920.

Baldwin, Richard, ed. *The Great Trade Collapse: Causes, Consequences, and Prospects*. A VoxEU.org Publication. London: Center for Economic Policy Research, 2009. Online at http://www.voxeu.org/reports/great_trade_collapse.pdf.

Barbera, Robert J. *The Cost of Capitalism: Understanding Market Mayhem and Stabilizing Our Economic Future*. New York: McGraw-Hill, 2009.

Basel Committee on Banking Supervision. *Review of the Differentiated Nature and Scope of Financial Regulation: Key Issues and Recommendations*. Basel, Switzerland: Bank for International Settlements, 2010.

Beber, Alessandro, and Marco Pagano. "Short-Selling Bans Around the World: Evidence from the 2007–09 Crisis." Centre for Studies in Economics and Finance Working Paper no. 241. Online at http://www.csef.it/WP/wp241.pdf.

Bernanke, Ben. "Nonmonetary Effects of the Financial Crisis in the Propagation of the Great Depression." *American Economic Review* 73 (1983): 257–76.

Blanchard, Olivier, and Gian Maria Milesi-Ferretti. "Global Imbalances: In Midstream?" IMF Staff Position Note, December 22, 2009. Online at http://www.imf.org/external/pubs/ft/spn/2009/spn0929.pdf.

Blundell-Wignall, Adrian, et al. *The Financial Crisis: Reform and Exit Strategies*. Paris: Organisation for Economic Co-operation and Development, 2009. Online at http://www.oecd.org/dataoecd/55/47/43091457.pdf.

Bordo, Michael D. "The Lender of Last Resort: Alternative Views and Historical Experience." *Federal Reserve Bank of Richmond Economic Review* 76 (1990): 18–29.

Bordo, Michael D., ed. *Financial Crises*. 2 vols. Aldershot, Hants., U.K., and Brookfield, Vt.: Edward Elgar Publishing, 1992.

Bordo, Michael D., and Barry Eichengreen, eds. *A Retrospective on the Bretton Woods System: Lessons for International Monetary Reform*. Chicago: University of Chicago Press, 1993.

Bordo, Michael D., and Andrew Filardo. "Deflation in a Historical Perspective." Bank for International Settlements Working Paper no. 186, November 2005. Online at http://www.bis.org/publ/work186.pdf?noframes=1.

Bordo, Michael D., Claudia Goldin, and Eugene N. White, eds. *The Defining Moment: The Great Depression and the American Economy in the Twentieth Century*. Chicago: University of Chicago Press, 1998.

Bordo, Michael D., and Harold James. "The Great Depression Analogy." National Bureau of Economic Research Working Paper no. 15584, December 2009. Online at http://www.nber.org/papers/w15584.

Boyd, John H., Sungkyu Kwak, and Bruce D. Smith. "The Real Output Losses Associated with Modern Banking Crises." *Journal of Money, Credit, and Banking* 37 (2005): 977–99.

Bruner, Robert F., and Sean D. Carr. *The Panic of 1907: Lessons Learned from the Market's Perfect Storm*. Hoboken, N.J.: John Wiley and Sons, 2007.

Brunnermeier, Markus K. "Symposium: Early Stages of the Credit Crunch: Deciphering the Liquidity and Credit Crunch 2007–2008." *Journal of Economic Perspectives* 23 (2009): 77–100.

Brunnermeier, Markus K., Stefan Nagel, and Lasse H. Pedersen. "Carry Trades and Currency Crashes." National Bureau of Economic Research Working Paper no. 14473, November 2008. Online at http://www.nber.org/papers/w14473.

Brunnermeier, Markus K., and Lasse H. Pedersen. "Market Liquidity and Funding Liquidity." *Review of Financial Studies* 22 (2009): 2201–38.

Caballero, Ricardo J. "The 'Other' Imbalance and the Financial Crisis." National Bureau of Economic Research Working Paper no. 15636, January 2010. Online at http://www.nber.org/papers/w15636.

Calomiris, Charles W. "Banking Crises and the Rules of the Game." National Bureau of Economic Research Working Paper no. 15403, October 2009. Online at http://www.nber.org/papers/w15403.

Calomiris, Charles W., and Larry Schweikart. "The Panic of 1857: Origins, Transmission, and Containment." *Journal of Economic History* 51 (1991): 807–34.

Capie, Forrest, and Geoffrey E. Wood, eds. *Financial Crises and the World Banking System*. New York: St. Martin's Press, 1986.

Case, Karl E., John M. Quigley, and Robert J. Shiller. "Comparing Wealth Effects: The Stock Market versus the Housing Market." *Advances in Macroeconomics* 5 (2005): 1–34.

Case, Karl E., and Robert J. Shiller. "Is There a Bubble in the Housing Market?" *Brookings Papers on Economic Activity* 2 (2003): 299–362.

Cassidy, John. *How Markets Fail: The Logic of Economic Calamities*. New York: Farrar, Straus and Giroux, 2009.

Cihák, Martin, and Erlend W. Nier. "The Need for Special Resolution Regimes for Financial Institutions." VoxEU.org, January 7, 2010. Online at http://www.voxeu.org/index.php?q=node/4446.

Cooper, George. *The Origin of Financial Crises: Central Banks, Credit Bubbles, and the Efficient Market Fallacy*. New York: Vintage, 2008.

Cottarelli, Carlo, and Jose Viñals. "A Strategy for Renormalizing Fiscal and Monetary Policies in Advanced Economies." IMF Staff Position Note, September 22, 2009. Online at http://www.imf.org/external/pubs/ft/spn/2009/spn0922.pdf.

Crotty, James. "Structural Causes of the Global Financial Crisis: A Critical Assessment of the 'New Financial Architecture.'" *Cambridge Journal of Economics* 33 (2009): 563–80.

Das, Satyajit. *Traders, Guns, and Money: Knowns and Unknowns in the Dazzling World of Derivatives*. Upper Saddle River, N.J.: Financial Times Press, 2006.

Dawson, Frank Griffith. *The First Latin American Debt Crisis: The City of London and the 1822–1825 Loan Bubble*. New Haven, Conn.: Yale University Press, 1990.

DeLong, J. Bradford. "Financial Crises in the 1890s and the 1990s: Must History Repeat?" *Brookings Papers on Economic Activity* 2 (1999): 253–94.

Desai, Padma. *Financial Crises, Contagion, and Containment*. Princeton, N.J.: Princeton University Press, 2003.

Diamond, Douglas W., and Philip H. Dybvig. "Bank Runs, Deposit Insurance, and Liquidity." *Journal of Political Economy* 91 (1983): 401–19.

Draghi, Mario. "Combating the Global Financial Crisis: The Role of International Cooperation." Hong Kong Monetary Authority Distinguished Lecture, Hong Kong, December 16, 2008. Online at http://www.bis.org/review/r081218b.pdf.

Eichengreen, Barry. "Out of the Box Thoughts about the International Financial Architecture." IMF Working Paper no. 09/116, May 2009. Online at http://www.imf.org/external/pubs/ft/wp/2009/wp09116.pdf.

———. "Sterling's Past, Dollar's Future: Historical Perspectives on Reserve Currency Competition." Tawney Lecture delivered to the Economic History Society, Leicester, U.K. April 10, 2005. Online at http://www.econ.berkeley.edu/~eichengr/research/tawney_lecture2apr29-05.pdf.

Eichengreen, Barry, and Kevin H. O'Rourke. "A Tale of Two Depressions." A VoxEU.org Publication, September 1, 2009, and original column of April 6, 2009. Online at http://www.voxeu.org/index.php?q=node/3421.

Eichengreen, Barry, and Richard Portes. "The Anatomy of Financial Crises." In Richard Portes and Alexander K. Swoboda, eds., *Threats to International Financial Stability*. London: Cambridge University Press, 1987, 10–58.

Felton, Andrew, and Carmen M. Reinhart, eds. *The First Global Financial Crisis of the 21st Century*. A VoxEU.org Publication. London: Centre for Economic Policy Research, 2008. Online at http://www.voxeu.org/index.php?q=node/4077.

———. *The First Global Financial Crisis of the 21st Century: Part II June–December 2008*. A VoxEU.org Publication. London: Centre for Economic Policy Research, 2009. Online at http://www.voxeu.org/index.php?q=node/3079.

Ferguson, Niall. *The Ascent of Money: A Financial History of the World*. New York: Penguin Press, 2008.

Fisher, Irving. "The Debt-Deflation Theory of Great Depressions." *Econometrica* 1 (1933): 337–57.

Fox, Justin. *The Myth of the Rational Market: A History of Risk, Reward, and Delusion on Wall Street*. New York: Harper Business, 2009.

Frank, Nathaniel, and Heiko Hesse. "Financial Spillovers to Emerging Markets During the Global Financial Crisis." IMF Working Paper no. 09/104, May 2009. Online at http://imf.org/external/pubs/ft/wp/2009/wp09104.pdf.

Friedman, Milton, and Anna J. Schwartz. *A Monetary History of the United States, 1867–1960*. Princeton, N.J.: Princeton University Press, 1963.

Galbraith, John Kenneth. *The Great Crash, 1929*. Boston: Houghton Mifflin, 1954.

Geanakoplos, John. "The Leverage Cycle." Cowles Foundation Discussion Paper no. 1715, July 2009. Online at http://cowles.econ.yale.edu/P/cd/d17a/d1715.pdf.

Ghosh, Artish R., et al. "Coping with the Crisis: Policy Options for Emerging Market Countries." IMF Staff Position Note, April 23, 2009. Online at http://imf.org/external/pubs/ft/spn/2009/spn0908.pdf.

Ghosh, B. N., ed. *Global Financial Crises and Reforms: Cases and Caveats*. London: Routledge, 2001.

Gorton, Gary. "Banking Panics and Business Cycles." *Oxford Economic Papers* 40 (1988): 751–81.

____. "Slapped in the Face by the Invisible Hand: Banking and the Panic of 2007." Paper delivered at the Federal Reserve Bank of Atlanta's 2009 Financial Markets Conference "Financial Innovation and Crises," May 11–13, 2009. Online at http://www.frbatlanta.org/news/conferen/09fmc/gorton.pdf.

Gross, Daniel. *Pop! Why Bubbles Are Great for the Economy*. New York: Harper Business, 2007.

Haldane, Andrew G. "Rethinking the Financial Network." Speech delivered at the Financial Student Association, Amsterdam, April 2009. Online at http://www.bankofengland.co.uk/publications/speeches/2009/speech386.pdf.

Huang, Rocco, and Lev Ratnovski. "The Dark Side of Bank Wholesale Funding." Federal Reserve Bank of Philadelphia Working Paper no. 09-3, November 2008. Online at http://www.philadelphiafed.org/research-and-data/publications/working-papers/2009/wp09-3.pdf.

Hubbard, R. Glenn, ed. *Financial Markets and Financial Crises*. Chicago: University of Chicago Press, 1991.

Hunter, William C., George G. Kaufman, and Michael Pomerleano, eds. *Asset Price Bubbles: The Implications for Monetary, Regulatory, and International Policies*. Cambridge, Mass.: MIT Press, 2003.

International Monetary Fund. *Global Financial Stability Report: Responding to the Financial Crisis and Measuring Systemic Risk*. Washington, D.C.: IMF, 2009. Online at http://www.imf.org/external/pubs/ft/gfsr/2009/01/pdf/text.pdf.

Izquierdo, Alejandro, and Ernesto Talvi. "A Stability Pact à la Maastricht for Emerging Markets." A VoxEU.org Publication, December 12, 2009. Online at http://www.voxeu.org/index.php?q=node/4360.

Jenkinson, Nigel. "Ratings in Structured Finance: What Went Wrong and What Can Be Done to Address Shortcomings?" Committee on the Global Financial System Paper no. 32, July 2008. Online at http://www.bis.org/publ/cgfs32.pdf?noframes=1.

Jorion, Philippe, and Gaiyan Zhang. "Credit Contagion from Counterparty Risk." *Journal of Finance* 64 (2009): 2053–87.

Kaminsky, Graciela L., and Carmen M. Reinhart. "On Crises, Contagion, and Confusion." *Journal of International Economics* 51 (2000): 145–68.

Kaminsky, Graciela L., Carmen M. Reinhart, and Carlos A. Vegh. "The Unholy Trinity of Financial Contagion." *Journal of Economic Perspectives* 17 (2003): 51–74.

Kaufman, Henry. *The Road to Financial Reformation: Warnings, Consequences, Reforms*. Hoboken, N.J.: John Wiley and Sons, 2009.

Keynes, John Maynard. *The General Theory of Employment, Interest, and Money*. New York: Harcourt, Brace, and World, 1936.

Kindleberger, Charles P. *Manias, Panics, and Crashes: A History of Financial Crises*. New York: Basic Books, 1978.

____. *The World in Depression, 1929–1939*. Berkeley: University of California Press, 1986.

Kindleberger, Charles P., and Jean-Pierre Laffargue, eds. *Financial Crises: Theory, History, and Policy*. Cambridge, U.K.: Cambridge University Press, 1982.

Klyuev, Vladimir, Phil de Imus, and Krishna Srinivasan. "Unconventional Choices for Unconventional Times: Credit and Quantitative Easing in Advanced Economies." IMF Staff Position Note, November 4, 2009. Online at http://www.imf.org/external/pubs/ft/spn/2009/spn0927.pdf.

Knight, Frank H. *Risk, Uncertainty, and Profit*. Boston: Houghton Mifflin, 1921.

Krugman, Paul. "How Did Economists Get It So Wrong?" *New York Times Magazine*, September 2, 2009.

____. *The Return of Depression Economics and the Crisis of 2008*. New York: W. W. Norton, 2008.

Laeven, Luc, and Thomas Laryea. "Principles of Household Debt Restructuring." IMF Staff Position Note, June 26, 2009. Online at http://www.imf.org/external/pubs/ft/spn/2009/spn0915.pdf.

Landier, Augustin, and Kenichi Ueda. "The Economics of Debt Restructuring: Understanding the Options." IMF Staff Position Note, June 5, 2009. Online at https://www.imf.org/external/pubs/ft/spn/2009/spn0912.pdf.

Lepler, Jessica. "The Pressure of 1836: Interpreting Atlantic Bank Wars." Unpublished paper.

Lo, Andrew W., and A. Craig MacKinlay. *A Non-Random Walk Down Wall* Street. Princeton, N.J.: Princeton University Press, 1999.

Mackay, Charles. *Memoirs of Extraordinary Popular Delusions and the Madness of Crowds*. London: National Illustrated Library, 1852.

Marichal, Carlos. *A Century of Debt Crises in Latin America: From Independence to the Great Depression, 1820–1930*. Princeton, N.J.: Princeton University Press, 1989.

Markwat, Thijs, Erik Kole, and Dick van Dijk. "Contagion as a Domino Effect in Global Stock Markets." *Journal of Banking and Finance* 33 (2009): 1996–2012.

Miller, Marcus, Paul Weller, and Lei Zhang. "Moral Hazard and the US Stock Market: Analysing the 'Greenspan Put.'" *Economic Journal* 112 (2002): C171–86.

Minsky, Hyman P. *Can "It" Happen Again? Essays on Instability and Finance*. Armonk, N.Y.: M. E. Sharpe, 1982.

____. *John Maynard Keynes*. New York: Columbia University Press, 1975.

____. *Stabilizing an Unstable Economy*. New York: McGraw-Hill, 2008.

Mishkin, Frederic S. "Anatomy of a Financial Crisis." *Journal of Evolutionary Economics* 2 (1992): 115–30.

Morris, Charles R. *The Trillion Dollar Meltdown: Easy Money, High Rollers, and the Great Credit Crash*. New York: Public Affairs, 2008.

Neal, Larry D., and Marc Weidenmier. "Crises in the Global Economy from Tulips to Today: Contagion and Consequences." In Michael D. Bordo, Alan M. Taylor, and Jeffrey G. Williamson, eds., *Globalization in Historical Perspective*. Chicago: University of Chicago Press, 2003.

Obstfeld, Maurice, and Kenneth Rogoff. "The Unsustainable US Current Account Position Revisited." National Bureau of Economic Research Working Paper no. 10869, November 2004. Online at http://www.nber.org/papers/w10869.

Obstfeld, Maurice, Jay C. Shambaugh, and Alan M. Taylor. "Financial Instability, Reserves, and Central Bank Swap Lines in the Panic of 2008." National Bureau of Economic Research Working Paper no. 14826, March 2009. Online at http://www.nber.org/papers/w14826.

Papadia, Francesco. "Central Bank Operations in Response to the Financial Turmoil." Committee on the Global Financial System Paper no. 31, July 2008. Online at http://www.bis.org/publ/cgfs31.pdf?noframes=1.

Philippon, Thomas, and Ariell Reshef, "Wages and Human Capital in the U.S. Financial Industry: 1909–2006." National Bureau of Economic Research Working Paper no. 14644, January 2009. Online at http://www.nber.org/papers/w14644.

Purnanandam, Amiyatosh K. "Originate-to-Distribute Model and the Sub-Prime Mortgage Crisis." Paper presented at the American Finance Association annual meeting, September 18, 2009, Atlanta, Georgia.

Rajan, Raghuram G. "Bankers' Pay Is Deeply Flawed." *Financial Times*. January 8, 2008.

____. "Has Financial Development Made the World Riskier?" National Bureau of Economic Research Working Paper no. 11728, November 2005. Online at http://www.nber.org/papers/w11728. Subsequently published as "Has Finance Made the World Riskier?" *European Financial Management* 12 (2006): 499–533.

Reinhart, Carmen M., and Kenneth S. Rogoff. "Growth in a Time of Debt." National Bureau of Economic Research Working Paper no. 15639, January 2010. Online at http://www.nber.org/papers/w15639.

____. "Is the 2007 US Sub-prime Financial Crisis So Different? An International Historical Comparison." *American Economic Review* 98 (2008): 339–44.

____. *This Time Is Different: Eight Centuries of Financial Folly*. Princeton, N.J.: Princeton University Press, 2009.

Richardson, Vernon J., and James F. Waegelein. "The Influence of Long-Term Performance Plans on Earnings Management and Firm Performance." *Review of Quantitative Finance and Accounting* 18, no. 2 (March 2002): 161-83.

Ritholtz, Barry. *Bailout Nation: How Greed and Easy Money Corrupted Wall Street and Shook the World Economy*. Hoboken, N.J.: John Wiley and Sons, 2009.

Rockoff, Hugh. "Walter Bagehot and the Theory of Central Banking." In Forrest Capie and Geoffrey E. Wood, eds., *Financial Crises and the World Banking System*. London: Macmillan, 1986.

Rose, Andrew K., and Mark M. Spiegel. "Cross-Country Causes and Consequences of the 2008 Crisis: International Linkages and American Exposure." Centre for Economic Policy Research Discussion Paper no. 7466. Online at http://www.cepr.org/pubs/ dps/DP7466.asp.

Roubini, Nouriel. "The Biggest Slump in U.S. Housing in the Last 40 Years . . . or 53 Years?" August 23, 2006. Online at http://www.roubini.com/analysis/38718.php.

____. "The Coming Financial Pandemic." *Foreign Policy*, February 19, 2009. Online at http://www.foreignpolicy.com/articles/2009/02/19/the_coming_financial_pandemic.

____. "The Rising Risk of a Systemic Financial Meltdown: The Twelve Steps to Disaster," February 5, 2008. Online at http://www.roubini.com/analysis/44763.php.

____. "The Risk of a U.S. Hard Landing and Implications for the Global Economy and Financial Markets." Speech at the International Monetary Fund, Washington, D.C., September 13, 2007. Online at http://www.imf.org/external/np/tr/2007/tr070913.htm.

____. "Why Central Banks Should Burst Bubbles." *International Finance* 9 (2006): 87–107.

____. "Why China Should Abandon Its Dollar Peg." *International Finance* 10 (2007): 71–89.

Roubini, Nouriel, and Christian Menegatti. "Vulnerabilities in Central and Southern Europe," June 6, 2006. Online at http://www.roubini.com/analysis/38622.php.

Roubini, Nouriel, Elisa Parisi-Capone, and Christian Menegatti. "Growth Differentials in the EMU: Facts and Considerations," June 1, 2007. Online at http://www.roubini.com/analysis/44809.php.

Roubini, Nouriel, and Brad Setser. *Bailouts or Bail-Ins? Responding to Financial Crises in Emerging Economies*. Washington, D.C.: Institute for International Economics, 2004.

____. "The US as a Net Debtor: The Sustainability of the US External Imbalances," November 2004. Online at http://pages.stern.nyu.edu/~nroubini/papers/Roubini-Setser-US-External-Imbalances.pdf.

Roubini Global Economics. *2010 Global Economic Outlook*. February 2010. Available to subscribers at http://www.roubini.com.

Schularick, Moritz, and Alan M. Taylor. "Credit Booms Gone Bust: Monetary Policy, Leverage Cycles and Financial Crises, 1870–2008." National Bureau of Economic Research Working Paper no. 15512, November 2009. Online at http://www.nber.org/papers/w15512.

Schumpeter, Joseph Alois. *Capitalism, Socialism, and Democracy*. London: Routledge, 2006.

Schwartz, Anna J. "Real and Pseudo-Financial Crises." In Forrest Capie and Geoffrey E. Wood, eds., *Financial Crises and the World Banking System*. London: Macmillan, 1986.

Shiller, Robert J. "From Efficient Markets Theory to Behavioral Finance." *Journal of Economic Perspectives* 17 (2003): 83–104.

____. *Irrational Exuberance*. Princeton, N.J.: Princeton University Press, 2000.

____. *The Subprime Solution: How Today's Global Financial Crisis Happened, and What to Do about It*. Princeton, N.J.: Princeton University Press, 2008.

Shim, Ilhyock, and Goetz von Peter. "Distress Selling and Asset Market Feedback." Bank for International Settlements Working Paper no. 229, June 2007. Online at http://www.bis.org/publ/work229.pdf?noframes=1.

Silber, William L. *When Washington Shut Down Wall Street: The Great Financial Crisis and the Origins of America's Monetary Supremacy*. Princeton, N.J.: Princeton University Press, 2007.

Sobel, Robert. *Panic on Wall Street: A History of America's Financial Disasters*. New York: Collier, 1968.

Sorkin, Andrew Ross. *Too Big to Fail: The Inside Story of How Wall Street and Washington Fought to Save the Financial System from Crisis—and Themselves*. New York: Viking, 2009.

Sornette, Didier, and Ryan Woodard. "Financial Bubbles, Real Estate Bubbles, Derivative Bubbles, and the Financial and Economic Crisis." Swiss Finance Research Institute Paper no. 09-15, May 20, 2009. Online at http://arxiv.org/PS_cache/arxiv/pdf/0905/0905.0220v1.pdf.

Soros, George. *The New Paradigm for Financial Markets: The Credit Crisis of 2008 and What It Means*. New York: Public Affairs, 2008.

Stiglitz, Joseph. *Freefall: America, Free Markets, and the Sinking of the World Economy*. New York: W.W. Norton, 2010.

Sylla, Richard. "Monetary Innovation and Crises in American Economic History." In Paul Wachtel, ed., *Crises in the Economic and Financial Structure*. Lexington, Mass.: D.C. Heath, 1982.

Taleb, Nassim Nicholas. *The Black Swan: The Impact of the Highly Improbable*. New York: Random House, 2007.

Temin, Peter. *Did Monetary Forces Cause the Great Depression?* New York: W. W. Norton, 1976.

Tett, Gillian. *Fool's Gold: How the Bold Dream of a Small Tribe at J. P. Morgan Was Corrupted by Wall Street Greed and Unleashed a Catastrophe*. New York: Free Press, 2009.

Tymoigne, Éric. "Securitization, Deregulation, Economic Stability, and Financial Crisis, Parts I and II." Levy Economics Institute Working Papers no. 573.1 and 573.2, August 2009.

VoxEU.org. *The Global Crisis Debate*. 2009. Online at http://www.voxeu.org/index.php?q=node/2824.

Wheelock, David C., and Paul W. Wilson. "Why Do Banks Disappear? The Determinants of U.S. Bank Failures and Acquisitions." *Review of Economics and Statistics* 82 (2000): 127–38.

White, Eugene N., ed. *Crashes and Panics: The Lessons from History*. Homewood, Ill.: Business One Irwin, 1990.

Wieland, Volker. "Quantitative Easing: A Rationale and Some Evidence from Japan." National Bureau of Economic Research Working Paper no. 15565, December 2009. Online at http://www.nber.org/papers/w15565.

Wilson, Jack, Richard E. Sylla, and Charles P. Jones. "Financial Market Panics and Volatility in the Long Run, 1830–1988." In Eugene N. White, ed., *Crashes and Panics: The Lessons from History*. Homewood, Ill.: Business One Irwin, 1990.

Wolf, Martin. *Fixing Global Finance*. Baltimore: Johns Hopkins University Press, 2008.

Wray, L. Randall. "Minsky, the Global Financial Crisis, and the Prospects Before Us." *Development* 52 (2009): 302–7.

Yehoue, Etienne B. "Emerging Economy Responses to the Global Financial Crisis of 2007–09: An Empirical Analysis of the Liquidity Easing Measures." IMF Working Paper no. 09/265, December 2009. Online at http://www.imf.org/external/pubs/ft/wp/2009/wp09265.pdf.

Zandi, Mark. *Financial Shock: A 360° Look at the Subprime Mortgage Implosion, and How to Avoid the Next Financial Crisis*. Upper Saddle River, N.J.: Financial Times Press, 2008.

Zimmermann, Klaus F. "Coordinating International Responses to the Crisis." A VoxEU.org Publication, October 9, 2008. Online at http://www.voxeu.org/index.php?q=node/2366.

INDEX